THE
OPEN UNIVERSITY

History and Evaluation
of a Dynamic Innovation
in Higher Education

Walter Perry

Forewords by

Harold Wilson

Cyril O. Houle

THE
OPEN UNIVERSITY

Jossey-Bass Publishers

San Francisco · Washington · 1977

THE OPEN UNIVERSITY
History and Evaluation of a Dynamic Innovation
in Higher Education
by Walter Perry

Library of Congress Catalogue Card Number LC 76–55917

International Standard Book Number ISBN 0–87589–305–8

Manufactured in the United States of America

JACKET DESIGN BY WILLI BAUM
FIRST EDITION

Code 7704

FOREWORD

This is a book written with the unrivalled authority of the man who has done more than anyone to ensure the success of what is now recognised in Britain, and in the wider world, as one of the most important educational and social developments of this century.

Sir Walter Perry, Vice-Chancellor of the Open University before and ever since its Charter, sets out the story, not only of the birth and growth of his charge, but also – of great interest to the political and social historian – its ante-natal history.

The decision to create the Open University, then known as the 'University of the Air', was a political act. It was announced as a firm commitment of the incoming Labour Government on 8 September, 1963; the text and outline proposals had been written out by hand in less than an hour after church on the previous Easter Sunday morning. It was never party policy, nor did it feature in Labour's election manifesto. But our political history is full of cases where the Prime Minister has a private hobby-horse and is determined to use the not inconsiderable resources of his office to get it through, whatever the opposition.

That opposition was pretty massive. The original proposals met an almost unanimously hostile press – Sir Walter quotes the judgements of *The Times* and others, words which read strangely today. I seem to remember one warm welcome, in *The Economist*. Opposition in the educational world, from the established universities to adult education and local authorities, was hardly less robust. As the book records, government departments, notably those of Education and Science and the Treasury, were uniformly critical, with a marked lack of enthusiasm on the part of certain senior ministers.

Then came the lift-off with the appointment of Jennie Lee as Parliamentary Secretary, and later as Minister of State in Education and Science, with the dual mandate of sponsoring the arts and creating the Open University. Less timorous than I had been, she, with Lord Goodman's backing and that of the Planning Committee under Sir Peter Venables, rejected any idea of a consortium of universities acting as an examining and organising body. The Open University was to be a chartered university in its own right, planning its work, producing its own teaching material – both printed and broadcast – and conducting its own research.

The second great turning-point, characteristically underplayed by the author, but at least as significant as Jennie Lee's appointment, was the selection of Sir Walter Perry as Vice-Chancellor in 1968. It is his record of the planning of the University, in a still hostile milieu, with grave doubts about its survival should there be a change in government, which makes this book historic. His problems in recruiting staff – where, as it turned out, every post was over-subscribed – and in estimating the numbers of students; the (successful) crash building programme; the decision to create foundation courses; the credit system; the widespread regional educational and counselling system; the establishment of the principal of open entry, with no insistence on prior formal academic qualifications; the creation of the courses, the departments, the 'course teams', the units; the mastering with the BBC of the formidable new broadcasting problems: these make up the story of the Open University. But leading and inspiring the attack on these problems, the Vice-Chancellor, with the full backing of the Senate, insisted on his great theme – *no compromise on standards*. Anyone even indirectly in touch – in my case my elder son, a former Oxford mathematics don, is an Open University lecturer, and my younger son halfway through his course as a student – can see how that uncompromising principle has been asserted.

For years now, when I have been abroad, especially in different parts of the United States, I have been besieged by University Presidents, Senators, Congressmen, and Presidents of the U.S. to tell them more about the achievements of the Open University. For years, too, I have been told that it will not be very long before every State of the Union will have its own Open University, or be in some way affiliated to one.

Those with only a limited knowledge of all the University does, and an even sketchier notion of how it was all achieved, will each have different interests in mind when reading the book. I have always been fascinated by the development work on scientific instruments, students' kits, microscopes and the rest. This is a success story, based on the combination of private enterprise design with economies of scale achieved through bulk-buying, guaranteed orders, re-design by the University's technical staff, new materials; a success to the point where such technological exports are now supplementing the sales of teaching material proper – books and films – to the universities and colleges of the world.

This book tells how the grand concept came into being, how apparently unyielding new ground was broken, what the hopes and problems are for the future – but above all how Britain led the world into a historic new educational dimension.

Harold Wilson.

London
September 1976

FOREWORD
TO THE AMERICAN EDITION

North Americans will find this book attractive for at least three reasons. First, it is the initial comprehensive account of an institution that has been a focus of world interest since it was first proposed in 1963, but whose nature has been obscured by fragmented or highly subjective journalistic viewpoints. Second, the author suggests answers to many problems that now confront leaders of universities in both the United States and Canada. Third, the book is written in an incisive style, in essence free from the localized references often characteristic of both American and British writing on education.

This volume shoulders its way at once to the forefront of the small but rapidly growing body of serious studies of the Open University. It is likely to retain its preeminence until—and perhaps even after—an official history is written. Since about 1970, people interested in education have been aware that an institution of world-wide importance was being created in the United Kingdom. The full magnitude of this venture is now apparent. For example, Eric Ashby recently observed that the founding of the Open University was the most significant event in the history of higher education since the establishment of land-grant colleges in the United States in the 1860s.

Lord Ashby's comment caused his audience to ponder the similarities and differences between the two types of institution. Each provided a serious sustained learning opportunity for large numbers of people for whom higher education had never been available. To achieve this aim, it was necessary in both cases to develop new methods, materials, instructional designs, and forms of administration. However, a major difference between the land-grant university (as it has now become) and the Open University is that the first institution took at least seventy-five years to achieve a fully established place in American society while the second had to be brought into full-scale operation in less than three years. Walter Perry took office in June 1968, and the University began operation in January 1971, with about 25,000 students—all of them embarked, as he says, on 'the most difficult way of getting a degree yet invented by the wit of man.' His account of how this goal was achieved, and of events until the Open University achieved a 'steady state', reveals far more about policies and problems than has ever been described in any book on this subject.

Leaders of American universities face some or all of the same challenges,

(ix)

particularly when the age and ability range of student bodies is broadened. Among the questions that must be answered are these:

In following a policy of completely open admission, how can the academic deficiencies of some students best be remedied?

What principles should a faculty use in designing a high-level course distinctively for adults?

In multimedia instruction, how can faculty members and technical experts work most effectively together?

Should an external baccalaureate program impose a minimum age for enrollment?

What are the values of an extended initiatory experience for students embarking on a long and rigorous program? How can such an experience be best designed?

How can creative staff members be prevented from settling into established routines?

How can costly innovative program materials be kept up to date?

Should independent study systems allow each student to work at his or her own rate, or should performance deadlines be established?

How can an institution determine in advance how many adult students will be attracted to a major new program?

How can the results of student achievement in an innovative program be best assessed?

In programs that place great emphasis on teaching, how can the research interests of the academic staff be fostered?

How can advance standing in a degree program be given to students who have already achieved some of its learning goals by other means?

In dealing with such questions, Sir Walter usually presents the range of alternatives considered by him and his staff, indicates the one chosen and why, and describes the results of the ensuing experience. Thus the reader learns not only what succeeded or did not succeed at the Open University but also discovers other options open to anyone who encounters similar problems.

Sir Walter writes, as he apparently administers, with verve and candor. In trying to explain why a perennially cautious British government undertook the gigantic gambles required by the Open University, an earlier author paid tribute to Jennie Lee, its strong advocate, as 'a politician of steely imperious will, coupled . . . with tenacity and charm'. Sir Walter does not seem imperious (though he implies that some of his associates may have so considered him), but he does give evidence of the other traits attributed to Jennie Lee. Certainly he speaks his mind very directly: In describing the intolerably difficult circumstances under which serious adult education had to take place in Britain until 1970, he refers to 'the loneliness of the long-distance learner'. In characterizing the early audiences whose support he had to win, he observes that 'it would have needed an ice-pick to cut the atmosphere'. He notes in relation to the work of course teams that 'there have been some bonny fights.' And, in an extended passage, he points out precisely why 'in statutory terms a Vice-Chancellor is in a position opposite to that of the harlot, and holds responsibility without power.'

Sir Walter surveys all he sees with an analytical eye. He is a thoroughly and deeply discipline-based scholar who had no concern for the needs of adult learners until he became Vice-Chancellor. Yet he now observes that 'departmental control of teaching is a root cause of much that is wrong with educational programmes in conventional universities.' Further, he remarks that 'clearly, if an applicant aged 35 wants to start a university level education, it is much more important to know what he has done in the twenty years since he left school at 15 than it is to know what ·bit of paper he obtained as a formal educational qualification on leaving, all those years ago.' The book is so full of personal opinions and distinctive interpretations of facts that almost every reader will probably disagree with some of the points Sir Walter makes. Certainly I do. But his directness of style, cutting through cant and evangelical fervor, provides the book's greatest immediate charm.

In the first months of its publication in Britain, this work has had a favorable press and acquired an enthusiastic readership. It deserves an equally strong and positive response in North America.

November 1976   CYRIL O. HOULE
University of Chicago
W. K. Kellogg Foundation

THE AUTHOR

Walter Perry has been Vice-Chancellor – the chief administrative officer – of the Open University since the institution was established in 1969 by the Government of Sir Harold Wilson. He was previously Vice-Principal of the University of Edinburgh, where he had also been professor of pharmacology since 1958.

Perry was educated in Scotland at Ayr Academy, Dundee High School, and at the University of St Andrews where he earned doctorates in Medicine in 1948, and in Science in 1958.

His early career spanned work with the Colonial Medical Service in Nigeria, with the Royal Air Force, and as a staff member of the Medical Research Council. From 1952 to 1958 he was director of the Department of Biological Standards, National Institute for Medical Research.

Perry was knighted in 1974 by Queen Elizabeth II, who had in 1957 awarded him the Order of the British Empire (OBE). He was elected a Fellow of the Royal College of Physicians of Edinburgh 1967; and received honorary degrees of Doctor of Science in 1974 from the University of Bradford, and Doctor of Laws in 1975 from the University of Dundee.

Among Perry's publications are papers in the *Journal of Physiology,* the *British Journal of Pharmacology and Chemotherapy* and, since joining the Open University, papers on its progress and the future of education; the latter include the 1974 Rede Lecture at the University of Cambridge, *Higher Education for Adults: where more means better* (Cambridge University Press, 1974).

Sir Walter Perry has four sons, three by his previous marriage. He and Lady Perry, with the youngest, reside at Wednesden House, Aspley Guise, close to the Open University campus at Walton Hall. Lady Perry practises medicine at the Stoke Mandeville Hospital in nearby Aylesbury.

CONTENTS

ACKNOWLEDGEMENTS

To write this book it was necessary for me to be freed from the day to day commitments of a Vice-Chancellor and I am most grateful to the Council of the University for allowing me to take six months of study leave to devote to the task. Even then I could not have completed the job without help and the Council agreed to provide me with a Research Assistant. I appointed Mrs. Dee Edwards, herself one of the first graduates of the Open University, and she has proved a tower of strength to me throughout the preparation of the manuscript.

I am indebted for comment on the early chapters to Sir Harold Wilson, who kindly agreed to write a foreword, and to Lady Lee. Mr. John Scupham and Professor Arnold Kettle both read the whole manuscript and made most helpful suggestions about it. I would like to thank my colleagues on the staff of the Open University, too numerous to mention individually, who have unstintingly provided me with facts and figures, often calling for special analysis, and to whom I have referred particular sections for correction.

Finally I must record my indebtedness to the Publishing and Media Divisions of the University who edited and designed the book and to the long-suffering secretarial staff who have typed and typed from my handwritten manuscript which only they, who work with me, can decipher.

PREFACE

I first began to think about the Open University early in 1968, when I applied for the job of being its first Vice-Chancellor. At that time I was Professor of Pharmacology and Vice-Principal of Edinburgh University. I had spent all my working life in medical research and teaching, but, over the years, had found that I particularly enjoyed the various administrative challenges that arose. Far from ducking out of such responsibilities I actively sought them. Sir Harold Himsworth, formerly Secretary of the Medical Research Council, recalls that in 1956, when I was a member of the staff of the Council, he had occasion to ask me what sort of job I would like to have; and that my answer was, quite simply, 'Yours'. By 1968, at the age of 46, I had reached the stage where it was not unrealistic to hope that I might achieve that sort of ambition: and one possibility lay in an appointment as Vice-Chancellor of a university.

I had, of course, heard about the University of the Air. Like most members of the established university world, I regarded it as a political gimmick unlikely ever to be put into practice, and likely, if it were, to produce only a few graduates of relatively poor quality. The idea that I might myself become involved in it had never crossed my mind. I had never been interested in adult education. I knew nothing of educational technology or of the use of broadcasting for educational purposes. I was wholly ignorant of the new developments in educational theory and philosophy that were challenging established patterns and practices. I had never been active in national politics and was not driven by any urge to extend educational opportunity to those deprived of it, although I would have been sympathetic to such an aim had it been put to me.

For various reasons I was, in 1968, anxious to move from Edinburgh back to the south of England, and my family was aware of this. One Sunday afternoon my son, Alan, immersed in *The Observer,* suddenly said 'Dad, here is the very job for you' and passed me the notice inviting applications for the Vice-Chancellorship of the Open University. I took his remark in the spirit he intended – as a joke. But over the next few days I began to think seriously, for the first time, about the proposal and the challenge that it presented.

The main attraction of the challenge was the extreme difficulty of effective teaching at a distance. I had long been concerned at the pitiably inadequate standard of most of the teaching that went on in the established universities. I had tried, in Edinburgh, tentative experiments in designing courses by teamwork, both within my own Department, and, on one occasion, jointly between the Departments of Pathology, Bacteriology and

Pharmacology, in a course on immunology. These experiments were stimulating but abortive; to accomplish anything significant called for a very large input of effort and time; and the whole concept ran counter to established practices. It struck me that a similar approach would inevitably be needed in the context of teaching at a distance. If it could be made to work in that context, it should ultimately spread back into the established universities and raise the standards of teaching everywhere. This was the motive that, on reflection, decided me to apply for the job. I consulted Michael Swann, then Principal of Edinburgh University, and he encouraged me in a typically Delphic way to go ahead. He had doubts about the practicability of the Open University, but was flattering enough to suggest that 'if anyone can make it work, you can'. His emphasis on the difficulty of the challenge was a further attraction and a goad, although he may have intended it to have the opposite effect.

I realised that I would have to learn a very great deal about whole new fields of which I was at that time ignorant, in adult education, educational broadcasting and educational technology. Nevertheless the prospect of starting with a clean slate was itself exciting. A few weeks after my appointment was announced, in June 1968, Tyrell Burgess, in an open letter to me in *The Guardian,* warned of the 'adult education jungle' that I was about to enter. I could reply, and did, that I would at least bring to the Open University an open mind, free of any prior commitment to a particular theory or philosophy and of any preconceived notions of which path to follow. It was in this spirit of pragmatism that I took up my appointment and began work.

After seven years of hard labour in what has turned out to be the most exciting and rewarding of jobs, I want to tell the story. I am no historian and the 'official history of the Open University' must await a more expert pen. I can provide only a personal account, based on my own prejudices and attitudes. I can hope to stimulate only when I am myself stimulated, to interest only when my interest is caught. Of what happened in the years before my appointment I can, of course, write only at second-hand. I have, however, met most of the people concerned and read most of the papers written, and the story has its own fascination. Thereafter I can draw on my own experience and memory to trace the progress of the ideas that have fired the imagination of the educational world.

The Open University   WALTER PERRY
September 1976

1

THE
BACKGROUND

1

THE BASIC IDEAS

The concept of the Open University evolved from the convergence of three major postwar educational trends. The first of these concerns developments in the provision for adult education, the second the growth of educational broadcasting and the third the political objective of promoting the spread of egalitarianism in education.

Since the Second World War the educational scene has bubbled with a continuous ferment of new ideas. Established practices have, almost without exception, come under challenge. Educational theorists have advanced radical, even iconoclastic, new philosophies. Amongst them are the concepts of 'education permanente', continuing education and recurrent education. Yet, despite continuing debates at national and international level, the inertia inherent in established educational systems is normally much too strong to permit of high speed change. Inertia stems both from the sheer complexity of educational systems and from the network of vested interests concerned with maintaining them.

Advances have usually been made only by pragmatists, who are prepared to modify and supplement existing systems to bring them more nearly into line with what is theoretically desirable, but who do so in ways that are acceptable to the establishment. Thus a system may, through a series of such piecemeal modifications, undergo radical change. This process takes longer but is much less painful than revolution would be.

In the UK almost every requirement of the total educational system has been scrutinised by government committees with a view to introducing such modifications. The tragedy is that an overall philosophy to provide a framework for change has never been defined and accepted, with the result that the modifications actually introduced have been random rather than designed. A host of good ideas is buried in the reports of the numerous committees – Plowden, Crowther, Hazelgrave, Robbins, James and Russell – which, if carefully selected and integrated, could provide much of the basis for a splendid new structure of educational provision.

What of the position of education for adults in such a structure? A lot depends on semantics. For administrative purposes in Britain the term 'adult education' covers only the activities of specified agencies, oriented neither towards vocational training nor towards any formal academic qualification; namely the Workers' Educational Association, the extra-mural departments of the universities, and the classes offered by Local Education Authorities. It does not cover all education offered to and taken up by adults. Adult education, in this sense, has always been the Cinderella of our educational world. Indeed Jennie Lee once described it as 'the patch on the backside of our educational trousers'. The whole spectrum of these activities was reviewed by the Russell Committee in its Report of 1973.[1]

University extramural departments were created primarily to extend the cultural influence of the universities to the adult population in their own localities. From the beginning the adults who enrolled in extramural classes were predominantly middle-class. Many of them had already benefited from higher education and were extending their interests and knowledge. More than 75% of all such classes are in the liberal arts or the social sciences; nearly all are 'non-vocational' and do not offer participants any opportunity of sitting an examination or of obtaining a certificate or diploma. They are, as the Americans put it, 'not for credit', being designed to suit those who want to study solely for their own self-fulfilment.

The pattern of Workers' Educational Association courses had, by this time, evolved into something almost indistinguishable from this. Originally the aim of the WEA was to stimulate and satisfy the demands of adults, and in particular of members of the workers' movements, for education. But over the years WEA classes had come to attract a predominantly middle-class audience, and the majority of classes were now 'non-vocational'. The third provider of adult education, Local Education Authorities, by 1968 undertook the lion's share of the task. In that year nearly 1.7 million adults enrolled for courses of study in LEA classes. Despite the fact that fees were kept at a nominal level, the bulk of the students was again drawn from the middle class; there was little sign of interest from those who were educationally under-privileged. Most of the courses were 'non-vocational' and, as the Russell Report emphasises, 80–90% of the programmes consisted of courses in physical activities, domestic subjects, arts and crafts, music and drama, foreign languages, and practical activities such as woodwork and car maintenance.

The value of all this in filling a need was undoubted; but the fact that the existing provision of 'adult education' was valuable did not mean that it satisfied all the needs for education that were felt by adults. There were two clear gaps.

First, there were very few opportunities offered to the adult who wished to embark upon vocational courses at the higher education level. That there were notable exceptions to this general rule did not invalidate it. My general impression, as a complete newcomer to the adult educational world, was that 'examinations' and 'vocational' were almost dirty words, that somehow study towards a qualification was felt to be intrinsically less worthy than study for the sake of study. This attitude inhibited the development of vocational courses almost everywhere.

If 'adult education' did not include all the provision of education for adults, who then provided the remainder of it? How far did the institutions of initial higher education, at that time the universities, the polytechnics and the colleges, cater for adults, for 'mature students'? British universities, unlike their counterparts in the United States, in Australia and in New Zealand, did not to any significant extent offer evening education, leading to a degree for part-time students. London University offered its external degree but this was a system of examination only. Virtually no teaching programmes were offered and adults scattered throughout the country had to make their own arrangements to prepare themselves for the examinations. Birkbeck College did provide part-time degree programmes for those who, living in London, could attend the College and was the shining exception to the rule. By 1968 it appeared that the polytechnics, which had been founded as Colleges of Advanced Technology with the part-time student very much in mind, were likely to gravitate towards full-time courses for full-time students. The technical colleges, although they had large numbers of part-time students, were catering in the main for people seeking an education at pre-university level, although they also offered courses intended to prepare students for London University examinations.

There was a gap, therefore, in provision. An adult who wished to take a degree, whether he was qualified to start the degree or not, would find it exceptionally hard to gain entrance to any university or polytechnic. This was true even if he was prepared to study full-time. Provision for mature entrants in most universities was extremely limited. There was tremendous demand from school leavers for the limited places available in the universities and most admission authorities gave preference to them. Money was better spent on training them than on training adults who could, at the end of their course, make a contribution to society only for a shorter period. The needs of adults who could not stop work to enter higher education on a full-time basis and who wished to obtain degrees by working part-time were often not met at all.

Such a student could register for a London external degree, study on his own and work towards that degree sometimes without any guidance or help. There are some classic examples of people who succeeded in obtaining qualifications in this way, amongst them Jennie Lee and Margaret Thatcher, but it was an extremely hard road. External students of London University could sometimes receive tuition by registering for part-time courses offered by technical colleges; others could take similar courses offered by the commercial correspondence colleges, but the number of such courses, except in subjects like Commerce and Law, was restricted, and the quality was often open to serious question. Correspondence colleges all too frequently lived on the profits made from those who paid fees but dropped out at an early stage, thereby making very little demand on the system, although the better colleges did provide a good service for those students who lasted the course.

Thus the gap in provision of vocational courses left by 'adult education' was in no real sense filled by other institutions, which provided higher education mainly for school leavers – 'initial higher education'. The existence of the gap was recognised fairly widely, but opinions also differed widely on whether there was any real need to fill it. Many authorities doubted whether there was a sizeable unsatisfied demand among adults for this kind of educational opportunity. Perhaps these doubts were a source of comfort, because few had any faith that it would be practicable

3

successfully to offer vocational higher education on a part-time basis.

The second gap in 'adult education' provision lay in its failure to attract those very members of the adult community for whom much of it had originally been designed: those who, at the stage of their initial education, had been under-privileged and deprived. To them the institutions of initial higher education offered nothing. They were the drop-outs of the educational system. Yet, amongst them, there were many who were highly intelligent and who would undoubtedly benefit from the experience of higher education if given the chance of it on a part-time basis. Yet, whether such an opportunity would be welcomed by the educationally deprived adult or would again be seized only by the middle-class aspirant, was open to question.

This debate was taking place against the background of a remarkable growth in the provision of educational opportunity for the school leaver. The Robbins Report (1963)[2] had made it clear that the universities must expand to meet the increased demand from qualified school leavers, and this expansion was under way. It insisted that places in higher education should be made available to all those capable of profiting from them. There was a growing awareness of the national need for trained brain power, and for the extension of opportunity to all classes of the population, as a positive step towards the replacing the elitist system that had been prevalent in Britain for many years. But most people would have given a higher priority to expanding the provision for school leavers than to providing new opportunities for adults who had had the misfortune to be born too soon to benefit from such an expansion.

On the whole the idea that initial education, up to and including university education, was the only way of providing the country with the graduates it required remained unchallenged. It is an easy system to organise. Full-time education has its established patterns, students are stimulated by the companionship of their contemporaries in a residential situation, and student life is full of social distractions that make for a full and enjoyable experience. The alternative idea of part-time study offers none of these advantages. The loneliness of the long-distance learner is hard to bear even for motivated and dedicated adults. It is probable that most 18 year olds would find it intolerable. Yet the idea of 'continuing education' as a viable alternative to initial education was gaining ground, especially on the Continent. The benefits of capitalising upon the greater motivation and sense of purpose that maturity conferred came to be recognised. The national wastage involved in educational drop-out was similarly noted and much was made of this factor in the Crowther Report of 1959[3] and later in the Robbins Report. Yet in Britain the remedy was basically to extend the provision of initial education, while the problems of the adult, though noted, were not tackled with any vigour.

The effects of the Robbins Report on initial higher education in Britain were profound. There was an enormous increase in the size and number of universities. This extension of opportunity was to be welcomed, though some of the traditional and best aspects of the old universities were lost in

4

the process. For the adult, on the other hand, nothing was done. It was hardly surprising that the existing institutions were not interested in their problems. They had enough difficulty in coping with the expansion induced by Robbins. The average academic was much more concerned with increasing the number of undergraduates in his care than with becoming involved in schemes to provide part-time adult education to degree level in the community. Academics regarded part-time education with great scepticism, considering that their vocation lay with full-time students.

It was often argued that an institution such as the Open University would be an unnecessary development, since all that it could do could equally well be done by the other universities acting in concert. This may be so in theory, but the idea that in 1969 the other universities of Britain might seriously have contemplated moving, either singly or collectively, into the field of part-time adult education is unrealistic. It could not have happened. The overriding view in the academic community was that this problem did not concern them; it ought to concern somebody else. It was this view that perpetuated the gap in educational provision.

The second major educational trend contributing to the evolution of the Open University was the growth in educational broadcasting. From its inception the BBC, under John Reith, had given education a high priority among its objectives in planning. As early as 1926, in an internal BBC memorandum, Mr Stobart put a proposal to Lord Reith for 'a wireless university' but there was to be no such formalisation of educational broadcasting at that stage. Even earlier there were moves to offer adult education in an informal way. In 1924 the Adult Education Committee of the Board of Education and the British Institution of Adult Education, together with the BBC, embarked upon a series of regular talks, and 20,000 copies of the printed syllabus were circulated. In 1927 the BBC set up their own adult education section, and later in the same year, possibly as a result of its creation, a committee of enquiry, under the chairmanship of Sir Henry Hadow[4], was set up by the BBC jointly with the British Institution of Adult Education. One of the recommendations of the committee was that there should be a separate radio station devoted to educational purposes, an idea which has survived for nearly 50 years but which has not yet been implemented. The story of this venture has been traced by Asa Briggs in his *History of Broadcasting*.[5] It was successful for a period of about 5 years, but thereafter the scheme faded away, for various reasons which have been analysed by Lord Briggs. It was succeeded by the establishment of a regular service of educational programmes for adults on one of the BBC's radio channels, financed from the Corporation's licence revenue. These were planned with the help of a Further Education Liaison Council, and included systematic language teaching supported by specially written textbooks and gramophone records.

The advent of television gave a renewed boost to the ideas of those who favoured the use of broadcasting for educational purposes. There were numerous experiments and much was written about the potential of the new medium, not only in the United Kingdom. In Britain one of the leading advocates of the use of television for higher education was R. C. G. Williams who over a period of two years (1962–3), while he was Chairman of the Electronics and Communications Section of the Institution of Electrical Engineers, argued strongly and continuously in favour of the creation of what he called a 'televarsity'.[6] Williams was concerned primarily with the field of technology, but his ideas were quite new in the sense that he raised the possibility of linking educational broadcasts with correspondence education and with visits to existing universities. In other words he produced a plan for a multimedia integrated programme rather than one concentrating on isolated educational broadcasts. In 1962 Michael Young wrote a paper[7] in which he estimated the probable growth of demand for higher education in the new decade. Amongst his proposals was one advocating the creation of an 'Open University' which would prepare people for the external degree of London University. He also drew attention to the increasing use of the broadcasting media for educational purposes in the United States and of correspondence teaching in the Soviet Union. He proposed the immediate creation of a National Extension College that would help students to achieve degrees through the London external system. These proposals were to reach fruition in October 1963 when the National Extension College was actually established, in Cambridge, and the first courses began to be designed.

The hours during which the BBC and the ITA were permitted to broadcast were controlled by the Postmaster General. In 1961 Mr Woodrow Wyatt introduced to the House of Commons, under the ten-minute rule, a bill designed to ensure that the Postmaster General would allow programmes of adult education to be broadcast outside the normally permitted hours. He too was concerned mainly with the need to provide further educational programmes for adults in the field of science and technology. No action was taken as a result of Mr Wyatt's bill because the Pilkington Committee on Broadcasting[8] was about to report, and this provided the Government with an excuse for deferring any action. The Report itself was presented to Parliament in June 1962. Although it was in favour of an expansion of formal adult educational television, the general conclusion was that there should be no segregated service of educational broadcasting, for three reasons: first, that an educational channel would isolate educational programmes, depriving other channels of any such component; second, that a separate educational channel would not reach the general public most in need of educational programmes; and third, that the production staff dealing with educational programmes would continue to benefit from association with other producers of more general programmes only if the services were offered on the same channels. These views were by no means confined to the Committee. They were held by the Ministry of Education, the BBC, the Association of Education Committees, the National Union of Teachers, the Workers Educational Association and the Universities Council for Adult Education. Indeed in the evidence submitted to the Committee by the BBC, they stated that 'to the best of the BBC's knowledge there does not at present exist amongst education authorities and organisations any demand for an educational service outside the context of the general services'. Nevertheless there was a contrary view even then. Professor George Catlin, a member of the National Broadcasting Development Committee, put forward to the Pilkington Committee an idea for the establishment of an educational trust which would control a new educational service. This kind of proposal was supported by bodies such as the Viewers' and Listeners' Association, and also, for reasons that were not clear and were almost certainly not wholly altruistic, by the ITA.

In parallel with this public debate about educational broadcasting and its future, things were happening behind the scenes. From 1961 the BBC was negotiating with the Universities Council for Adult Education and other educational bodies about the development of programmes for adult education. John Scupham, then Controller of Educational Broadcasting at the BBC, was anxious to move into this area and the UCAE in 1961 asked the extramural departments of the universities to encourage their staffs both to examine ways in which talks on radio and television could be used for educational purposes, and to make concrete suggestions about such a service. These discussions also involved officials of the Department of Education and Science, resulting by September 1962 in a government memorandum proposing the introduction of adult education programmes on television.[9] Despite some experimental attempts by extramural departments in the country to act on these recommendations there was little evidence of success by the end of 1963. The main hindrance to progress in this whole field was usually the lack of adequate transmission times. It is, however, important to note the valuable experiments carried out under the direction of Harold Wiltshire at the Extramural Department of the University of Nottingham in collaboration with one of the independent television companies, and of Michael Young at the National Extension College in collaboration with the Further Education Department of the BBC, in offering courses that combined radio and TV broadcasts with correspondence education. These were clear forerunners, in the years between 1963 and 1969, of the Open University.

The growth of interest in the potential of educational broadcasting in the United States was no doubt part of a national response to the technological challenge from Russia presented by the success of the 'Sputnik' programme. Enormous advances were made but they were scattered and inchoate. The primary causes of this lay in the national structure of provision both for education and for broadcasting. Education was the responsibility of state legislatures and only indirectly of the Federal government, so that a coherent national programme for education did not emerge. Broadcasting was organised almost entirely by commercial companies. Neither within a state, nor on a federal basis, was there any controlling organisation like the BBC so that, again, there was no coherent national programme, either for broadcasting or for educational broadcasting. The result is that, despite progress and experimentation both earlier and more extensive than that which took place in Britain, nothing comparable to the Open University has emerged so far in the United States. In the Soviet Union the use of educational broadcasting was extremely limited. They had, however, successfully pioneered the development of education by correspondence for external students and indeed, some 40% of all graduates in the Soviet Union had by 1960–61 followed at least a part of their course by correspondence. There was no comparable provision of correspondence education either in the United States or in Great Britain and this was a factor which had impressed itself on Harold Wilson's mind during his successive visits to the Soviet Union during the early years of the 1960s.

The third major trend was the increasing concern expressed throughout the world (during the 1950s and the early 1960s), about elitism in education and the effects of this on the nature of society. The Crowther report had indicated that the social background of children was a large factor in determining their educational career and that steps should be taken to make opportunities more easily available to the lower socio-economic groups. This point was taken up and developed very fully by Brian Jackson and Dennis Marsden in their book *Education and the Working Class,* first published in 1962.[10] The Robbins Committee, set up in 1961, also tackled the question in some detail. They showed that 45% of young people whose fathers were in the 'higher professional' group entered full-time higher education compared with only 4% for those whose fathers were in skilled manual occupations. In March 1962, the Labour Party, at that time led by Mr Gaitskell, set up a study group under the chairmanship of Lord Taylor to examine Labour's attitude towards higher education, whose report was presented in March 1963.[11] It again drew attention to how greatly the lower socio-economic groups were deprived of opportunities for higher education. Within the report it was proposed that an experiment should be mounted on BBC radio and television and by ITA, in organizing a 'University of the Air' for serious planned adult education; and that, as an alternative, the fourth television channel might be used exclusively for higher education.

By 1963, the time was ripe for someone to grasp the significance of these three trends and to crystallise them into a coherent pattern. It was Harold Wilson who seized the opportunity thus afforded. There was clear evidence of a gap in the provision of part-time higher education for adults; there was a strong political motive for promoting educational egalitarianism, a motive that was particularly suited to Labour Party philosophy; and the developments in educational broadcasting offered a new means both of filling the gap and counteracting elitism.

In a speech delivered in Glasgow on 8 September 1963,[12] as part of the pre-election programme of the Labour Party, Harold Wilson presented his synthesis of the ideas that had been germinating in his mind from all these sources. He proposed a set of nationally organised correspondence courses, primarily for technicians and technologists, designed for adults who had left school at 16 or 17 but who could reasonably be expected to acquire new skills and qualifications by working part-time at home.

'What we envisage,' he said, 'is the creation of a new educational trust representative of the universities and other educational organisations, associations of teachers, the broadcasting authorities, publishers, public and private bodies, producers capable of producing television and other educational material. This trust would be given state financial help and all the government assistance required. Broadcasting time could be found either by the allocation of the fourth television channel together with the appropriate radio facilities or by pre-empting time from the existing three channels and the fourth, when allocated. Educational programmes would be made available for supplementary study at educational institutes such as technical colleges.' In other words, Mr Wilson's plan was for a consortium of various interests, in education and broadcasting, designed to make available study by external means including broadcasting and correspondence. In his speech he laid little stress on educational egalitarianism although, as I have said, the time was ripe for it. He was much more concerned with the need for expanding technological education and for harnessing technological advances in the media of mass communication to the service of education.

Mr Wilson's plan for a 'University of the Air' may bear little relation to the Open University as it exists today; but it was to be the key that opened the door. It was the first expression of interest, by a powerful political figure, in the provision of opportunities for higher education to adults, studying part-time while in full employment, through a multimedia system that harnessed educational broadcasting to correspondence teaching and other methods.

2

THE POLITICAL HISTORY

Although Mr Wilson's speech in Glasgow on 8 September 1963 un-doubtedly represents the political birth of the 'University of the Air', the concept that he advanced did not command, then or later, the support even of those who were thinking along similar lines. This is not surprising for he himself described his concept as 'an inchoate idea', saying that he wanted to obtain reactions to it before going any further.

The only immediate reaction was that of the national press. The general tone was highly critical. An editorial in the *Times Educational Supplement* of 13 September 1963 is typical. The University of the Air was a 'heady prospect' but Mr Wilson defeated his objective by the sheer magnitude of his dream. Through the existing systems of education, those who really wanted to advance their education had all sorts of chances to do so. 'How far is it really true that people are hindered by lack of facilities?' the leader went on to ask. 'If the resources that were to be poured into Mr Wilson's pipe dreams were to be spent on improving the schools then more young people would come out resolved to continue learning. When this was done and the demand was still unsatiated, then, and not till then, will be the time for Mr Wilson's imaginative leaps.' This leader accurately reflected the prevailing mood in the academic world at that time.

Mr Wilson was not to be deterred. At the Annual Conference of the Labour Party in Scarborough on October 1st his speech, as Leader of the Party, dealt with the challenge of the new technological era. The Party was preparing for the next General Election; it was full of enthusiasm and hope. Mr Wilson's theme was the need for Labour to drag Britain into the twentieth century. 'At the very time that even the MCC has abolished the distinction between amateurs and professionals, in science and industry we are content to remain a nation of gentlemen in a world of players.' Labour must not be so content; technology must be harnessed to the service of society. One way to do this was to create a University of the Air, thereby harnessing the technology of mass communication to the service of education.

The Labour Party was to gain power a year later in the election of October 1964. Throughout the intervening year of intensive prepar-atory work within the Party, little notice was taken of the Leader's new suggestion. The Taylor Report had proposed a crash programme of ex-pansion of existing university opportunities. It had, almost as an aside, suggested that 'as an experiment, the BBC sound radio and television and the ITA should be required to co-operate in organising a university of the air, for serious planned adult education'. The Party did not respond to this suggestion either. The Manifesto for the election of October 1964 referred to the Taylor Report, but not directly to the University of the Air. A paper, written in May 1964, which outlined Party thinking on the subject as far as it had progressed at that time, concluded only by posing a number of questions which remained to be settled. The fact was that the University of the Air was not an element in official Labour Party policy, only an element in the Leader's ideas about what policy might be. It was not a subject that was discussed at the Party Conference, nor at the National Executive Committee. Despite the large number of working parties operating in the months before the October 1964 election there was no working party on the University of the Air.

Mr. Wilson told me that, as far as he could remember, he did not feel any need to put the matter to the Party for debate. He intended to introduce the idea into government thinking when he became Prime Minister. He said to me, 'I just knew it was going to happen; a Prime Minister can, you know.' When Mr Wilson formed his first government in October 1964 he had a tiny majority and was faced with a formidable series of problems. His Ministers were inexperienced in office and there was just too much else to do for there to be any time left for further consideration of the University of the Air. Mr Wilson made it quite clear to me that at no time, until Jennie Lee went to the Department of Education and Science in March 1965, did he request the Department to take any action about it; nor did he recall any proposals from the Department itself about educational broadcasting during that period.

Yet the Department was by no means inactive. During 1963 and the early part of 1964, under the Conservative government, it had been actively pursuing the idea of using educational broadcasting for a 'College of the Air'. Departmental officials working with John Scupham of the BBC were trying to design an experiment, using BBC 2 but financed by government to a total cost of some £2 million a year, to test the feasibility of allocating the fourth TV channel eventually for educational use.

This proposal was ready to go to the Cabinet before the 1964 election, but Lord Hailsham decided not to go ahead with it in the current economic climate. After Labour gained power in the 1964 election, the Minister of State at the DES was Reg Prentice. The proposal, which had been prepared for the previous government, was put to him and by March 1965 everyone was ready for it to be taken to Cabinet.

The concept of a College of the Air was essentially based on a combination of broadcasting with correspondence teaching over a range of subjects at pre-university level for adult students. It had much in common with the experiment of the National Extension College. Michael Young, who had been a member of the Labour Party's Secretariat, and was influential in Party circles had, immediately after Mr Wilson's speeches, set up the National Extension College in Cambridge as a pilot study for what might be developed later. He was primarily concerned with education at pre-university level, recognising the need for qualifications at General Certificate of Education Ordinary and Advanced levels, rather than for university qualifications amongst the adult population. The National Extension College carried out several key experiments during 1963 and 1964 in combining correspondence teaching with the use of television and radio.

It is therefore clear that reactions to Mr Wilson's speech of 1963 had taken a number of forms, none of them closely related to Mr Wilson's own concept, and that by March 1965 several projects had either begun or were about to be launched. It was at this critical moment that Jennie Lee first came on the scene.

The advent of Jennie Lee was the flashpoint of the whole story. Until then the Prime Minister's concept, although it was a matter of public record, had been endorsed neither by the Labour Party nor by the Labour government. The DES was ready with a completely different scheme of its own: suddenly a Minister arrived with a clear brief to explore and promote the Prime Minister's own concept.

Mr Wilson invited Jennie Lee to be Minister with special responsibility for the Arts. He had made up his mind that responsibility for the Arts must be moved from the Treasury and, during his first administration, Jennie Lee was found a position as a Junior Minister at the Ministry of Works. During that period Lord Goodman, who was the Prime Minister's personal solicitor, was made Chairman of the Arts Council. He was thus Miss Lee's closest colleague in her work on the Arts and he was to become a key figure in the development of the Open University.

As part of a Cabinet reshuffle in March 1965 Mr Wilson asked Jennie Lee to accept responsibility not only for the Arts, a task that everyone knew lay close to her heart, but also for the University of the Air. These were strange bedfellows and the arrangement was only possible because Miss Lee was now to operate as a Junior Minister within the DES. However, it meant that the Minister of State with responsibility for all the rest of higher education would *not* be concerned with the University of the Air; and that no part of the civil service machine concerned with higher education would be reporting to Jennie Lee. Thus the new university was effectively isolated from the normal bureaucracy of government. This enabled corners to be cut, but only at the price of alienating, to some extent, those whose support would be required later.

The reasons why Mr Wilson put Miss Lee in charge of the University of the Air thus seem to have been, at least in part, fortuitous. She was already in charge of the Arts, she was to be at the DES and she had the necessary time and energy to take it on. She was, of course, a close personal friend, yet there seems little doubt that, until March 1965, she had had no direct involvement either formally or informally with his ideas about the University of the Air. Her main briefing seems to have been his speeches of 1963. Nevertheless, as Brian McArthur put it,[13] Mr Wilson 'knew that by selecting Jennie Lee to steer it into being, he had chosen a politician of steely imperious will, coupled both with tenacity and charm, who was no respecter of protocol and who would refuse to be defeated or frustrated by the scepticism about the university, which persisted not only in the Department of Education and Science, but also in the universities, among MP's and among the community of adult educators'.

His confidence was not misplaced. Jennie Lee had, within a few days, not only assimilated the ideas that the Prime Minister had advocated, but had in adopting them added her own. They were very stark and very clear and she was to stick by them without wavering. The University of the Air was to be an independent university, offering its own degrees, making no compromise whatever on standards and offering an opportunity to all, without any entrance qualification. These principles are not to be found in Mr Wilson's speeches. I can find no record of their having been put to Jennie Lee by any political person or organisation and they did not represent the thinking of her new Department. She formulated them as soon as she took up her new office, and they seem to have been 'pure unadulterated Jennie Lee' in origin. They were, she told me, inevitable conclusions from the philosophy she had long held: nothing but the best would do. Amongst her very first acts as the new Minister she scrapped, without hesitation, the proposals that had been worked out within the DES for an experimental College of the Air. After discussing with Jennie Lee the brief she now held from the Prime Minister, Reg Prentice agreed to drop the scheme entirely although, I am told, he was somewhat shaken by this *volte-face*. So, indeed, were the people who had worked so hard to formulate the proposals. There was considerable resentment at what appeared to be a high-handed dictat arrived at without any consultation, which was exacerbated by the fact that within the Department there was a good deal of opposition to the Prime Minister's own concept. The University of the Air was held to be a diversion of effort to the wrong ends, an unnecessary frill at a time when resources for badly needed developments over the whole range of education were extremely scarce.

Miss Lee's other early decision was to put the whole idea of the University of the Air before the Ministerial Committee on Broadcasting, a standing Cabinet Committee. This was to lead to two separate chains of events. In the first place the Ministerial Committee referred the matter to its Official Committee with a request that a report be prepared on the organisation and finance of the University of the Air. Secondly, the Ministerial Committee set up an Advisory Committee to explore the 'educational functions and content' of a University of the Air. These two chains of events were to lead to very different results.

The Advisory Committee on the University of the Air was a very unusual Committee indeed. In the first place, Jennie herself was to be Chairman; she insisted on this as a matter of principle. It meant however, that, as the responsible Minister, she could not remain independent of the findings of the group (this is an almost unheard-of situation in Civil Service terms). Senior civil servants at the DES were taken aback at the whole idea, but had no way of stopping it. The general view was that the Advisory Committee would proceed under Jennie's leadership, but that sooner or later the whole idea of the University of the Air would be dropped like a hot potato.

13

The second unusual feature of the Advisory Committee was that its terms of reference were extraordinarily specific – the group was to advise on the possibility of a University of the Air as described by Harold Wilson in his 1963 speech in Glasgow, and was not to examine anything else. Thus the concept first described by Harold Wilson and elaborated by Jennie Lee had, through the Ministerial Committee on Broadcasting, been imposed on the Advisory Committee without what most civil servants would have regarded as proper consultation beforehand. Furthermore, throughout the short life of the Advisory Committee, Jennie worked directly to the Prime Minister and to a considerable extent ignored the normal Whitehall machinery. It was equally true that the latter virtually ignored the existence of the Advisory Committee, in the belief that it would be a 'flash in the pan' and that the whole thing would die a natural death in a relatively short time.

The first meeting of the Advisory Committee was held on 8 June 1965 and it had completed its work by 4 August. The membership, under the chairmanship of Miss Lee, was:

PROFESSOR K. J. ALEXANDER, Professor of Economics, University of Strathclyde.

LORD ANNAN, Provost, King's College, Cambridge.

DR E. W. BRIAULT, Deputy Education Officer, Inner London Education Authority.

DR BRYNMOR JONES, Vice-Chancellor of the University of Hull.

MR D. J. G. HOLROYDE, Director, University of Leeds Television Centre.

MR PETER LASLETT, Fellow of Trinity College, Cambridge.

MR N. I. MACKENZIE, Lecturer in Sociology, University of Sussex.

MR A. D. C. PETERSON, Director, Department of Education, University of Oxford.

DR O. G. PICKARD, Principal, Ealing Technical College.

PROFESSOR F. LLEWELLYN-JONES, Principal, University College of Swansea.

MR J. SCUPHAM, Retired Controller of Educational Broadcasting, British Broadcasting Corporation.

PROFESSOR H. WILTSHIRE, Professor of Adult Education, University of Nottingham.

Also in attendance were Civil Servants from the DES, including members of the inspectorate, together with officers of the University Grants Committee, the Ministry of Technology and the Scottish Education Department. Members of the Committee produced their own versions of how they would like to see the University function. From these papers and from discussions at six meetings held over this very short period there emerged a report from the Committee. This report was produced unchanged as paragraph 8 of the White Paper which was eventually published in February 1966.[14]

The Advisory Committee's Report was basically an academic one; it embodied the principles that Jennie Lee had herself laid down and offered a first outline of possible courses of study. It did not, however, concern itself with questions of resource or of finance. These had been referred to the Official Committee on Broadcasting, composed of civil servants from the departments headed by the members of the Ministerial Committee on Broadcasting.

The work of the Official Committee took rather longer and its Interim Report was sent to the Ministerial Committee on 17 January 1966. Its conclusions were admittedly tentative, but in essence they were that the University of the Air would necessitate the establishment of the fourth television network, at a total capital cost of £42 million and an annual operational cost of about £18 million. The Committee considered that to accommodate the University of the Air within available resources would be extremely difficult and might depend upon financing the University from advertising income. In this case the University would have to be placed under the administration of the Independent Television Authority just as, in a similar manner, the Schools Broadcasting Council fell under the jurisdiction of the BBC. The report ended by indicating that, in the absence of any pilot scheme, it was unlikely that any reliable assessment could be made of the likely viewing audience or of the number of serious students, but that it was probable that the number of degrees gained would be relatively small. The entirely negative tone of the whole of this Report was perhaps typical of the scepticism with which the concept of the University of the Air was viewed by the academic world, and by senior civil servants whose views, at a personal level, would be much coloured by those of their academic advisers and friends.

The Report went to the Ministerial Committee on Broadcasting on 2 February 1966. There is no record that any decision was reached. It is clear, from letters that Jennie Lee wrote at the time, that she was convinced that the establishment of the fourth television channel for the use of the University was a *sine qua non*. There is equally no doubt that there was a great deal of opposition to allocating it for this purpose. This basic divergence of views among Ministers was leaked to the Press from an indeterminate source during January.

On the 23 January, Colin Chapman, writing in *The Sunday Times,* talked of a split in the Cabinet holding up the plans for the new university. He suggested that the announcement of the government's intention to set up the University of the Air would be postponed indefinitely. Chapman indicated that the main objections came from Mr Crosland, Minister of Education, who was arguing that any money available should be devoted to the schools programme and to raising the school leaving age in 1970, and from Mr Wedgwood Benn, Postmaster General, who was taking the line that until the future of the fourth channel was determined nothing could usefully be done about the University of the Air. I suspect that Chapman's account is accurate and that it is a fair representation of the feelings of individual ministers. Jennie Lee was thus fighting hard against a formidable body of opposition to get a firm announcement of the government's intention to proceed with the University of the Air. She wanted to publish a White Paper that would embody the academic Report of the

Advisory Committee and that would commit the government both to allocating the fourth channel to the University and to providing all the necessary finance.

One critical meeting took place on 6 February 1966. At that time the Labour Party held office only tenuously but they had just won a by-election in Hull which helped to maintain their tiny majority. The Press were convinced that there would be no election that spring. Mr Wilson thought differently and says that he had always intended to hold an election then. 'There could be no legislation during the summer with Mr Heath and Mr MacLeod in full cry against the policy of the government and only a very tiny majority to sustain us,' he said. In consequence, on 6 February there was a meeting at Chequers of members of the Cabinet and of the National Executive Committee of the Labour Party. One of the features of the meeting was that Jennie Lee presented the case for the University of the Air.

According to Harold Wilson, it was a very moving occasion and nearly everyone, including himself, was convinced by the new firm proposals. The University of the Air was likened to the National Health Service and the achievement of his widow to that of Nye Bevan. This discussion, informal as it was, almost certainly formed the basis for the inclusion in the election Manifesto for March 1966 of the following statement.

> We shall establish the University of the Air by using TV and radio and comparable facilities, high grade correspondence courses and new teaching techniques. This open university will obviously extend the best teaching facilities and give everyone the opportunity of study for a full degree. It will mean genuine equality of opportunity for millions of people for the first time. Moreover for those who prefer not to take a full course it will bring the widest and best contribution possible to the general level of knowledge and breadths of interest.

This was the very first formal commitment by the Labour Party to the creation of the Open University. Nevertheless it was a commitment that gave no date and no particulars of how the new institution would be set up. Furthermore a Party commitment was not a government commitment, and Jennie Lee had still not abandoned her conviction that the fourth television channel must be made available. In a letter to Jack Diamond, Financial Secretary to the Treasury, dated 7 February, the day after the Chequers meeting, she asserted that to launch the University of the Air on the scale publicly announced demanded a more coherent and substantial television coverage than could be provided by residual broadcasting time on existing services. She maintained that certain financial arguments put forward by Mr Diamond were irrelevant since no University based on the use of residual time would be academically viable. It was, in the opinion of all the experts she had consulted, indisputable that the fourth network was indispensable to the establishment of the University of the Air.

This was plain speaking indeed. Yet at a Cabinet meeting the very next day she compromised. I do not know what was said but she must have realised that to insist on the fourth channel *ab initio* would inevitably mean the end of the project; the opposition was too strong. She therefore agreed to proceed on the basis of using BBC 2 initially, on the assumption that a fourth channel would become available in the future. This change of tactic, for it was not a change of heart, is apparent in the letter she wrote to Lord Goodman on 8 February after the Cabinet meeting. She stated that there was unanimous agreement that the University should be launched if it could be made financially possible. She said that the questions that remained were cost and the television channel to be used, and continued, 'the real choice lies between BBC 2 and the fourth television network. Many members of the Cabinet suggested the hours 6–9 pm, five days a week on BBC 2 for this project. I consider this the ideal solution. In these 15 hours all the original programmes we needed could be presented and the repeat programmes could be offered on other channels.' Later in the letter Jennie Lee said that it was vital that the programmes should have a regular place in a single network and that it would be hopeless to expect the teachers of the institution or indeed the students to 'grope around from one channel to another'. She then went on to discuss the possibility of obtaining at a later date the fourth television channel in colour and of sharing it between the University of the Air and the ITA, who would buy time. It had been felt in the Cabinet discussion that the ITA would not be interested in this particular arrangement. The last paragraph of the letter is significant: 'What we need now is a realistic assessment of the relative costs of launching the University of the Air on BBC 2 and the fourth channel. The Cabinet are convinced that you (Lord Goodman) are the best person to help on this and were unanimous in asking me to approach you.'

If Jennie Lee had accepted a compromise at the Cabinet meeting on 8 February, so indeed had the opponents of the University of the Air. The invitation to Lord Goodman clearly overrode the Report of the Official Committee on Broadcasting; it was a request for an independent assessment of costs. But the election programme would not wait even for Lord Goodman's report. It was, in the Prime Minister's view, necessary that a White Paper on the University of the Air be published before the election in March. The text of the White Paper,[14] when it appeared, was itself a compromise produced by the DES in the light of these discussions of early February. Paragraph 2 included one revealing statement: 'The government believe that by imaginative use of new teaching techniques and teacher/ student relationships, an open university providing degree courses as rigorous and demanding as those in existing universities can be established' – not that it 'will' be established. Thus the government was still not committed to the venture.

However, paragraph 4 states that 'From the outset it must be made clear that there can be no question of offering to students a makeshift project inferior in quality to other universities. That would defeat its own purpose, as its status will be determined by the quality of its teaching. Its aim will be to provide, in addition to television and radio lectures, correspondence courses of a quality unsurpassed anywhere in the world. These will be reinforced by residential courses and tutorials'. There is thus a firm commitment to the university level and quality. Then, in paragraph 8, the Report of the Advisory Committee is given in full, ending with a firm recommendation that a Planning Committee be established. In paragraph 9 the White Paper simply states, 'The government are now discussing with the broadcasting authorities arrangements for the television and radio programmes that will form part of the new structure of a University of the Air'. So the issue of BBC 2 versus the fourth television channel was shelved. By neatly avoiding a final decision on the two most crucial questions, it had become possible to produce the White Paper in time for the forthcoming election, and copy was sent to the Government Printer in mid-February.

At that time there was a delay in the Government Printer's office because of an industrial dispute. As a result of this one of the officials in the DES advised the Prime Minister's private office that publication of the White Paper might be delayed. The message that came back is said to have been 'Sack the Government Printer'. This was a measure perhaps of Mr Wilson's anxiety that something should be on record before the general election.

A clear indication that the University of the Air had so far progressed outside the normal working of the Whitehall machine was contained in another White Paper, published at the same time, which emanated from the Post Office and dealt with the future of broadcasting. The draft of this Paper did not even mention educational broadcasting and it was only through the efforts of Miss Lee and officers in the DES that a paragraph was subsequently written in.

When the White Paper appeared press reaction was again hostile. *The Times*, in an editorial on 26 February, suggested that the only available air time would be on BBC 2. It continued, 'the big question is whether all the money the University of the Air will cost will be worthwhile. There may well be a relatively high audience to begin with, but how fast and how far will it run down?' It ended with the statement that 'the cost per degree would be fantastic'. This, in my view, was once again a fair reflection of feeling in the academic world at the time. *The Times Educational Supplement* began its editorial on 4 March, 'Mr Wilson's pipe dream of a University of the Air, now adumbrated in a White Paper, as vague as it is unsubstantial, is just the sort of cosy scheme that shows the Socialists at their most endearing but impractical worst.' It went on to say, 'Can we really afford the cost of what this would entail? The government give no estimate. It is just as well. This is one of those grandiose schemes that does not bear inspection when so much else that is already begun remains half done'; and it ended, 'Can anyone by any stretch of imagination justify a priority for this well-intentioned but untimely caprice?' A week later in *The Times Educational Supplement,* after the debate in the House on broadcasting policy, the principal opposition spokesman, Mr Paul Bryan, was reported as saying that 'The obstacles to the University of the Air were the cost, the channel on which it could be transmitted and the problem of one set to a house'. He referred to the experiments at Strathclyde and other progressive universities and contended that all experience so far did not seem to recommend a University of the Air as envisaged in the White Paper. *The*

Observer on 27 February, in slightly less definitive terms, took the same line as *The Times:* it ended, 'The plain fact is that Miss Lee's project still has a good many enemies within the Cabinet. Even the educational world is far from sold on it. Many adult education experts doubt that there would be sufficient demand to justify running all degree courses on TV.'

In *The New Statesman*, traditionally a supporter of the Labour Party, Magnus Turnstile on the 11 March wrote a fairly lengthy and thoughtful article about the White Paper. He summarised the reactions to it in the following words, 'The Press was lukewarm, educators were doubtful about ends, broadcasters were dubious about means and the public was apparently unstirred'. He went on to suggest that the small group of educationally deprived that the new University would cater for – those who missed college – were the least important of all this category in the country. He argued in favour of filling the enormous gaps in the educational system by providing for people at a lower educational level. Having asked all these questions he concluded, 'But why were they not faced before the Cabinet approved the White Paper? Why was the Advisory Committee given so little time to produce a report and instructed most firmly that it must not discuss any major alternatives to the Glasgow speech? Those questions like so many others about this project remain unanswered.'

In voicing all these doubts the press was undoubtedly reflecting feeling in the world of adult education and of education generally. This is shown very obviously in a letter to *The Times* on the 7 March from Tom Kelly, then the Secretary of the Universities Council for Adult Education. He thought that the proposal in its present form was premature, as not enough was known about the potential number and needs of students. He argued in support of the Universities Council for Adult Education proposal to establish an adult education broadcasting council which would seek to identify the urgent needs and relate these to the efficient use of available resources. He felt that meanwhile the money available should be devoted to the existing adult education agencies. This, then, was the situation when the country went to the polls on the 31 March 1966 and returned the Labour government with a very much bigger majority.

When Mr Wilson set up his second administration in April 1966 Miss Lee was back in the same job. Her battle to induce the previous government to commit itself to the University of the Air had been at best only partially successful. There was, it is true, a Labour Party commitment in the Manifesto, and the White Paper had been published – but without the firm government commitment she had sought.

It might have been expected that, in the new situation, things would begin to hum immediately. But this turned out to be far from true. There was a deathly hush for a very long time, in fact until September 1967. This was partly due, no doubt, to the overall state of the economy. By July 1966, the sterling crisis had resulted in a bank rate of 7%, in tax increases, in credit restraints, and in a prices and incomes standstill. But despite the silence there was throughout this period continuous activity, all aimed at settling the outstanding questions: 'What would it cost and who would pay for it?' and 'on what channels will the programmes be broadcast?' The key figure in both sets of negotiations was Lord Goodman.

He had been working away at the task since accepting the invitation of 8 February 1966. By the 23 February he had seen Hugh Greene, Director-General of the BBC, and had had preliminary discussions about the costing of the new institution. It is quite clear that the two men hit it off together from the very start. From the tenor of the letters exchanged between them it is evident that Miss Lee had no thought of delaying the creation of the institution. The BBC completed careful analyses of the overall cost of putting on programmes on television and radio to meet the needs of the new institution. They were calculating on a start in 1968, which involved the appointment of a Vice-Chancellor of the University of the Air by the summer of 1966. They estimated that 32 hours per week of broadcasting time could be made available on BBC 2, at a total annual cost for both production and transmission of about £2 million at 1965 prices. Even at that stage they envisaged an educational partnership between the University and the BBC and they had gone into considerable detail concerning the necessary staffing and backup facilities that would be required. The BBC had in fact reached a view which was almost identical to that which they put forward nearly two years later.

Lord Goodman's report was prepared and sent to the Prime Minister on the 25 May 1966. In essence it recommended that BBC 2 should be used to launch the Open University, the real basis for this decision being that no major capital costs would be involved such as would arise if the fourth television channel were initiated. The report envisaged that the early years of the institution would be experimental. Modifications might be made in the light of experience and, should substantial expansion be required, it might involve transferral to a fourth television network. The report was equally firm that neither BBC 1 nor Independent Television should participate in the scheme. A start was proposed in 1968 with 10 hours of television per week rising to 30 hours in the third and subsequent years. The estimated cost of the whole project was £3.5 million annually with an initial capital expenditure of just over £1 million. Lord Goodman knows that he greatly underestimated the total cost. He takes credit for having made it a practicable proposition—by accident. On 23 May 1974 he said in the House of Lords, 'When I see the figure I mentioned and the figure it is now costing I ought to blush with shame.' But he did not because it 'might not have been established except for my foolish miscalculation'. Had the real cost been known at the time, it seems quite probable that the whole idea would have been dropped.

Lord Goodman's report was submitted to the Secretary of State, Tony Crosland, and was referred by him to the Ministerial Committee on Broadcasting with a covering memorandum, dated September 1966, pointing out that there had been a lot of public reference to the Open University since February and that a firm decision could no longer be delayed.

He asked his colleagues to announce the intention of establishing the Open University in 1968 or as soon as possible thereafter with programmes on BBC 2 and supporting correspondence courses. He proposed that the Advisory Committee be reconstituted and asked to work out a plan for the establishment of the University as an institution, created by Royal Charter and grant-aided by the Department of Education. As far as I can make out the delay between May 1966, when Lord Goodman's report arrived, and September 1966, when this submission was made, was primarily because the DES was not as convinced as Jennie of the desirability of submitting the project yet again to the Ministerial Committee on Broadcasting and, through it, to the Cabinet.

Thus the second question had been answered by September 1966 in a way that was formally acceptable to the government. Nevertheless it was by no means a popular answer in all circles. Although an early agreement had been reached by Lord Goodman and Sir Hugh Greene, there was a large element of scepticism within the BBC's own staff about the future of the project and widespread resistance to the idea of giving up potential peak transmission times for these educational programmes. Furthermore, the Further Education Advisory Council of the BBC wished to expand their own provision of further education and were in competition with the University of the Air for some of the times that were available. In addition, the future of broadcasting was still under review and the Postmaster General and his Department feared that plans for the allocation of the channels would be prejudiced by early decisions about the University of the Air.

Progress over the finance of the institution was much slower. Lord Goodman had also been asked to see whether he could raise money from sources other than government funds in order to get the University established. Two possible sources were suggested by the Prime Minister himself through his personal contacts in the USA. He had long been friendly with Senator William Benton, who owned the Encyclopaedia Britannica and was a fervent supporter of the idea of a University of the Air. In addition Mr McGeorge Bundy, a former member of the Kennedy administration, had just become President of the Ford Foundation. Lord Goodman visited both in the USA in February 1966. He returned with expressions of interest but it was clearly too early to make any formal request for funds.

There is little evidence of what actually went on during the following year in respect of finance. By May 1967, in a letter to Lord Goodman, Jennie Lee was able to say, 'The only thing holding us, as you know so well, is finance. From the outset it has been clear between Tony Crosland and myself that a new project must not be launched at the expense of existing commitments such as school building programmes in the priority areas. I am also most anxious that the University Grants Committee, which is permanently short of funds to meet present claims, should see in an Open University an easing of its problems, not an additional burden.'

Almost certainly no money could be found from within the existing funds available to the DES and the Treasury was by no means anxious to vote additional funds to the Department to cover this new venture, for which they had never had any enthusiasm. There is also no question but that Jennie, with the help of Lord Goodman, was still trying to find sources of money from outside the government area.

In May 1967, Lord Goodman met Mr McGeorge Bundy for a second time. He explained to Mr Bundy how enormously helpful it would be for the government to be able to present an experimental scheme like the Open University as having the support of his great Foundation, not merely on financial grounds, but in justification of the decision to proceed. Mr Bundy expressed general interest in this proposal, said it was one which would certainly be considered by the Foundation, and invited the submission of a detailed request. Meanwhile Miss Lee was making the first tentative approaches to individuals, with a view to setting up the Planning Committee of the Open University, despite the absence of a firm decision to get the Committee started. She made this clear in a letter to Lord Goodman in July, but ended by asking whether on a further trip to the United States he was once again going to speak to Mr Bundy, looking for some word of the latter's willingness to support the project. By this time, Miss Lee had put in a very large bid to the Ford Foundation for funds to get the University of the Air off the ground.

Mr Bundy considered that the bid was much too large to be met by the Foundation alone and he indicated this in a letter to Lord Goodman in the same month. There seems to have been some crossing of wires at this time, since it is Mr Wilson's impression that Miss Lee was to have approached Mr Bundy and that her bid was to have been limited to getting supplementary help to government money that would be made available for the Open University. By the 31st of the same month, in any case, Lord Goodman was able to indicate to Mr Bundy that the government had given a positive indication of its willingness to subscribe to a fund and he asked him if the Foundation could make a similar contribution.

On 24 May, Jennie wrote to the Prime Minister describing the result of the talks between Lord Goodman and Mr Bundy and telling him that Mr Bundy wanted the Vice-Chancellor of the Open University to visit America to meet his trustees. She asked urgently for an official announcement about the setting up of the Planning Committee, but there was no response to this letter in the sense that no announcement was made for another three months. In late June of 1967, Jennie was still trying to get the backing of Mr Callaghan at the Treasury, which had given considerable help in formulating the application for funds to the Ford Foundation, but was still dragging its heels about the setting up of a Planning Committee. Jennie made it perfectly plain that there was considerable pressure coming from Sir Hugh Green and the BBC, who needed a firm decision if they were to take steps to implement the programme that they had presented to Lord Goodman in the previous year. But even at this stage there was no enthusiasm at all from the Treasury. Indeed Jennie was told that it was hopeless to try to arrange further meetings with the Chancellor and that it would be better to carry on discussion by correspondence.

The decision to set up the Planning Committee for the new university could be taken only by the Cabinet, for the creation of the Planning Committee, and the impossibility of rejecting the Report it would produce, would effectively commit the government to going ahead. This was therefore the next great hurdle. It was jumped in September 1967.

I can find no record to explain why the Cabinet finally agreed to set up the Planning Committee. There was no promise of funds from the Ford Foundation or indeed from anywhere else. There is no evidence of any change of heart in the Treasury. It is almost as if Jennie's continued pressure finally wore down the opposition. I asked the Prime Minister the precise reason why the Cabinet finally agreed that a Planning Committee should be set up, but he told me that he did not know, he felt that it was just 'the natural process of things'. He felt that the delay had no obvious cause. 'Maybe,' he said, 'I did not give Jennie enough backing and support, maybe I left too much to her.' As far as I can gather from discussion with officials at the DES, the Prime Minister never gave any special instructions, but left the whole thing in Jennie's hands. It may well be that the Chancellor was finally persuaded to withdraw Treasury opposition through the Prime Minister giving way on some other issue dear to the Chancellor. Such political 'horse-trading' is not unusual and there seems to be no other explanation of the final change of heart.

Throughout this long period of silence on the part of the Government, from April 1966 until September 1967, there was inevitably a good deal of press and political comment and speculation. In June 1966, *The Times Educational Supplement* carried another editorial about the University of the Air which began with a paragraph of renewed hope. 'The idea of a university of the air did not at first get a good reception from some people in adult education; it was called 'impractical' and a 'diversion of resources'. Three months after the publication of the White Paper, informed opinion in the world of adult education is far more optimistic about the idea.' Asa Briggs, at that time President of the Workers' Educational Association, suggested that an essential part of the setting up of the University of the Air should be that more money be given by the state to existing bodies working in the field of adult education. He felt that the WEA could play a big part in making the scheme work but that the new organisation should not be centralised in any sense, but should depend, like the WEA, on full consultation with local bodies.

In Parliament too, a series of questions about the costs of the whole operation were thrown at Miss Lee. She stalled for time, but always in a tone that indicated total conviction that the new institution would come about. Thus, on 28 July 1966, in response to a supplementary question from Mr J. E. B. Hill, who asked whether in view of the economic crisis and the need to concentrate all available educational resources where they were most needed, the proposals for a University of the Air would now be shelved, her answer was short and sweet, 'Most certainly NO, sir'.

In November 1966, in response to Mr William Hamilton who asked when the university would be established, Miss Lee replied that the preparatory work was far advanced and that she hoped to make a full statement in the next two months. In March, she hoped to make the statement soon. In April and in June, the same reply was given. By July, Mr Hamilton, in a supplementary question was asking 'How soon is soon? Is the project being held up by finance, or by disagreement on principles as to the operation of the scheme?' Miss Lee replied that the scheme was not being held up on either point. Sir Edward Boyle suggested in a supplementary that the House was becoming somewhat impatient, and that the whole question was becoming something of a non-saga of rather considerable length. Since it was over a full year since a statement had first been promised, this seemed to be a reasonable comment at the time. By July Jennie Lee was sufficiently sure that she was nearing victory to begin to consider the membership of the Planning Committee. By this time, too, there had been a change in the name of the institution from the 'University of the Air' to the 'Open University'. A number of individuals had been approached one after the other and asked to serve, but no decision had yet been taken over the key question of the Chairman. The reasons why the choice fell upon Sir Peter Venables are not documented, but his appointment was a fateful one, since it brought on to the scene the next key personality in the development of the Open University.

The fact that the Planning Committee was formed at all surprised most academics in this country. Doubt about the whole venture was still the order of the day, and how the idea had remained as part of the programme throughout successive financial crises, nobody could quite understand. Undoubtedly Jennie Lee was the key figure, but equally she could not have sustained the concept without the known and overt support of the Prime Minister. This enthusiasm and dedication undoubtedly kept the project alive while others were sacrificed. On the other hand, her decision (taken as soon as she assumed responsibility for the University of the Air) that it should be at university level, termed a university and offering its own degrees, aroused even more reservations in the academic community, and especially in the world of adult education.

She showed no signs of moving from this stance and, with hindsight, it seems to me that she was right. Had she given way, had she attempted to start with a scheme offering education through the media to adults, at school or pre-university level, I think the concept would have disappeared. Its cost would have been no less, its status would have been much less, it would have had no glamour. It was the glamour of a university in name and in actuality that enabled her to win her way. It was perhaps this too, that led her to seek advice from the university world, but largely to ignore the world of adult education, including the extramural departments, the Workers' Educational Association and the local education authorities. This undoubtedly caused a great deal of resentment amongst those who were working hard in this field who felt that they were, especially in the eyes of the DES, the Cinderellas of the educational world. Once the Open University began, it took us a very long time to overcome this early resentment. The appointment of the Planning Committee was announced by Jennie Lee at a press conference on Monday, 18 September 1967. At the same time she gave its membership and revealed that its chairman was to be Sir Peter Venables, Vice-Chancellor of the University of Aston in Birmingham.

Miss Lee went on to reiterate the major features of the new university as outlined in the White Paper: that it would make no compromise on standards, that its degree-giving system would be modelled on the credit system common in Scottish and American universities, that the programmes would be distributed on BBC 2 and that the cost would be met from the University's funds and not from the BBC's licence revenue. There would be short seminars, residential courses and local viewing centres which would probably have to be provided as a responsibility of local education authorities. Miss Lee gave figures for the total cost of the operation: they were based on Lord Goodman's exercise of the previous year, and estimated capital costs of about £1 million, and running costs, when the University was fully operational, of between £3 and £4 million. Students, she said, would have to pay fees, but these would be in line with the usual levels of fee for correspondence courses. The rest of the money would be provided by direct grants-in-aid from the DES.

In response to questions, Miss Lee repeated that there would be no entrance qualifications and that students would be allowed to work at their own pace, but that the standard of the degree would be quite definitely equivalent to that of any other university. Press comment as a result of the conference was not extensive. There was a singular absence of enthusiasm but there was no sign of any major criticism.

The Planning Committee, which was to begin work immediately from offices in Belgrave Square and was expected to report in about nine months, consisted of the following members:

SIR PETER VENABLES, Ph.D, FRIC, Chairman (Vice-Chancellor of the University of Aston in Birmingham).

SIR WILLIAM ALEXANDER, Ph.D, MA, M.Ed, B.Sc (General Secretary of the Association of Education Committees).

SIR ERIC ASHBY, FRS (Vice-Chancellor of the University of Cambridge).

DR E. W. H. BRIAULT, MA (Deputy Education Officer of the Inner London Education Authority).

PROFESSOR ASA BRIGGS, B.Sc (Econ), MA (Vice-Chancellor of the University of Sussex).

LORD FULTON, MA (former Vice-Chancellor of University of Sussex).

LORD GOODMAN, MA, LL.M (Solicitor; Company Director; Fellow of University College, London; Chairman of the Arts Council).

MR BRIAN GROOMBRIDGE, MA (Education Officer, Independent Television Authority).

PROFESSOR HILDE T. HIMMELWEIT, Ph.D. (Professor of Social Psychology, London School of Economics).

MR I. HUGHES, LL.B (Warden of Coleg Harlech).

SIR BRYNMOR JONES, Ph.D, LL.D, Sc.D, FRIC (Vice-Chancellor of the University of Hull).

DR F. J. LLEWELLYN, B.Sc, D.Sc, LL.B, FRS (NZ) (Vice-Chancellor of the University of Exeter).

MR NORMAN MACKENZIE, B.Sc (Econ.) (Director of the Centre for Educational Technology at the University of Sussex).

MR RODERICK MACLEAN, MA, M.Ed (Director of the University of Glasgow Television Service).

DR A. J. RICHMOND, B.Sc (Eng.), F.I.Mech.E (Principal of Lanchester College of Technology).

PROFESSOR LORD RITCHIE CALDER, CBE, MA (University of Edinburgh).

MR J. SCUPHAM, OBE, BA (former Controller of BBC Educational Broadcasting).

PROFESSOR ROY SHAW, BA (Director of Adult Education, University of Keele).

PROFESSOR HAROLD WILTSHIRE, MA (Professor of Adult Education, University of Nottingham).

The Committee, by its very creation, took the job of drawing the blueprints for the new university out of the hands of the politicians for the first time. It was a wholly academic group and a remarkably strong one: there were five Vice-Chancellors and an ex Vice-Chancellor among the members. There was representation from the local education authorities, from the fields of adult education and broadcasting and from the world of educational technology.

The Chairman, Sir Peter Venables, had no direct political affiliation, but was an experienced and well respected educationalist who had long been interested in widening educational opportunities. He had been a member of the Crowther Committee and was especially interested in the section of its work which dealt with increasing the opportunities for technical education. He was also a very able and hard working Chairman. In my experience, having sat on many committees in my time, he was one of the two best chairmen I have ever known. The critical task of a Chairman is to have done a complete job of homework, so that he starts each meeting knowing what he thinks should be done on each item of the agenda. He should then allow all members of the Committee a chance to express their views and, unless in a particular case he considers the majority view to be disastrous, he should adopt the consensus of opinion. Should he sense any lack of a clear view among the members he should be ready to give a lead by expressing his own view, worked out in advance. Sir Peter had all these attributes and combined with them a lightness of touch, a gift for mordant comment and a bubbling good humour that kept the Committee a happy as well as a very industrious one throughout its life. I know that my opinion of his Chairmanship was shared by every member of the Committee.

The Planning Committee, being as it was of immense academic distinction, brought an aura of respectability and of authority to the concept of an Open University, which had been looked on as a 'gimmick' in the academic world as a whole. This was all in line with Jennie Lee's main aim of making sure that the University was a university in all senses of the term and was launched in accordance with that style. She had worked very hard to gain the co-operation of these powerful educationalists, a number of whom have confessed that they were by no means supporters of the idea until they joined the Committee. It is no part of the political history of the Open University to discuss the work of the Planning Committee itself. The work was primarily academic and administrative rather than political, as befitted the membership, and I will be discussing these aspects in later chapters.

The Committee worked from September 1967 until January 1969 (a period of fifteen months, instead of the nine originally forecast by Jennie Lee). Its first public statement was in the form of a press release in March 1968. This statement emphasised the recognition by the Planning Committee that its function was to draw up outlines along which the University would develop rather than to set out a complete blue-print. Although there were still many unknowns in the academic and logistic equations, partly because of the innovatory nature of the institution, the Committee believed that the pattern they had worked out would be feasible.

The press release continued with details of the degree pattern: no formal academic qualifications would be needed for entry; a degree could be obtained by the accumulation of six credits; and a diagram setting out the pattern of lines of study was attached. Later the statement emphasised that courses would not depend exclusively on live broadcasting but that correspondence courses and a network of viewing and listening centres would also be provided. It concluded by saying that the provision of professional and refresher courses was under consideration but that the University would not organise or run preparatory courses; the Committee hoped that other organisations would assume this role.

My appointment as Vice-Chancellor of the Open University was made in May 1968 and announced at a press conference in London the following month. The political significance of this choice was that I came from a traditional academic background and would therefore be seen as a respectable Vice-Chancellor and not as an eccentric or gimmicky one. As further academic appointments were made during 1968 and early 1969 it became clearer to the academic world that the Planning Committee was as determined as Jennie Lee had been that only the best would do and that the university should have a status at least as high as that of any other.

The Times however, on 7 June 1968, linking its editorial to the announcement of my appointment, did nothing to reassure me or any future applicant for vacant appointments. It repeated the old cry: 'Is there a demand for the service? The Committee as yet have given no answer. The Open University is to begin in early 1971, but we still have no consumer research.' They quoted the example of the Chicago experiment, where some 53,000 out of a total population of 8,000,000 participated in 'credit' courses; of these, only 122 (0.2%) gained a degree and 1,100 (2%) gained some form of credit. The suggestion was clearly that the Open University would be lucky to end up with comparable results. They queried the budget, with a certain amount of justification, and argued that not enough information was being made available for adequate judgments to be made. They quoted Asa Briggs who, a year before he became a member of the Planning Committee, had said that if the Open University was not done well it was likely to be done deplorably. They finished by saying, 'It is time for the Planning Committee and Miss Lee to convince us all that the University is something more acceptable, feasible and desirable than just an expensive memorial to one who may well be its original mentor, that most brilliant of genuinely self-educated men, Aneurin Bevan.' This attitude continued in isolated press comments throughout the year. Because of the relative silence of the Planning Committee there were continued questions in the House about the progress that was being made, and most had a certain snide element to them.

At that time I was acting as the main public relations officer for the new institution, although I was still in fact a member of the staff of Edinburgh University. Nevertheless, I never turned down an invitation to speak and I travelled around the country talking about the future of the Open University. It would have needed an ice-pick to cut the atmosphere. Although it would get perceptibly warmer after I had spoken, the tenor of the questions often indicated scepticism, and sometimes downright ridicule. I believe that I was able to remove the topmost layer of scepticism, but I could reach only a small fraction of the academic world.

If the atmosphere in the academic world was unpropitious, it was no better in that of politics. During the life of the Planning Committee the Conservative Party never went on record with any public statement about their attitude to the Open University. Nevertheless, as we discovered later, any potential applicant for a job in the University who wrote to the Party for advice was, throughout the whole period, advised not to apply as the future of the institution was considered to be in doubt. I do not know how many potential applicants withdrew as a result of such advice: I only know that a number were undeterred by it. Nevertheless it may explain in part the left of centre bias amongst the academic staff of the Open University as a whole.

The next step in the political progress of the University came with the publication of the report of the Planning Committee in January 1969.[15] The report had been submitted to Mr Ted Short, Secretary of State for Education and Science, on 31 December 1968. He was extremely anxious to have it published quickly. He had been a supporter of Jennie Lee on Ministerial Committees since the earliest days of the Labour Government, and was the first Minister of Education to have shown any public enthusiasm for her project. Consequently the report was printed within a month and published on 28 January 1969.

On the same day Mr Short announced in the Commons that the government fully accepted the plan of development as outlined. This was a firm and explicit commitment: the government intended to go ahead.

In his short account of the history of the University,[13] Brian MacArthur says Mr Short had got the backing of the Cabinet at that time. I asked Mr Wilson about this and it appears that the report of the Planning Committee was not submitted to the Cabinet at all. Yet the Secretary of State indicated that it was not he who accepted the report, but the government. It seems in retrospect that he took the Cabinet decision to proceed with the appointment of the Planning Committee a full fifteen months earlier as sufficient reason to justify acceptance of its Report on behalf of the government. However, Mr Short did run some risk by his immediate endorsement of the Report since, even at that late stage, there were several Ministers in the Labour Government who remained fairly doubtful about the scheme.

In his statement to the House, Mr Short said, 'It will now be for the University authority, as an autonomous and completely independent institution to carry the project forward, and in this it can count on the support of the government.' Immediately thereafter, Sir Edward Boyle, chief opposition spokesman on Education, rose to set out the Conservative Party's views on the published report. Until that time they had made no public statement. But we knew that they had no love for the scheme, and comment in the House and in the press indicated that there was rampant hostility to it amongst many influential members of the Party. For this reason, Peter Venables and I had arranged an interview with Sir Edward on the day before the debate, when we tried to put to him some of our underlying beliefs about the future of the University. Edward Boyle is a very liberal man and we expected that he would be able to see our point of view, as indeed he did. On the other hand he was under severe pressure from his constituency parties and from the back benches in the House to take a strong line against the Open University. In the event his speech the next day was a carefully worded blend of the two sides to the story. He did not say the Conservatives would not support the new venture but, on the other hand, he carefully gave no guarantee that they would. His statement actually read:

> The report sets out a project embracing interesting experiments in the use of broadcasting for educational purposes and in the development of part-time degree courses, with both of which objectives we on these benches are very much in sympathy. But is it not a fact that this proposal comes at a time when resources for essential educational tasks are more severely stretched than any year since the war? Does the Right Honourable Gentleman really think that it makes sense for him to commit himself to funds of about an annual rate of £3.7 million as mentioned in the report, particularly as this report may well suggest techniques and innovations that could be adopted more efficiently and less expensively by existing institutions providing part-time degree courses and other forms of adult education?

It was probably the mildest attack on the Open University that Sir Edward felt he could get away with. Reports in the Conservative press suggested that his words were much stronger than they had, in fact, been.

Thus, instead of being an educational establishment outside politics, we remained a pawn in the party political game and our future was by no means as assured as we would have liked. The thought of a General Election bringing the Conservatives back into power before we had established ourselves as a respectable and practicable institution in the eyes of the academic world and the community at large, was a bogey we could not face with equanimity. Things were to get worse before they got better. Many of the Conservative spokesmen were much less liberal-minded than Sir Edward and at one point during the next year the Open University was castigated by Iain McLeod as 'blithering nonsense'. This seemed to me a remark that was grossly out of character for a man who was so liberal on other issues. Perhaps he was influenced by the fact that the university had been originally proposed by the Prime Minister, for he was in those days very much the self-appointed 'Hammer of Harold Wilson'. In the summer of 1970 the next General Election took place and, against all the previous forecasts, the Conservative Party won handsomely. We were up against our fears in a real form: Iain McLeod was the new Chancellor, and we had to worry about survival.

Some months earlier the Officers of the Open University, who had made a habit of meeting together over dinner about once a month, invited Margaret Thatcher, then the opposition spokesman on Education, to join them to discuss the future of the University. It was a memorable occasion. Margaret Thatcher, who is a lawyer by instinct as much as by training, came prepared to attack on all fronts. She suggested first that our main activity would be to offer courses on 'hobbies'. I fear that I needle very easily and this attack got under my skin in no uncertain manner – as she no doubt intended. The exchanges were sharp, short and furious. I am happy to say that, despite it all, we ended on a friendly note. Mrs Thatcher went away admitting that not only was she much better informed but that, even if she was not yet persuaded of the validity of the whole concept, at least the edge of her criticism had been blunted. When she became Minister of Education after the Tory victory in 1970 we had reason to be glad of that dinner.

In any case we survived, albeit with a cut in our total budget, during the Conservative Party's hold on power, and throughout the years of their administration we gradually won their political acceptance. I think it is fair to say that by now, in 1976, the University has achieved its proper position as an institution outside politics and is no longer a pawn in the party political game. It has been a long haul and this position has only been achieved as a result of the academic success of the University: through the fact that it has, despite all the initial opposition, won its spurs as an institution that can and does offer a chance to the many people who have the dedication and drive to succeed.

3

EARLY PROBLEMS

When my appointment as Vice-Chancellor was announced in June 1968 there were two and a half years to go before we were due to start teaching our first students. At first sight this seemed to be a timescale long enough for my needs. I was to find out very quickly just how wrong first impressions could be.

I came to the Open University from a wholly traditional background, having spent most of my working life as a member of the staff of the Medical Research Council and as Professor of Pharmacology in the University of Edinburgh. At the time of my appointment I was also acting as Vice-Principal of Edinburgh University. This had led me to face some of the problems, challenges and techniques of university administration. It was however administration in a university with a long history and deep seated traditions, which by no stretch of the imagination could be regarded as an innovative institution. I had had no experience of any of the new universities in Britain, nor had I ever been involved in adult education in any of its many forms.

My first task was obviously to make myself informed about what the Planning Committee had done and what it proposed to do. With the help of Peter Venables, the Chairman, and of David Stafford, an officer from the Department of Education and Science who had been seconded to act as secretary of the Committee, I studied the files of all its previous meetings and attended all its meetings thereafter. This was a relatively privileged position for me since I was able to influence the nature of the Report of the Planning Committee without assuming responsibility for its content. This lack of personal commitment to the detailed recommendations of the Report left me with a freer hand once the University was created. Throughout 1968 I remained an employee of the University of Edinburgh, but Michael Swann, then Vice-Chancellor, was very understanding and allowed me to devote most of my time to my new task. Nevertheless I was still commuting to and from London and trying to do two jobs at the same time.

There were two primary tasks that faced me: the first was to build the University, and the second was to try so to influence the atmosphere within which it would be built that it would be welcomed as an exciting new venture in the field of education at large. The second task was urgent and vitally important; it involved two kinds of problem. The first concerned the place of the new university in the context of adult education in general. In the next two years I was to meet nearly all the key people in this field. It was a wholly different world from that in which I had moved in the past and it was hard to find one's way in the new ambience. Some of these people I encountered at the meetings organised by the Planning Committee; others came to see me on their own initiative and I came across still more as I went about the country talking and lecturing about the new institution. The main problem stemmed from the feeling, prevalent amongst most people working in the field, that the government had for many years starved adult education of funds and support. If it was going to spend more money, they felt, it ought to be directed to those agencies already in being, rather than being spent on a new institution and, furthermore, on an untried, unproven institution that many people thought would be serving a need much less important than the needs with which they themselves were concerned. Some of this doubt and resentment had been provoked by Jennie Lee's insistence, without what was regarded as adequate consultation, on setting up a university rather than providing opportunities at a lower educational level.

The situation was therefore plain enough. The world of adult education was interested in the foundation of the Open University, would have liked it to have been an institution to fulfil the needs that they themselves felt to be particularly urgent, would have liked to have been consulted very much more fully than they had been, and were suspicious that what would come out at the end would be something they themselves would not have wanted or approved of. It was vital to convince them of the need for the institution and to describe for them precisely what it was going to tackle and how it was going to do its job. I had to try to ensure that it was not regarded by the rest of the world of adult education as a threat, a take-over bid designed to reduce the effectiveness of the Workers' Educational Association or of the extramural departments of the universities. Finally it was necessary also for me to ensure that it was not regarded by the local education authorities as a central government device to force them to channel their limited funds in different directions. I had to learn all this for I was not at first aware of all these undercurrents. Without such awareness I could not hope to persuade those working in adult education that what we were doing was a good thing and would complement their own activities rather than compete with them.

A further set of problems lay within the world of higher education, from which I had sprung and about which I was much more knowledgeable. Here there was no welcome for the new institution at all. Most of my colleagues in universities regarded my move to the Open University as a sign of incipient senility; they thought I was quite mad! They did not believe that education through the media could conceivably work. They largely shared the views that had been expressed both by the Conservative Party and by the national press. I had to persuade them that there would be absolutely no compromise on standards. Jennie Lee had made this point over and over again during the past few years, but a political assurance is very different from an academic assurance and they required some evidence of academic intent before they would begin to believe it. Most academics still thought of the new institution as one that would teach primarily by television and, quite justifiably, refused to believe that anyone could get a degree just by watching the telly. This attitude had arisen as a result of the original name of the institution – 'The University of the Air' – which had created a totally wrong impression. Although it had been made clear in the Report of the Advisory Committee, and in all subsequent writings, that television and radio would form a relatively small part of the teaching programme, which would largely consist of correspondence materials, this had not percolated through to the consciousness of the academic world. Consequently people were very surprised when I told them that television would make up only about 5% of the teaching programme. The whole concept of 'The University of the Air' had properly been regarded as a gimmick, as an unrealistic idea. I had to explain that I was not forming a University of the Air, that the Open University was not a gimmick, that it was a serious attempt to educate people at a distance and, above all, that it had a reasonable chance of proving successful. At the same time I had to convince people that the institution was needed, for there was great doubt about the demand for it. Many people felt that any initial demand would not be sustained and that we would be providing simply for a small pool of dissatisfied individuals which would rapidly be drained. At this stage, therefore, I also accepted every invitation I possibly could from the university world. Going back over my diaries I find that between my appointment in June 1968 and the end of 1970 I spoke about the Open University, and what it intended to do, in 22 British Universities.

Another area of public relations in which I had to operate during this period lay overseas. There was enormous interest in the experiment of the Open University, emanating from almost every country in the world. It was marked by an enthusiasm and an absence of the criticism so common in this country, and did much to offset the depressing effect of the continuous flow of adverse comment at home. We were indeed in the position of the prophet without honour in his own land. We were constantly being asked for information about what we were doing and were besieged by overseas visitors wanting to study our plans and programmes. This was a reflection of the interest in the extension of opportunity for higher education that had developed over two decades in almost every part of the world. It led in 1969 to the creation of our Information Office, designed to help the Officers of the University to cope with the demand.

So much then, for the atmosphere in which the new University was to be built. What about the problems that faced me in June 1968 of building the University itself? I prepared a chart in late 1968 to help me decide what were the critical steps in the programme. (Figure 1). The chart represents my efforts at a 'critical path analysis', although at that time I did not know what the phrase meant. First of all I had to work forward from the date at which I found myself, namely 1 January 1969. It would take time to insert advertisements to attract staff, to interview applicants for the jobs and to wait for successful applicants to work out their periods of notice. Most would be unable to take up their appointments before September

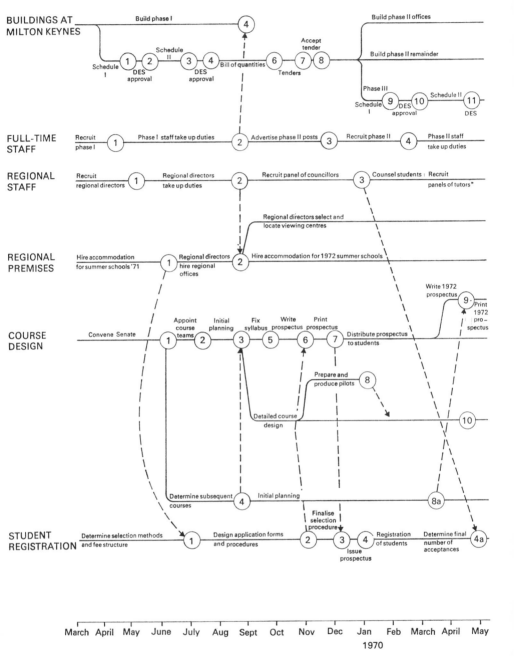

FIGURE 1   Flow chart for 1970–1971 (see p. 33)

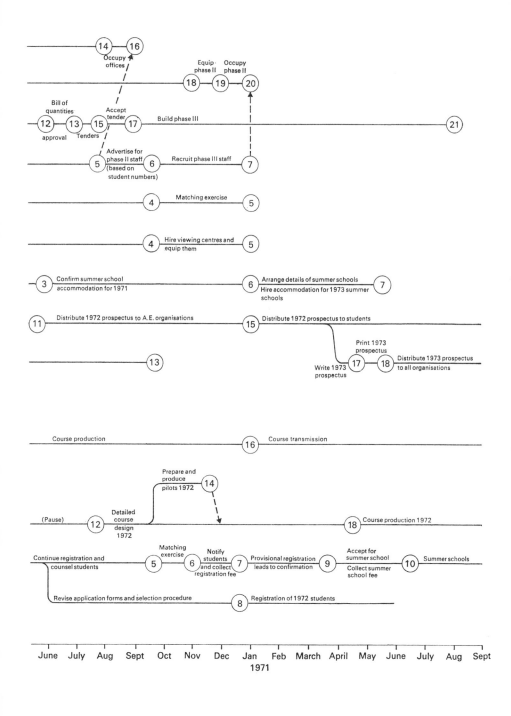

June July Aug Sept Oct Nov Dec Jan Feb March April May June July Aug Sept

1971

1969. Then, again, the building programme had to be planned forward from January 1969 in order that new staff should have somewhere to work.

On the other hand I had also to work backwards. If we were to start teaching students in January 1971 then courses must be available and students must be enrolled before then. I had to work out when applications from prospective students were first to be invited. Before we could invite such applications we had to know what we were going to offer the students, and consequently we had to write a Prospectus. My chart soon made the problems of timing horrifyingly clear.

My first task in the Summer of 1968 was to appoint the Secretary of the University, the man who was to be my prime administrative aide over the years to come. This was a critical appointment. The Planning Committee had advertised concurrently for this post and for a Vice-Chancellor, and we had a number of very worthy applicants. But we were looking for more than just a worthy university administrator. We needed someone of outstanding quality who could cope with the unprecedented administrative tasks that the new University would throw up. It was suggested to me that Anastasios Christodoulou, at that time Deputy Secretary of the University of Leeds, might be tempted, although he had not actually applied for the job. I arranged for him to come and see me in Edinburgh. He spent an entire day with me and I tried to explain to him what the whole venture was about. He started off with a healthy scepticism (indeed I had started the same way myself) but over the course of the day I persuaded him that it was an exciting idea that offered the prospect of success. I also came to discover in him the sort of qualities that I was looking for and I was very relieved indeed when, after thinking it over, he decided to join me in building the new institution. Thereafter he, too, attended the meetings of the Planning Committee and began to play a major part in the development of the Open University. I was able to pass over to him the whole problem of recruiting the non-academic staff of the University and of designing its administrative structure. Many of these appointments turned out to be amongst the most important that we were ever to make.

The next task was to recruit the first members of the senior academic staff of the University. The Planning Committee had determined that there should be four Directors of Studies who would be in charge of the first 'lines of study' or faculties, and two more who would be in charge of Regional Tutorial Services and Correspondence Services respectively. These appointments were to be tenured, in other words there was a clear adoption of the idea of appointed rather than elected Directors of Studies. These first six appointments were made in the latter months of 1968.

I persuaded the Planning Committee that the minimum number of academic staff in any one discipline should be four, for reasons that are discussed in Chapter 5. It was decided to recruit them in two phases. The first would begin early in 1969 and the staff thus appointed would form the nucleus of the course teams for the first four foundation courses, which must be ready for use in January 1971. The second phase would be a year later and these staff would be involved in the production of later courses.

These plans, tentative as they were, had to serve as the firm basis of planning throughout 1968 and much of 1969.

As the chart shows, all the interviewing for the first phase jobs, some 34 of them, would have to be completed by the end of April 1969 if we expected the staff to be in post in September. This arrangement would allow the teams for the foundation courses to be appointed in June so that, during the long vacation, the new staff could at least begin to think about the structure of these first courses. They might also give some preliminary thought to provisional titles for later courses. Haste was essential because during September we would have to settle on a syllabus that could be published in our first Prospectus. If this were to be available in print for prospective applicants by the end of the year, then all copy would be needed by the end of September.

Advertisements for academic staff were therefore inserted in appropriate journals towards the end of 1968 and I sat back to await results. I waited in some trepidation, for I had no means of knowing what the outcome would be: whether we would receive an adequate number of applications, or whether those who applied would be of suitable quality and qualification. In fact I need not have worried at all, for we received for the 34 jobs some 1,200 applications, many of which came from very highly qualified people. This was extremely gratifying but it posed a new problem for me. An application for a Professorship or a Senior Lectureship at a University is not written on the back of an envelope. It takes the form of a curriculum vitae in which the individual concerned traces his academic career which, for those applying for senior jobs of this kind, stretches over many years. Thus one application may run to 20 or 30 pages of typescript, and 1,200 applications make up a perfect deluge of paper. All this must be read and digested in order to arrive at short lists of candidates to be interviewed. Normally the work is shared by members of a selection committee for each post but we had no academic staff to sit on such committees. In consequence the burden of this first stage fell wholly on me as the only academic member of the staff in post. I remember lying in bed every night with a bundle of applications. The 'possibles' I dropped out of the right side of the bed; the non-starters went out on the left. This preliminary sorting of physicists, philosophers, psychologists was essential if we were to keep to the timetable.

I then chose external assessors in each of these disciplines from amongst colleagues in other universities. This was in fact the very first time I had asked for help from other institutions of higher education, and it was given willingly by many people in a heart-warming way, at a time when the general scepticism about the whole venture was still at its height. Although I had prepared a preliminary short list in respect of each job, I had all the applications looked at by the appropriate external assessors to make sure that I had not made gross errors of judgement. Thereafter we held, in the first three months in 1969, what seemed a never-ending series of meetings of selection panels composed of the external assessors, members of the Planning Committee and myself. For each job we interviewed an average of about eight applicants, so that in this period some thirty working days were spent doing nothing but attending selection panels.

There were three important results of this exercise. The first, the obvious one, was that we did successfully recruit the first group of academic staff. The second was that I learned a great deal about the background of a number of University disciplines about which I had previously had little direct information. I was also forced, in answering the questions of many of the applicants, to think very clearly about some of the implications of what we were doing and to formulate more precisely my ideas about the future of the University. The third outcome of this exercise was perhaps the most important of all, namely that some fifty or sixty external assessors helped us to make our choice. These eminent men, from many of the most important branches of university academic life, usually came to the panels almost totally ignorant of what the Open University was about. During the long sessions of listening to questions and answers and taking part in the general discussion about the philosophy of the University, they learned a lot about the new institution. This was, I believe, a major factor in spreading information in the academic world about the Open University. These men also saw the quality and calibre of the people who were appointed, and this was a great help in establishing our respectability as an academic institution amongst the universities of Britain. The University owes a debt of gratitude to all those who helped us in this way at that critical time.

It proved necessary, when discussing the structure of the different disciplines with applicants for jobs on the academic staff, to clarify in our minds what back-up services and ancillary staff would need to be made available to those who joined us. Consequently, in these early months, we made tentative decisions about staffing which have stayed with us over the years. We decided, for instance, that the group of four academics in each discipline would be doing a job in which the end product was largely paper. In consequence, a ratio of secretarial staffing to academic staffing much higher than that normally available in other universities would be essential. We also decided to provide technicians in each laboratory discipline even though we would have very little laboratory space available. The staff would be planning experimental work for the students and would therefore require technical help to design and make the necessary apparatus.

It was perhaps too much to expect that, at the beginning, with no buildings and no library, people would be able to maintain their research effort by their own unaided work or could to be expected to raise money for research projects from the Research Councils. Consequently we agreed to fund research assistantships, so that staff members might arrange for their experimental work to be continued; and research studentships (normally provided by the Research Councils) to provide for a few postgraduate research students. All this was little enough but it was an earnest of the intent of the new University to promote the research activities of its academic staff, an intent from which the Open University has never wavered.

At the same time Christodoulou had made initial projections of the staff he would need to provide the administrative back-up services of the University. When he and I put all these estimates together in late 1968, we could see that we must expect to provide, by September 1969, for a total staff numbering about 170. We were at that time occupying a very splendid house in Belgrave Square that had been obtained as the office of the Planning Committee by Jennie Lee. Jennie had always held that visitors to the Open University from Oxford or Cambridge must be met and entertained in surroundings equal to those encountered by visitors to Oxford or Cambridge. She had spared no effort to convert the Belgrave Square premises into a really attractive and prestigious main office, going as far as to take the Minister of Public Works himself to the house and tell him precisely what she wanted. In my own office I felt rather like a caricature of Mussolini, sitting at an enormous glass-topped desk with acres of floor for visitors to cross before they reached me. The splendour of the Belgrave Square offices was good for morale at that stage: candidates for jobs could at least see that we were not going to have to live in squalor due to inadequate financial support. But it wasn't all joy. For the main public room of the house Jennie had ordered a superb chandelier. Unfortunately the weight of the new fitting was so great that it pulled the ceiling down and we thereby lost the use of our only large meeting room; but this was probably a small price to pay for such surroundings.

However, the premises in Belgrave Square could under no circumstances be expected to house 170 staff the following September. Yet, in October 1968, no thought had been given to where the Open University would find its permanent home. I think this was because, until I arrived on the scene, the Planning Committee had envisaged a total staff for the new institution which was much smaller than turned out to be necessary. Whatever the reason we clearly had to move fast if we were going to be able to house our staff in September 1969. We referred the problem to the Ministry of Works, asking for their help in finding a suitable permanent site for the University.

We laid down two parameters for the site. First, our permanent home must be within one hour's commuting distance of Alexandra Palace, for it was here that all the television and radio production was going to take place. This caused quite serious problems since at that time, Government policy placed a restriction on the creation of any new offices in the London area, and we were at some risk of being directed to a development area in the north. We asked for political help over this and I understand that Prime Ministerial intervention by Mr Wilson himself was necessary in order to get us permission to build the permanent home of the University in the south east. The second parameter was that there should be adequate space for future and unforeseen development of the University. I had some difficulty in establishing this principle. Pressure developed within the Planning Committee itself for us to stay in Greater London. There were strong reasons for this. In the first place London was the centre of almost all the agencies with which the University would have to work in close co-operation. It was as near as one could get to Alexandra Palace and the other BBC premises, and it was also easy to gain access to a wealth of library and audio-visual resources. Nevertheless there were, to my mind, very serious disadvantages. The first was that the cost of land and buildings in the area of Greater London was very high indeed, making it virtually impossible to acquire sufficient space to allow for later development. In addition, I myself felt that an urban setting for the Open University would make it difficult to create anything like a University ambience on a campus where there would be no undergraduates. We would tend to become more and more an office and less and less a university.

Despite these strong feelings on my part, pressure from the Planning Committee was sufficiently heavy to make it necessary to examine several potential sites in North London, mainly in office blocks available on lease. These visits reinforced my view that here was no place to begin the infant university. The Planning Committee eventually accepted this view and we then asked the Ministry of Works to try to find a country house with space available for new building. They suggested several properties – mainly National Trust ones – including Cliveden, Knebworth and Dropmore Lodge, and inspection parties from the Planning Committee spent many happy hours wandering over these very attractive houses. Although each of them would have provided a marvellous central facility the constraints on new building were almost absolute, and there seemed little chance of developing the additional premises required to serve the many specialised functions that would be necessary.

By January 1969 our choice had become a matter of extreme urgency and we had refined it down to two possibilities. The first was a property near Didcot which had been used by a commercial company as a research centre and which had, as a result, a number of buildings which could be rapidly adapted for our use. There was a certain amount of land available for further development and little restriction on new building. On the other hand there were considerable planning difficulties, since the access roads were already heavily used and the local authority was reluctant to have a further influx of full-time staff in the area. In addition, it was a little too far removed from Alexandra Palace for comfort, being outside my limit of an hour's commuting distance. We were therefore extremely glad when, through the good offices of Lord Campbell of Eskan, the Chairman of the Milton Keynes Development Corporation, we were invited to examine two sites within the boundaries of the proposed new city as possible homes for the University. The Development Corporation on its part was keen that the new city should have a University. No other new town could boast a university and it was felt that this would be a source of attraction to new industry. The Corporation was consequently willing to offer us the sites at very low rentals. Furthermore, land was available for building and there would be few restrictions from the planning point of view. It was, of course, an advantage to have landlords who were themselves in process of creating a completely new city of 250,000 inhabitants. It seemed to me that if we were to set ourselves up in a new and developing city, the staff of the University would have an additional source

38

of local interest and could play a full part in the growth and development of the cultural life of the new city. Milton Keynes lies in an area bounded to the south by Bletchley, which has a main-line railway service direct to Euston, and to the north and east by the M1 Motorway, which offers rapid access by car not only to London but also nowadays to almost the whole of the country. In fact, there are in England only three universities, Newcastle, Durham and Exeter, which are not within three hours' drive of the Open University on this site.

In mid-November I paid a visit to Milton Keynes to see the two available sites. It was a wild and wintry day and North Buckinghamshire is not attractive in such conditions. It is flat and exposed to the elements and there is little in the way of scenery to leaven the gloomy outlook. In the spring, when the foliage burgeons, the trees are a glory and the whole prospect changes, but on that first day there was no such joy. We saw the two sites in the worst possible circumstances. One of them was a very modern farm in beautiful condition, with a large amount of land available. On the other hand, it was still occupied by the original owner and there was obviously going to be a long delay before we could acquire the property. The other, Walton Hall, was empty. It was already the property of the Development Corporation and we could move in right away. It was a relatively small house, in a poor state of repair, but lay in a park of some 70 acres bordered on one side by the River Ouzel. It had potential, the sort of potential that we had to have if we were going to develop in the way I foresaw.

Lord Goodman, himself a member of the Planning Committee, came out to see the site at our request and was clearly in two minds about its desirability. In the first place, he agreed with me about the future potential of the site and the advantages of being within the boundaries of the new city. On the other hand he foresaw very clearly the sort of problems which would beset us initially and remarked that 'You will have nothing to do out here except commune with the pigs'.

Meanwhile the Planning Committee embarked on the task of appointing development architects and after careful consideration we chose Fry, Drew & Partners Limited. That was on Thursday 6 February and on the following Saturday I accompanied Max Fry and Jane Drew on a site visit to Walton Hall. They were enthusiastic about the potential of the site and we discussed the immediate needs of the University. Christodoulou and I explained to them our basic timetable and indicated that we would have to have temporary buildings for 170 staff by 1969. To our amazement they responded by assuring us that permanent buildings could be erected within the same period, given that we had Government backing. Over the Sunday they produced sketch plans of the first block of University buildings, designed to provide office accommodation for all the staff who would be in post by the following September, but also to serve as the permanent home of the Arts-based Faculties. I took these plans to Jennie Lee at the Department of Education and Science on the following day and explained the urgency of the situation. She managed to get the Department to agree to a negotiated contract in order to avoid the long period of detailed drawings and estimates of quantity that would have been necessary in order to go out to tender. As a result of this the contract was negotiated with Y. J. Lovell and building began on the site on 1 April 1969, only five weeks after we had appointed the consultant architects. This must represent an all-time record for the planning of a university building.

It was of course an extremely simple building, a shell into which we could put pairs of modular rooms, choosing the sizes carefully so that the bigger one would be exactly the dimensions of the room permitted under University Grants Committee regulations for a professor, and the smaller, the size permitted for a lecturer. The negotiated contract called for the completion of this brick-built building within a period of five months. The contractor in fact met this deadline and the building was ready for occupation on the due date. Furthermore the whole building was put up at a price well below the cost limit per square foot at that time approved by the University Grants Committee. The building was thus available in time to house the new staff when they took up their posts in September of 1969, and that stage of the critical path shown in the chart was completed. There were two other buildings that formed part of this first phase of our building programme, namely a refectory and a set of preparation laboratories. Both were essential but of lower priority than the main Arts Faculty building and so, although they were put up concurrently, they were not completed quite so quickly.

The move from Belgrave Square to Milton Keynes took place in October of 1969. The renovation of the old Walton Hall had not been completed and all the staff arriving on the site were housed temporarily in the new building. It was not a good season of the year to move in. Due to the weather and the contractors' activity the whole place was a sea of mud. Moving from the car parks to the buildings was a hazardous occupation. The new building was carpeted wall to wall and the carpets looked like being permanently impregnated by the thick clay of North Buckinghamshire. One of the first things that I did on arrival at the site was to send the Purchasing Officer to Northampton to buy 100 pairs of cheap carpet slippers, which were issued to members of staff in an effort to protect the new carpets.

Because of the slower completion of the refectory it was necessary to operate an emergency catering service, and our new catering superintendent performed miracles in the improvisation of makeshift lunches. The University was in the middle of the green fields, there were no restaurants within easy reach, and there were only one or two scattered country pubs. The design of the refectory building had been another problem dependent upon guessing the size of the new University. The responsible Officials at the Treasury and the DES could not conceive that we would require a staff as large as we were estimating for and continually cut down the size of the proposed refectory. As a result the refectory was, on the very day that it opened, already too small for the numbers of staff on the site. The same applied in later years when an extension was built: by the time it was enlarged the staff had enlarged even more, and we have never had an adequate catering service.

The other item in the first phase of the building programme was our preparation laboratory. If we were going to teach science we would not only have to provide Home Experiment Kits, but would also have to demonstrate experiments on television. Such demonstrations demand a great deal of careful preparation and often require the building of special apparatus suitable for the purpose. It was therefore necessary to have, at the very minimum, a preparation lab for each discipline in which these experimental techniques could be worked out and practised and in which the apparatus could be designed and built.

In addition to these buildings in the first phase we required, in order to be operational in 1971, a large building to house our correspondence services unit and all that went with it. It was therefore necessary to plan a purpose-built building – a very different task from building a modular office block – and to plan it very fast. All the rules governing university building projects had been bent in order to get us started; we could not hope to be allowed to bypass normal tendering procedures a second time. Plans were therefore required by May 1969.

The main parts of the complex that made up the second building were a set of offices for administrative staff; a sort of factory block that would include a print shop, an area for despatch of the correspondence materials, stores to hold the printed materials prior to despatch, a post office, rooms for handling the receipt of assignments written by students and their despatch to the tutors; and a suite for the computer that would handle all the records of the University. To plan the new building, we had to assess the space needed to serve each of these different functions, and we had virtually nothing to guide us. How much material, for instance, would a course team write for despatch to students in any one week? Nobody knew the answer, yet upon it depended the size of the print shop, the size of the stores, the size of the despatch room and the size of the post office.

We did our best to gather information that would help us to make an intelligent guess at the answer. In the Autumn of 1968, as a representative of Edinburgh University, I attended the Commonwealth Universities Conference in Australia and took the opportunity of seeing some of the Australasian arrangements for correspondence education. Then in May 1969 I made a special visit to the University of South Africa, in Pretoria, which was the largest correspondence-based university in the western world. We also inspected mail order stores and football pool offices to see how they handled the problems of mass mailing. Tom Robertson, who was recruited from Rapid Results College to manage our Correspondence Services Unit, brought with him much experience of the methods of handling correspondence education, albeit on a smaller scale.

Yet even with all the information thus collected my guess at the answer to the critical question was out by a factor of between 8 and 16-fold. My estimate was much further from the mark than was Lord Goodman's estimate of the total cost of the University. I too should blush with shame.

But once again the error of judgement turned out to be, in one sense, advantageous. We found in practice that there is much to be gained from contracting with commercial printers instead of printing ourselves. We were indeed forced to adopt this preferable arrangement because the print shop that I built can nowadays handle only about 10 per cent of our total printing needs.

On the basis of such guesses, however ill-judged, we drew up definitive plans for the second building. Then plans had to go through the further stages of detailed architectural drawings, preparation of bills of quantity, tendering procedures and the various steps needed to obtain governmental approval. All these stages had to be completed, as the chart shows, by the end of 1969 so that building could start in January 1970.

The time scale was extraordinarily tight. We relied very heavily on the goodwill of the officials at the DES, and with their help in cutting a certain number of corners we met our deadline. Before we had had final approval to go ahead with the building, Jane Drew told me one day that there was a world shortage of steel. The second building was to be constructed on a steel frame, and she pointed out that, unless we pre-ordered the steel, we ran the risk, even if the DES approval came through in time, of being unable to obtain the building materials necessary in order to make a start in January. I took my courage in both hands and personally authorised the pre-ordering of some £100,000 worth of steel. Fortunately, in the event, we did get approval to build and the steel was used. Had approval to build been withheld I would have been personally responsible for the un-authorised expenditure. In fact the world price of steel rose sharply over these few months and I could have re-sold it at a very considerable personal profit.

This was the sort of heady atmosphere in which we worked in those early days. We knew that we could rely on the goodwill of the government to help us get things moving in time to make a start. It was the honeymoon period, the atmosphere of which we could never recapture once we became a recognised institution subject to all the usual rules of procedure.

At about this time too, I began to try to provide more amenities for the staff than could be made available from public funds. Unlike most new universities we had no other source of money, for there had been no appeal for private endowments, and indeed the atmosphere was not such as to have made such an appeal successful. I did, however, persuade Senator Benton to make a grant from the Benton Foundation to enable us to add a staff common room and a squash court to the second building. Another endowment came to the University at about the same time. Jennie Lee, at the instigation of Jane Drew, our development architect, came to see Walton Hall while it was being renovated and I went with them to inspect the basement of the old house. It was a welter of old pipes and discarded junk and as I stood there the two ladies looked around the vaulted ceiling of the basement and said 'We see here a splendid faculty club'. I must confess I was sceptical, but Jennie obtained a grant for us from the Aneurin Bevan Memorial Trust, and the renovation was an outstanding success. It provided our first common room on the new site and was a godsend, as we had literally no social life available within easy reach of the campus. The Club became the focal point for much of the early discussion and planning.

If the development of the full time staffing of the university and the buildings to house them was scheduled from January 1969 looking forward, the whole problem of students had to be faced in the reverse direction. I had to begin with the start of the teaching programme in January 1971 and work back. This necessitated a further series of guesstimates. When, for instance, should we invite applications from students who wanted to start courses in January 1971? How many applications would we receive?

We had to play safe and allow a very long period during which applications could be made in case we were to be inundated by, say, 100,000 applications and by the sheer physical problems of handling them. Once we had accepted a given number of students and knew their geographical distribution in the country we would have to recruit part-time staff and allocate students to them; we must leave adequate time for this matching exercise. We therefore came to the conclusion that the admission of students should be completed by June 1970, leaving the latter half of the year for processing and for the matching exercise; and that applications should be received from January 1970 onwards, thus giving people a clear period of six months to decide whether or not they wished to apply. It followed that we would have to issue our final prospectus by the end of 1969 and this, in turn, meant that copy for the printer must be ready by October. Since most staff would not be in post until September 1969 we would have only a few weeks in which to make all the final decisions about the nature of the syllabus and the content of the first prospectus. This was the narrowest bottleneck in the planning exercise of the first two years.

At the beginning of 1969 many critical questions remained unanswered. How many first degrees (eg BA, BSc, BComm, BEd) were we to offer? What would they be called? What were to be the regulations about examinations and re-sit examinations? What programmes of study were students to be offered in later years? What was to be the fee structure? What were to be the regulations governing the award of a degree? All of these decisions had been left by the Planning Committee for the University Senate to take, but there could not be an effective Senate until September 1969. In fact much preliminary thinking was done by the small nucleus of academic staff who joined the University in the spring, and firm proposals were ready for consideration by the Senate in September and October. Nevertheless the members of Senate, wholly inexperienced as they were, had little real choice in the matter. They could do no more, in the time available, than endorse the proposals put to them. I wrote the first prospectus virtually single handed, but frequently had to delay completing a paragraph in order to refer to one of the Senate Committees for a decision endorsing its content. With hindsight I am sure that, had the Senate been in session much earlier, we would have taken even longer to come to these decisions, and we might well have failed to meet the deadlines. A participative democracy is a very slow and cumbersome method of decision-making. On the other hand a closer and more thoughtful examination of the procedures involved might have spared us some of our early mistakes. Yet speed was of the essence if we were to survive. So perhaps it is just as well that, despite the mistakes, our participative democratic structure was not in operation in this early formative stage.

The creation of a suitable regional structure through which we could maintain direct contact with our students all over the country raised another set of problems. I decided to relegate them to a second order of priority since I knew that we would not have any students until 1971 (see Figure 1). What I failed to appreciate was that applicants would need the same sort of services as students, and that we would have the applicants to deal with a year sooner. I realised this too late for us to be able to catch up with the time we had lost. I had asked Robert Beevers, our Director of Regional and Tutorial Services, who had been one of HM Inspectors and was familiar with the world of adult education, to determine how the country should be divided into regions and to plan the siting of our regional offices and study centres. I had intended to defer the recruitment of Regional Directors and their ancillary staffs until 1970. When we realised that they were needed much sooner, we advertised at once, but it turned out to be more difficult to recruit Regional Directors than academic staff. We were creating a cadre of posts which had no counterpart in the conventional university world. We underestimated the magnitude of the job, and we did not know quite what qualities we should demand of applicants. In consequence we may have deterred many potential applicants. It was only after much effort and worry that we were able to recruit a satisfactory band of Regional Directors. Even so, in a few instances we ended up with misfits in the sense that the man we appointed, able as he was, would have been happier and more effective in a different kind of post.

The delays in organising the regional structure also affected the acquisition of suitable premises for Regional Offices and study centres and, during the early part of 1970, the best that can be said of our organisation was that it muddled through. I describe some of these problems in more detail in Chapter 7.

In support of the central and regional organisations we were creating, we had also to organise a reliable system of records. During 1969 I shed the entire responsibility for this onto the broad shoulders of the University Secretary. This was a very difficult and highly technical task, for which we had to obtain the advice of consultants (Urwick Diebold Ltd) on the nature of our needs for a computerised system, on the acquisition of the computer itself and on the preparation of the necessary programmes for it. The most urgent of the latter was a programme to handle the admission of students, since this would be required in 1970.

At the beginning of 1969 the Planning Committee was still trying to produce a first draft of the Charter of the Open University, and I had been

44

deeply involved in this exercise as early as the previous June. We modelled the Charter, at the suggestion of the Privy Council's assessor, on those of the other new universities. The main difficulties arose from the entirely new structure of the Open University, so that often there was no precedent to guide us, and from the ever-present fact that none of us had a clear vision of what form the institution would take. I will return to this topic in Chapter 14.

One section of the Charter did, however, require detailed completion very urgently. The first Officers of the University were to be named in the Charter itself. Thus we needed to choose a Chancellor, a Pro-Chancellor and a Treasurer, the other Officers being myself as Vice-Chancellor and Christodoulou as Secretary.

The Charter laid down that the Pro-Chancellor was at the same time the Chairman of the Council of the University. The members of the Planning Committee, Christodoulou and I had no difficulty in making our choice: everything pointed to Sir Peter Venables. By selecting him we would ensure a smooth transition from the rule of the Planning Committee to the rule of the Council and we would have an absolutely first-class chairman. Furthermore Sir Peter had just retired from the Vice-Chancellorship of the University of Aston and would thus have rather more time to devote to the affairs of the Open University.

The question of selecting the first Chancellor was not so easily settled. Peter Venables and I spent many hours investigating possible names and discussing the procedures to be followed. The Planning Committee was consulted and individual members of the Committee made various suggestions. We wanted, above all, a titular head of the institution who had no strong party political affiliation, so that the University could be removed from the political arena as soon as possible. At the same time we wanted a man (or woman) of such stature that he would have unquestioned access, when necessary, to all political levels up to and including the Prime Minister. Furthermore we preferred someone who could combine with all this a knowledge of the business world and an overt interest in education. We eventually emerged with the name of Geoffrey Crowther and immediately wondered why we had spent so much time on the problem – for it seemed to us we should have thought of him immediately, so well did he measure up to all the specifications. As a life peer he sat on the cross-benches, and he could command access anywhere in politics. As Chairman of Trust Houses he was a well-known figure in the City. The Crowther Committee Report was a monument to his deep concern for widening educational opportunity. As a bonus his years as Editor of *The Economist* had established his reputation in the field of scholarly journalism. In the difficulties of the early years my task as Vice-Chancellor was greatly eased by his backing. He had a mind of exceptional quality, and seemed unfailingly able, having listened to garbled accounts of a complex problem, to isolate the critical issues and state them with complete clarity. I never heard him make an irrelevant comment. It was a privilege to have gained his friendship. It was a tragedy that his early death was to rob the

University of his services after all too short a period of office.

The selection of a Treasurer was also a difficult task. We badly needed someone from the financial world who could guide us wisely at the outset, when we had no factual basis for our estimates of expenditure and no precedents to guide us, and therefore had to depend upon intuition and a sort of 'feel' for the quantification of costs. Our choice fell upon Sir Paul Chambers. He had, as a senior civil servant, been responsible for the introduction of PAYE; later he had become Chairman of ICI; now, in 1969, he was Chairman of the Royal Insurance Group. His political tendencies were known to be conservative and he had been a vocal critic, when at ICI, of the alleged failure of British universities to produce graduates suited to the needs of industry. We were able to persuade him that the Open University, as a complementary educational agency, might help to change this picture, and he soon became a convinced supporter of its academic objectives.

As Treasurer, Paul Chambers gave devoted service. I never knew him miss a meeting of the Finance Committee of which he was Chairman, and he was present at almost every meeting of the Council throughout his whole period of office. He had the great talent of combining total financial propriety with imaginative and flexible acceptance of wholly new principles. He turned out to be the ideal man for the job and the University owes him as well as Geoffrey Crowther a tremendous debt of gratitude for the effort they put in over that period.

The announcements by the Planning Committee of the names of our first Chancellor and Treasurer caused a certain stir in government circles. There is no doubt that a Chancellor drawn from the ranks of committed Labour Party supporters would have been more acceptable. Paul Chambers' political views were anathema and his appointment was at first regarded as a big mistake. But these initial doubts were rapidly dissipated, and the doubters became first reconciled and later enthusiastic about both men. There had been no prior consultation with the DES, either at ministerial or officer level, before the announcement of the names of the Officers by the Planning Committee. This was deliberate policy. Peter Venables had been adamant from the outset that all appointments must be made, and must be seen to be made, by academics and on academic grounds; there must be no hint of a political appointment. Indeed in June 1968, the Prime Minister had expressed a wish to announce my own appointment in the House of Commons and Peter Venables had had to argue strongly to prevent this happening. He was absolutely right to do so; such a method of announcing the appointment of a Vice-Chancellor would have been wholly out of keeping with normal practice and could only have prejudiced my own academic status.

We were still, in 1969, very conscious of the importance of establishing the academic status of the Open University, and we decided to stage our first ceremony with all the pomp and circumstance we could muster. The occasion was the installation of Lord Crowther as Chancellor, and the first meeting of the Congregation of the University was held in July 1969.

46

The ceremony was combined with the award of the Charter by the Privy Council and we had considerable fun in disentangling the extremely interesting and novel problems of procedure which it threw up. It was in two parts. Until the Charter was formally awarded the University as such did not exist – it was a creature, as it were, of the DES. Therefore, the Secretary of State for Education and Science was the host and it was agreed that the chairman for the ceremony should be the Chairman of the Planning Committee, which had been set up by the DES. The second part of the ceremony was a University occasion; the Planning Committee ceased to exist once the Charter was awarded. In consequence Sir Peter, as Pro-Chancellor, stayed in the chair until the Chancellor himself was installed. Because of the change in the constitution of the meeting halfway through, it followed that the platform party had to include two wholly different groups of people. The ceremony was further complicated by the fact that we had invited the Prime Minister, as the originator of the whole idea, to address the Congregation during the latter part of the ceremony.

We had also to decide whether to follow tradition in having the regalia common to other universities. Would we have gowns and hoods, a mace, all the trappings characteristic of mediaeval universities which had been copied by the modern ones? Amongst the staff of the Open University there were some who felt that these trappings should be swept away but on the whole I felt, in common with most of my colleagues, that the students themselves would come to demand just the same sort of ceremonial as was provided by any other university. Decisions about ceremony were therefore left in the hands of the Officers, and we did in fact borrow the necessary gowns to make this first ceremony into a traditional university one. I have never regretted this decision. There is no substitute for ceremonial to mark such great occasions. We also took advantage of the occasion to invite, as other universities do for the installation of their Chancellors, the Vice-Chancellors of all the other British universities. It is interesting, looking back on this, to see that, in 1970, despite the general scepticism about the Open University, the invitation was accepted by all but one of the British universities. Most Vice-Chancellors attended, others sent representatives.

We also had a problem in deciding where to hold the ceremony. We had no suitable lecture theatre or assembly hall of our own, and did not feel that it would be appropriate to borrow a hall from any other academic institution. We were very fortunate in that Lord Blackett, then President of the Royal Society, was sympathetic to our aims and ideals, and he offered us the use of the handsome new premises of the Royal Society. They made a magnificent setting, and the presence of the Prime Minister ensured a heavy press coverage for our first formal appearance as an independent institution. On the whole we had a good press.

Another of my early preoccupations was the governmental structure of the new institution. From the outset we foresaw that we would be operating not only an academic establishment, but in a very real sense a sort of commercial establishment as well. The latter would require a form of government quite different from that which was common in conventional universities. Yet this structure had to be consistent with the terms of the Charter. In Chapter 15 I trace the whole history of the government structure of the institution. I was very anxious that we should not become committee-ridden, and that decisions should be taken by individuals given the responsibility for making them. I hoped to streamline the University's structure in such a way that decision-making was quick and rational and easy, but I fear that it was a forlorn hope!

One particular question in this area that needed early resolution was that of the financial structure under which we would operate. Jennie Lee had decided, very early on, that the Open University would be financed directly from the DES, and would not fall within the ambit of the University Grants Committee.

Although it had been decided that we were to be separately funded, we still had to arrange the mechanism by which this funding would take place. Other Universities were funded by quinquennial grants. In the opinion of the Department and the Treasury, five years was too long a period to use for the Open University and it was agreed that we should operate on a triennial system. But there were all sorts of details to sort out. Would we draw money in regular monthly instalments or, alternatively, at need?

My main aim was not to achieve any particular preferential treatment for the Open University, but to stay as nearly as possible in line with the other universities. Perhaps I was over-sensitive about this, but I felt that, without comparability of this sort, our task would be that much more difficult. We were recruiting our staff from the ordinary university world. In time they would wish to return to it, and it was therefore vital that we should have the same kind of salary structure, of promotion prospects, of terms and conditions of service as applied there. It was equally necessary that we should be seen to be a university not only in name but in actuality. It was vital that the Research Councils and the charitable trusts saw us as a university supported and financed by government in the same way as it backed all the others. As soon as we became something different there was a chance of differential treatment and this, in my view, we had to avoid at all costs. Yet this desire to conform is sometimes at variance with the need to be innovative and new. On the other hand, with hindsight, I cannot blame myself too much. I believe we were innovative in such a very large number of ways that it paid us in the long run not to try to be so in others but to stick within the accepted sets of rules.

Finally, as Vice-Chancellor, I had to maintain the Open University's ongoing relationship with the BBC. Here the situation was quite different. The BBC was very much further ahead than was the University with the planning and preparation of their side of the educational partnership. They had worked out their proposals for the production and transmission of our programmes in the days of the discussions between Lord Goodman and Sir Hugh Greene. Little had changed since then. They had a clear idea of their recruitment policy and of what the timescale had to be. I fear that in those days we were a drag upon them rather than the other way round. They wanted to know what our decisions were before we had had time to make them. Furthermore, there was a deep-seated feeling of mistrust amongst many of their staff that, in giving final authority to the University, they were abrogating a valued privilege, and that they would have to protect the independence of their producers. On the other hand there was a feeling amongst the staff of the University that they might become engulfed in the BBC machine, and be unable to maintain the separate academic authority that they had been guaranteed.

During the latter part of 1968 the nature of the educational partnership between the BBC and the Open University had been discussed at length, and the Report of the Planning Committee included in an Appendix, the following statement

The Planning Committee and the BBC have been engaged in discussion upon securing the most effective practical working relationship between the BBC and the University. Both parties are pleased to record their complete agreement in the following statement, which in due course will be followed by appropriate internal procedures as the work develops.

The radio and television programmes, required by the University and provided by the BBC, are to be planned on the basis of an educational partnership between University and BBC staff. In practice, this partnership will extend over the whole range from the conception of the course to the final production of the programmes. The success of this partnership rests on the recognition by both parties that, while effective education is the over-riding objective, and the ultimate responsibility of the University under its Charter, each has a specific professional role to play. The University will prescribe the academic objectives and general character of the broadcasts in relation to the other component parts of each course, while the BBC will provide the necessary presentation and production skills. In the overlapping area – where the inter-relationship of content and presentation is worked out – a reasonable degree of flexibility on both sides is essential in order to secure the proper concern of the academic staff and the fullest use of the experience of the broadcasting staff.

Within this area, such matters as the choice of principal academic contributors to programmes and the inter-connection of subject instruction and broadcasting method will be of first importance to both partners. While the BBC recognises the right of the Open University finally to determine any such points that may be at issue, the University agrees that full participation of BBC staff in all discussion pertaining to these matters is a necessary condition of working effectively together.

The key relationship between contributors and production staff jointly engaged in producing material and programmes for broadcasting will thus be secured.

There will be a continuing need to secure the educational effectiveness of the programmes by the application of organised feedback, research and other evaluative procedures to all the elements of the University courses, and appropriate provision will be made accordingly.

There was thus no doubt of the intention of the partnership, only about its interpretation in practice. At the personal level of working relationships the interpretation evolved over the years. At the formal and legal level there was an urgent need to draft an Agreement that covered, *inter alia,* financial arrangements, problems of copyright and mechanisms for handling possible disputes. This turned out to be a time-consuming and difficult job and much of my time in 1969 and 1970 was spent in arriving at a final version. The Agreement that was finally signed in December 1971 was to last for five years in the first instance.

Taking it all in all, there was no time to weary. Things were moving inexorably forward towards the day when we would be on view to the world, and we were determined to succeed. This determination called forth from virtually every member of staff an output of work quite unusual in an academic environment. I think consciousness of the scepticism of the academic world was perhaps the greatest spur, but a real excitement about the potential value of the institution ran it a close second. Whatever the particular drive of any individual, all of them laboured mightily. Without that dedication we could not have met the deadlines of the time-table and we might not have survived the change of government in June 1970.

For me the workload was particularly heavy. I worked eighteen hours a day, seven days a week, with only one break for a round of golf, throughout 1969 and 1970. I ended up, in December 1970, with a coronary thrombosis which put me out of commission for three months just as we began the teaching programme. Fortunately I made a complete recovery and can therefore accept it as having been the price I had to pay for leading the team that brought the Open University into being. It was surely one of the most exciting and rewarding opportunities that could have fallen to anyone, and I shall always be grateful that it fell to me.

2

THE
COURSES

4

DEGREE STRUCTURE

The traditional concept of a university is of a place where, through teaching and research, the scholarship of the past is nurtured and the sum total of human understanding extended. It is a concept that is held almost universally by academics. Before the expansion of the British universities that followed the Robbins Report there were, I believe, many among the academic community who would have gone even further. For them, the primary output of a university was the scholars of the future, and the production of graduates to fill essential posts outside the academic world, whether their university education was highly vocational, like medicine, or 'liberal' and non-vocational, was a by-product only, though useful and even essential in commanding the income from government that sustained the primary output.

Whether or not this view was consciously held, there is no doubt that the nurture of scholarship had become the over-riding motive in the design of teaching programmes. Academics have a very well-developed reproductive instinct and to turn out scholars in their own image was the highest peak of their ambition. It is, indeed, a worthy aim and an essential ingredient of any worthwhile system of higher education. To provide the best possible environment for what Ashby has called 'the thin clear stream of excellence' must always be one duty of a university.

But it was never the only duty, and after the Robbins-induced expansion its supremacy came under more severe challenge. The number of natural scholars among students was always limited and their proportion fell as the universities expanded. 'More means worse,' said Kingsley Amis. If he believed that expansion would lead to a fall in the average level of intelligence of the student population I think he was wrong; but, if the catch-phrase is interpreted to mean that there would be a smaller proportion of scholars in it then he is probably correct.

This would not matter if the teaching programmes of the universities were suited to those able students who are, nevertheless not scholars and who came to university to study, not primarily because of the love of learning for its own sake, but to fit themselves for a fuller and more rewarding role in life. It is an empty sneer to refer to universities as 'diploma mills'. We do not need scholars in abundance but we do need a population educated to the limit of their individual capacities. Most students are students because they want qualifications.

But the teaching programmes of the universities were not suited to the non-scholars. Perhaps it was a realization of this, felt rather than comprehended, that was one of the major, if not *the* major, source of student unrest in the 1960's. They felt that their courses were not 'relevant' and of course they were right, but for the wrong reasons. Their teachers, in making the needs of the scholars paramount and in making the courses 'relevant' for them, were neglecting the needs of the non-scholars.

It is, of course, arguable that the expansion of the universities that followed the Robbins Report was ill-advised. Expansion of opportunity for higher education was vitally necessary, but perhaps this should have been catered for through institutions of non-university status, leaving the universities to provide only for the scholars. In a sense this is now beginning to happen through the growth of the polytechnics, but it is happening after the universities have been severely diluted by the earlier expansion and their nature quite drastically and probably irrevocably altered. It may well be that, in the future, scholarship will have to be nurtured primarily in 'centres of excellence', in post-graduate schools, rather than in the universities themselves.

The Open University inherited from the Advisory Committee and the Planning Committee guidelines along which they felt that degree programmes should develop. But these could in no way be binding since a new autonomous and independent university had been created with its own Senate as the supreme academic authority. When the Senate of the Open University met for the first time in April 1969 it consisted only of those members of the academic staff in post before the Charter was granted and its primary task was to develop, according to its own principles, programmes of study leading to a degree that would be equal in status to those offered by other British universities.

The Senate was, however, constrained by the nature of its members. The Planning Committee had authorised the recruitment of the academic staff and, acting with that authority, I had recruited primarily from other British universities. To what extent would their ideas of an academic plan for the new university coincide with the tentative ideas of the Advisory Committee and Planning Committee? To what extent would they be influenced by their background in the traditional British universities? Could equivalence in the status of the degree be achieved without falling into the old trap of designing a degree primarily to suit the scholars?

I think that the answer that has emerged, seven years later, is a very clear affirmative. There are a host of reasons why this should be so, and I shall try to trace some of them in detail. One is undoubtedly that those who were attracted to the Open University were not typical of the academic community in general. They joined because they were excited by the prospect of breaking with tradition and of designing something new, with more relevance to the twentieth century.

I had joined the university for much the same reason. While I was sympathetic to the idea of offering new opportunities to adults who had been deprived, and was to some extent stimulated by the challenge of harnessing the mass media to the service of education, I was primarily motivated by my belief that university education, as we had known it, was in a state of flux. Applicants for the post of Vice-Chancellor had been asked to state what they considered to be the significance and scope of the work of the Open University, and in February 1968 I wrote:

I believe that the established academic world has, in expressing scepticism [about the Open University] assumed that the common educational pattern in the established universities is both inevitable and inherently desirable. It is this assumption that I would challenge. [. . .]

If the Open University were successful, even in a limited sense, its impact upon development [in other institutions of higher education] could be profound, and, as a new institution, it can experiment with new patterns of teaching with a freedom that would be impossible to achieve in established universities.

Most of my colleagues in the Senate of 1969 shared these views which were crucial to the Open University in developing its academic strategy. They coloured our approach to all the other factors that were to affect the academic plan, whether these were the actual objectives of the new university or whether they arose from the problems, both political and academic, that we faced in implementing these objectives.

We were to be self-constrained, then, in a number of ways. I shall describe certain of the major strands in our thinking: these include a consideration of the principle of 'open entry', the need for a 'credit system', the 'standard' of the courses to be offered as compared with courses in the degree programmes of other British universities and the 'nature' of the courses themselves. All these ideas had to be integrated before we could arrive at an overall academic plan.

The principle of 'open entry', of making enrolment as a student open to everyone, irrespective of educational qualification, had been implicit in Harold Wilson's speech of 1963. It was made explicit in the report of the Advisory Committee. Yet, even at this early stage, the principle was a frightening one for most academics. Other university degree programmes, after all, started off on the basic assumption that all entrants would recently have passed appropriate Advanced level GCE examinations (or their equivalents), and had assumed entry behaviour based thereon. How could adults who had left school many years before without such qualifications be expected to succeed in courses that must be of equivalent standard if the degree to which they led was itself to be equivalent to other degrees? There would have to be, thought the Advisory Committee, a counselling service for applicants 'to help them select suitable courses, for some of which a minimum starting level of qualifications would be advisable'.

The principle of open entry was reiterated even more strongly in the report of the Planning Committee. 'We take it as axiomatic,' they said, 'that no formal academic qualification would be required for registration as a student.' The Planning Committee, composed as it was largely of academics, clearly shared with the Advisory Committee the same fears about the results of holding to this principle. They had tackled it in two ways. First they had, at the suggestion of their Working Group on Students and Curriculum, chaired by Asa Briggs, agreed that the first-year courses of the Open University would be 'Foundation Courses'. The concept was that one such course in each 'line' of study, multidisciplinary in scope, would serve the dual purpose of re-introducing adults to serious study in that 'line' and of explaining rapidly and succinctly, by ruthlessly pruning out all content other than the essential basic information in all the disciplines covered, what was required in order to proceed to second-level courses. I have not been able to trace the actual originator of the concept of the Foundation Courses, but the idea was accepted at the very first meeting of the Working Group. The experience of Keele University with its Foundation Year was no doubt pertinent. Members of the Working Group thereafter produced their sketch outlines of appropriate Foundation Courses. Ritchie-Calder, for example, submitted his plans for a Foundation Course in the science 'line' called 'Understanding Science' and argued in favour of a course based on a historical survey of each major 'breakthrough' in scientific understanding and of its relevance to everyday life. Yet the Planning Committee obviously doubted whether these foundation courses, even if successful, could really enable entry to be open to anyone who wanted to start. They therefore adopted, as their second method of tackling the problem, the same solution as had the Advisory Committee, and stressed the importance of 'preparatory courses'. They made it perfectly clear that the creation of preparatory courses should not fall within the work of the University itself, but they were very sure of the need for the development of a network of such preparatory courses in other institutions. 'There will clearly be many potential students,' said the report, 'who require a preliminary introduction or re-introduction to the academic topics to be covered in the foundation courses.'

The position is still the same and we still face the same fundamental dilemma. The principle of open entry remains as a pillar of our structure, yet many of those who wish to start in the University are ill-prepared and fall by the wayside through inability to cope with the demands even of the foundation courses. Many more, no doubt with a greater gift of insight, see and recognise their own inability to cope with a foundation course before starting, and are therefore inhibited from 'having a go'.

It was, indeed, feelings of this kind that led many people, when the University was founded, to suggest that an open secondary school should have been founded first, to make provision for those in the adult population who had really been deprived of any chance of an education, so that they could start off with a challenge at a much lower level than that demanded by the University courses themselves. There is little doubt that they were right, and that the social need for this kind of education is even greater than the social need for education at university level. The trouble was that an open secondary school, founded at that particular time, would not have had enough glamour to survive the financial stresses which almost put paid to the idea of the Open University itself.

The situation in 1969, when we began work on the foundation courses, was therefore not an easy one. Our main aim was to offer courses to those who, for any reason at all, had not taken advantage of the opportunities for higher education normally available. After a lot of debate we agreed to restrict open entry to people over the age of 21. At that time 21 was the age of majority and we could therefore say that we were providing for all adults. We were, of course, to be overtaken very soon by the change in the age of majority, which was reduced to 18 in 1971. The choice of 21 as the youngest age for students to begin – and this was to be a requirement that could be waived in the case of younger applicants who for reasons of physical disability, or early marriage and young children, were unable to go to a conventional university – was not a decision that was lightly taken. We were well aware that the country faced an increase in demand from school leavers for university education and it was in some ways tempting to offer to meet some of that demand. If we were right in assuming that our education would be cheaper than that in a conventional university, we could offer substantial savings to whatever government was in power. On the other hand, most of us felt that to follow a course of study in isolation demanded qualities of maturity that would usually be lacking in people as young as 18. I also believed, as did many of my colleagues, that a young person of 18 would be missing a great deal if he were denied the opportunity of studying in a regular residential university with all that it had to offer in the way of social life and the stimulation of colleagues. I think we all felt that what we could offer was very much a second best for people of this age. We offered a chance to those who had not been able to go to regular universities, the only chance that such people could have.

There were, of course, other reasons for making the choice that were less academic and more political. We were extremely anxious not to enter into apparent competition with other institutions – universities, polytechnics, technical colleges and teacher training colleges – for students of 18. We realised from the outset that nearly all of the peripheral activities of the University would depend for their success on obtaining the support and co-operation of other institutions in the higher education sector. Only they could provide our part-time staff and the space we needed for study centres and for summer schools. Politically, therefore, it behoved us to stay on good terms with such institutions. For both these sets of reasons, therefore, it was decided to make 21 the minimum age for entry and I have never regretted this. As a result we were able definitely to set our sights on adults living at home, in full employment, studying part-time in isolation, and we could write the courses with them particularly in mind. We believed that an appreciation of their special needs would be critically important and that the failure of correspondence teaching elsewhere might well have stemmed from the fact that the courses offered were often identical to those offered 'on-campus' to full-time students and consequently unsuitable for adults studying in isolation.

This decision, by a circular argument, reinforced the need to stick to the principle of having no formal entrance qualifications whatsoever. Clearly, if an applicant aged 35 wants to start a university level education, it is much more important to know what he has done in the twenty years since he left school at 15 than it is to know what bit of paper he obtained as a formal educational qualification on leaving, all those years ago. I myself passed Scottish Leaving Certificate examinations at the higher level nearly forty years ago. My sons passed these examinations some ten years ago. They hold the same certificates as I do, but the mathematics that they learned in order to pass that examination bears no relationship to the mathematics that I knew when I got mine. Thus the formal qualifications that adults hold may be of little value in determining the starting level of a course at university.

If we were to accept students at 18, we would, I think, be more sanguine about the chances of those who had left school at 15 and spent three years in gaining some experience of life, than we would be about those who had tried to obtain a formal qualification at 'A' level and failed. They would have nothing to offer to offset the failure to achieve an academic qualification. The others, who had not even made the attempt, would at least have that wider experience of life which might help them to cope. Certainly at that time I was extremely anxious that we should not end up as a sort of dustbin for all those people who had tried and failed to get into conventional universities. For we would then be dealing with an embittered and disillusioned population of students who felt they had been given second best and who would not have the right sort of motivation. We would also be under fire from the other universities and colleges for attempting to do what they claimed they could not do.

We have often re-examined the idea of offering preparatory courses at pre-university level, for people who wanted to start our degree programme. Each time we came to the same conclusion as that already arrived at by the Planning Committee, namely that, if we were to do this, we would be seen by the outside academic world as admitting that the principle of open entry to universities was not a tenable one. We would be seen to be starting off at a pre-university level and would therefore prejudice the possibility of achieving that status as one of the 'family' of British universities that we were very anxious to achieve. At the same time we were all too aware that there is, and must be, an 'assumed entry behaviour', for students who begin any sort of course at university level. One must assume that all students can read, write, add, subtract, multiply and divide. On the other hand, one clearly cannot start off by assuming that they have all the knowledge that is in the heads of those who have just, a few months before, passed 'A' level examinations.

It therefore followed that the foundation courses were the most difficult courses that we would ever have to write. Yet these were the very courses that were going to be on show from the beginning, by which we would be judged by the outside world. It would have been so much easier to have started at the end. If one had begun by writing a final course in a specialist honours programme one could have assumed entry behaviour that was equivalent to the immediately preceding course in the same subject. This, however, was not a practical proposition: we had to start at the beginning.

It was here that the educational technologists began to make their impact. The first thing one has to do in writing the first unit in a foundation course is to state plainly the assumed entry behaviour and the objectives of the unit. This sounds easy but is, of course, extremely difficult. In the fields of arts and social science much of what is assumed as entry behaviour is the sort of general information that adults have picked up, read about, and learned in an unsystematic way throughout their working lives. In the case of science and mathematics however this is just not true, except of select groups of entrants such as those school teachers who have been working in these subject areas for several years.

The course teams in mathematics and science adopted similar approaches to the problem. Those students who did not have the assumed entry behaviour for the unit were provided with additional background information to study before going on to the unit proper.

The great danger of a system of open entry that does not demand any entrance qualification is, of course, that a great many students will drop out. The critics of the idea of the Open University held this out as the likeliest prospect before us and, had they been proved right, our very survival might have been in jeopardy. We were, therefore, most concerned to minimise drop-out. There was another very cogent reason for our concern. One is anxious not to inflict the trauma of failure on students who are trying very hard and have perhaps bitten off more than they can chew. Certainly, in a part-time non-residential university like the Open University, it is probably much less severe than it would be in a conventional institution. The individuals concerned are self-supporting and are not slung out without a job to go to; far fewer people need be aware of their failure since their friends, relatives and employers need not know that they have been students at the Open University. Nevertheless, it is a trauma to be avoided if at all possible.

It was known, from the experience of the University of New England at Armidale, New South Wales, where they taught students in the outback by correspondence unsupported by television and radio, that the biggest drop-out occurred in the first year of study – indeed, in the first few months of the first year. We had been fortunate in attracting to the Open University in 1969, for a spell of three months, Mr. Howard Sheath, who had been Head of the Extension Division of the University of New England for many years. I was most impressed by his arguments on this point. It was this knowledge that led me to suggest to the Admissions Committee that there should be a provisional registration period. However hard we tried, many adult students could not know before they actually began whether or not they could cope with our courses. We needed to let them test the temperature of the water before plunging into it. The general idea was that all new entrants to the University would pay a registration fee which would bring them all the teaching materials for the first three months. At the end of this period they would be required to pay the full tuition fee. If, at the end of the three months, they discovered that the work was beyond them or that they lacked the necessary motivation or opportunity, they could drop out at minimal loss to themselves or to the University. This pattern was adopted and we have used it ever since. Of those admitted on a provisional basis in January roughly 75% pay the tuition fees in April (see Chapter 11), and we have always calculated our student population from this final registration date. Students who after three months do not finally register are not considered as having been part of the University at all.

Over the years that we have been teaching the results have to a large extent vindicated our principle of open entry, although there are inevitably drawbacks to it of which we are all conscious.

The second major strand in our thinking about the degree structure concerned the need for a credit system. Both the Advisory Committee and the Planning Committee had envisaged a system which, by providing for examinations at the end of each course, would allow the student to obtain a 'credit' in that particular course which he could carry forward as a mark of achievement, whether or not he proceeded to the completion of a degree programme. This was felt to be extremely important, especially when dealing with adult students who might not all wish to continue on the long hard road towards the accumulation of six or eight credits for a degree, but might want to stop at some point along that road.

English universities are, in respect of the credit system, out of step with much of the rest of the world. The Scottish degree has for long been based on a credit system, although it is not so called, and almost every American university uses one. It is only in England that students can go, as one of my sons did, to Oxford, take one examination after six months, and thereafter spend the remainder of three full years of study without any formal examinations whatsoever. At the end of three years he was faced with a period of no less than three weeks in which he sat a multiplicity of papers which were as much a test of stamina as of anything else! This system may work perfectly well for the natural scholar for whom it was designed. It does not suit the non-scholar who requires some indication that he is making adequate progress at regular points along the road. In vocational programmes of study such as medicine where a multiplicity of different subjects have to be studied and mastered, the need for a credit system has always been overriding and is uniformly used.

There are great differences in the credit systems in operation in different parts of the world, but perhaps the comparison of America with Scotland will serve as an adequate illustration. In America they work to a system of 'credit hours'. Each credit hour represents the equivalent of one hour of instruction per week throughout a term or a semester and most courses in American universities rate only three or four credit hours. The student makes up his programme from a very large number of courses. In Scotland, on the other hand, the courses are very long by comparison, being the equivalent of something of the order of fifteen American credit hours. In other words, the modules of credit that go to make up a degree are of very different lengths. We chose to follow the Scottish pattern and to adopt the large module as our 'credit'. This at least has the merit that the examinations are not too frequent and that a fairly large area of study is examined on each occasion.

There are, of course, those who believe that the Oxford system, whereby the whole of three years of work is examined concurrently and the student has a chance to display how far he has integrated all his studies, is the best, indeed the only valid way of awarding a degree. I do not myself share this view but, even if I did, it would be wholly inapplicable in the situation of the Open University where, for better or worse, we have to follow a system based upon individual credits. The usual criticism levelled at the credit system by those who support the Oxford pattern is that a student who has a free choice of courses that he can take for credit is liable to end up with what has been called 'a miscellaneous rag-bag of credits' – a second rate degree with no internal coherence. Such people argue strongly that teachers must determine the pattern of studies that is most suited to the individual student and that direction of this kind is of the essence of education. Opponents of this view, on the other hand, argue equally strongly that a student is the best judge of what he wishes to learn and that he should be given the maximum freedom of choice consistent with a coherent overall pattern. They hold that this is doubly true when one is dealing with adults who, after years of experience of life, ought to be in a better position to judge what precise studies they wish to undertake than is the school leaver who has no experience outside the school-room. For this reason too the credit system has much to commend it when one is dealing with adult students. We therefore determined to put an absolute minimum of constraint upon the individual student in his choice of course. In practice it is remarkable how conservative our student body has been and how coherent are the patterns of study that have been chosen. It is extremely uncommon for a student to take a set of credits which any academic could call a miscellaneous rag-bag. One can in fact trust adult students not to abuse their freedom of choice.

It was partly for this reason, too, that we determined to offer only one undergraduate degree. There was a good deal of feeling that we should offer several. Many scientists and technologists, arguing for a BSc, felt that a BA would not properly indicate the nature of study in their faculties and might mislead potential employers of our graduates; there were similar arguments in favour of offering a BEd. Yet to allow students to choose their credits freely from more than one faculty would cause considerable problems if each faculty were to offer a different degree. One could start, it is true, by ensuring that regulations for the award of all the degrees were the same. But over the years faculties would want to impose new constraints, new restrictions, even new freedoms, on the students following the course pattern leading to their own faculty-based degree. Soon flexibility would be lost and students would more and more tend to fall into predetermined patterns of study. For this reason we decided to offer only a BA degree. We perhaps made a virtue of necessity by arguing that the same decision had been taken by both Oxford and Cambridge and was therefore hallowed by tradition.

All our foundation courses were full credit courses, each one counting as one credit towards the award of a degree, but it soon became quite clear that second and subsequent level courses might be better planned if a shorter module of work was adopted. This led most faculties to develop half-credit courses. These were spread over the same number of weeks as were full-credit courses but at half the intensity. There is always a tendency on the part of academics to make two half-credit courses rather more demanding than one full credit course, and we have struggled hard, but sometimes I feel unavailingly, to avoid this pitfall. On the other hand, the choice available to students within the limitations of the number of courses that we can offer is greatly increased by offering half-credit courses. Courses of less than half a credit in length have frequently been mooted but so far we have eschewed them.

Both the Advisory Committee and the Planning Committee made it clear in their reports that the University would offer courses leading to a degree offered by the new institution in its own right. Although it was, I think, implicit in both reports that the standard of the degree would have to be equivalent to that of any other university, it was not explicitly stated in either, and nowhere was any indication given of how equivalence was to be achieved. I therefore had to work out how the Open University degree could be made comparable with the degrees of other institutions.

This may sound easy but in practice it was extremely difficult. In the first place, England is, once again, very much out of step with the rest of the world in the pattern of its degree structure. In English universities students normally take an honours degree in three years. If they opt for a general, or pass degree, they also take three years. This unusual situation is made possible by the existence of the Advanced level examinations of the GCE. I personally regard the 'A' level as a pernicious influence on the whole pattern of education in England. In order to achieve, at school, a level of education normally reached in other countries after at least one year at university, children are forced to specialise at the age of 15 or 16 in two or three subjects only. Thus a child proceeding towards a scientific education abandons study in languages, history, literature and the liberal arts in order to concentrate upon physics, chemistry and mathematics. Conversely, a child proceeding towards an education in the humanities is no longer exposed to science and mathematics. This has two results. First, our graduates in the arts are largely innumerate, and our graduates in the sciences largely illiterate. Second, and perhaps even more important, advanced secondary schooling for all the intelligent children who are not going to university bears little or no relationship to their real needs in later life.

It has been shown over and over again by the odd examples of students who change direction in mid-stream, abandoning one educational line for another, that it is possible, in one year at university, to catch up with a subject not studied for 'A' level at school. There is, therefore, no real need to suffer all the disadvantages of the 'A' level system. The only advantage that it offers is a financial one, namely that it is cheaper to teach a sixth-former than to teach a university student. For this marginal financial gain the English educational system is held to a wholly unsatisfactory pattern that penalises most educated adults throughout their working lives.

In most of the rest of the world a pass or general degree takes three years and the equivalent of an English honours degree four years. The nearest example of such a degree structure is just across the border, in Scotland. I suppose it was natural, being a Scot by birth and education, that when I began to look at ways of comparing our degree in the Open University with those of other universities, the Scottish pattern should come to my mind. I thought, indeed, that I had had a new idea but years later when I read through the papers of the Advisory Committee, I discovered that Jennie Lee, also a Scot educated in Scotland, had had the same thought as early as 1965. Both of us came independently to the same conclusion, that the Scottish example provided the most useful standard of comparison.

For the ordinary degree of the ancient Scottish universities students are required to take, normally, a minimum of seven courses. In the majority of cases only two 'levels' of course are required and a student is required to take either five courses at first level and two at second, or four courses at first level and three at second, making a total of seven in all. The former is the normal pattern in Faculties of Arts and the latter in Faculties of Science, where the need for sequential courses is much greater.

The Planning Committee had fixed six course credits as the minimum number for the basic degree of the Open University. I was a little unhappy that we should be asking for one course fewer than did the Scottish universities, especially since we planned to allow students to take two credits concurrently, so that even as part-time students they could complete their degree programme in a minimum of three years. I did, in fact, make one attempt to persuade the Senate to increase the minimum number of credits from six to seven, but this was regarded as a major change to the policy laid down by the Planning Committee and the proposal was not accepted. I was therefore forced to justify on other grounds the conclusion that the Open University's general degree would be equal in standard to that of the Scottish ordinary degree.

First of all, we intended to teach each course of our degree programme over a period of 36 weeks each year, plus a one week summer school, and this was to be compared with an average of about 26 weeks' teaching in a regular university. Our academic year was thus significantly longer. The second point was that ordinary degrees in the Scottish universities were awarded after obtaining five credits at first level and only two credits at second level, whereas in the Open University, the proposal was that all students should take two courses at our foundation or first level, plus four at second level, in order to qualify for a general degree.

We were then faced with the critical question: are our foundation courses equivalent in level to the first courses in a Scottish University? This is not easy to answer. The 'level' of any course is ultimately governed by the achievement of students at the end of the course but that in turn depends on the level of knowledge assumed at the start of course, on the length of the course, and on the rate at which students can progress during it. At the start of a first-level course in a Scottish university, students are assumed to have reached a level of knowledge equivalent to a pass in the Scottish Certificate of Education at Higher grade. This is taken in four to six subjects, compared with the two or three subjects taken in 'A' levels in England, but the examinations are taken a year earlier. It is therefore a qualification of less depth but greater breadth and, in this sense, is one to which our unqualified students would more nearly approach. Yet they probably could not be expected to have achieved it, and we had to work on the assumption that most of them would have achieved something more like the Ordinary grade of the SCE, normally reached by school children at about 15. We felt that our adult students, with their greater maturity, could be asked to progress at a faster rate than Scottish first year students. We therefore set our sights on achieving, at the end of the foundation courses, the same level of achievement as that reached by the end of first-level courses in the Scottish universities.

If, then, we were to accept that our foundation courses were the equivalents of Scottish university first-level courses, we could quite properly award an ordinary degree on the basis of credits in them and in courses only one level beyond them. Even if our foundation courses were of a lower level, we could still argue that our degree would be of equal standard, since we were to demand a (2 + 4) pattern of course levels as compared with the (5 + 2) pattern of the Scottish universities.

We then proceeded to examine the number of hours work that would be demanded of students in the two systems. This could at best be only a rough and ready guide because, as is well known, students vary enormously in the effort they put into their course work. Their innate ability determines the amount of work they have to do in order to pass. They may wish simply to scrape a pass or they may wish to achieve distinction: many students spend their time at university doing other, and perhaps more interesting things, than working towards their examinations and are content with a bare pass. We assumed that, over a period of 26 weeks, an average student in a Scottish university might be expected to work a 30 hour week. This would include the time he spent actually in face-to-face contact with teachers, plus the time he spent on private study and reading. On this basis he would actually work a total of 800 hours in each year. We determined that each one of our courses would require a student to spend an average of 10 hours of study in each of the 36 weeks that he followed the course, plus a one week summer school connected with that course. If we assume 30 hours of work at the summer school we get a total of 390 hours of work for each course.

Thus, a full degree programme for a Scottish ordinary degree would require of the student 2,400 (3 × 800) hours of work over a three year period; a full degree programme for an Open University pass degree would also require nearly 2,400 (6 × 390) hours of work of the student. On this admittedly rough and ready basis it therefore seemed that we were going to ask for a comparable effort from our students. Just as my figure of 30 hours a week may be an underestimate of the amount of time spent by the average undergraduate in a Scottish university, so also might our figure of 10 hours a week be an underestimate of what was actually demanded of our own students. The figures shown by surveys of students over the last five years indicate that the average time spent by a student per week is closer to 12 hours than 10. This would be comparable to a 36 hour week worked by undergraduates in the Scottish universities.

It must be remembered that these arguments to justify the structure of our degree were going on at a time before any courses were actually written and on display to our colleagues in other universities. The ultimate decision as to whether our degree was up to standard would depend upon the courses themselves. But it was initially very important that our course and degree structure should appear to match existing ones.

When I spoke in public on these matters, I was usually faced with two other questions. The first was, 'How are you going to teach without an element of face-to-face tuition of fairly sizeable proportions?' The answer to this, of course, was that if the whole concept of teaching at a distance, of home-based study, of working in isolation, was valid, then we must dispense with face-to-face teaching. We must put our faith in the idea that it was possible for students to achieve the same level of education without a significant face-to-face element.

The second was, 'How are you possibly going to be able to teach science and technology, where laboratory work is a significant part of the total course?' The answer to this was much more complex. I used to argue that we could teach the laboratory element of scientific disciplines in three ways. The first was by television where demonstrations of experiments can usually be carried out more efficiently than in the practical classroom. All students can see what you are trying to show them, not just those in the front row. The second way in which we could approach laboratory teaching was by developing what we called a 'home experiment kit' for each course where needed. This used to be laughed at, since for most people it conjured up the vision of a sort of child's chemistry set. But what we actually designed over the years was very much more sophisticated than that (see Chapter 6). The third way in which we could provide laboratory experience was at the summer school, where the whole week could be devoted to laboratory work. Some first level science courses in the Scottish ordinary degree programme actually called for as little as one afternoon of laboratory work per week for 26 weeks (i.e. 13 full days). A summer school provided six days in the laboratory and this, coupled with television demonstrations and home experiments could well be regarded as equivalent in terms of laboratory time.

This was our justification for the programme that we adopted. It did not question the need for the usual amount of laboratory experience although many of us privately did so: prolonged spells spent in laboratories by junior students in science and technology are often a waste of time. In laboratory sessions, one is actually trying to do one of two things. For most students one is trying to illustrate the principles of experimental work, so that students can recognise the difficulty of obtaining good data and appreciate just how carefully one has to examine it in the literature before accepting the conclusions of the author. For the small group of students who are actually going to become practising scientists one is also trying to provide a training in laboratory techniques. It is my belief, shared by many university teachers, that most courses lay far too much stress on provision for the latter group and thereby force the much larger group to spend much too long doing experiments in the laboratory.

When it came to the honours degree, we were arguing on a different basis. Here we returned largely to the idea that had been advanced by several members of the Advisory Committee, notably by Harold Wiltshire, that to achieve an honours degree in a single subject required a minimum of four years of work in that subject area. Our version of this was that the additional two credits required to upgrade a pass degree to honours degree level should be spent either studying two further subjects at third level or one further subject at both third and fourth level. Although the pattern of honours degrees in the Scottish universities is not the same as that, it seemed a justifiable structure for us to adopt and one which would still maintain the principle of the credit system. We were, therefore, reasonably happy that we had achieved a pattern of degree structure and a pattern of courses within it which would stand comparison with at least one group of British universities. It remained only to translate the pattern into the reality of courses on offer to students.

We had decided, then, that we would stick with the principle of open entry without qualifications, and that we would start off with a foundation course designed to bring students who had been out of education for a long time back to an awareness of the general problems that would face them within any particular field of studies. We had been innovative in the sense of abandoning entry qualifications and of offering multi-disciplinary courses within one line of study. We were also innovative in the sense that our courses would be multi-media ones, designed to bring education to a student in his home, rather than to bring a student to education in an institution. The question that remained was: what would the subject matter of these courses be and how innovative could we afford to be in designing them?

Here we made a clear decision not to innovate but to stick to the traditional fields of study typical of conventional universities, and I suppose that we could therefore legitimately be charged with having had 'cold feet'. The decision was, in my view, determined by our overriding need to achieve academic respectability. Had we embarked on a series of courses that broke too far with tradition, that based themselves on a desire to achieve what students have called 'relevance', that appeared to deal only with superficial aspects of learning because they did not explore traditional fields of knowledge in depth, we would have achieved nothing at all. The other universities, our colleagues throughout the country and throughout the world, would have regarded the degree of the Open University as something so different as to be second-rate, even if the standard of the courses themselves was acceptable. We were not, after all, dealing with students who were simply anxious to achieve a degree of equivalent standard; they also wished their degree to be recognised by employers as of equivalent content. This was especially significant in those lines of study, such as science and technology, where the courses were regarded as 'vocational'.

There is a great deal of nonsense talked about 'vocational' and 'non-vocational' studies. Much of adult education has fallen into such a trap throughout the years. Courses that led to a qualification were frowned upon. What adults really wanted, it was maintained, were courses of study that led to no qualification, that were designed to broaden the mind, to appeal to those who wished to study for the sake of study, without any thought of bettering their careers. A great deal of emphasis was laid on the fact that a 'liberal' education was not a training for any particular type of work but a training of the mind, fitting a student to embark on a non-scientific career, and great play was made of the fact that a classical education was the basis for all true education. What utter nonsense! If one goes back to the earlier days of the universities, it is quite true that there was an absolute demand for all students to have a mastery of the classics. The reason was that later courses of study were designed to fit a graduate to embark on a career in the Church, in Medicine or Law, three 'vocations' if ever there were any. Reading for any one of those three vocations was possible only for those who had mastered the classics, because all the literature was written in Latin or Greek. This was the real basis of a so-called 'liberal' education. It was designed primarily to lead on to a vocational education. The idea that an education in science and technology, simply because it is vocational in aim, is less liberal and more to be sneered at than an education in the classics and the liberal arts is, in my view, quite unacceptable.

We also had to decide what would be the main motives driving adult students to seek degrees with the Open University. There was a great difference of opinion about this but I, for one, was quite sure that most students would want primarily to obtain a qualification which would fit them for promotion, for a change of job, for a better job, for more money, – in other words, for the perfectly proper end of furthering their own careers. This is not to say that other students, especially the older ones, would not be studying for reasons of self-fulfilment, or improving their general knowledge and of learning to enjoy life rather more fully. Even amongst this latter group, however, many welcome the challenge that a course leading to a qualification offers. Many of our current students, when asked why they chose our courses rather than others in further or adult education, give the answer that it is because ours, which are examined for degree purposes, are therefore more rigorous.

What was true of the individual courses was also true of the degree itself. When the graduate emerged he should have a total spectrum of knowledge and training comparable in all respects to that which he would have achieved elsewhere. There was thus great pressure on faculties to consider offering specialist honours degrees in subjects such as psychology, where the standards for professional recognition were laid down by the professional associations themselves, rather than by the universities offering the degrees in the first instance. I shall return to this topic in a later chapter.

In the Faculty of Arts it was agreed that the second level courses should allow the literature, the fine art, the philosophy and the religion of selected periods of history to be examined as a coherent whole. Beyond second level there should be an opportunity for students to specialise in one discipline, in literature, history, philosophy or the fine arts. In the Faculty of Social Science, where professional recognition was an issue, disciplinary studies would begin at second level, so that students could obtain sufficient credits within any one of the five disciplines of the faculty to obtain a more specialised degree. A similar view pertained in the Faculty of Science, where studies at second level in chemistry, in physics, in geology and in biology were, from the beginning, a part of the planned development of the faculty. The Faculty of Educational Studies was primarily concerned with the needs of the very high proportion of teachers who were expected to be amongst the first entrants to the Open University. The non-graduate certificated teacher must be able to obtain an appropriate degree, which called for courses in the theory and practice of education as well as in the disciplines offered by the other faculties. The Faculty of Technology decided that specialised honours degrees in the various branches of engineering were beyond the capacity of the Open University. It was therefore much more interested in turning out graduates who were trained in the broad area of engineering science, rather than any one particular branch. As a result, many of the courses (apart from electronics, which lent itself as a discipline to our particular methods of teaching) were designed to give a broad understanding of the principles of technology. Courses in systems and in design were quite clearly of this kind. The Faculty of Mathematics aimed at teaching an understanding of the nature of mathematics, rather than the particular applications of the discipline. The 'new' mathematics, which involved a completely new language for most adult students, was to be the basis of all courses. Nevertheless, the need to provide service courses in mathematics for those who were proceeding in Science, Technology and the Social Sciences, were obvious from the outset. Such students, whose comprehension of 'new' mathematics was zero and who had been trained in the language of the old mathematics, could not be expected to cope with these courses. Yet we could ill afford to mount duplicate courses. Even at the time of writing we have not wholly solved this particular problem.

Thus, as things developed, the faculties adopted different patterns of course planning and there was no overall policy to guide them. Things grew rather like Topsy because we were working in an area wholly unexplored and had no clear idea of the range of courses that we would ultimately be able to offer.

We were also faced with the problem of re-thinking the range of the 'lines of study' that had been determined by the Planning Committee and of deciding whether these were in fact the appropriate ones for the University to be following. We were not in much doubt about the need for lines of study in the arts, in social sciences, science and mathematics. We separated mathematics and technology at an early date because we felt that the area of engineering science was one that we could deal with even though we could not handle the individual branches of engineering. We added education because of the clear need to provide for certificated teachers.

Other very pertinent suggestions were made. Great pressure was put upon us by successive Lord Chancellors, first by Lord Gardiner of the Labour Government and then by Lord Hailsham of the Tory Government that took office in 1970, to offer a line of studies in Law. I have found no trace in the files of the Advisory Committee and the Planning Committee that the thought of offering courses in Law was ever raised. It is a subject that is commonly dealt with by commercial correspondence colleges, and I have no doubt that we could successfully have mounted courses of this kind. Another new line, which we considered, was the whole area of Business Studies, the sort of field that is covered by conventional universities in a Bachelor of Commerce degree. Here again, there would have been nothing to stop an institution like the Open University from embarking on courses of this kind. They lend themselves to correspondence teaching and again, the commercial correspondence colleges offer a great many such courses.

We were, in the event, too late to introduce any new lines of study. We had embarked on fulfilling the promises made by the Planning Committee in their report and, by the time alternative lines of study were suggested, there was no money left further to expand the activities of the institution. There is no question in my own mind but that, in the long term, we ought to offer courses of study both in Law and in commercial subjects, in order to meet a deep need in the country as a whole. In the present financial climate, this must however remain an aim for the future, rather than becoming a part of our current programme.

It was with all of these underlying principles in mind that we embarked upon our first attempts at devising a profile, a spectrum of courses that would count as credits towards a degree.

All the early writings about a University of the Air placed much emphasis on the social purposes of an institution which would rely for its teaching programme upon the mass media of communication. Similarly, all lacked any clear account of the courses of study that would be offered. The first mention of any profile of courses is to be found in the papers that were submitted to the Advisory Committee on the University of the Air in 1965. Here, for the first time, people began to examine the problems realistically. The main constraint that was envisaged was the inevitable limitation on air-time. To most people the very name, the University of the Air, conjured up a vision of an institution which would rely upon television and radio for

69

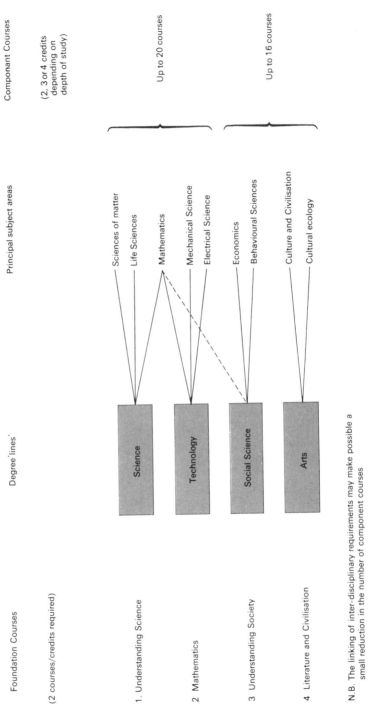

Foundation Courses

(2 courses/credits required)

1. Understanding Science

2 Mathematics

3 Understanding Society

4 Literature and Civilisation

Degree 'lines'

Science

Technology

Social Science

Arts

Principal subject areas

Sciences of matter
Life Sciences
Mathematics
Mechanical Science
Electrical Science
Economics
Behavioural Sciences
Culture and Civilisation
Cultural ecology

Componant Courses

(2, 3 or 4 credits depending on depth of study)

Up to 20 courses

Up to 16 courses

N.B. The linking of inter-disciplinary requirements may make possible a small reduction in the number of component courses

FIGURE 2   Planning Committee's degree structure.

its formal teaching programme. Dr. Pickard, the Principal of Ealing Technical College, pointed out that one relatively small technical college offered no less than 35,000 hours of instruction in an academic year: a new television channel, used exclusively for educational broadcasting for 18 hours a day, 7 days a week, for 40 weeks, would provide only 5,000 hours of instruction in a year. Two lines of thought stemmed from such assessments. The first concentrated upon the need to make a start with a very restricted number of courses; the second led to a fuller recognition that broadcasting must become only one, and a relatively small one, of a number of components in a multi-media form of instruction. Furthermore, Jennie Lee became more than ever convinced that the University of the Air must, as a *sine qua non,* be provided with the Fourth television channel.

There was, however, fairly general agreement amongst the members of the Advisory Committee that the total number of courses that could be offered within the constraints of broadcasting time was about 20, and that main lines of study should be in the arts and the social sciences. Science and technology, the Advisory Committee considered, were very important but could only be tackled in partnership with technical colleges. It was, however, recommended that the University of the Air should offer, from the outset, degree courses in mathematics and in the foundations of science.

The Planning Committee, on the other hand, had more ambitious ideas. It envisaged four main lines of study, namely the arts, the social sciences, mathematics and technology, and science. Within each line it suggested courses at three levels, foundation level plus two higher levels, with about four component subjects in each line of study, each of which could be taught at both these higher levels. Thus the number of courses offered in each line would be nine, and the total number of courses would be 36. This therefore represented a virtual doubling of the scale of operations envisaged by the Advisory Committee.

There was another change of emphasis between the plans of the Advisory Committee and those of the Planning Committee. The range of subjects suggested by the Advisory Committee was never made explicit, but in John Scupham's scheme, which formed the basis of the eventual White Paper, he foresaw the ten main subjects as being:

English	Economics	Mathematics
History	Social Sciences	Physics
Philosophy		Biology
French		
German		

The Planning Committee however developed its own outline of proposed subjects for courses (Figure 2) which was issued in a press release in 1968. It shows a considerably greater departure from the traditional range of university courses than did the Advisory Committee proposals. There was also an obvious and deliberate dropping of all courses in languages, for three reasons: first because of the large number of courses that each language would pre-empt, second because university language teaching normally assumes a knowledge of the language as an entry qualification which would be contrary to the principle of open entry, and third because conversational language courses are well provided for by the Further Education Advisory Council of the BBC.

The Planning Committee also extended the Advisory Committee concept of the general degree to include a 'general honours' degree. If we use a notation whereby the numbers of courses required at each 'level' are given *seriatim*, then the pattern proposed by the Advisory Committee can be written as (5 + 2); the pattern proposed by the Planning Committee for the ordinary degree was (2 + 4); for the general honours degree various schemes were suggested by the Students and Curriculum Working Group (such as (2 + 4 + 2) and (2 + 3 + 3)); but the Planning Committee decided to leave the final decision to the Senate of the new University.

This, then was the position when I took up office in January 1969 and began to recruit the first group of academic staff. To do so I had to draft advertisements. What was I to look for? There was no way of advertising successfully unless I could define the academic disciplines from which I wished to recruit the staff. Thus more definitive decisions about the components of each line were essential and urgent. I submitted proposals to the Planning Committee which were approved, and resulted in advertisements for senior academic staff for each of the following 17 disciplines.

HUMANITIES:

| Literature | Philosophy |
| History | Fine Arts |

SCIENCE:

| Physics | Geology |
| Chemistry | Biology |

SOCIAL SCIENCES:

Psychology	Economics
Sociology	Geography
Government	

MATHEMATICS:

| Pure Maths | Computer Science |
| Applied Maths | Statistics |

During the spring of 1969 I was heavily committed in chairing the Selection Panels for these 34 posts. During the interviews of the short-listed candidates it became clear that the majority were very anxious to know whether there was any prospect of teaching to honours level in their own discipline. I took the line, supported by other members of the Planning Committee who sat on the Selection Panels, that the immediate tasks were to prepare multi-disciplinary courses at foundation level and also at second level; but that, given adequate numbers of students and adequate financial support, there was no reason why in the long term honours courses in individual disciplines should not be prepared. Although the Report of the

Planning Committee had described courses at only three levels, the Students and Curriculum Working Group had considered fourth level courses as possible components of honours degree programmes.

I became more and more certain that we should evolve an academic plan that did not exclude the possibility of such fourth level courses or of more specialised honours degrees, at least in some selected subjects. I therefore prepared a paper, outlining a long-term academic plan, which was submitted to the second meeting of the Senate of the Open University on June 23rd 1969. This was the first version of a profile of courses.

In this plan I proposed that each line should offer a foundation course and three inter-disciplinary second-level courses, together with one third and one fourth level course in each of the component disciplines of that line. I suggested that an ordinary degree could be obtained by a minimum programme of (2 + 4) credits (using the nomenclature outlined above), a 'general' honours degree by a minimum of (2 + 4 + 2) and a 'special honours' degree by a minimum of (2 + 4 + 1 + 1). The Senate accepted this general pattern at its third meeting on September 5th 1969.

By this time we had agreed to add two further lines to the original four, namely Technology and Educational Studies, but the latter would not offer a foundation course. The component disciplines of these lines were to be

TECHNOLOGY:	EDUCATIONAL STUDIES:
Electronics	Psychology of Education
Materials Science	Sociology of Education
Design	Curriculum Planning
Systems	Educational Administration
Engineering Mechanics	

The new proposals therefore embodied five foundation courses, 18 second-level courses (three in each of the six lines) and third and fourth level courses in 26 component disciplines, making a total of 75 courses in all. Thus the Planning Committee's academic plan was once again doubled in overall size.

Those were halcyon days for planning. The Open University had been created; it was no longer just a dream. But we had no concept of the level of demand and even less of the workload of course preparation. There was no reason why we should limit our long-term targets, since we had come to terms with the amount of available air-time.

Over the next two years there was little change in the accepted academic plan – the first version of the profile – although the faculties interpreted it in different ways. We were all too busy creating the first courses to have much time or energy for longer term planning. Two things did emerge slowly but inexorably. One was the gross underestimate we had made of the time and effort needed to produce one course. The other was the need for more and more courses to support the sort of special honours degrees that we had envisaged. Even in my plan of 1969 there was room, for instance, for only three courses in subjects like literature or history. A special honours degree, to be comparable with those in other universities, would call for many more, even if there were to be few options. (In Edinburgh University there are some 32 options amongst the final year History honours courses alone.)

It was not until 1971 that these pressures led John Sparkes, then Pro-Vice-Chancellor (Academic), to call for a reappraisal of the whole academic plan. As a result, the Senate agreed to the profile of courses shown in Figure 3. The Sparkes profile laid particular emphasis upon the need for interfaculty courses and these, together with single faculty courses, were defined for each faculty ('Lines' had by that time become 'Faculties'). The total number of courses envisaged had grown to 111.

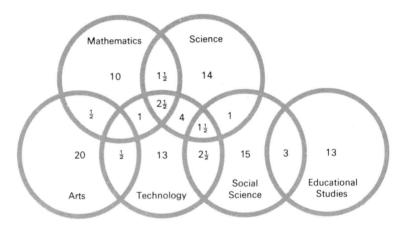

FIGURE 3   The one hundred and eleven credit profile.

Almost immediately this new profile of courses came under challenge. The reasons were now both academic and financial. There was a growing awareness that the expansion in the numbers of courses being offered was leading to a situation where one of the basic purposes of the Open University, namely to provide a more general education, was being eroded in order to try to provide an honours degree of the classical specialised kind, and that the Open University could not always offer such specialised honours degrees successfully. We were in danger of abandoning something we could do very well for something we could do only poorly, if at all. In parallel to this development we became aware that with the sort of resources at our disposal and the sort of student numbers we could accept, it was just not feasible to aim at a target of 111 courses. (See Chapter 18).

We therefore went through a further agonising reappraisal in 1974. Paramount in this was the consideration that, if the profile were reduced, some of the courses already written to fit into the larger profile would have to be abandoned and some of the planned courses, very dear to the hearts of individual academics, would never be written. Add to that the tensions between different faculties, each of which wished for a more extensive programme of courses, and the agony is readily understandable. However, the reappraisal, guided by Arnold Kettle, successor to John Sparkes as Pro-Vice-Chancellor (Academic), was nevertheless completed and accepted as the new plan.

TABLE 1

	A	D	E	M	S	T	University	Total
Undergraduate academic profile	16	17	10	10	15	15	4	87

The final revised profile provides for a total of 87 credits, which are distributed as shown in Table 1. We accepted that we could not offer special honours degrees at all. We are now pledged to try to offer instead a choice of 'coherent programmes of study' in selected 'fields of study' and the Faculties are currently working towards this end. The aims are at last clear. It remains to be shown whether we can achieve them.

5

COURSE CREATION

In Chapter 4 I described the evolution of the structure of the Open University degree. It was to be gained by obtaining credits in a number of 'courses'. The basic elements of each 'course' had been described by the Planning Committee. There were to be specially written correspondence texts sent to the student through the post and these were to be integrated with television and radio broadcasts transmitted on open circuit. The specially constructed teaching materials would refer to set text books and to additional background reading lists. Students would be required to undertake written assignments which would be marked by a 'correspondence tutor' and this activity was seen as a method of teaching as much as a method of assessment of performance. In addition students would be required to attend short residential summer schools and would be offered, optionally, the opportunity of meeting a counsellor (and later a tutor) and other students at one of a network of local study centres. Each course would end with a final examination to be held in local examination centres.

We were therefore faced with all the problems involved in setting up the machinery to operate courses of this kind. It is possible, with hindsight, to analyse these problems and to see that they fall into four separate categories. First we had to create the course, to determine its objectives, its content, the method of its presentation. Second, we had to produce the course as printed books, recorded videotapes, and other materials suitable for presentation to the student. Third, we had to transmit the course to the students, and this involved not only the use of the postal services and open-circuit broadcasting, but also the organisation of all the regional back-up services – of study centres, part-time counsellors and tutors and summer schools – needed to support the teaching-learning process. Finally, we had to accredit the course by assessing the students' work, both throughout his period of study and in a terminal examination so that we could award credit for the course at an approved and recognised standard.

In the conventional university course creation occurs in the mind of an individual teacher, who sorts out his own thoughts and ideas in preparing his lectures. There is often no stage of course production, except when printed lecture notes are reproduced. Course transmission consists in delivering the lecture in the classroom (and distributing any printed lecture notes). Only in the process of course accreditation are there elements that closely resemble those of the Open University system. I shall try to describe these four stages of devising a course as they developed in the context of our new system; in this chapter I shall consider the creative phase.

To produce the drafts of the various 'course materials' that would enable an adult, working in isolation, to reach a predetermined standard of performance in a given area of study, called for the combined skills of a number of groups of people. First we had to have not just one university teacher, with his thoughts and ideas about the objectives, contents and methods of presentation of the course, but several, because our courses were to be multi-disciplinary as well as multimedia in nature. This, in turn, meant that each teacher would have different and inevitably conflicting thoughts and ideas which would somehow have to be reconciled with each other to lead to an agreed final version. Second, since the university teachers that we could recruit would mostly be unfamiliar with the special problems both of educating adults and of teaching at a distance, we would need the advice of other experts, in particular educational technologists and television and radio producers, in order to determine the method of presentation of the course. The need for educational technologists had been foreseen by the Planning Committee which had said that the aim must be 'to provide the necessary expertise in the educational technologies associated with specialised course design, with correspondence tuition, with radio and television broadcasting, with the special problems of adult education and with the problems of programmed learning and with the assessment of student performance'. This was an aim that was relatively easy to state but turned out to be excessively difficult to achieve.

We therefore needed three separate groups of specialist staff, and we had to set about attracting them. The academic staff were recruited as already described, the radio and television production staff by the BBC. The educational technologists had still to be found. All three groups had then to learn about each others' problems and to work together on a common task. We had to operate by teamwork and this was the whole basis of the concept of the 'course team'. I believe this was one of the most important and far-reaching concepts of the Open University which, it seems probable, will become more and more widely used all over the world.

The reports of the Advisory Committee and the Planning Committee give very little indication of their thinking about the real nature of the academic staffing of the Open University. The Advisory Committee envisaged that the University would require a central professional staff of between forty and fifty. This total included not only the academic staff but also the administrative and operational staff that would be required. In respect of the academic staff the Advisory Committee mentioned only 'a group of highly qualified heads of faculties, who would be responsible for the planning of courses in their own subjects and for the selection of lecturers and tutors'. As far as I can make out from the papers submitted to the Advisory Committee and from the discussion with members of that committee at a later date, this very small nucleus of full-time academics would select lecturers and tutors from amongst the staff of other universities and colleges. These lecturers and tutors, on secondment from their normal duties would make programmes within the courses devised by the small group of full-time staff. The Planning Committee envisaged academic departments 'staffed by full-time university teachers who will be employed under conditions of service comparable to those which apply in other universities'. The academic departments would be grouped into a number of lines of study corresponding to faculties, each line being under the administrative control of a Director of Studies who would be the counterpart of a Dean of a Faculty.

The Planning Committee went no further, leaving the staffing of each individual department for determination by the Senate of the new university once it was set up. Nevertheless, when I joined the Planning Committee after my appointment in June 1968, I became aware that their concept was similar to that of the Advisory Committee, namely of a small nucleus of full-time academic staff aided by a large number of people from other universities employed on secondment or for short-term periods as consultants. When I was faced with issuing the first advertisements for academic staff, I had to make some estimate in my own mind of how many would be employed in any one discipline. I had to argue very strongly with the Planning Committee to get them to accept my minimum figure of four members of the academic staff per discipline. This was a figure which I virtually drew out of the air. I knew that any smaller number could not provide for that cross-fertilisation of ideas through which academics maintain their drive and interest in their own subject. Working in isolation is not a happy situation for most people. At that time too I had the naive idea that one full-time member of the academic staff could probably write a full credit course in one full year of work. Since any one discipline would offer only two courses of its own (one third level and one fourth level course) and would participate in four multidisciplinary courses of the faculty concerned (one foundation course and three second level courses) it seemed to me that four full-time staff could cope with this total load and still allow one of the four to be on study leave in any one year. I was not alone in this misconception, as all my early colleagues in these first meetings of the Senate concurred in that judgement. How wrong we were! And how fortunate it was that we were so wrong! For at that time I was also planning the first buildings. Had I foreseen with any accuracy the real needs in terms of staff numbers, our demands for building would probably have frightened off even our most faithful political supporters.

The Planning Committee had made a very significant stride forward in determining that the academic staff would be employed on terms and conditions of service comparable to those in other universities. This, I always felt, would be absolutely crucial in attracting an adequate staff. I decided that I would make no attempt to select staff on the basis of experience in the techniques of broadcasting, of communication at a distance, or of adult education but that, on the contrary, I would use precisely the same criteria as I would have used in the University of Edinburgh. I would be looking for academics of a quality recognised by any other university in the country. I was determined to ensure that the Open University would as early as possible gain academic acceptance as a reputable institution. We therefore recruited these first staff by issuing advertisements in normal form in the normal journals that attract academic applications. I was more than relieved when we received more than 1,200 applications, emanating overwhelmingly from reputable candidates with an academic record comparable to, indeed often better than, that of applicants for jobs in other universities. This was really the first time that I began to believe in my heart of hearts that we would succeed.

We soon became aware that the academic staff would need help of a kind we had not foreseen. The phase of creating a course was to be followed by the phase of production, and it transpired that the interface between the two presented a whole series of day-to-day problems. Thus, if a course were broken down into 36 individual 'units' of work for a student, the first units would go into the 'production phase' at the same time as later units would still be in the 'creation phase'. Academic staff, labouring over the creative effort, could not easily attend to the more mundane problems associated with converting their earlier creations into finished 'course materials'. Yet problems about the selection of graphics and photographs for the illustration of texts, about the editing and lay-out of drafts for the printers, the packaging of finished materials for students, the scheduling of the whole complex process, arose daily.

For this reason we began to recruit a number of junior graduate staff to carry out such functions. We have had great difficulty with this group over the years. In the first place it was very difficult to define in any precise way just what their duties would be. We were developing our systems as we went along and new tasks arose at frequent intervals. No one liked to be a 'dogsbody' but it was the inevitable fate of our first recruits in these jobs. The second problem was that there was no obvious career structure for them, because this was a job for which there was no counterpart in other universities. At the time that we were recruiting, the job market in the university world in general was very depressed. Consequently we attracted people of a calibre and quality much higher than we had expected, whose career aspirations were therefore much more ambitious than we had allowed for. These people developed very considerable skills in handling the particular system of the Open University and became virtually irreplaceable. There were no comparable jobs available to them in other institutions, and promotion within the University can only be to a lectureship when a vacancy arises. This is only one example of a problem that we have encountered all too frequently. A wholly innovative institution is bound to require categories of staff that have no counterparts elsewhere. When such a category calls for senior positions – career grades – the situation is tenable, but where this is not so, the difficulty can become well-nigh insuperable. Either one is bound to create senior positions without really needing them and with a consequent escalation in costs, or one creates frustration and disaffection amongst the staff concerned, there being nowhere for them to go. A number of these problems remain unsolved.

We were also faced with the necessity of providing an adequate library service to back up the work of the academic staff. We needed more than a conventional library: we were really setting up a 'department of media resources' and a collection of audiovisual materials was therefore as important as a collection of printed materials. As far as the students were concerned, scattered as they were throughout the whole of the country, it would not be feasible to offer a library service. They would have to rely on the public libraries and on inter-library loan services to acquire the reading material that they would need. Support for libraries in other universities is geared to and determined by the student population as well as by the number of academic staff. Consequently we could expect only a very small library grant, since we had no student users to justify a large one. We had to cut our coat according to our cloth, and we determined that we would build an absolutely first class collection in the field of educational technology but would not, indeed could not, attempt to build comparable collections in all the academic disciplines that would be represented within the university. Our staff in these disciplines would likewise have to rely on inter-library loans and on the use of other university libraries. This policy has been modified over the years and the collection is now considerably better than we had at one time feared it might be. But it is still far from adequate as compared with the libraries of other universities. One of the moves that I have long hoped to make in a more favourable economic climate is to launch an appeal for funds to build the library up to an adequate size.

When I began work in 1969, educational technologists with the range of skills which we required were extremely rare birds. Furthermore, although the need for such people in the early days would be paramount, the academic staff of the university seemed likely, or so I thought, rapidly to acquire such skills, both by association with educational technologists and by the continual application of their techniques, so that the need for this kind of specialist help would probably decline. Yet the immediate need was acute, not only for the development of the courses themselves but also for the academic planning of the various systems that we had to develop. It was clear that we could not hope to recruit to our own staff enough skilled educational technologists sufficiently quickly to satisfy these urgent needs. This crucial gap was filled by contracting with a group of consultants (Instructional Systems Associates) to provide the help we needed. During the course of their contract the consultants became so intimately involved with, and fascinated by, the development of the Open University that the company went into voluntary suspension and the three senior partners all accepted full-time posts in the university. Meanwhile we proceeded to recruit educational technologists to our full-time staff as fast as we could. How were we to fit this group into the new university? We decided to create a Department of Applied Educational Sciences. We were well aware that the phase 'educational technology' tended throughout the world to be interpreted as meaning knowledge of the 'hardware' associated with education – teaching machines, computer-aided instruction, audiovisual aids and so on. We were concerned primarily with the development of 'software', of the methodology of teaching, and the title 'Applied Educational Sciences' seemed to describe more precisely what the new department was trying to achieve. But we were soon to make a further change.

The Planning Committee had recommended most strongly an on-going programme of research into the operation of the University. How effective would our educational system turn out to be? What would happen to those adults who succeeded in obtaining degrees? A whole host of problems of this kind called for investigation and we would need a staff of experts to undertake the research. We had made a small start by appointing two research officers to study the effectiveness of the so-called 'Gateway' courses that were being offered in 1970 by the National Extension College in association with the BBC, as preparatory courses for the Open University. This was only a small, almost a token start on what the Planning Committee had hoped would be a major activity of the new university. There was continuous pressure to increase the scale of our institutional research from members of the Planning Committee and later of the Council of the Open University. Yet our resources were very limited and the needs of course production and transmission inevitably took priority. The need for institutional research was clearly going to become acute as the first students began work in 1971, and the volume of such research would certainly grow as the size of the student population increased in subsequent years. This prospect suggested to me that there was a potential correlation between the growing need for institutional research and the declining need for advice on course construction, as the academic staff themselves became more and more experienced and skilled in such tasks. I therefore proposed that the Department of Applied Educational Sciences should be combined with the group of Research Officers into a single Institute. I considered that the staff of the Department of Applied Educational Sciences would be just the sort of people who could most happily and successfully undertake institutional research as the need for this advisory service declined. My suggestion was accepted, although with some misgivings, by the staff concerned and the Institute of Educational Technology was born.

The misgivings were justified in part. As it turned out, the need for advisory services increased over the years rather than declined. This was partly because the academic staff expanded each year so that we have always had many who had neither associated with educational technologists nor had had experience in applying their techniques, and partly because, even amongst experienced academics, a substantial number turned out to be either unwilling or unable to assimilate the principles and practices of the educational technologists. Although this particular burden on the staff of the Institute has grown heavier, the staff of the Institute have become more and more deeply involved in institutional research, supported increasingly both from our own funds and from research grants, to enable the work to be significantly extended. Consequently they have had less time to devote to the advisory services, the need for which has not declined.

Regarding the development of BBC production facilities, it is apparent
from the tone of the statement issued jointly by the BBC and the Planning
Committee* that there were considerable doubts on both sides as to just
how this partnership would work out in practice. The tradition within the
BBC was plain; the producer was the boss. What he said went and, within
the limits of the budget provided, he had full control of the content and
shape of each broadcast. This was clearly unacceptable to the University,
where the broadcast had to fit into the pattern of a multimedia course. The
University thus feared that the BBC might exert too great an influence on
the shape of programmes. On the other hand the BBC feared that the
University would insist on what would turn out to be bad television. These
fears were a reflection of the unhappy outcome of many attempts at
educational broadcasting both in this country and even more overseas,
which had led to confrontation and conflict between two creative artists,
namely the academic and the producer.

Most of the suspicion stemmed from ignorance. To remove it required
that each of the partners got to know much more about the other. To this
end we held a number of meetings, both formal and informal, so that staff
would get to know each other as well as finding out about organisation and
technique. Most of our staff had no experience of television and required a
considerable indoctrination into the principles and practice thereof. Most
of the BBC production staff were newly recruited and themselves had to be
trained in their own expertise. Such production staff were recruited from
amongst the graduate population of the country at the same time as the
University was advertising for its academic staff. In a number of cases the
same individuals applied for jobs both in the BBC and in the Open
University. As a result the production staff of the BBC were of very high
academic quality, comparable in almost every respect to their academic
counterparts in the University, and this made for increased mutual trust.
New production staff were trained by a small nucleus of experienced
producers from the BBC's general educational service who were dedicated
to the idea of the Open University, and they were splendid promoters of
a happy relationship. However, it was necessary for the University's
academic staff to learn the ways of production studios and to be introduced
to the problems and difficulties of teaching through these media. In
consequence, at that time there was perhaps more to-ing and fro-ing
between the University and Alexandra Palace than at any time since. I
remember being taken by Don Grattan behind the scenes at Television
Centre to see how a studio worked. I fear I was an inept pupil but at least
I, like others, gained some appreciation of the enormous technical
difficulties.

It was very hard for those of us without experience of television
production to accept that it would take a whole day – sometimes two whole
days – in a studio to produce a programme lasting only twenty-five
minutes. It was sometimes hard for the BBC to realise that the academic
who was working flat out to prepare a correspondence text could not spare

*See p. 49 for the full text of this statement.

the time to work out the precise details of a broadcast related to that text until the text itself had taken on a reasonably final form. It was equally difficult for some of our staff to accept that the nice things they would like to show on television would be vastly too expensive and time-consuming to create on videotape. Finally, it was sometimes difficult for the BBC production staff to realise that an attractive visual presentation of a particular technique would actually carry very little pedagogic weight when shown to students. The two partners had to get to know each other's foibles and prejudices much more intimately than they did at the outset before the partnership could be said to work happily. These early contacts culminated in the production of pilot programmes, two for each faculty, that were made only to be discarded, but the exercise greatly helped both sides to understand the techniques, systems and attitudes of the other before course production actually began.

From the very beginning the Planning Committee was anxious to ensure that responsibility for the nature, the content and the teaching of each course offered by the University should be vested in the University as a whole. It should not be left to the whim of the individual department or the individual member of staff. Thus in our recruitment policy we made it clear that each professor, while he would be head of his discipline, would not be head of a discrete department with its own budget. I had long believed that departmental control of teaching is a root cause of much that is wrong with educational programmes in conventional universities. It permits individual academics to produce courses designed primarily for the scholars of the future and militates against the provision of courses more suited (relevant!) to those whose careers will lie outside the pursuit of the discipline concerned.

At the same time I firmly believe that departments are necessary units in a university. The department is the spiritual home of the members of a discipline; the head of department is the focal point for research in that discipline and must be the leader of the research team, controlling recruitment of team members and finding and allocating funds and other resources for the research. But the department, efficient though it is as a base for university research, is not a good base for university teaching. We might well have had departments as administrative units in order to fulfil the functions of research and administration, but we were aware that with only four members of each discipline these units would be so small as not to be viable. Thus we made the smallest administrative unit the faculty, in the hope that both the administration, and indeed the research, would be inter-disciplinary in nature. However, staffing of the disciplines is still the responsibility of the appropriate head of subject and this frequently determines the nature of the on-going research.

Since responsibility for teaching preferences was not to be vested in academic departments, a new form of control had to be found. This led to the concept of the Course Team. Essentially each Team was to consist of three groups of staff: academics, educational technologists and BBC production staff. Once set up the Team would have delegated to it authority for the content, nature and method of presentation of the course, together with full responsibility for its standard and for creating it at the proper time and the proper price. We hoped that a Course Team of this kind would provide an excellent vehicle for the creation of the sort of course we had in mind. It would bring together academics from a number of disciplines, a vital factor in the creation of a multi-disciplinary course, and would provide the expert knowledge that was needed to make the course suitable for adults working in isolation through correspondence texts and radio and television broadcasts. It offered a real hope of creating a course that would be a balanced, logical and integrated whole.

Each Course Team is, essentially, a sub-committee of the Senate. This is very proper, for the primary duties of the team are to ensure that the course is of proper quality and that credit in the course reflects a proper standard of achievement. The Vice-Chancellor, as Chairman of Senate, is ultimately responsible for ensuring that the course teams carry out these primary duties. In practice this responsibility is delegated to the Dean of the Faculty concerned who, in turn, delegates it to the Chairman of the Course Team.

On the other hand the Vice-Chancellor, as chief academic and administrative officer of the university, has, to quote the Charter, 'a general responsibility to the Council and the Senate for maintaining and promoting the efficiency and good order of the university'. In exercising this responsibility he must ensure not only that course materials are of the necessary quality and standard (in which he is clearly acting for the Senate) but also that they are produced in time for their transmission to students, and that their cost falls within the budgetary limits laid down. In these latter capacities he must act with the authority not only of the Senate but also of the Council, as the employer of both the academic staff and the administrative and operational staff who are involved in the later stages of course production and course transmission. Thus the course team must not only create a course of quality and standard, they must create it at a time and a price consistent with the efficient functioning of the University as a whole. Consequently the authority of the Council, as well as that of the Senate, is delegated by the Vice-Chancellor to the Dean of the appropriate Faculty and, through him, to the Course Team Chairman in respect of these latter duties.

Obviously the two sets of responsibilities may clash. Such a clash, when it occurs, does so in the persons of the Course Team Chairman, the Dean of Faculty and the Vice-Chancellor, each of whom has a dual responsibility and each of whom must, on occasion, exercise a balance of judgement. Quite clearly it would be fatuous for them to insist on the distribution of material to meet appropriate deadlines if its quality and standard were below that which would be acceptable to the Senate. Equally clearly, it would be fatuous for them to allow a Course Team to prolong the recasting and polishing of the creative work that goes into making a course unit to such an extent that deadlines were missed and the material, however good, failed to reach the students in time.

In 1969 there was very little difficulty in appointing the course teams for the first four foundation courses. All academic staff in post in September 1969 in any individual faculty were *ex officio* members of the foundation course team of that particular faculty and the Dean of the Faculty was course team chairman. In addition, we arranged for cross-faculty representation, thus providing a means whereby one faculty could influence another, so that the four foundation courses would not be too divergent in style or structure.

From our nucleus of trained educational technologists we seconded at least one to each of the four course teams. In addition, the BBC production staff, chosen by the BBC itself to be responsible for the broadcast element of each of the foundation courses, sat as full members of the appropriate course team.

In 1969 the foundation course teams numbered 9 to 16, but they were to get bigger. Additional academic staff, recruited a year later to help in the preparation of second level courses, were often made full members of foundation course teams so that the final size was two or three times the original size. The structure of the foundation course teams did not, however, become the pattern for the future. The very fact that each faculty was preparing only one course and that the chairman of that course team and the Dean of the faculty were one and the same person meant that there was no divergence between the roles of the faculty and of the course team. These two bodies were virtually identical, and this led to a deferral within the University of any clear definition of their respective responsibilities or those of the Dean and the course team chairman. When the need for such definition became urgent it was therefore based upon experience in practice rather than on any preconceived notion of how precisely the administrative structure should work.

I have never actually been a member of a course team. Thus, although I have from time to time attended meetings of individual teams, others are very much better able to describe their detailed mode of operation than I am. John Ferguson in his recent book *The Open University from Within*[16] has given his own impressions of the working of the foundation course team in the Faculty of Arts. In the earlier book, *The Open University Opens*[13] edited by Jeremy Tunstall, a number of other members of the academic staff give graphic accounts of their experience in their course teams.

Looking at the operation of the foundation course teams from the outside I soon became aware that considerable differences in practice were developing in the various faculties. In a subject like literature, the raw materials of teaching are the written works of the authors of the past, and the teacher is essentially writing a structured commentary on them. Such a commentary will clearly be a personal view, and a team will never produce a commentary that is as provocative and interesting as that written by a single individual. It thus became the practice in the Faculties of Arts and Social Sciences for the major part of the course materials to be written by individual members of staff, to appear under their own names, and also to be identified as their own work. Other members of the course team might comment on and criticise the initial drafts of the main author, but it remained his responsibility as to how far he accepted their suggestions, provided always that his final draft was acceptable to his colleagues. In the Faculties of Science and Mathematics, the whole concept was different. Although the first draft of any one unit would be prepared by one person, it was never regarded as his own individual work, and the ultimate draft was the result of the work of all the members of the group concerned. Consequently, drafts did not appear under the name of an author, but as the work of the course team itself. Furthermore, they tended to be themselves the raw material of the course and the number of texts to which they referred was very small. Indeed in the foundation course in mathematics there was no set text-book at all and the correspondence texts themselves formed the entire written substance of the course.

These differences were to have unexpected and profound effects on the development of the university. It is much quicker to proceed by the method whereby one individual is primarily responsible for a course unit, and where his colleagues have the job only of criticising and commenting on it, than it is for a whole committee to arrive at an agreed draft of each unit in a course. The productivity rates in the faculties of Arts and Social Sciences therefore soon became much higher than those in the faculties of Science and Mathematics. This inevitably affected the levels of staffing required.

Each course team found that academic quality always took priority in the initial stages of making a course. Consequently deadlines were frequently missed and this imposed a heavy burden on the production and distribution divisions of the University, which were faced with catching up on the time lost by the academic side. On the whole this burden was willingly accepted by the non-academic staff who became aware of the extreme difficulties under which the academics worked. In all cases, however, the course teams had to work to a schedule which was usually determined by the Dean of Faculty concerned. No attempt was made to ensure that all faculties followed precisely the same pattern, and practices varied widely.

The first task of the course team was to determine the syllabus of the course. The general experience was that this was the most difficult stage of all. It invariably took a very long time, and sometimes involved bitter and acrimonious argument. The process by which each member of the team had to achieve an understanding of the ways in which the minds of his colleagues worked, before the group could get going, provided a fascinating illustration of group dynamics. Thereafter, I am told, things became much easier. The syllabus was divided into manageable portions, sometimes initially into blocks of work, and ultimately into individual units, each of which represented one week's work for a student. Sometimes a team would delegate responsibility for a block to a sub-group, and ultimately the writing of the first draft of each unit became the responsibility of one member of the team.

We had agreed to allocate an equal amount of television and radio transmission time to each of the foundation courses. We were aware that the pedagogic need for broadcasting might be different in each case and that, ultimately, the rations of broadcasting time for courses should vary according to that need. In the first year of operation of the University, these courses would also be its main shop window, allowing the academic and political worlds to see what precisely we were trying to do. Since we had no experience of trying to estimate the pedagogic need for broadcasting it therefore seemed sensible to allow each foundation course team to work out its own way of making the best use of the same amount of time on television and radio.

Each unit of a course consisted essentially of a correspondence book, a television programme and a radio programme. The texts for all three had to be prepared in parallel so that the integrated relationship between the media would be preserved. They also had to go through a number of drafts so that the criticism and comments of members of the course team could be taken into account. The course team chairman remained in overall control and had to read all these drafts himself to make sure they were up to the standard that he was setting for himself, as guided by his own course team. In some instances drafts might be prepared by external consultants, asked to undertake a broadcast or the preparation of a bit of correspondence text. Such consultants would be supernumerary members of the course team in respect of the units or blocks with which they were concerned. The creation of an integrated multimedia course in which the broadcasts reflected the correspondence text and could be understood in association with that text, raised all sorts of problems with scheduling. The number of days available in the BBC studios for the production of the courses did not allow much margin of safety. For example, the television studio schedule might require that a course team produce the videotape for unit 17 on a particular day. It followed that the correspondence text for unit 17 had to be prepared in parallel. If it were delayed and the studio date were consequently missed, not only did we incur the expense of running the studio with no output, but it became increasingly difficult to provide another free day in the studio.

We were anxious that the course units, once written, should be subjected to some form of pilot testing. Various methods were used for this, but essentially it meant that the text must be ready many months in advance of teaching actual students, so that it could be tried out on 'guinea-pig' students and their comments taken into account in preparing the final version. In addition to this, we had agreed to submit the final drafts of all texts to external assessors, who were academics on the staff of other universities. All these precautions to ensure the standard of our teaching materials were regarded as essential, but imposed severe time constraints on the staff of the University. The finished correspondence texts had to be passed over to the production side of the University for printing 18 weeks before the mailing date to the students. A lecture, to be delivered in a classroom, can frequently be prepared 24 hours beforehand. The comparable cycle in the Open University is a matter of many months at the very least. Yet it is extremely hard to finalise a course unit in July when you know that it will not actually reach your students until January, six months later. The temptation to bring the material up-to-date during that long gap is very strong, and resisting it is difficult. There is, of course, an opportunity to make corrections in galley proof or in page proof, but this is expensive and must be resisted if the cost of printing and production is not to become overwhelmingly high, and even page proofs must be returned to the printer many weeks before the mailing date.

One result of all this was an increasing demand from academics for extra material that could be prepared much nearer the actual time of teaching. These came to be known as 'supplementary materials'. They could be printed by reprographic methods quite quickly, and despatched to the student along with the course materials. This device is used for many other purposes such as the provision of broadcast notes, instructions for using home-experiment kits, and assessment questions (which are changed annually). It is, however, an extra expense and adds considerably to the volume of material sent to the student.

As the foundation course teams got going we began to find out just how much effort was needed to create these courses, and just how wrong our estimates of 'productivity' had been. We were already falling behind our timetables and getting worried about whether the courses would be ready for our first students in 1971. We needed extra manpower and thus everyone available was soon involved with these critical first four courses. The planning of the second level courses needed in 1972 had to be put off. This decision was forced upon us for we simply could not afford to fall down on the job in our very first year of public appearance. Yet the consequent delays in planning second level courses imposed even greater constraints on our subsequent production schedules; and this was of particular concern to our producers at the BBC.

In the first year of production the BBC produced some 130 programmes for the four Foundation Courses but by the second year this number had more than doubled. The recording schedules became very tight with little room to manoeuvre and as Course Teams came under increasing pressure, broadcast and print production tended to get out of phase on some courses. Furthermore, in order to give Course Teams and the BBC sufficient time to view completed programmes, write the associated broadcast supplementary notes and put the programmes into the BBC's transmission system a deadline of 16 weeks was fixed between recording and transmission. The result of this was that some programmes were recorded too early and last minute changes and reappraisals of the print component sometimes conspired against the most effective integration of the broadcast component.

These were very serious matters which might adversely affect the quality of our later courses and we spent many many hours trying to devise ways, some facile some ingenious, of overcoming the difficulties. One vital need was to increase the number of full-time academic staff; external consultants, although valuable and necessary in many situations, worked more slowly and produced material which, despite its high intrinsic quality, still required amendment by the full-time staff to make it fit in with the rest of the course and to make it suitable for teaching adults at a distance. Thus any spare resources that could be found were devoted to this increase in our full-time academic staff.

By 1975, things had changed very considerably. In the first place, the number of academics who could be spared to sit on individual course teams got smaller and in the second place, as the courses became more specialised the number of academics who had anything to offer to the construction of a given course became smaller. As a result, the size of course teams itself became smaller and this has both advantages and disadvantages. With a large course team it inevitably takes longer to agree on the syllabus, and indeed on the individual units themselves; with a small course team one tends to reach a situation where the work becomes more like that of an individual member of the academic staff than that of a team. This means that the standard and quality of the course becomes more dependent on the standard and quality of individual members of staff themselves, which is inevitably bound to vary.

I had hoped that as time went on the academic staff of the University would become more expert in the techniques of educational technology so that the members of the Institute of Educational Technology would be less essential to the course teams. This has not turned out to be quite so true as I had anticipated. In the first place the forty-odd members of staff who started in 1969 are now only one-seventh of the total staff of 280 academics, many of whom have joined the University relatively recently and have had little opportunity of acquiring the necessary skills. In the second place, although it is true that many members of the academic staff have become extremely expert in the principles and practice of educational technology, others find these difficult to grasp and to apply; they require the continuous stimulation of educational technologists to keep them in the forefront of their minds. Yet the staff of the Institute of Educational Technology has not increased in parallel with the academic staff, and the burden on the educational technologists sitting as members of course teams has got steadily heavier, so that sometimes the contribution made to a particular course team by the educational technologist concerned is very small indeed. This is a very different situation from that applying to the BBC, whose production staff has expanded in parallel with our own academic staff and whose producers have always been full members of every course team.

It also followed that the number of members of staff acting as course team chairmen increased very greatly. No longer was it true that the Dean was the course team chairman and doubled in two administrative roles. As more and more junior members of staff became course team chairmen, so the difficulty of maintaining the balance of control became more acute. Course team chairmen tended to be chosen because they were expert in the subject matter of the course concerned. This unfortunately did not mean that they were necessarily skilled administrators. I have gradually become convinced that course team chairmen should be appointed for their managerial skill, not because they are expert in the subject matter of the course. Yet it is easy to see that this could create a tricky situation. If a course is clearly the academic product of one or two key members of staff, it is hard to insist that another member of staff should be given the responsibility for controlling the content of the course. I have little doubt that there will be fierce arguments over this question in the years to come.

A course team's job was not over when the course was written. Every year new assignments had to be written and new examination papers prepared. Furthermore, we were not infallible; we made some bad programmes, we wrote some bad texts and we had to correct these errors as soon as possible. There was thus an ongoing problem of maintaining existing courses, which was tackled by what came to be called 'caretaker course teams', small groups of people whose prime responsibility was to keep the course up to scratch throughout its life. We had originally fixed the life of each course at four years, because we were determined to ensure that outdated courses should not be used simply because of a shortage of funds to remake them. I had therefore insisted that the University should not be empowered to extend the life of a course without the agreement of the course team which had made it. This provision, while it can make things very difficult for the University, has the merit of giving those who create a course the authority necessary to ensure that its standard is maintained.

Although I had originally envisaged that courses would be written much faster and that they would be much shorter than they turned out to be, I had always allowed for an 18 month period of gestation. Thus courses for one year would be in preparation at the same time as courses for the following year. In fact it now takes much longer than 18 months for a course to be thought of, designed, written and produced. Furthermore, with correction and maintenance as ongoing tasks we are not completely free of a course once it has been written. Thus an individual member of staff may be directly concerned at one and the same time in several different courses, all at different stages of preparation and maintenance. This imposes further strains on the staff, who can never concentrate on just one new course.

It is in the individual course team that one finds the drive for innovation that is an essential part of maintaining the Open University in good health. There has been no shortage of new ideas, many of them extremely good ones, about how to create better courses. Even amongst the foundation course teams innovative ideas emerged. For the foundation course in the Humanities, for example, the course team produced gramophone records which were distributed to all students in order to cover some aspects of their musical education. The course team for the Mathematics foundation course, determined that all students must learn the basic techniques of computer programming, arranged for the setting up of the Student Computing Service, which enabled students to have access to computer terminals in study centres, the terminals being linked to one of the computers that we installed in each of three different regions. Great inventiveness was shown by the Faculties of Science and Technology in devising home experiment kits to enable students to acquire necessary practical experience. Course teams frequently arranged for the production of readers, consisting of reprinted extracts from the literature, to provide students with source materials which they would find impossible to obtain from their local libraries. For the foundation course in Technology, all students were supplied with tape recorders which enabled us to distribute pre-recorded tapes. These were just a few of the many ideas put forward from time to time by individual course teams.

We now have very tight financial constraints on every course team, but when the foundation courses were being written there were very few since we had no idea of what the whole process would involve or what the overall cost would be. Furthermore, we had not then developed a workable cost control mechanism. Nowadays course teams put up an overall plan for their course requesting financial support, and within the limits of their overall budget, their new ideas will be implemented if they are practicable. But practicability is not just a question of money. The ideas must be workable in the distance teaching situation and must be compatible with the regional structure of the University.

What, then, have we learned from our experience of the course team method? There seems to me no doubt that a course produced by this method will inevitably tend to be superior in quality to any course produced by an individual. The concept of the course team is, I believe, the most important single contribution of the Open University to teaching practice at the tertiary level. It is, however, true that it is a very expensive way of writing courses, that can be justified only if the course materials are used for a very large number of students. It is not, therefore, a method that can easily be adapted to the needs of conventional institutions and, perhaps, they do not need it. If they make mistakes in the initial presentation of their courses they can, in the face-to-face situation, correct these mistakes and put them right. Yet I believe that there ought to be a modified form of course team control of courses in all institutions. I think it would be advantageous for a course team to be made responsible for the syllabus of every course, even if the detailed presentation of the material within that syllabus were left to the usual methods of classroom teaching and individual departmental control.

If other institutions were to adopt courses already prepared elsewhere by the course team method they would be saved all the expense of initiating their own courses. On the other hand it is difficult for academics to accept that anybody else can teach their subject better than they can. Our teaching materials are however already being used by many other institutions in this way. The potential danger that if this practice were to be adopted too widely, the dull hand of uniformity might adversely affect our university teaching can be easily exaggerated, for the commentaries of staff using the same basic course materials would still be personal and idiosyncratic. The method of course construction typified by the course team approach can be applied to courses of any kind and is by no means appropriate only to university level. It could be used for school teaching, in colleges, or in adult education. Indeed, we are frequently approached to give advice on these matters by countries in the third world whose educational needs are far removed from the provision of traditional types of university education on the British pattern.

I believe that the validity of the course team approach has been proven by the quality of the materials that the Open University has produced to date, which are second to none anywhere in the world. This is not said in any mood of complacency, for I believe we still have a great deal to learn. We are not very good at arranging that the feedback obtained from our students is adequately used in improving the quality of our teaching materials for following years. We are not yet good enough at incorporating new ideas into the pattern of the courses themselves. Sometimes we fall down very hard because a course team doesn't 'gel' and fails to produce the materials on time. There is no sanction that can be applied to creativity. You cannot make academics write good courses, you can only provide encouragement and facilities and an ambience in which they can indulge their creative impulses.

The fact that the academics creating our courses are full-time members of the staff of the institution seems to me to be all-important. This factor of primary loyalty has often, I think, been overlooked. Many institutions across the world have tried to prepare multimedia courses by contracting very skilled, very distinguished academics on the staff of other universities to make the necessary programmes. On the whole, these have been failures and the primary reason for this, I believe, is that the academics so contracted give their primary loyalty to the institution that employs them full-time. They take on the task of making a multimedia course for another institution as an additional chore. They may do it well, but they are not primarily concerned with the welfare of the students to whom these programmes are directed. They are much more concerned with the students in their own institution. Consequently, the editing, re-writing, polishing, changing and adoption of the educational technologists' ideas are not so readily undertaken in a situation of this sort. I am quite sure that we were right to employ as our main course creators full-time academics of the Open University, and to eschew the original idea of the Advisory Committee, and indeed of the Planning Committee, of using mainly consultants or people on secondment from other universities. Our success in creating courses, in other words, seems to stem from the fact that those who joined the Open University staff put their whole careers at risk. Their success was contingent on the success of the Open University. This is never true of someone on secondment.

Before closing this account of course creation it would seem appropriate here to touch on the vexed question of academic freedom. In a conventional university this includes *inter alia* freedom to teach. That freedom is not unqualified. Any university teacher is told the titles of the courses that he is asked to undertake. He may request permission to offer a course on a different topic and that request may or may not be granted by the department or, indeed, by the Senate of the university. But once he is given the task of teaching a particular course he is not constrained at all in how he presents it, in what opinions he inculcates in the minds of his student audience, or in his choice of illustrative material. In this respect conventional academic freedom would not, and could not, be available to members of staff at the Open University. This was made clear to all those who joined the staff of the University during their initial interviews; the need to put the control of teaching in the hands of teams rather than of individual departments or of individual members of the academic staff was made abundantly plain. The loss of academic freedom is greater the larger the size of the team responsible for a particular course, and this is especially true when a course is inter-disciplinary, for larger teams are absolutely vital when creating multi-disciplinary courses.

Members of staff take to this new situation in different ways. Some find it relatively straightforward, others extremely difficult. There have been some bonny fights in course teams before opposing views of the method by which any particular topic should be treated have been reconciled. It is of course healthy that there should be such differences of opinion. The outcome of the argument and the final compromise may take away something of the sharpness of one particular view but, on the other hand, what is left is likely to represent an agreed synthesis of what is most important in the topic concerned. In some cases where the differences of view are so important that students should be made aware of them, it is perfectly proper for the course team to present both points of view in the text so that the students can see that there is no consensus amongst their teachers, or indeed in the world at large, and can make up their own minds on the question. Nevertheless it is unarguable that team responsibility implies a loss of freedom of action on the part of the individual teacher in determining what is presented to the students.

A second limitation on individual academic freedom stems from the fact that the courses are not lectures presented in private behind the closed doors of a lecture theatre to a relatively small group of students. They take the form of course materials that are open to view by the world at large, presented in open-circuit broadcasts, and in texts which are on sale in bookshops. It follows, therefore, that what is taught to the students is open not only to their criticism, but also to that of students in other institutions, of professional broadcasting critics, of politicians and of the general public. This very openness results in the academic staff responsible for designing the courses taking greater pains over what is offered than they would if they were presenting such materials behind the closed doors of the classroom. Statements will tend to be hedged in with reservations and qualifications, rather than made boldly and vested in the authority of the pedagogue. Furthermore, the teacher must recognise that most of the cost of the exercise is being paid for out of public funds and must wonder just how those responsible for the disbursement of public funds will react to what it is that he is telling his students.

If there is a loss of academic freedom for the individual there is an even bigger one for the institution. The students of the Open University pay fees but these represent only about 15 per cent of the actual cost of the teaching. The rest is paid by central government in the form of a block grant to the University amounting in 1976 to over £20 million. The situation is the same for all universities in the United Kingdom, but there is a convention that, although the government pays for most of the cost of university education, governments do not interfere with the freedom of the universities to teach. This restraint on the part of governments has been meticulously honoured over the years, but the power to interfere, to intervene in what universities teach, always remains with the government. The fact that it is not used is solely a convention, and there are no rules about the matter. The new feature of the Open University is that it commands considerable time on the mass media. The effect of its teaching can potentially spread very widely and have a powerful impact. The student audience is enormous by comparison with that for any individual lecture in a conventional university, and there is always the possibility of an overspill audience of almost unlimited size.

There are therefore two sources of political power potentially available to the Open University. In the first place total academic freedom on the part of all its staff could lead to use being made of the teaching programmes to indulge in polemic, enabling an individual member of staff to preach disaffection or even sedition to a very large audience. In the second place, when institutional control is imposed on the content of courses, the institution could use this power of control for propaganda purposes. It is therefore essential, in my view, to the survival of an institution of the nature of the Open University to recognise that its freedom to teach precisely what it wishes cannot be total. It must be extremely careful, in its choice of courses, to avoid the charge from any political party that its freedom to use the mass media is being misapplied. In consequence, it must retain some sanction over the individual teacher, and this is another root cause of loss of individual academic freedom.

In the traditional universities the main objectives were to teach, to research and to nurture scholarship. To these modern society has added two more: first, to provide services to government, industry and society through, for instance, work on advisory committees; and second, to promote the educational wellbeing of the community, largely through the extramural departments of adult education. Yet the highly selective system of university entry in the United Kingdom, which leads to a low drop-out rate amongst student entrants and a high quality of degree, also means that higher education is offered only to a relatively small fraction of the population. It was the elitism and the preservation of the meritocracy, implicit in the traditional university system, that led Harold Wilson to propose the creation of an Open University which would provide an opportunity for anyone, and which would harness technology to the service of education. These aims for the new Open University appeared to be unexceptionable, yet are they? There has been in recent years an explosion in communications, and travel has become available to many people. Post and telegraph, telephone and radio have brought instant availability of news from across the world to everyone. The development of the mass media have given such news an immediacy and an impact that they never had before. In consequence the public at large has become aware of and concerned about problems on a global scale, and increasingly demands a right to participate in finding solutions to them. A great increase in the education of the adult population adds to all this an understanding of the problems, and understanding brings in its train intensification of all the other effects. The introduction of mass education thus makes a return to elitism and to meritocracy more unlikely, and there are therefore quite clear political implications in the creation of the Open University, whether these are regarded as desirable or not.

It would have been perfectly possible for the Open University to have been given, quite overtly, a further political objective, namely that of offering courses which were themselves designed to change society. This was prevented in a sense by the very conventions that are set up to safeguard the academic freedom of all universities. But a new innovatory institution with access to the mass media undoubtedly attracts staff who are left of centre. Nearly all universities tend to attract such staff, for radicals seem to flourish in the academic community. Undoubtedly this tendency was, for a variety of reasons, intensified in the creation of the Open University, some of whose staff have an avowed personal objective of changing society. When such people are employed by conventional universities to teach behind the doors of the classroom, polemic on their part is acceptable. It is then an understood part of the life of a university, but when polemic can be transmitted through the mass media it is much less acceptable. The Open University has faced this intrinsic dilemma from the beginning, but it becomes more intense as the courses become more specialised and deal more directly with the global problems that face society today.

Should an institution like a university have the objective of changing society? Should it take a public stance on the issues of vital importance to mankind? Certainly individual academics must and should take such stances. Universities raise no barriers in their recruitment policy on the grounds of race, colour or creed and this is implicit in the charter of every one of them. We would therefore expect a community of scholars in a university to exhibit all shades of opinion on global issues. In my view this is the essence of a university community. On the other hand, I believe that it would be contrary to the spirit of a university that the institution itself should adopt a stance or policy simply because it is favoured by a majority of its staff at any one time. The institution should stay clear of such involvement, accepting that all members of its staff have their own individual views and that the melange of all these views will have its own impact on society without the institution itself proselytising for a majority view.

We have, over the first six years of our life as a teaching institution using the mass media, avoided any major confrontation outside the university in relation to the choice of materials that we teach and the way that we teach them. This is not to say that there has not been criticism. It comes to me in a variety of forms – such as letters from members of Parliament or hurt reactions on the part of a company or a public association – but to date we have managed to give reasonable answers to these representations and there has been no major row. At any moment such a confrontation could blow up into a cause célèbre, but on the other hand we may well continue to muddle through in true British fashion.

There remains a much more difficult question. The methods used by the Open University to design its teaching system are now under close examination by a number of countries interested in adopting them for use in their own societies. This interest stems from the growing knowledge across the world of the high quality of Open University materials and of the relative cheapness of this way of providing an education. More sinister is the realisation in certain countries that our methods keep students off campus, and campus populations have become a major political threat in a number of countries. A further attraction of the Open University system, especially in the third world, is that it enables the maximum use to be made of a very small number of skilled teachers, who are often scarce in such countries. If such a system is introduced in countries with a less liberal form of government than ours then the dangers that I have been describing are intensified. There is a very real possibility that a despotic government could use it as a vehicle for propaganda. On the other hand there is also the danger that an Open University system which got into the hands of dissidents could be used as a vehicle for revolution. There are no guaranteed ways of avoiding these dangers, but it is as well to be constantly aware of them.

6

COURSE PRODUCTION

The choice of the courses that we would offer and of the ways in which they would be created were matters that raised philosophical problems and could be settled only by making a series of decisions about the aims and objectives of the university. The second phase of our overall academic plan, which involved the whole process of converting the courses that had been written into materials that were ready for transmission to students was, by comparison, a mundane one. The problems presented were, in the main, neither academic nor philosophical, but administrative, logistic and financial; but that did not make them any easier to solve. They are problems that, in the world of higher education, are unique to the Open University.

Most of the difficulty in course production stemmed from the nature of our publishing methods. I hasten to add that neither I, nor any of my colleagues, had any advance insight into the problems that were to arise; nor did we deliberately plan our particular method of publishing. Rather did we tackle the problems as they happened to arise, and my analysis of the situation is wholly retrospective.

There have been, especially in the United States, many attempts at producing 'packaged courses' of instruction of varying degrees of sophistication. Nearly all such packages of course materials, whether they consist only of text or of a combination of audiovisual materials and text, have been produced by established publishing houses. The general pattern has been that the commercial publisher has contracted academics and audiovisual producers to create the contents of the package; has arranged for illustrations, copyright clearances, layout, format, and copy-editing to be carried out within his own establishment; has commissioned the printing; and has controlled the sales and distribution. Thus the production of the 'package' has followed the same pattern as is normal for a book where, although the author is the creative artist, control of the finished material rests primarily with the editor, who is appointed by the publisher himself.

The original descriptions of the Open University in the Reports of the Advisory Committee and the Planning Committee envisaged only a small nucleus of full-time senior academic staff. Had this pattern been followed they would have inevitably become *de facto* editors. In respect of course creation and course production, the university would have been little different from a conventional publishing house and most of the problems that we have encountered would never have arisen. In fact we developed into something quite different. The academic staff is much larger than was then envisaged and, consequently, we have a new situation where the authors are to a considerable extent in control of the finished article. Yet the university must, at the same time, function as a large-scale publisher. How were we to handle this unprecedented arrangement? The short answer is that we did not know and that we have had muddle and mess as a result.

An editor in a commercial publishing house is primarily concerned to ensure that the product is such as will satisfy the market at a viable price and his influence over the author is directed towards these goals. Our market is our students and it is perfectly proper that their satisfaction should be the direct responsibility of their teachers. On the other hand the purchaser is, effectively, the government and, quite clearly, control of costs cannot be left wholly in the hands of the authors.

Price control depends upon a host of factors in addition to the length of the basic academic content of the course materials. Amongst the most important are: the number and nature of the illustrations, the degree to which colour printing is used, the 'layout' – size of margins and typeface – the quality of paper and the cost of 'permissions' to reproduce copyright material. Furthermore the unit cost could be greatly influenced by the number of corrections made in galley and page proof and by the length of the print run.

As a publisher the university required not only to determine the methods to be used to control such variables but also to employ the staff to take all the decisions needed daily to implement them. For this purpose we set up a Publishing Division to handle copyright, house style and copy editing, and a Media Production Division to process all illustrations, graphic and photographic, and to be responsible for layouts and briefing the printers, including our own internal print-shop. These divisions were not created in their present form, but evolved gradually and with numerous changes in organisation and structure.

How far would the staff of these divisions control course production and its cost? At first sight it might appear that most of the factors affecting price control lie outside the proper interest of the academics as authors, but this is far from true. The layout, the use of colour printing and the illustrations are all factors that can significantly affect the efficiency of the teaching/learning process for the isolated student. The same teaching materials cyclostyled in single-spacing on both sides of foolscap sheets would lose much of their value. If the interest of the student is not held by a stimulating visual presentation his motivation flags. Not a little of the success of the university in achieving a relatively low drop-out rate amongst its students can, I am sure, be attributed to the attractive presentation of our courses. It was thus vital that a balance be struck between the pedagogic quality of our course materials and their cost. Quotation from copyright texts and reproduction of copyright illustrations are also a matter of academic as well as of financial concern, and authors are very properly concerned to ensure that, when they are pedagogically necessary, they are not excluded on purely financial grounds.

All these problems may seem relatively trivial, and capable of easy resolution. It is the scale of our operations that raises them to a level of importance that can provoke acrimonious dispute. Our graphic unit produces about 10,000 illustrations and the copyright office clears about the same number of 'permissions' each year. We print, in all, some 200 new titles annually. It is easy to see that relatively trivial over-expenditure on each unit can, with such multipliers, become a real embarrassment.

Extra costs can also be incurred by delay in the submission of course material from the academic authors because printers may have to work overtime to meet deadlines. Further costs can arise from changes in course materials at the galley and page proof stage. I was staggered in 1970 at the magnitude of the extra charges that arose on this last head. At that time the paramount need to meet deadlines for our first courses and our first students over-rode all questions of cost, but it was clear even then that this could not be allowed to go on. On the other hand sanctions against a course team would harm not the team but only the innocent students.

The length of the print-run would appear to be even less a matter for academic concern, but once again appearances are deceptive. In 1971 copies of each foundation course unit were needed for 7,000 students and 1,500 part-time staff, so that almost the maximum economy of scale in printing costs could be obtained by running off only one year's supply, namely some 10,000 copies. This obviated the need to store copies for use in the later years of the life of the course and at the same time allowed course teams, at minimum cost, to modify, correct and update the material for the second and subsequent printings. These great advantages could not be expected to continue. The number of students studying each second level course would, as I have described, inevitably be smaller. To achieve the economies of scale in printing, it became necessary to print all the copies needed for the whole life of the course in a single run. Course teams had to accept, often with great reluctance, that it would not be possible to modify the texts in later years save in exceptional circumstances where errors were so gross that the copies already printed must be scrapped. Less vital corrections could be made only by issuing errata sheets. The economics of printing also imposed severe warehousing problems that made a nonsense of the small amount of storage space I had provided in the original buildings. By 1975 we had in stock printed materials valued at about £1 million, and our total warehouse space had grown to some 10,000 square metres.

Thus the establishment of specialised units to cope with all the publishing functions did not in any sense solve the basic problem of controlling the balance between pedagogic value and the commercial cost of the course materials. Rather did it aggravate some of the tensions. The academic staff had a legitimate interest in nearly all the factors that affect costs, and naturally wished for a voice in the control procedures. The specialist staff inevitably brought with them their own preconceived notions of where the balance of control should lie. The most striking example was to be found amongst the editors who were recruited to the

Publishing Division. They were drawn largely from commercial publishing houses, people able and accustomed to contribute more to the complex process of transforming manuscript into print than the mundane performance of copy-editing and proof-reading. Some course teams gladly accepted the assistance of a professional editor. Others resented it, making the editors feel that their skills were unappreciated, their assistance superfluous, and their jobs unrewarding.

Clearly the nature of our academic appointments precluded any possibility of editors being given the ultimate control of the form of our teaching materials. We have compromised by seconding editors to work on a day-to-day basis in the faculties. Each editor is attached to a course team, in which he can be accepted as an academic colleague, and where he can accordingly bring his wider talents to bear, by influence if not by direct control. We have not yet produced a tidy solution. We have got steadily better at controlling costs but not by appointing any one individual as the 'controller'. Academic staff have become more aware of the problems and have tried to come to terms with them. Nevertheless the basic problem is still unsolved and much thought and effort is still being devoted to it.

BBC producers were made members of the appropriate course teams, and played a full part in determining the syllabus of the course and the choice of topics that required audio or video signals for their efficient presentation to the student. When it came to the phase of converting the scripts written by the course teams into recordings for subsequent transmission the control of cost once again became a vital factor. All broadcast production was controlled and financed by the BBC, and the Open University simply paid a block sum for the services rendered. In the studio there was never any question but that the producer was in control, and his primacy also extended to 'outside broadcast' activities. He had a definitive programme allowance and was charged by the BBC with completing the programme within it.

Academic control of the finished programme remained with the University but it could in practice be exercised only before and after the production and not during it. Before the event the course team made the decisions and the producer was only a member of the team. He would naturally be influential in determining the nature of the broadcast but he could not dictate. Furthermore the course team decided on the participants wherever practicable. This was cheaper, quicker and generally more effective than any other method. It did not preclude the use of external academics or, indeed, of anyone else. Yet the general policy was to eschew the professional presenter and the professional actor in favour of the academic himself. What may be lost in slickness is gained in realism, and I am sure that, for pedagogic purposes, the pedagogue is the best performer. After the event the finished recording was submitted to the course team and their approval was necessary for its acceptance. The University could thus reject the work of the producer, but only at a substantial cost, for a remake was expensive and the bill fell to be paid by the University.

In practice the partnership worked very much more smoothly than either partner had anticipated. I believe that this was a direct outcome of the course team approach.

When the Open University was established there was considerable concern in the Publishers' Association and the Booksellers' Association about the ways in which we would affect their markets. There was an understandable fear that if we were to become large scale publishers, we would be competing unfairly in the marketplace, using government funds instead of having to raise risk capital. There was also a strong feeling that we could unfairly cut out the retailer by supplying books directly to students. It was clear that we would depend very heavily upon the goodwill of the trade for our future success and we made strenuous efforts to consult with both Associations at all stages. Much of their initial concern turned out to be misdirected. In the event they were not at all worried by our publishing and distributing our own course materials. I suspect that this was because, like many others, they envisaged a set of cyclostyled lecture notes rather than the attractive course books that we were ultimately to produce. They were in fact primarily interested in our set textbooks, which we had no strong ambition either to publish or to distribute. Consequently our relationship with both Associations has become a harmonious one.

Our main dealings with commercial publishers have related to the price and availability of set books. Most courses prescribe as set books conventional texts that the student is expected to buy. Since one of our first priorities was to keep the costs that fell on students as low as possible, we set an upper limit to the total cost of the set books for any course. Negotiations with publishers to obtain reductions in price, often by the production of a paperback edition, were vital, and could make the difference between a particular textbook being used or not. Set books are prescribed for the whole life of a course, and the University thus insists on a guarantee from the publisher that the book will be available throughout this period. This enables the publisher to fix a price based on the longer print run needed for all the students over a period of at least four years, and this often makes possible a substantial reduction on the previous list price. One American textbook was chosen only after the publisher had agreed to produce a paperback edition at £1.25, when the original hardback had been priced at over £7.00: as a result the book was, within a few years, adopted as the prescribed text for students in more than a dozen other British universities. Interest among the general public is often aroused by the fact that a book is chosen as a set text, and publishers have found that it pays them to mark all reprints of such books with the Open University colophon, stating that it has been adopted as a set book, because of the resulting increase in general sales. Indeed, in some cases students have found that the whole stock of set books has been sold by the time they have been informed of their courses, necessitating a further printing or the import of copies from abroad. Our interest has also enabled publishers to keep in print books of which the low sales would not otherwise have justified a reprint, and in certain cases we have been able to arrange for special reprints of important books.

In a series of negotiations with the Booksellers' Associations we agreed not to embark on a policy of direct supply of set text to students, but to sell only through booksellers. In return the Association undertook to provide an adequate service to our students, and a scheme embodying local and regional stockists was evolved which, despite all the difficulties, is a viable operation. Booksellers and publishers realise the good business involved when 60,000 people are regularly purchasing set books, and their total annual turnover from this source is now of the order of £500,000 and is still rising.

From the beginning we accepted that the carrying out of experiments at home by students would be a vital part of offering correspondence tuition in science and technology, and we were determined, as a university, not to exclude these faculties. On the other hand, had we envisaged just how complex and difficult the whole programme of the supply of home experiment kits would be, we might well have had second thoughts. The first home experiment kit to be dealt with was that for the foundation course in science, and we embarked upon ordering and supplying it very light-heartedly. We made no special arrangements in advance for the storage, purchasing or maintenance of the kits and we learned our lessons the hard way, by bitter experience. The course team decided upon the various experiments that students would be asked to perform and drew up the list of equipment necessary to enable them to do so. This turned out to include a total of 136 components, ranging from test tubes and a rubber ball to an analytical balance and a microscope. Members of the course team and of the purchasing division, set out to obtain the best bargains they could in ordering some 7,000 of each of the 136 components.

When the manufacturers of the various components started to deliver the goods, we found that we had been as foolish as the Sorcerer's Apprentice. Our despatch department became fuller and fuller of cartons and crates. We had arranged for polystyrene packing cases to be supplied to house the individual items of equipment in a safe and compact form, and 21,000 of these polystyrene packs (over 4,000 cubic metres in volume) also arrived on our doorstep just before Christmas 1970. During the Christmas holidays most of the staff of the University, from professors to porters, together with their wives, children and friends, lived in the University busily engaged in packing these cases. There was a communal spirit at work, and an utter determination to get the kits delivered so that we could begin the course on time. I missed all the excitement because of my illness of December 1970. We could not hope to recapture this spirit in later years and we obviously had to take steps to ensure that the muddle did not recur.

Kits were supplied to students on payment of a deposit, which was returnable when they came back in reasonable condition. We had to work out ways in which the individual items of equipment could be checked when they were returned by the first generation of students, to make sure that they were in working order for the second generation. Technicians in the faculties of science and technology designed instruments which could be used for these checks, which are now a routine activity during the turn-round period between the end of one academic year and the beginning of the next. By 1976 the number of different kits that were being sent out to students had risen to 31. Storage, distribution, checking and maintenance of kits is now carried out in our warehouses, and the total value of the kits is well over £1 million. We are very cheese-paring in the number of kits that are ordered for any one particular course, and this forces us to impose a strict quota on the number of students that can be accepted for it. It would be much easier to order more kits than we required so that the burden of maintenance and distribution would be lightened, but the problem of finding the additional capital to tie up in these extra kits would be a major one. We have had no capital grant from government to cover the costs of our stocks either of print or of home experiment kits. They have been bought out of recurrent income.

In purchasing home experiment kits, we were able to use our economy of scale to make quite dramatic savings. When one is ordering many hundreds or even many thousands of an item the unit price is a great deal less than that for a single one. For large instruments this was of vital importance. The MacArthur microscope, which had been on sale for £98, was made available to us in a redesigned plastic casing at under £10.

In later years many items, especially of electronic equipment, were designed and built in our own workshops. The prototypes were then passed to commercial companies who undertook to manufacture in bulk to the specifications supplied. This in turn kept the price of items much lower than it might otherwise have been. The cost, for instance, of a mini-computer was kept as low as £65 in 1974 yet students could learn on this machine all the principles of programming.

I am aware that, in this short chapter, I have picked out only a few of the practical problems that arose in translating the final drafts of course teams into finished course materials; and that I have, even in respect of those few, given only the veriest sketch of the ways in which they were tackled and sometimes solved. Much of the more detailed story is, however, only of domestic interest. That these intractable problems were solved at all in the time available to us was due to a combination of luck, dedication and drive on the part of my staff rather than to any element of good management. Much as I would like to claim credit, I cannot do so. I could not envisage the problems until they arose, and my method of management consisted of hasty improvisation to cope with successive emergencies. The wonder is that we came through at all.

7

COURSE DISTRIBUTION

It is of course artificial to divide up the whole academic system of the Open University into discrete sub-systems of course creation, course production and course distribution, for all of them interact. The nature of the course material determines in part the distribution system, and an established distribution system imposes constraints on the types of course materials that are practicable. Which was to be the chicken and which the egg? There was no time to wait either for the chicken to lay an egg or for an egg to hatch. Both had to be derived concurrently and, as a result, we sometimes ended up trying to hatch an ostrich out of a sparrow's egg. Because of the long life of the courses on the one hand and the complexity and consequent inflexibility of the distribution system on the other, we are still living as best we can with such difficulties. It will, indeed, take years to eliminate them.

In 1969 the Open University was generally regarded as an institution that would teach primarily through television and radio broadcasts, and was not infrequently taken to be a branch of the BBC. The University attracted hostile and sometimes bitter criticisms for wanting to hog, for a minority group, a substantial proportion of the limited available air time which could, on a more democratic basis, be used to bring other kinds of programme to the much bigger audiences who did not want education. As Mrs. Thatcher once put it, 'the Open University, if awarded the fourth channel, would sterilise it as a means of mass communication'. Even the 30 hours of time on BBC 2 that had been allocated to us were resented in many quarters and not least among several of the senior BBC staff. At that time there was, however, no more effective alternative way of ensuring that a video-signal would reach all our scattered population of students, and we were certain that this would be an essential part of our teaching/learning package.
  Nevertheless we were aware of the strength of the criticism and we were concerned to explore other potential ways of bringing video-signals to our home-based students. The prospect of relatively cheap video-recordings was attracting the attention of almost every major organisation in the audiovisual industry. Thus, in the lectures that I delivered throughout 1968 and 1969 I repeatedly indicated that our need for open-circuit air time might be only temporary, and that the despatch of cheap video-recordings to home-based students could become the pattern for the future. The prospect was a distant one, but it served to blunt criticisms about our use of the mass media and about the impossibility of ever having enough air-time

to offer an adequate profile of courses. We also studied in detail all the new methods of video-recording that were being developed since, even if open-circuit broadcasting were to be the main method of distribution, there was a need to provide recordings of the broadcasts in study centres, both for those students who lived in areas not yet covered by BBC 2 and for revision. I was sure however that we would never want to abandon open circuit broadcasting altogether, having always believed that it had two critical parts to play in any system of open education. The first was the shop window role, allowing us to show what we could do to a very much wider segment of the general population than the registered students. This would be vital not only to bring home to the academic world the quality of what we were intending to do, and to attract into the university a larger proportion of the adult population, but also to reach those who would not want to register as students but who could benefit from simply watching and listening to educational broadcasts. Second, I believed that the broadcasts would act as a pace-making mechanism for many students. This runs counter to the frequently expressed view that the great advantage of correspondence education is that students can follow courses at their own pace, and do not have to start or finish at a fixed date. Open University courses depend on broadcasts as an integral part of the learning materials. They are transmitted at fixed times and consequently all students must begin a course at the same time and finish at the same time. This is certainly a constraint on students' freedom of choice but, on the other hand, many individual students require this kind of continuous stimulus in order to keep up with the work at all. Most correspondence teaching is characterised by the very large student drop-out rate, and I am convinced that one reason for this is that many people lack the drive and dedication to maintain their work over a long period without an enforced pacing mechanism. I would therefore be very sad to see open-circuit broadcasting dropped in favour of individual recordings. I think it would penalise those students most in need of help. Natural scholars do not require such pacing; they will work at their own pace and satisfactorily complete a course in a reasonable time. It is the non-scholars who need this sort of help in order to keep them at a job that is being tackled less for the love of the subject itself than for the advantages that a qualification will ultimately bring.

These were, however, arguments about the future. In practical terms no technique was available in 1968 for making video-recordings cheaply enough to make it possible to supply individual copies even to study centres, far less to individual students. The cost of the transducing hardware, the playback machines, was also very high. All such methods were hopelessly expensive for the individual student, and this, I fear, is still true, despite the fact that the cost both of video-tapes and of machines has fallen dramatically. Detailed comparisons of the cost of open-circuit broadcasting with the cost of providing recordings to students were made by Dr. A. W. Bates for our submission to the Annan Committee[17]. The first, and obvious advantage of open-circuit broadcasts is that the capital cost of the transducer (the television set) has already been met by the students: surveys reveal that virtually all our students have access to a receiver. The second advantage is that the actual cost of transmitting a programme on open-circuit is much cheaper than alternative methods of distributing audiovisual materials. Nevertheless the problem remains that air-time is also a valuable resource and we cannot, therefore, decide between the two on the basis of financial comparisons alone.

The provision of recordings in study centres is a problem of a different order of magnitude. Here we only have to supply one for each centre – about 300 in all – instead of an average of 1000 for each programme if we were to supply copies for all students and part-time staff. Instead of having to send out 20,000 transducers each year, each centre is provided with one, which should last for several years. In 1971 each centre was equipped with a film cassette projector and we provided from Regional Offices copies of all broadcasts as 8mm. film-loops in cassettes. We are now converting to the use of quarter inch video-tape with suitable playback machines.

We soon discovered that we could not afford to stock copies of all the films in every centre and we had to settle for a halfway house. There were only 14 study centres in Britain which could not receive the BBC 2 signal directly, and these we supplied with a complete library of films. All the other centres were supplied, on demand, from a library of films held in each regional office. Thus a student who wished to see a film had to ask his counsellor at the study centre to obtain it from the regional office. Each centre was also provided with a cassette sound recorder and cassettes of the foundation course radio programmes.

It had been agreed between Lord Goodman and Sir Hugh Greene that the Open University would be provided with up to 30 hours per week on BBC 2. We had also decided that all programmes would be repeated so that students who could not be at home or at a study centre to see the first broadcast would have a second chance of seeing it. This presented no difficulty in the first teaching year when we only had four courses on offer but it has made programming increasingly difficult as time has gone on.

The BBC agreement did not specify the time of day at which the 30 hours would be provided and we have had continuously to fight for our share of peak hours on BBC 2. Even in 1971 arguments arose over the allocation of time between 7.00 and 7.30 pm. The Further Education Advisory Committee of the BBC (FEAC) were already broadcasting two half hour programmes per week on BBC 2 between 7.00 and 7.30 and they were naturally most reluctant to give up this time to the Open University. The controversy over two half hour 'slots' between 7.00 and 7.30 is not as petty as it seems at first sight. The proportion of the adult population at home and free to watch programmes shows a very rapid increase as the time advances between 6.00 and 7.00 in the evening. Between 7.00 and 7.30, 92% of the adult population are at home and free to watch, but between 6.30 and 7.00 the figure is only 83% and between 6.00 and 6.30 as low as 70%.

By 1975 we were so short of good viewing times, having filled up the weekday evenings between 5.00 and 7.00 and the whole of Saturday and

Sunday mornings, that we had been pushed into bands of time in the very early morning or, occasionally, very late in the evening. Our students do not appear to object to early rising too strongly, but even so it is virtually impossible for them immediately to reinforce these broadcasts by reading. Immediate reinforcement is a very necessary feature of the learning process and if delayed, even by as much as a whole day spent at work, is not as effective. I cannot advance hard evidence to support this assertion, but it is certainly true for me – what is crystal clear in my mind immediately after a broadcast, is lost very quickly if I do not reinforce it at once. Our difficulties will undoubtedly increase as time goes on and, as we have indicated in our submission to the Annan Committee, we will be unable to satisfy all our needs for television time under the present agreement with the BBC, once we approach the steady rate of course provision and the total profile of 87 undergraduate courses. This will be true even if there are no developments in the provision of other courses in the continuing education programmes as discussed in Chapter 21.

The distribution of the broadcast elements of our courses was thus based on a centrally controlled system backed up by the provision of copies of the broadcasts in regional centres. An exactly similar system was used for the distribution of the printed course materials. We knew that we faced a task of some magnitude, but not even Tom Robertson, the Manager of our Correspondence Services, with his experience of working in a commercial correspondence college, had any clear concept of just how immense it would become.

Clearly we would have to use mechanical methods wherever possible. During my visit to the University of South Africa in Pretoria, which handled a large number of external students by correspondence, I was struck by the simplicity of their administrative system. Students were sent all the correspondence material for a whole year's work on one course in a package at the beginning. It seemed to me that this was not psychologically sound. To send a student a large volume of material before he has even started the course impresses upon him the immensity of his task before he has even begun. We therefore decided that we would not send out more than three or four weeks' work in one mailing. Since we were to work to a 36 week teaching year, this meant a total of about nine mailings for each course. In 1971, our first teaching year, there would therefore be 36 mailings covering the four foundation courses. Thus, if we could schedule our system properly, (and this was very difficult in practice) we would have to arrange one mailing per week. With student numbers of between 7000 and 8000 in each course, plus all the part-time staff concerned with that course, this meant a despatch of anything up to 10,000 packages in each mailing. To write out 10,000 names and addresses and to pack 10,000 envelopes, each containing up to nine or ten individual items, is not a job that can be tackled by hand without a very large staff. By 1975, we would be dealing not with four courses, but with something nearer 70. There would then be not one mailing per week, but four mailings per day in a five day working week. The need for mechanisation was obvious.

By 1975 we were despatching several tons of mail a day. When we moved to Walton Hall in September of 1969, the incoming mail was delivered by one man on a bicycle; the huge increase in mail since then, both outgoing and incoming, has naturally imposed a severe burden on the local Post Office authorities, who have risen nobly to the occasion.

We have in the last couple of years been hit extremely hard by the increases in postal charges that have been imposed by successive governments. The bill for postage in 1975 reached the staggering figure of nearly £750,000. As a result, we have been forced to re-examine the whole basis of our course distribution system and reluctantly to consider alternative methods.

Thus far I have been describing the dissemination of the course materials; but the term 'course distribution' also includes the teaching and support services that are provided for the student. This back-up is provided through the regional structure of the University. I have never worked in a Regional Office, so that I cannot draw on my own experience in describing how the regional service developed. I therefore asked Ron Cosford, Regional Director of our Southern Region, to prepare an account of his early experiences and have drawn heavily upon that. The opinions expressed are however my own.

The Planning Committee had realised that the academic staff who created the courses would not necessarily know anything about the problems of adult education, of which many of them had had no previous experience. It was therefore considered vital that the regional tutorial and counselling services should be undertaken by men with a long experience of the particular problems involved in that kind of work. Consequently Regional Tutorial Services (RTS) was set up as a separate division from the beginning, and each Regional Director was made responsible to the Director of RTS, to whom I delegated responsibility for organising this very large segment of the new institution.

However, with hindsight it is clear that course teams in fact have a real interest in the precise nature of the tutorial and counselling services. Over the years the central academic staff have gained greatly in their knowledge and appreciation of the problems of their adult students and have begun to demand a greater share of control of the regional services. The organisation of the University into Course Teams has been successful in co-ordinating the work of BBC production staff, educational technologists and academic staff, but the teams have often worked without any direct contact with Regional Tutorial Services. Course teams may therefore demand types of service that the RTS staff know cannot be provided at regional level and this has inevitably led to much dispute and argument. I think that we chose the wrong structure at the beginning, that we would have done better to have created an Institute of Regional Tutorial Services, with an advisory rather than administrative function, and to have had the staff of the Institute as members of every course team. This is in no sense a criticism of the Director of Regional Tutorial Services or his staff, who have worked hard and efficiently within the limits of the structure imposed upon them. They have, despite these limitations, provided our students with a whole range of vital services that have worked in practice. It may well be that a radical change, now, of the kind I have suggested, would create more problems than it could solve; yet I keep wishing we had started out differently.

A Regional Director, on appointment in 1969, found himself carrying a large share of the burden of attempting to enlighten public opinion about the Open University and of fending off some of the most ill-informed criticisms of our objectives. Just as I met criticisms nationally, so he met them in local circles, where there were numerous instances of a real sourness of attitude about us, especially amongst local councillors and adult educationalists. He had to counter local convictions of the need for an Open School or an Open College rather than for an Open University. Just as I had been faced with fears on the part of the Library Association about the likely demands of hordes of Open University students, so similar criticisms were levelled at the Regional Director by local librarians. Librarians were particularly aggressive at that time because they, better than any other group, foresaw the growth in demand from Open University students, but in an exaggerated form. In my experience the average undergraduate in a vocational subject reads remarkably little apart from his set textbooks. Librarians would find this sad, would hope for better things, and would thus fear the resulting effects.

The Regional Director also found a tremendous fund of goodwill, which had to be nurtured and channelled into positive outlets. He was often inundated with offers of help and, if he was wise, would not treat them casually, even if they seemed of little value. He had to respond to an immense interest in and ignorance of what the Open University was going to be. He was swamped with requests to speak to all sorts of local organisations on all sorts of occasions. He was invited to present prizes, to speak to Rotary Clubs and Round Tables, to go to conferences, to visit factories. He was in other words the 'front man' of the new institution in his own region, and was for a long time virtually single-handed in carrying out this uphill task.

In determining the geographical boundaries of the Open University regions in England, we had followed as closely as possible those of the Regional Advisory Councils for Further Education. The early papers of the Advisory Committee and the Planning Committee envisaged co-operative academic work between the Open University and the WEA, the extramural departments of the universities and the Local Education Authorities. In practice such direct academic collaboration has developed, if at all, only very slowly. The academic relationships that did develop were with the universities and the world of higher education. Collaboration with the adult education world at the non-academic level was, on the other hand, very real from the beginning. We were parasitic on it, needing its accommodation for study centres and its full-time staff to act as part-time counsellors and tutors.

One of the first tasks of the Regional Director in 1969 was to choose the locations of the study centres in his area. Most were to be in individual institutions such as colleges. The size of the student population served by each potential centre was obviously a critical factor but it was unknown. The objective was plain; each centre should be readily accessible to the Open University students and as far as possible adaptable to their special needs. We did not want our students to feel alienated from the main stream of activity of the host institution. In other words the latter should be, wherever possible, an institution that was providing teaching programmes of a standard and level roughly comparable to our own and directed at students like ours. It was hard to satisfy both these conditions. A conventional university was not necessarily a good site because its students were so different from ours, but in a technical college, although the students might be comparable, the level of courses was not.

We were in practice governed by more mundane considerations. Did the host institution actually want us as tenants? What would it offer us in the way of accommodation? What would it charge us for rental? We hoped that LEAs would provide us with space at rates as reasonable as those charged to other educational organisations making use of their premises and, in the end, they did. In 1969, however, this was in some doubt. The Local Education Authority Associations had made it plain that they would expect the entire cost of the Open University to be met from central funds, and this could imply that they would charge us commercial rentals. It was an anxious time and Regional Directors had to exercise great patience and tact to establish the mutual trust that has fortunately characterised our relationship with the LEAs.

Perhaps the most striking example of our failure to comprehend the nature of the organisation we were planning is that we had, initially, made no provision at all for the establishment of a strong link between the part-time tutors and counsellors and the full-time academic staff. I was naive enough to think that the Regional Director would himself provide the link necessary. It was Robert Beevers, the Director of RTS, who first realised the seriousness of the gap. Early in 1970 he submitted a paper making two proposals. The first was that the part-time tutors, who would mark the correspondence assignments submitted by the students, should be linked to the full-time academic staff at the centre, who had set the assignments, through a group of full-time academics called Staff Tutors. The second was that the gap between his central Regional Tutorial Service unit, which must organise a national counselling service, and the part-time counsellors employed in the Region, should be filled by a group of full-time Senior Counsellors. These proposals were unexpected and costly, for every new post had to be replicated in each of the twelve regions. In our initial evaluation Christodoulou and I had made no provision for such staff and we had to go back to the DES cap in hand. Yet there was never any doubt, once the existence of the gap was pointed out, that it must be filled.

The proposals were therefore accepted. The nature of such appointments, their terms and conditions of service, and their relationship to other full-time staff, had to be determined, and new space and facilities in the Regions had to be found for them. Staff Tutors, it was considered, should be selected by the academic staff of a faculty under the control of the Dean, and should be full-time members of that faculty on secondment to a particular region. The general idea was that they would live and work in the Region but would be required to spend some 20% of their time on the main campus, so that they could become fully aware of the views of the central academic staff about each course and what it was intended to demand of students. This inevitably means that a Staff Tutor has a dual loyalty: in the first place to his Dean and professional colleagues in the faculty, but also administratively to his Regional Director to whom he is responsible on a day to day basis for the organisation of the tutorial service in the Region. It is a difficult job to serve two masters, especially when they may be pulling in different directions, for the reasons I have already discussed. In some Regions, by the exercise of tact and sympathy, these difficulties have been overcome, but in others things have been less happy.

Senior Counsellors, on the other hand, were to supervise the work of part-time counsellors and the operation would primarily require knowledge of and sympathy with the problems of adult education. It would only marginally be concerned with course creation, distribution and accreditation, so there was no need to involve the faculties. Consequently recruitment of Senior Counsellors was left wholly in the hands of RTS and the Regional Director and presented no particular problem.

Our idea of a regional office in 1969 was very modest. Indeed some regions started without any offices at all and the Regional Director had to operate from his own house for several months until we could acquire suitable premises. Later we rented a few rooms from the local university or college. When the need for a much larger number of full-time staff in each region became apparent this sort of arrangement became inappropriate. In one region where, for instance, we planned initially for an office of 130 square metres, we now occupy 1700 square metres. In many regions the office has had to be moved twice, in the relatively short life of the University. Since our regional offices are mostly sited in major cities the cost of renting office accommodation has of course become very high. It would have been much cheaper to buy office space outright but only recently have we persuaded the government that this would be a good plan.

The first group of part-time staff was needed during 1970 to provide a counselling service to applicants, and Regional Directors made *ad hoc* arrangements to obtain these 'admissions counsellors'. The prevailing mood in the regions was one of dedication, but the intensity of this effort was coupled with a real anxiety about the likely quality of both the courses and the students. It seemed to most Regional Directors that the Planning Committee might well have exaggerated student demand for the Open

University. They suspected that many applicants would be over-optimistic about their ability, especially their ability to follow two courses concurrently. They considered that the full-time staff did not appreciate the grassroots problems of adult education and in this they were almost certainly right. In their admissions counselling they tried, therefore, to avoid over-optimism, to inject a note of realism. They grappled with these problems both in individual counselling interviews and at a series of induction meetings for new students held in the last two months of 1970.

The recruitment of the main body of part-time staff for 1971 began with a national advertising campaign. The response was not uniform across the whole country but in most regions it was very encouraging. We received over 12,000 applications for our 3380 vacancies. The main problem was not to choose the best applicants but to reject the others. This meant, in many cases, turning away local people who were known to be enthusiastic, helpful and keen, but whose keenness and loyalty were not matched by their academic excellence. To reject such people without giving offence was never easy. Indeed in some cases educationally dubious appointments were made for reasons of expediency and this dead wood had to be pruned out in the second and subsequent years. Nevertheless even at that stage offence was sometimes caused, and some of the grudges that resulted still simmer and cause difficulties between the University and some members of the staff of host institutions.

The main criteria for the appointment of part-time staff were academic qualification, experience in teaching unqualified or adult students and experience in teaching at university level. Over 60 per cent of those appointed actually held full-time teaching appointments in institutions of higher education. The recruitment was left very largely in the hands of the regions although certain minimum criteria were laid down by the faculties. In fact in many regions some of the most competent staff turned out to be those who had little or no previous experience and who learned on the job. In later years, therefore, the formal selection criteria were modified and we came to depend more on personal knowledge of individual staff by Senior Counsellors and Staff Tutors than upon paper qualifications. No doubt a careful examination of the particular qualities which make for success in a part-time tutor or counsellor of the Open University would yield interesting results, but time has not so far permitted such a study.

The availability of high quality tutors in all regions, and indeed in nearly all localities, led to a change of policy which was to have a profound effect upon the university. It opened up the prospect of providing an element of face-to-face tuition for our students. This was a very attractive idea, for both staff and students knew that face-to-face teaching worked and was enjoyable. Consequently we introduced 'class tutorials' over and above the original provision of 'correspondence tuition'. Part-time tutors would thus operate not only by marking and commenting on assignments by post but also by meeting students at study centres. While this undoubtedly provided a safety net for our untried system of teaching at a distance, it was potentially dangerous. We had many students who could not travel to study centres and for them, we had to continue to rely wholly on distance teaching. Again, as our advanced courses became more specialised we could not hope to provide class tutorials for them all, as there could not be enough students (or enough skilled tutors) in any one locality to justify the cost. We therefore insisted that class tutorials must be regarded not as an integral part of the teaching programme but as 'remedial' – available as an optional extra to those who could attend them and who were having difficulty in comprehension.

Thus the very size of the foundation classes was allowed to erode the principle of relying solely upon teaching at a distance. It was an erosion that was welcomed by students and part-time staff alike, and by a large number of the full-time academic staff. In the first year the class tutorial undoubtedly played a part in improving the success rate by diminishing the drop-out from the foundation courses. The long term effect is much more difficult to assess. It is almost impossible to withdraw from students a service which many find valuable and attractive. It is all very nice to be able to meet a tutor and discuss your problems with him, but for advanced courses with small numbers of students this kind of service is prohibitively expensive and wholly impracticable. We must hope that students who have reached a late stage in their studies will find it possible to struggle along without such a service.

The fact that so many of our part-time tutorial staff were drawn from the full-time staffs of universities, polytechnics, technical colleges and teacher training colleges greatly improved the reputation and status of the university in the academic world. These people became familiar with our courses and with our students, and came to see the institution in a wholly new light. There were so many of them that knowledge about the Open University spread quickly in those days.

Perhaps I have already said enough to indicate that I am not at all certain whether we have evolved the right balance between the regional structure of the University and the central organization. To some extent an imbalance was inevitable in view of the fact that we had no coherent plan for the regions when we started; they were simply allowed to evolve. I am sure that Robert Beevers was fundamentally correct in deciding that students would need continuous counselling, but it was not a view that was shared widely by academics. They tended to believe that most of the advice that students would want would come best from the academic staff who were teaching them (the tutors) and that counselling would become a relatively peripheral and minor activity. This runs counter to the experience of most people who have worked in the field of adult education, where the belief is fairly general that adults need a great deal more supportive help, in areas divorced from their purely academic studies, than do students in conventional residential institutions. The views of the RTS division have accordingly not been the only influence in determining the ways that individual regions have coped; the views of faculties, expressed through Staff Tutors, have often prevailed. No doubt valuable experience has been acquired as different solutions have been applied in different regions, but we have not learned much from that experience because people have in general been too busy to have the time or the inclination to learn from others. We are now trying to put this right, but perhaps it is already too late in the sense that things have become institutionalised to such a degree that it is increasingly difficult to change the system. The staff of the RTS division have probably had an impossible job of trying to co-ordinate the regional operations. They were faced by the scepticism of many of their academic colleagues, they had to represent the regions in the evolution of the central organisation and they had to give guidance and leadership to the whole of the regional operation. With only a handful of full-time staff to do all these jobs the one that got least attention was the co-ordination of regional activities and the development of an overall policy. The result of this was that regions increasingly became more independent of central control. Paradoxically this has led to a different form of criticism from the central academic staff who claim, sometimes with justification, that the regions have too much influence over the teaching operations of the University. In fact, however, each Regional Director was forced to work out his own salvation and in so doing sometimes achieved a reputation for arrogance amongst the central academic staff who did not understand the reality of the situation.

I have described how we provided libraries of cassetted recordings of television and radio programmes in study centres. We also decided that the student must be able, at the study centre, to watch and listen to our open-circuit broadcasts. We thought that many of our students would be members of large families who would have only one television set in the house, and foresaw family battles between the student who wished to watch an Open University programme and other members of his family who wanted *Coronation Street*. We believed that many of our students, who would be out at work all day, would find it easier to reach a study centre to watch a programme at six o'clock than to go home to do so. I think we were wrong. On the whole the families of Open University students have been intensely loyal and have performed miracles of family reorganisation in order to ensure that our students have uninterrupted opportunities to see their television programmes. Students do not seem to enjoy communal viewing or listening and much prefer to watch or listen at home. We did, however, equip all our study centres with television and radio sets and, although they are little used, they offer an additional facility that is sometimes valuable.

Each study centre is also equipped with a complete library of the texts of foundation courses, and selected centres have those of higher level courses. Once again I suspect that this facility is under-used and represents a fairly large capital investment for a relatively small return. However it is a facility that is useful to our own students on odd occasions, and it may often be very valuable to the staff and students of the host institution.

Study centres are open every weekday evening and some also at weekends. At these times there is normally a part-time counsellor in attendance. We originally thought that students would wish to consult counsellors regularly, but many students make little use of the opportunity, while others make heavy demands. The counsellor is a vital figure at the study centre. He can stimulate the foundation of self-help groups; he can provide background information about the University; he can oil the wheels of the machine by helping students to obtain copies of library books and to gain access to local institutions and their facilities. The general idea is that the student will stay with the same counsellor throughout his time with the University, unless he moves from one region to another, in order to give him a sense of continuity in his studies. This concept has been maintained throughout all the various changes that we have made in the organisation of tutorial help.

Part-time tutors present a much more complex problem. It would be inordinately expensive to have a tutor in each subject discipline on duty at every study centre every night of the week. This would be to create a mini-university at each of 270 study centres. Consequently we originally decided that tutors would not attend at study centres, but the introduction of class tutorials changed all this. For these, the tutor in a particular discipline is in attendance at the study centre on certain specified evenings. We knew that some students would get stuck. We were particularly concerned to get them unstuck to prevent their dropping out simply because they came across a conceptual difficulty and could not, without a face-to-face tutorial, get themselves going again. This problem arises more frequently in courses such as mathematics than it does in the arts. It is inevitable that a student who fails to comprehend Unit 6 in a mathematics course will find it impossible to comprehend Unit 7. In arts-based courses the subject material for one week does not depend on complete understanding of the material for the preceding week, so that even if the student comes across an intellectual problem in week 6 he can usually proceed to the work of week 7 without any great difficulty. He can therefore afford to wait much longer to have his conceptual problem unravelled. For this reason we arranged that remedial tutorials would be available more frequently in mathematics than in arts-based courses. However, if more than an absolute minimum of such tutorial help is provided we run the risk, both of pricing our system out of the market and of relying more and more on the tried and proven method of face-to-face tuition, thus denying the validity of our claim that learning at a distance is a feasible alternative. We have therefore had to resist, over and over again, demands from the students for more face-to-face tutorials.

In 1971 we had no shortage of applications for part-time tutor posts. The multi-disciplinary nature of the foundation courses made it possible to recruit people with a wide range of backgrounds. Two-thirds of those that we selected were in full-time employment in universities, polytechnics or colleges, and it was vital that we should not prejudice the value of their services to their full-time employers. For this reason I insisted that no part-time tutor or counsellor should be asked to undertake a work load greater than 10% of a full-time load. Most institutions would regard extra spare-time work of this magnitude as acceptable; it was unlikely to affect their capacity to carry out their full-time jobs satisfactorily. As a result we had to employ no less than 3380 part-time tutors and counsellors to cover the needs of our students in 1971.

The amount of the actual cash payments we could make to members of part-time staff was restricted. This did not matter too much in the early years as they tended to be highly motivated and to wish to be associated with the new venture. They enjoyed their teaching duties and found their reward in the enthusiasm of the adult student. Over the years this initial drive was bound to slacken as novelty wore off and the heavy burden imposed on tutors became more and more evident. As advanced courses were produced the burden was to increase dramatically. The number of students registered for such courses was small and consequently tutors had fewer students and, on a *per capita* basis, a smaller income. Yet they had to master increasingly difficult subject material before they could act as tutors. We therefore plan to introduce into the payment system an 'initial' fee designed to cover the work involved in mastering the subject.

During the last two or three years the total remuneration of academic staff, especially in the polytechnics and colleges, has increased dramatically. In consequence, despite cost of living increases in our payments to our part-time staff, the additional money that they can earn by working for the Open University has become less attractive. It has to be added on to a much higher salary and is consequently taxed at a much higher rate. We have therefore had increasing difficulty in recruiting adequate numbers of part-time staff, especially in certain highly specialised subjects.

This whole problem of paying part-time staff is aggravated by the system of finance employed by government. Nationally agreed increases in salary for full-time academic staff have always attracted automatic compensatory increases in government grant, but this principle is not extended to part-time staff. Most universities employ very few part-time staff so that increases in their salaries, even if not automatically compensated, raise no financial problem. In this respect the Open University is quite different. No less than 12% of our total budget goes in payments to part-time staff. If inflationary pressures cause us to incease the rate of payment to them and if we do not get supplementation for this increased outlay, we divert a higher and higher proportion of our total resource into the part-time staff budget. However strong the case for paying more may be, we may therefore have to resist it, and this in turn is likely to prejudice recruitment of part-time staff in the future. The irony of this situation is that, had we set up a system whereby the tutorial and counselling work was done by full-time staff, we would have had no financial problem of this kind, since their salaries would have been automatically supplemented.

Yet it would have been a more expensive and probably less efficient way of providing the service, and we would have failed to forge the link between the University and outside institutions which has, I suspect, done more to influence the standards of teaching used in these institutions than any other single aspect of our work.

The final element in our present system of course distribution is summer schools. My initial commitment to these, as a requirement for all students proceeding to a degree, stemmed from my association with Howard Sheath, who had for many years been Director of External Studies in the University of New England in New South Wales. On his prolonged visit to us early in 1969, he laid very great stress on the advantages of summer schools in motivating and holding the interest of scattered students studying by correspondence in the Australian outback. He advised against making summer schools voluntary, maintaining that they were critical to the success of students. I was impressed by his arguments and determined that we should follow the same pattern.

I therefore proposed that all students taking a foundation course should be required to spend two weeks in a summer school, and this proposal was accepted. We realised, however, that some students would choose to study two foundation courses concurrently, and that a requirement to spend no less than four weeks in residence at summer schools might well prove an insuperable difficulty for them. Many of those in full-time employment had only relatively short holidays and could not expect their employers to give them additional leave of absence.

I felt that the best answer would be that these students should be required to attend only one of the two summer schools, but this found little favour with the faculties who were already planning on the basis of the summer school programme being an integral part of the overall course design. This was especially true in the Faculty of Science, where the summer school was to consist almost wholly of laboratory work. Consequently we were forced to reduce the summer school requirement for any one course to one week in residence. I am not at all sure that this was a wise decision, but it pinpoints the dilemma that arose in defining what precisely the objectives of summer schools should be.

From the beginning I regarded the summer school less as an integral part of a multi-disciplinary multi-media course than as a necessary extra – a learning experience that the student could not otherwise undergo and a chance to taste the flavour of an on-campus situation in contact with many other students. Here students would learn for the first time that many other students were having just the same difficulties as they were and would discover how other undergraduates worked. It would be an intensely motivating experience which would reinforce students halfway through their course with the determination necessary to carry them through to the end.

I did not believe that the subject matter studied during the summer school need necessarily be directly related to, and integrated with, the subject material of the rest of a course. It seemed more important that the students should just be there. This view was challenged by a number of my colleagues. They were particularly concerned by the fact that we would be making a demand on busy adults which would take them away from home for a spell in the summer. They considered, therefore, that students would become very rebellious if they were expected to attend a summer school that was not directly related to the course that they were following. This view was adopted, and it may well be that it was the right one, but it did impose severe constraints on the later development of our summer school policy.

The general idea was to run summer schools over a twelve week period during the long vacation of other universities, and to provide accommodation in some twelve or fourteen such universities so that students could be offered a choice both of time and place. This was easy to arrange in 1971 with only four courses; by 1975 the situation was different. We then had some 70 courses on offer, 34 of which demanded or shared a one week summer school. A pattern had emerged whereby some students, taking four half-credit courses concurrently, might be required to spend four weeks in summer school, while other students might have no summer school requirements at all. This clearly has repercussions on students' choice of courses. If they are unable to take such periods off work in order to attend summer school, they may be forced to choose to study courses of less value to them in the future.

We have found it impossible to offer a separate summer school programme in each course, and have been forced to develop programmes that fit a number of courses in the same discipline. By such means we have been able to hold the number of separate summer school programmes at 26. To achieve this, the objectives have to some extent had to be modified in the direction of the alternative policy of having summer schools that are not strictly integral parts of individual courses. Even with these limitations it is becoming increasingly difficult to organise 26 different summer school lines and at the same time to offer students a choice of time and place. This situation can only get worse as we approach our full profile of courses.

The cost of running summer schools goes up constantly, and it falls upon the student. The financial stringency of recent years has forced the universities to increase their charges to us for accommodation, and we have had no choice but to pass this increase on to the students by raising summer school fees. This has meant, particularly for students on the science side, a considerable increase in the overall cost of getting a degree, except where, as often happens, the summer school fee is met by grant from the local authority.

Taken all in all, however, the summer schools still remain one of the most exhilarating of all Open University experiences, both for the staff who are concerned with them and for the students themselves. The students, who are determined to get the maximum benefit out of their short stay on campus, make enormous demands on the staff. At the end of each summer there is nothing but enthusiasm for the continuance of summer schools, but in the spring, when the labour of organising summer schools for up to 40,000 student weeks is at its height, I hear only about the difficulties and snags of the summer school system. At this time there are endless arguments with the host institutions about the price and the nature of the facilities; endless problems in organising the programmes, collecting the necessary equipment and shipping it to the various centres; endless bickering about staffing the summer schools and arranging for central academic staff to be in attendance at each and every one. All of this is an exhausting and debilitating experience but in the event it brings its own reward in the tremendous success that these schools achieve. There are many students who enjoy them not only for their academic content but for the social occasion that presents itself. They are away from the constraints of their homes, and are free to indulge in both work and play to the fullest possible extent. I do not believe they go back rested as if after a holiday, but they probably do so motivated and enthusiastic as they have not been since the course began. Thus, despite all the problems, I am quite certain that we must press on with our summer school programme and not abandon it for reasons of difficulty or price.

Our course distribution has been built up by making use of existing systems of communication. It depends on the BBC and its transmission networks that reach out to well over 95% of the population. It depends on the Post Office, which despite the brickbats cast at it and the increasing cost of its services over recent years, is still an efficient organisation in the sense that it delivers letters very quickly by comparison with most countries of the world. It is based on the existence, in almost every town in Britain, of a conventional educational institution that is able to provide us with space for study centres and with part-time staff to use in teaching our students. It is also able to rely on the existence of a very highly developed system of public libraries and an inter-library loan system which allows our students to gain access to almost all the reading material that they require without great difficulty. These are all existing systems of communication that are by no means common to all nations of the world.

We have, by operating in this way, kept our investment in new hardware for new methods of communications to an absolute minimum. In this we have differed greatly from other innovative ventures, especially in the United States, which have devoted literally millions of dollars to developing very sophisticated hardware systems for communication between teacher and students. From the beginning we have been interested in such developments, intending all the time to latch on to and make use of them as soon as they had been developed to a point where they were available to us in a form that was sufficiently cheap to be adaptable to our use.

In successive visits to the United States over the past six years I have seen, in a number of institutions, some extraordinarily sophisticated hardware systems, ranging from computer-aided instruction (CAI) to two-way television link-up. These are enough to make my eyes gleam with jealousy, and I would simply love to have them available for our students. But their cost is prohibitive.

We have been able to make increasing use of the telephone for teaching purposes and telephone tutorials have been a growing feature of the teaching programme in some of our more advanced courses, where tutor and student are often far apart. We have also experimented with conference phone linking which would enable us to hold class tutorials making use of the telephone system. Unfortunately the British telephone switching system is very much more difficult to adapt to conference phone linking than is the switching system in use in America. I am told that the only way to set up a conference telephone call in Britain is to send a man with a soldering iron to doctor the switchgear: this is naturally a brake on the development of such telephone calls! Our technologists are also working on a new cheap 'telewriter' which would allow a picture drawn by a teacher on a sensitive board to be reproduced on a television set through a telephone link. This would be a new method of communication of great significance for our work if the prototype could be developed into a commercially viable product.

We want to remain open to all new suggestions of this kind, but I fear that, in this area, institutionalisation is equivalent almost to ossification. The whole of the Open University communication network is now so complex that to make a change of any kind is a costly enterprise, and we need therefore to be very sure of our ground before embarking on one. It would be nice to be able to experiment with new methods on a pilot basis: I trust that we can devise ways of doing so,· in the hope that a successful experiment might justify the cost of modifying our whole network.

8

COURSE ACCREDITATION

One of the principles laid down by Jennie Lee was that the 'University of the Air' would offer its own degrees which would be of a standard equivalent to the degrees of any other British university. There were two ways of ensuring this: first by providing, within the structure of the new institution, appropriate checks to ensure that the staff of the University, were they to be foolish enough to try to achieve a high pass rate by reducing standards, could not act in this way; and second by appointing a staff who would themselves be concerned to ensure that standards were maintained, and who would determine rigid and precise assessment procedures leading to the award of the degree.

Two checking mechanisms were built into the structure of the University. Both are applied uniformly in all universities in the United Kingdom, but very seldom in other countries. Consequently it is often difficult for foreign academic communities to appreciate just how important they are to the whole British system of higher education. The first is the creation, under the Charter, of an Academic Advisory Committee. This has been a uniform practice in the Charters of all new British universities over the past two or three decades. Until each new university has established itself by recruiting an adequate number of high quality academic staff, the control of its teaching programmes, its examinations and the quality of its degrees is vested in the Academic Advisory Committee which has power, under the Charter, to override decisions of the Senate. Normally, the life of the Committee is five years and thereafter authority is vested in the Senate of the new university. Academic Advisory Committees are appointed by the Privy Council and usually consist of about eight very senior and respected academics drawn from other universities, together with the Vice-Chancellor of the new institution; this was exactly the pattern adopted for the Open University in its Charter. The membership of the Academic Advisory Committee appointed in 1969 was as follows:

PROFESSOR HILDE T. HIMMELWEIT, Ph.D, Chairman (Professor of Social Psychology, London School of Economics).

PROFESSOR J. C. GUNN, MA (Cargill Professor of Natural Philosophy, University of Glasgow).

DR SIDNEY HOLGATE, MA (Master of Grey College, University of Durham).

DR KATHLEEN KENYON, CBE, D.Litt, MA (Principal of St. Hugh's College, Oxford).

PROFESSOR K. W. KEOHANE, B.Sc, Ph.D (Vice-Principal of Chelsea College, University of London).

MR FRANK THISTLETHWAITE, MA (Vice-Chancellor of the University of East Anglia).

DR BRYAN THWAITES, MA, Ph.D (Principal of Westfield College, University of London).

LORD WYNNE-JONES (Emeritus Professor of Chemistry, University of Newcastle-upon-Tyne).

THE VICE-CHANCELLOR

As Vice-Chancellor I attended all the meetings of the Academic Advisory Committee, and found that its members took a very keen interest in what we were trying to do. They came fresh to the job, with minds that were open to the new ideas, but without any preconceived notions of what shape or form the new University would take.

We submitted to the Committee our plans for each new course and got back from it thoughtful comment that was often incorporated by the course team into the design of the course itself. The Committee was thus able to influence the standard and the nature of the course materials in addition to being able to fulfil its other major role, that of ensuring that the assessment procedures were properly designed. Thus the Committee monitored the nature of the assessments, both continuous and final, approved the appointment of all external examiners and, in general, took care that the award of credit in any particular course was made only to those who had fulfilled a programme that was unexceptionable. The Charter also gives power to the Academic Advisory Committee to monitor the methods by which staff are appointed to the University and to approve the government structure for the academic side of the University. To all these tasks the Committee brought wisdom and authority.

British universities also ensure a uniformity of standard amongst the degrees awarded in the country through the system of appointing external examiners from amongst the staffs of appropriate disciplines in other universities. It was agreed from the outset that the Open University should follow the same practice. In theory an external examiner has the final say, not only about the precise form of the examination and the questions that are asked in it, but also in determining whether any particular student has passed or failed. Although he has no statutory right to determine results in this way, no examination board would be willing to issue a pass list with which the external examiner fundamentally disagreed, since he would be free to criticise such a decision in public, and this would undoubtedly bring the institution into disrepute.

In the Open University, the problems of using external examiners properly were very different from those which apply in other universities. We had decided to use continuous assessment in addition to final examinations on each course. The number of 'examination' papers that were sent to students throughout the year was therefore very large and monitoring them was a task out of all proportion to that normally expected of an external examiner. In the second place, in each of our four foundation courses there were several thousand students, and the idea that the external examiner could play a part in actually marking the scripts of even a sizeable sample of such a number of students was not feasible. We knew that it would be impossible, when all the results were in, to give individual scrutiny to every paper or set of papers and that we would consequently have to rely on some other method of collating the results of the examinations that could be operated through the computer. In turn, we would have to arrange to have a system of monitoring the results of the collation procedure so that the external examiner could properly exercise his influence and authority at the time of determining the pass list. These were the sorts of problems put before the Academic Advisory Committee for solution, for which we had to evolve a system that would meet with the approval both of the Committee itself, and of the external examiners who were to act for us.

What then, were the methods of assessment that we should use? There was considerable concern in the academic world about the inadequacy of many of the examination systems that were in use throughout the country, both at university and at pre-university level. Furthermore, in the world of adult education, the idea of examinations was an unpopular one: adult education, it was maintained, was provided for the benefits of adults who wished to learn for the sake of learning, and examinations were at best an unnecessary frill and, at worst, a positive hindrance to free and untrammelled study.

Much of the pressure within the University was in the direction of using continuous assessment as the major method of determining the progress of students. This was less for the purposes of examination than as an absolutely integral and necessary part of the learning process. To work successfully at a distance, a student required continuous reinforcement of his awareness that he was making progress, and continuous assessments were of the essence in the successful maintenance of such a system. Many people believed that, if this arrangement were to work satisfactorily, there would be no reason for any final assessment of the student at the end of the process. It is probably true that if one could rely utterly on the absolute integrity of every student this would be a wholly adequate system. Unfortunately, when one is dealing with very large numbers of students, one cannot take this attitude. If, in the award of a credit or a degree, one is providing certification that a particular individual has achieved a given standard of performance and knowledge of a subject, one must ensure that it is a truthful certificate. If students are assessed solely on the work they do at home, there is no way of ensuring this: they may have obtained help from wives or husbands who already hold degrees in the same subject or they may have relied entirely on information obtained from reference material. Such cheating achieves nothing for the individual, since he will almost certainly be found out when he starts to make use of his qualification in later life. On the other hand, when such individuals are discovered, it brings disrepute upon the institution that provided the certificate. This sort of reasoning led us to decide that we could not rely wholly on continuous assessment to provide the evidence upon which we would award degrees.

It is for precisely the same sorts of reasons that universities in general apply examination systems of particular stringency in disciplines where their degree award is at the same time a licence to practice the vocational subject that has been studied. A good example of this is medicine, where external examiners are required by the General Medical Council as a condition of accepting the degree of a particular university, both as a licence to practice and as a qualification for the entry of a graduate on the Medical Register. Such constraints on universities in vocational subjects are not applied in respect of degrees in arts or social sciences, but the practice of using external examiners is customary in all degree examinations.

We therefore set about considering the particular form of the final examination. We decided from the outset that an examination would be held in respect of every individual credit course and would not be deferred until a student had completed his full programme of six or eight credits towards a degree. In other words, the examination for one particular credit would be a separate and complete entity, and a student, once having achieved such a credit, could carry it forward and be awarded his degree when he had accumulated sufficient credits.

This pattern is common to the universities of Scotland and the United States and to many universities throughout the rest of the world, but is relatively uncommon in English universities, except in faculties like Medicine which are highly vocational in nature.

Those who most vocally criticise the written examination as a method of assessment are usually also those who argue strongly in favour of new forms of assessment. The trouble is that when one asks them what new forms they would use they are generally unable to give a constructive answer. In fact, nearly all the current methods of assessment have been in use for many years.

One can use an examination paper in one of two forms. The first is the traditional one which requires the student to write answers to a number of questions, each in the form of an essay that attempts to provide the information called for. The second form of examination paper consists of multiple choice questions which each call for a single word response. The paper can thereby cover a much wider total field of knowledge than can be attempted in essay-type question papers. Both of these types of examination are held under the eye of an invigilator who ensures that students do not receive help in arriving at their answers, either from other students or from written materials. The problem is that they impose a great strain on candidates, whose performances in such circumstances are conditioned by whether they feel well or ill, and by the effect that the psychological stress of the examination has upon them as individuals. Some people react well under such conditions, others very badly. When one is examining adults, one has to be aware also of all those other stresses that may apply, very unevenly, to adults living at home and in full-time employment, I am thinking in particular of family problems, children's illnesses and various problems at work, all of which may adversely affect the performance of a student.

As a replacement for the written examination paper at the end of a course, one can substitute a *viva voce*. Here, the candidate is put in a different sort of stressful situation, before one or more examiners who will simply ask him questions and assess the quality of the replies. I have in my days in Edinburgh carried out a large number of *viva voce* examinations of medical students and have no doubt that if one sets out with the intention of failing a candidate, there is nothing easier than to do so. However good a student may be, one can by the nature of the questions one puts, and by the way in which one puts them, confuse and trap him into error. I have seen colleagues actually do this in examination situations, and it is the duty of the other examiners present to ensure that the candidate is not failed by such disreputable tactics. In general, however, examiners do everything possible to help a candidate to overcome shyness and stress and to perform as well as he can under these difficult circumstances. Despite this, the *viva voce* is no less and often more stressful than the written examination. It is also a very much more subjective assessment and unless the whole proceedings are recorded there is no way of subsequently checking that it is an accurate one. This is not the case where answers are written down and can be re-checked to make sure that no error has been committed. The great advantage of the *viva voce* type of examination however is that, should the answer to a particular question appear to be ambiguous, it can be explored in greater depth at the time, and a proper judgement made as to whether the candidate has a real understanding of the problem with which he is faced, or just a vague recollection of something he has read.

There is one other way of making a final assessment of the performance of a student. It is widely used in postgraduate work and requires a student, at leisure and in his own time, to write a thesis or dissertation about the topic that he has studied over a long period. This is undoubtedly a fair way of assessing a student who has been involved in a research project, about which no-one can know quite as much as he does himself and where he cannot obtain significant help from other people in writing up his conclusions. It is not easily applicable to more elementary subject material where one can never be sure how much help the student has obtained, working in private on his answers. At this level it therefore offers no advantages over a system of continuous assessment.

This then was the spectrum of different forms of assessment from which we had to derive our own system. It was not an easy choice! There was no opportunity for innovation: the only new thing we could do was to use existing forms of assessment in a different mix.

Continuous assessment was to be a very important part of the learning process, quite apart from its value in determining standard of performance. We decided that our teaching materials, as part of their

125

structure, would call for responses from the student throughout the whole progress of his reading of each unit. This was 'self-assessment' in the sense that the answers were provided within the text, and it enabled the student to check his comprehension of the subject matter at frequent intervals throughout a unit.

In addition he would be provided every three or four weeks with a separate set of assessment questions. His answers to these would be marked by a correspondence tutor who, in addition to grading them, would be expected to comment on them in a helpful and stimulating way. A record would be kept of the student's performance on these questions and would form a basic part of the overall assessment of a student at the end of the course.

These assessment questions were, from the beginning, of two kinds: one, the traditional essay type and the other, multiple choice. It was possible to devise means of marking multiple-choice papers by using the computer, and such assessments came to be known as 'Computer Marked Assignments' or 'CMA's', for short. The essay types had to be marked and assessed by correspondence tutor and became known as 'Tutor Marked Assignments' or 'TMA's'.

The great advantage of the CMA is that the student sends his answer direct to the University where it is marked by the computer and the score returned direct to him. He thus gets a rapid feedback which can help him in the next units of the course. The main disadvantage of CMAs is that they are extremely difficult to set. It takes a long time for academic staff to devise suitable questions of the right level of difficulty, which will provide a fair test of a student's comprehension.

Not all academics are persuaded of the value of this form of examining; many hold that it is only when a more extended essay type answer is written that they can really tell whether a student has the level of understanding that they are seeking. Others argue that the form of the multiple-choice question inevitably gives all the necessary information and that a student is then required only to differentiate between correct and incorrect information; there is thus no required recall of information. Detailed analysis of multiple-choice papers does show, however, that it is possible to devise very sophisticated multiple-choice questions which do require a great deal of recall and of judgement. Nevertheless, there is no doubt that it is more difficult to construct such questions than to devise essay questions. Furthermore, this difficulty is very much greater in the liberal arts than in mathematics or in science, where multiple-choice questions are generally accepted by academics as a means of covering a wide area quickly and where, in general, answers are either right or wrong and do not call for value judgements. For this reason, multiple-choice papers are used much more frequently in science and mathematics than they are in arts, though all faculties in the Open University make use of them to some extent.

Over the years the computer has never been shown to have made a mistake in marking a CMA, although this is often suspected by a student.

Mistakes do occur when wrong instructions are given on CMA forms or when the student misinterprets instructions by, for example, selecting too many answers to a question. This is then scored as a 'technical error' and the student gets no credit even though the correct answers were included in his selections. Similarly if a student does not use an HB pencil, as he is told to do, the document reader misses the student responses and an incorrect grade is given. Human errors cause the trouble; there has not been any machine error, in our experience.

Another overwhelming advantage of the CMA is that the cost of operating the procedures, once the questions have been written, is extremely low. The expensive element is the academic time involved in constructing the questions. Thus it would be easy for us to extend the number of CMAs without much additional cost, but this is by no means true of TMAs.

We knew that we could not rely wholly on CMAs as the method of continuous assessment, especially in the liberal arts. Thus, in all courses, TMAs were regarded as necessary and important.

TMAs are processed by a 'circular' system: the student sends the essay direct to the tutor, and the tutor forwards it marked to the University, which then returns it to the student having recorded the result. Why not go one step further and simply have the tutor record the result and send the essay directly back to the student? Here we come up against an awkward fact of the Open University system. Since we were going to rely on several thousand part-time tutors, the standards they used in assessing the work of a student could vary greatly. If their assessment was to be used in determining the final performance of a student for the award of credit, then it was essential for us to have some system of monitoring the marks they awarded. We therefore arranged that a sample of marked scripts would be extracted from each batch sent to the University, and photocopied for monitoring. The number of scripts retained for this purpose depends upon the length of time the tutor has worked for us and upon the monitor's reports. Normally a new tutor starts at a high level of monitoring which decreases over the years. After all the assessment grades have been entered on the computer file of each student, the photocopied essays are distributed to full-time staff tutors who re-mark them. Through this procedure they are able to discover any tutors who have marked all the essays either too stringently or too leniently, or who have made irregular assessments. If necessary, the staff tutor then offers the tutor appropriate advice. At the end of the year tutors identified as being out of line are reported to the Award Meeting of the Examinations and Assessment Board, which can make allowances where necessary, particularly in the case of a borderline student.

This system for dealing with TMAs is clearly much more complex and reliant on human factors than that used for CMAs and there is consequently more room for error. On the whole, however, the system has worked reasonably well and students generally get the result of their TMA within about fourteen to twenty-one days of completing each assignment.

This says a great deal, not only for the conscientious way in which tutors have tackled the problem, but also for the efficiency of the much-maligned British Post Office. On average each full credit course of the Open University calls for students to undertake eight TMAs in the course of each year. Since part-time tutors are paid fees that are directly related to the number of TMAs that they mark, it is clearly an expensive system. Indeed if we were to increase the number of TMAs per annum from eight to nine in each course, it would cost us an additional £100,000. When we are short of resource there is always considerable pressure to reduce the number of TMAs required.

In the case of both CMAs and TMAs the student is assessed on the best 75% of the tests that he undertakes. This allows us to ignore his worst performances and takes account of the fact that, especially in multi-disciplinary courses, there may well be certain aspects of the course – for example, music in the arts foundation course – which are conceptually or aesthetically difficult for him.

A further problem for the University, presented by both TMAs and CMAs, arose from the necessity to use them as another pacing mechanism for students. If the results of an assignment are made known to all students who have submitted answer papers on a given date, it is obviously not proper to accept later submissions from other students, since the bush telegraph might well enable such late entrants to have gained access to the correct answers. We have therefore had to determine a 'cut off date' for the submission of each assignment beyond which it will not be marked, so that a student must progress at a reasonable rate if he is to submit his assignments in time.

Every course offered by the University has a final examination, which we realised would be a complex and costly exercise imposing hardship on many of our students. We simply had to face this fact, although we took what steps we could to minimise the degree of disturbance. Thus in 1971 each examination was held on two separate occasions. By arranging for one diet to be held in the morning and the other in the afternoon we offered an alternative to people such as shift-workers or housewives, for whom certain times of day are much less practicable than others. This meant, however, that every examination board had to write two separate examination papers of equal standard and demand. Since it is almost impossible to achieve such equality examination boards may ultimately have to adjust the grades awarded in one or other diet.

We go to great lengths to try to ensure that no student is disadvantaged by our examination system. Examinations have been held, for instance, on merchant ships where the captain has acted as invigilator and a member of the crew has been the only candidate, in prisons, and in foreign countries, to which a number of students have had to move through the exigencies of their work. All this adds to the complexity of the organisation and to its cost, but it has been accepted as necessary and desirable to provide such a service to our students.

The examination scripts are sent to the examiners, who are usually selected from the part-time tutorial staff, together with a marking scheme. All the examiners attend a co-ordination meeting of the Examining Board, where they are briefed about the way in which they should mark the papers and the standards that are expected of the students.

Once marking is complete the examination board meets to arrive at an overall collation of the performance of each student and to determine the award of credit. The computer produces for each student a print-out of the

Course Result Matrix

Overall continuous-assessment grade

	A	B	C	D	F	R
A	W^1	W^1	W^2	W^2	X	Y
B	W^1	W^2	W^2	W^2	X	Y
C	W^2	W^2	W^2	W^3	X	Y
D	W^2	W^2	W^3	W^3	X	Y
F	X	X	X	X	Z	Z
R	Y	Y	Y	Y	Z	Z

Examination grade

Key

'W' All students in these cells will achieve at least Pass 4 (or Pass in the case of foundation courses).

'X' The Board will normally consider students in these cells individually to decide whether they should be awarded Pass 4 or be failed. Those students with a high grade on one or more elements of the assessment will be more favourably considered.

'Y' Students in these cells will normally fail.

'Z' Students in these cells will automatically fail.

FIGURE 4   Course result matrix

overall grades obtained in continuous assessment and in the final examination. These results are then laid out in the form of a matrix which shows the number of students falling into each cell (Figure 4). It is clear that if a student obtains a grade A both on continuous assessment and in the final examination he will be awarded a credit with distinction. This is not a difficult decision. Similarly if a student obtains a failing grade of F on the continuous assessment and on the examination he will fail. The problem is what to do with students who obtain a passing grade only in the final examination, or vice versa. The cells in the shaded area in Figure 4 represent the area where judgement has to be exercised.

It was recognised from the beginning that this would be a major problem and many of us, including myself, argued very strongly that there should be a 'third assessment'. My original idea was that this could take the form of a subjective judgement of each student made at the summer school. If a student had performed very well on continuous assessment but very badly in the final examination there were two possible explanations. The first was that he had obtained help throughout the whole course from some third party and that his continuous assessment was, therefore, a spuriously high estimate of his capacity. The second was that he was really a very good student but that under the stress of the examination, because of illness or psychological trauma, he had performed much below his proper capacity. A judgement about which of these explanations was correct could be made on the basis of a 'third assessment' from a tutor of the performance of the student at summer school in a face-to-face situation.

It became clear that two factors would militate against this idea. The first was that some course teams held very strongly that the whole benefit of a summer school would be lost if a student knew he was liable during the week to be assessed for examination purposes by his tutor. The second was that some later courses did not require a summer school. Some other solution was necessary. The one that found most favour was that of calling on students who fell in the shaded cells in Figure 4 to attend for a *viva voce* examination after the written examinations were over, and this has in fact been the custom ever since. Thus the *viva voce* becomes the 'third assessment' when this is needed. We hope that thereby, we come to fair decisions in those cases represented by aberrant results in the matrix.

The whole process is monitored by the external examiners, who are in attendance at the meetings of the examination boards. Great efforts are made to be fair and to award credit only where it is due. On the other hand errors of judgement are bound to creep into the system from time to time, leading to injustice being done. For this reason we have established an appeals procedure whereby a student who is aggrieved may write in and ask for a re-scrutiny of the results. Unfortunately a very large number of disappointed students take advantage of this offer, and as a result a great deal of extra work is imposed on course team chairmen and chairmen of examination boards. Most of these appeals are rejected because they are found to be unsupported by adequate evidence. A few are accepted and no doubt thereby a certain number of injustices are put right, but it is an expensive way of operating and I am in some doubt as to whether it is a justifiable additional expense.

Immense pains have to be taken to try to ensure that the system used by the Open University for the accreditation of courses is a fair and efficient one. It is also a relatively expensive system to operate and the average cost of the examination system per student per annum comes out at £6. Consequently it is not surprising that many of us wish that we could come up with a better system of assessing student performance, which could be operated with less difficulty and with equal fairness. This, however, remains a pipe-dream. Every other university that has tried to experiment with new ways of arriving at an assessment of performance has had the same experience. The hard fact of the matter is that a new method of assessing performance remains a mirage. It seems that for the foreseeable future we will have to struggle on with the methods that are available despite their problems, stress and high cost.

3

THE
STUDENTS

9

THE DEMAND FOR ENTRY

When the Open University was established as a degree-awarding institution offering courses of university standard, many of its critics challenged the assumption that there would be a large and sustained demand from adults for this type of education. What was the evidence that the demand would be forthcoming? What has the demand actually been?

When people first started talking and writing about a 'University of the Air' they often waxed eloquent about the need for such an institution. Almost to a man they seem tacitly to have assumed that there would be no shortage of demand for it from the adult population. This assumption was presumably based on the fact that very large numbers of adults did seek education through one of the bewildering variety of opportunities that already existed. Since, as we have seen, virtually all these opportunities were of a kind quite different from that which was to be offered by the Open University, this assumption was not necessarily valid. Yet even the Advisory Committee in its Report of 1965 ignored the problem of demand.

On the other hand the Planning Committee saw clearly, and for the first time, that the estimation of demand would be a matter of critical importance. Yet the evidence available to them was exceedingly sparse. They tackled the question in two ways: by a combination of calculation and assumption, they made rough estimates of the sorts of populations that they could expect to serve, and they commissioned through the National Institute for Adult Education a survey of a sample of the adult population.

Their first set of calculations and assumptions was based on figures from the Robbins Committee Report. These showed that the number of places available in higher education in Britain was, and had been for many years, considerably lower than the demand for higher education – and very much lower than the number of people who could benefit from higher education but had not made any demand for it. Many people had, in fact, been born too soon for them to benefit from the expansion that followed Robbins. Rough calculations indicated that, of the adult population of Britain between the ages of 21 and 50, well over a million people fell into this category. The Committee was realistic in recognising that only a small proportion of this vast group of adults would, at a later age, wish to go back into higher education. The question at issue was what proportion would be so willing. The Committee guessed that 10% might be a reasonable figure, and some 100,000 people might therefore want to take advantage of the opportunity that the Open University would offer. Similar calculations were made for particular occupations. In England and Wales there were known to be more than 250,000 certified teachers who were not graduates. Many of these could enhance their salaries and their expectation of promotion by achieving graduate status. The Committee again assumed that some 10% – about 25,000 – might wish to take up the Open University places.

These figures represented, at best, a pool of motivated adults who might want to better themselves. If the pool were to be drained would it be continually refilled by new adults who had been denied the opportunity of higher education? Or had that denial been eliminated by the expansion in the number of conventional university places that had followed Robbins? One answer to this question was the fact that the expansion had not materially increased the proportion of school leavers going to universities. At best it was coping with the 'bulge' and the 'trend', with the enormous increase in the numbers of qualified school-leavers. The Universities Central Council for Admissions figures, published in 1969, showed that only about 50% of those who applied for university entrance were actually admitted. Nevertheless the increasing opportunities in polytechnics and teacher training colleges were probably having an effect in reducing the number of qualified entrants who were being denied places in higher education.

If that were true of the qualified school-leavers, what was the position of the unqualified? How many children, capable of entering higher education, actually left school at 15? A figure had been recently published,[18] based on an opinion poll conducted amongst school-teachers, indicating that there were no fewer than 40,000 such children each year. On this sort of argument the Committee concluded that the pool of motivated adults would be continually topped up and that the Open University would be meeting a continuing, not an evanescent, need.

To these rough calculations and assumptions the Committee wished to add something firmer, and for this reason they commissioned a survey of a sample of the adult population. The general public knew nothing about the nature of the programme to be offered by the Open University and it was therefore essential to inform the individuals in the survey about it. A sample of 3000 adults was selected by the National Institute for Adult Education in seven areas of the country and was given as much information as was then available about the new institution and the courses that it would offer. These adults were asked to say whether they were interested in the idea, and whether this interest was so strong that they would certainly be amongst the first applicants for entry.

TABLE 2   NIAE survey of 7 areas (excluding London)

	Sample	Returned form	Very interested	Would definitely join
Total	3000	2100	150	27
%	100	70	5	0.9

Despite the difficulties of the operation and the relatively small sample, a number (0.9% i.e. 27 people) said that they would definitely be amongst the first applicants (see Table 2). By extrapolating this figure to the whole adult population of Britain, it was estimated that the immediate demand for places at the Open University would be somewhere between 170,000 and 430,000. The validity of this estimate depended, however, on the assumption that the entire adult population of Britain would be as well informed about the Open University as were the individuals in the sample, an assumption that was very unlikely to be valid. We have since proved just how invalid it was. We have commissioned, in March/April of each year, a survey of the adult population designed to discover what proportion of the general public was aware of the existence of the Open University. The results of this series of surveys are given in Table 3.

TABLE 3   Level of awareness – 1971–1976

% knowing of the Open University (in the Spring of the Year: March/April)

Socio-economic groups	1971	1972*	1973	1974	1975	1976
All	31	40	49	65	62	64
AB	66	78	78	85	87	88
C_1	50	58	71	82	77	78
C_2	21	30	40	57	58	56
DE	12	22	30	50	44	47
C_2, DE	19	27	33	53	51	50
All men	33	43	54	65	64	70
All women	29	37	45	65	60	58

* January

By the end of 1970, just before we admitted our first students, some 31% of the total population had heard of the Open University but only about 19% of those in classes C_2, D and E, (the working classes) had heard of it. Awareness has increased steadily since then, but even in 1975 more than half of those in the lower socio-economic groups remain ignorant of the opportunity offered by the Open University. The general public is usually slow to become aware of new developments of this kind. Should we have spent money on advertising our existence more widely in order to attract applications from the more deprived classes of society? The cost of trying to persuade the population of this country to wear seat belts in motor cars ran into millions of pounds and was only partially successful. The cost of persuading them that an opportunity exists for them in the Open University would have been no less. It is perhaps surprising that so many people have already heard about us.

In any case, it is clear that the assumptions made, when the results of the sample survey carried out for the Planning Committee were extrapolated to the entire adult population, were wholly invalid. Since in 1970 less than one in three adults had actually heard about the University, the figures from the survey might have been more realistic had they been reduced by two thirds to give an expected demand for entry of between 50,000 and 150,000. But in 1969 we had no such estimate of awareness to guide us and the figures from the survey were the only ones available for planning purposes and on which to base the crucial decision as to how many students would be admitted in 1971.

If we planned to admit a very large number of students in 1971 we would run the risk of having too few applicants to fill the vacancies. Such an outcome would have been politically disastrous. On the other hand, to plan for a small intake might disappoint many people and thus discourage other applicants in future years, and would nullify the cost benefits arising from economies of scale. Although we had no knowledge of the precise cost of the programmes that we were still to develop, it was apparent that certain costs would fall into the category that could be termed 'overheads'. We knew, for instance, that we would have to pay the BBC nearly £2 million per year, whatever the student number, be it one or a million. The costs of maintaining the central academic and administrative staff would similarly be constant, whatever the number of students. Whatever happened, these overheads would account for a large fraction of our total expenditure. We knew much less about the other teaching costs. Each student would require one copy of the correspondence material, which would have to be printed, packed, and posted to him; and would also need the services of a tutor and a counsellor, and a share of accommodation at a study centre. These so-called 'direct student costs' would increase in proportion to the number of students.

Calling the overhead expenditure A and the direct cost per student B, then our total expenditure T could be expressed as

$$T = A + Bn$$

where n is the number of students. The cost of educating a single student would then be

$$\frac{T}{n} = \frac{A}{n} + B$$

and would fall as n increased.

The Planning Committee estimated on the basis of the rough and ready budgets that Christodoulou and I had prepared late in 1968, that the overhead expenditure (A) would be of the order of £3.5m a year. Consequently, the cost of the overhead per student (A divided by n) would be £140 if we had 25,000 students but would rise to £700 if we had only 5,000 students. To each of these figures we would have to add the unknown value of B to obtain the total annual cost of educating a student. The comparable figure in other institutions in 1968 was about £670, and we were anxious to hold our costs well below this. We could not afford to start on a pilot scale but we must aim to be as big as possible from the very beginning. On all the evidence before us, inadequate as it was, we could expect to have at least 25,000 applicants in the first year.

Accordingly, the Planning Committee fixed the target for student admissions in 1971 at 25,000. It was not a figure that was to go unchallenged. Although large numbers of students reduced the cost per student they clearly increased the total cost. We had to persuade the Department of Education and Science and, even more difficult, the Treasury, to accept the figure of 25,000 admissions and the total cost for the university that would result. It was accepted immediately by Jennie Lee and by Edward Short, the Secretary of State, but was challenged by the Treasury and the Chancellor of the Exchequer, Roy Jenkins.

Peter Venables and I were summoned to meet Mr. Short and asked if, on consideration, we wished to stick to our proposal to admit 25,000 students. We were virtually asked to guarantee that we would attract more than 25,000 applicants and that the University would be in a fit state to accept that number and teach them properly. We felt we had no choice but to take our courage in both hands and say 'yes' to both questions. Mr. Jenkins had suggested that it would be wise to begin the Open University with a much smaller number of admissions – 5,000 or at most 10,000. He was motivated in part by a desire to curtail the total expenditure, but he also argued that it would be wiser to start on a small scale as we were an experimental institution. This was an argument with which most of us had considerable sympathy, and we rejected it only because of our overwhelming desire to achieve economy of scale. We felt that if our costs per student were as high as those of other universities we would be very vulnerable.

Our proposal was eventually accepted by the Treasury and we were given authority to proceed. In the summer of 1970, following the change of government, we were faced with the same questions, emanating perhaps from the same officials in the Treasury who had suggested them to Mr. Jenkins about a year earlier. By that time we knew the exact number of applications: during the first six months of 1970 we had received 43,000 of them. We stuck to our guns and successfully gained the agreement of the new government to proceed with the admission of 25,000 students in 1971. No doubt they were swayed by the actual number of applicants, for the votes of 43,000 adults and their families could not be utterly disregarded by any politician.

I am however anticipating by a year. In 1969 the target figure of 25,000 admissions for 1971 was fixed. They would have to be selected from a number of applicants that was wholly unknown but could be as high as 430,000. How was this to be done? How were we to handle such numbers of applications? To answer these questions we set up in 1969 our first standing committee, the Admissions Committee. So important were the implications that I felt it necessary to be Chairman of the Admissions Committee myself. Our first decision was that the basic method of selection should be that those who applied first should be admitted first; 'first come first served' was as good a principle as any that we could devise. We could not use educational qualifications as the basis for admission for there were to be no entry requirements. Yet we knew that 'first come first served' might, if applied without constraint, produce a completely unacceptable group of students. We would have to balance the intake of students to each foundation course, for we could not have all our students studying humanities and none studying science. There would thus have to be a quota of places for each foundation course. We would also have to balance the intake across the country by setting regional quotas; as a national institution it would never do if all the students came from Scotland and none from Wales, or if we had too many from London and not enough from the North of England.

We also had long and anxious debates about the need to provide places for deprived members of the community. We guessed that they would be among the last to hear about the new institution. How then could we help them? Could we give them priority in the entrance stakes? In the event we decided that the best we could do would be to have a quota for each occupational category. Then, by setting the quota higher for those occupations which included blue collar workers we might be able, within the limits of the numbers in each category who had actually applied, to give some preferential treatment to the deprived adult. We also wondered whether we should do something to try to balance the intake between men and women, especially since women were even more greatly deprived of opportunities for higher education than were men. On the other hand, we expected that women would be especially attracted to the institution and that this problem would solve itself. We also thought we might prove very attractive to elderly and retired people who had a great deal of leisure in which to embark on educational programmes. It was well known for instance that middle-aged and elderly students formed the bulk of many of the classes offered by the LEAs, the WEA and the extra mural departments. We did not feel that the Open University would be fulfilling its place in society if it were to cater largely for this group. They should not be excluded, but it was even more important that younger people should have the opportunity of qualifying, thereby increasing the contribution that they could make to society during their active working lives. We therefore set up a system whereby we could apply a weighting factor against older applicants; but we decided that we would not apply it unless the bias was very large.

Finally we were concerned that we might attract a significant number of applications from adults who by no stretch of the imagination could be regarded as ready to embark on a programme of education at the higher level. We did not want to reject any application, even from an individual who was considered wholly unprepared. A compromise was therefore adopted whereby we might advise an applicant to withdraw and embark instead upon more elementary preparatory studies; if he chose to reject that advice, however, we would allow his application to stand. In the event only 565 candidates (about 2%) were so advised and, as far as we know, most of them accepted the advice. These then were the basic decisions taken by the Admissions Committee in 1969 and endorsed, not without some misgivings, by the Senate.

We further agreed that we would not select and offer places to any students until all the applications had come in. It was only by this means that we could run a computer programme incorporating the agreed quotas and weighting factors. This programme would have to be written and 'debugged', and would be run during August so that we could make offers to the selected 25,000 students in September 1970.

Our immediate need was to design an application form, which would have to be printed and despatched to all enquirers from the beginning of 1970. There were long and anxious discussions about its precise nature. It was often said, and may well have been too true to be funny, that the ability correctly to fill in an application form would be the first real test of an applicant's suitability for the Open University – it was even suggested that we should award a credit for so doing! But there were other more serious questions. How far could we ask for information about educational background and educational qualifications? Clearly we would want to have access to such information for purposes of analysis afterwards. Yet if we were to ask for more than a minimum of information we might well be accused of using it in the admissions procedure. In the event we chose a relatively simple form of enquiry about the age at which formal education had ceased and the maximum level of qualification achieved. How much information should we ask for about the nationality and birthplace of our potential students? We knew that we could offer courses only to students who were domiciled in Britain, but we did not wish to imply that there would be any sanction against either the immigrant or the itinerant population. We therefore felt it safer not to ask for such information, although we knew that we might later regret being unable to analyse for this kind of factor. The only information we did ask for under this heading was the first language of the applicant.

It was difficult to decide how much of the information contained on the application form should be transferred to the computer record. The research staff of the University wanted the computer to store as much data as possible but I doubted whether we could afford to do this or could recruit the extra number of computer staff it would necessitate. I therefore pressed to have the absolute minimum of information put on the computer. In the event, the actual number of applications was not all that large and I have no doubt that historians will blame me for a decision that was imposed for reasons of expediency.

By the end of 1969 we had finished the preparation of our first prospectus and 100,000 copies of this, together with copies of the application form, were packed in envelopes, ready for despatch to enquirers. The big question was how to promote enquiries. We printed about half a million leaflets giving a brief description of the University and inviting people to send an attached coupon for the prospectus and application form. Similar information was published in one issue of *The Radio Times* and in a number of national journals. The leaflets were distributed all over the country, through such outlets as institutions of further education, professional associations, employers and trade unions. The opening date for receipt of applications was set at January 15, 1970. By Christmas 1969 we had done everything we could think of, within our limited budget, to attract applications from people who wanted to be students. We now faced the onset of reality when all the estimates that had been made would be put to the test.

We set up in the Registry a bulletin board on which we recorded day by day the number of enquiries and of applications received. It became an almost daily habit for senior members of the University to drop in there to see how things were going. It was an anxious time. The graph in Figure 5 indicates the rate at which enquiries and applications were received throughout the six months that followed.

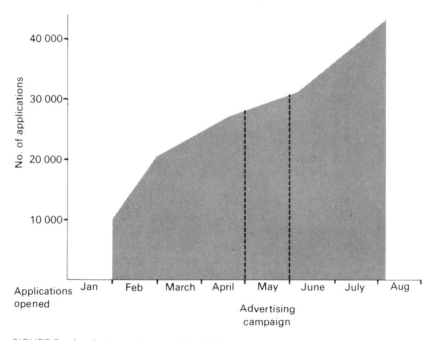

FIGURE 5   Applications January–July 1970

After the initial rush of early applications there was a gradual falling away and we became concerned about our ability to fill all the 25,000 places. The Information Office then launched a second-phase advertising campaign in carefully selected journals and this produced a marked increase in the flow of enquiries and applicants. Towards the end of the phase the number was accelerating steadily, reaching nearly 43,000, which we considered a reasonable total. But it was not until July that we were able to breathe freely, knowing that we had enough applicants to fill all the places that we had fought so hard to secure from the Treasury. Overall, 130,000 enquiries yielded no fewer than 43,000 applications. This ratio of 1 in 3 was remarkably high, greatly exceeding that commonly achieved by other institutions of correspondence education or, indeed, by other campaigns carried out by mail in the fields of commerce and industry.

We were all of course intensely interested to know what would be the profile of the applicants. How many of them would be from women, how many from men? What would be the age and regional distribution? How many would apply for each foundation course? Detailed figures for the breakdown of applications in these categories have been published annually both in my Annual Reports and in compendia published from the Survey Research Department, and I summarise in Chapter 13 some of the trends over the first five years.

In this first year there were two prominent factors: first, the very high proportion of school teachers amongst the earlier applicants and, second, the preponderance of applications for arts-based rather than science-based courses. In the first month or two applications from school teachers represented nearly 50% of the total. These rather fell off during the application period and ended up at just over one third. The reasons are easy to see. The Open University had attracted tremendous publicity in the educational press and in consequence a very high proportion of school teachers had heard about us. In the second place certificated school teachers were particularly motivated to become graduates, not only because graduation led to an immediate guaranteed increase in income under the Burnham scales, but also because it offered a much better . prospect of promotion to a headship. Thirdly, we made it clear in the prospectus that we would give exemption from some parts of the degree for those already in possession of diplomas, including the teacher's certificate; in consequence the school teacher knew that he could obtain advanced standing as a student in the Open University and could expect to graduate in a shorter period of time than would be necessary for the non-qualified entrant.

The second prominent factor was the distribution of applications between the arts side and the science side, between the foundation courses in humanities and social sciences on the one hand and in mathematics and science on the other. The ratio amongst the applicants was approximately 60% for the first group to 40% for the second. The agreed quotas for admission to the University called for a ratio of 55% on the arts side to 45% on the science side. This meant that we had to attract a total number of applications considerably in excess of the total number of available places in order to fill all the places in the less popular courses.

Given the uneven distribution of public awareness about the Open University revealed by our surveys, it was to be expected that, amongst the 43,000 applications that we actually received, the proportion emanating from the lower socio-economic groups would be low. It soon became apparent that this was indeed the case. Only about 10% of our applicants gave as their occupational category one which could, by any stretch of the imagination, be held to fall within the working class, and it seemed probable that the real proportion of working class applicants was less than 5%. The great preponderance of applications came from middle class people of whom school teachers made up a considerable part. I should like to make it perfectly clear that this came as no surprise at all. It was precisely what we expected. Nevertheless, it attracted very considerable adverse publicity in the national press. The result was contrasted with the objectives that were said to have been put forward in the early days by Harold Wilson and Jennie Lee. The original objectives however make no explicit mention of any special provision for the deprived adult. The opportunity was to be available to anyone who felt himself able to benefit from higher education, not restricted to deprived adults. That is not to say that my colleagues and I did not share in a desire to increase the proportion of working class applications and admissions and to do something for the deprived groups in the community; but most of us felt that we could not hope to achieve this in the early years of the University's life. Indeed, since 1970, the proportion of applications coming from the working class has steadily increased, if only slowly. This increase is reflected in the growth of awareness of the Open University over the same period.

Nevertheless, the adverse publicity provoked me to defend the situation, both on these grounds and for the following reason. Applicants to other universities, being largely school-leavers, were placed in socio-economic groups by the occupations of their parents; our applicants on the other hand, being adults, were categorised by their own occupation. But what had been their fathers' occupations when they themselves were 18? It seemed to me probable that many of our students might be just those people who had not gone to a regular university when they left school precisely because they came from homes where they had been discouraged either for financial or social reasons. I asked Naomi McIntosh, Head of the Survey Research Department, to investigate this and she discovered that, in fact, some 85% of all our students had working class parents. My hunch had been right. Many of these students had, because of their own ability and drive, already climbed a few rungs of the social ladder before applying for admission, so that, by the time they did apply, they were in occupations that were regarded as 'middle-class'. We were in fact reaching many more people who had suffered the effects of early deprivation than we were given credit for. The fact that most of them had successfully struggled to overcome the effects of their early deprivation was itself a virtual guarantee that they would be highly motivated students.

I confess that I was not unhappy at the way things had turned out, despite the adverse comments in the press. Taking the longer view, there was one thing that would certainly be of no benefit at all to the educationally deprived adult – namely, for the Open University to be remembered merely as a glorious failure. This could well have been its fate had we admitted only those in working class occupations, many of whom would have been ill-prepared; the consequent high drop out might have been politically damning. It was much better to have as our first students a large number of school teachers who were motivated, well prepared and with time for study. If we succeeded with them we would not only have gained the time needed to polish our methods so that ultimately they might work effectively for less well prepared entrants, but we would also achieve the academic recognition that would enable us to tolerate higher drop out rates.

We also categorised the entrants to the Open University according to whether or not they had passed the minimal qualification for entry to other British universities, i.e. two subjects at Advanced level GCE ('A' levels), or their equivalent (see Table 4). Almost two thirds of all the entrants did possess such qualifications and only one third was unqualified in this sense. We have, through the years, studied the relative performance of these two categories and it is fascinating to look at the results, which are summarised in Table 10 in Chapter 13.

TABLE 4   Percentage of 'qualified' and 'unqualified' entrants

	1971	1972	1973	1974	1975
Less than 2 As	32.6	42.1	41.8	38.3	46.4
2 As or more	61.8	56.6	57.3	59.2	52.4
No data	5.5	1.1	0.9	2.1	1.1

When applications closed we began the selection programme on the computer, but before that we had been able to simplify the programme. Our applicants were much younger than we expected. The age distinction, from the cut off point at age 21 was very skewed, with a modal age of 27 and a very long tail upwards to a single applicant aged 82. Since only 7% of all applicants were aged 50 or more we decided that we need not after all apply any weighting factor against elderly applicants.

No less than 60% of all our applicants had applied to do two foundation courses concurrently, so that we had nearly 70,000 applications for individual courses. The view of those who were experienced in adult education, that a load of two full credit courses would be too heavy for most students, was amply confirmed in practice. Over the years students registered for two courses have tended to drop out of one of them, finding the load too heavy. This view was the more readily accepted when we came to realise that we simply could not afford the cost of teaching 70,000 student courses. We therefore decided that only the best prepared students would be permitted to register for two courses concurrently. We had graded all applicants for suitability (although their grades were not in fact used for the selection process) and only those graded A or B, amounting to some 20% in all, were registered for two courses. This greatly simplified the student programme by reducing the number of student courses from 70,000 to just over 50,000.

We then set in operation the computer programme that we had struggled to produce over the previous twelve months. It dealt with the applications in date order of receipt so that it was principally a programme of first come first served; but it had also to cope with the quotas for regions, courses and occupations. Essentially the programme dealt with the applications in date order, carrying them to the cells of a three-dimensional matrix, the dimensions being region, course and occupation. Since each dimension was handled independently the computer worked towards the desired quotas by a series of successive approximations, and in 1970 no less than 13 computer runs were required to reach a satisfactory result.

In early September we sent offers of places to 25,000 students; we also sent out letters to 5,000 other students putting them on the 'reserve list'. All remaining applicants were sent letters saying that we were sorry but that there were no places available for them in 1971. The next phase of the admissions process required those who were offered places to pay the registration fee by a given date, or the offer would lapse. Tacit rejections of this kind occurred much more frequently than we had expected and 20% of those offered places failed to register. This was probably a result of the mobility of our student population. They are mobile in a number of ways: they tend to have jobs which may require them to go to different places in the country; to be in the age group where their families are growing in number; to be faced with all sorts of new and unexpected difficulties that lead them to change their minds about starting an Open University course.

The vacancies that resulted were filled by making firm offers to those on the reserve list, but this turned out to have been too short. To reach our target we had to offer, as late as the end of November, some places to applicants whom we had previously rejected. This caused severe operational problems but we felt that it was absolutely necessary to achieve as nearly as possible the target of 25,000 students for which we had fought so hard. At the end of this topping up process we reached a final number of provisionally registered students for 1971 of 24,200, slightly short of our target figure but near enough to be acceptable.

Over the years we have made only minor changes in the admissions system, but we have become much more sophisticated in handling it and few of the difficulties experienced in that first year have recurred.

The main worry in 1971 and 1972 was the decline in the number of applications received for entry to the University in the second and third years of its teaching programme (see Figure 6). Was the pool of motivated adults being drained after all? Despite an accompanying reduction in the number of new admissions (for the Conservative government had reduced our budget and with it our target student population from 55,000 to 42,000), the drop in applications made it difficult to fill the course quotas for science and mathematics, the less popular choices; and in 1972 we only just managed to fill the available places in science from amongst the 32,000 applications that were received. To do so we had virtually to exhaust the reserve list of applicants and some students were offered the course in science even though it had been their second or even third choice of foundation course. Applications for humanities and social sciences continued at a higher level and we continued to turn away applicants for these courses. We were increasingly worried by the prospect that the number of applications would progressively decline to a level too low to sustain the University as a cost effective institution.

Fortunately our anxiety was unfounded, for in 1973, as Figure 6

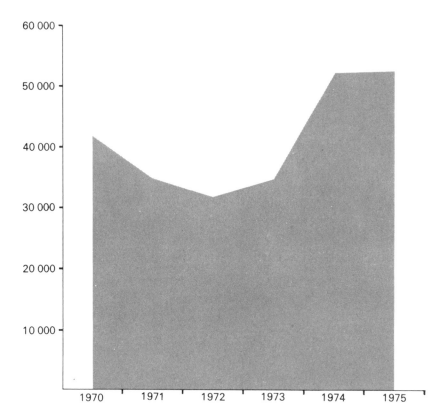

FIGURE 6   Applications 1970–1975

illustrates, the number of applications started, albeit slowly, to increase; a dramatic increase followed in 1974. I think there were two main reasons for the upward trend of the graph. The first was the increasing awareness of the existence of the Open University amongst the general public, which in turn increased the pool of potential applicants. The second and probably the more important was that we produced our first graduates. Only about 900 students graduated at the end of 1972, after 2 years of study, because only those who were awarded credit exemptions and who successfully completed two full credits in each of two successive years could possibly do so. Nevertheless, the first graduation ceremony in June 1973 attracted publicity and was followed by a new influx of applications. Nearly every graduate was the subject of an article in his or her local paper, and this represented a tremendous free advertising campaign for the University. No doubt many people waited for this smell of success before risking their own future in such a new and untried venture. In the following year we produced some 3,500 graduates and there was a corresponding upsurge in the application rate from 35,000 to 52,000.

The rising number of applications was, however, accompanied by a fall in the number of people that we were able to admit. From the beginning our total permanent grant was tied to a fixed target figure for the total number of students in the University. The relatively low drop-out rate for our students meant that a high proportion registered for courses in succeeding years, leaving fewer places for new students. The Conservative government reduced our target total student population from 55,000 to 42,000.

The return of the Labour government in 1975 saw an increase again, to 50,000, and our intake in that year went up to 20,000. Although the intention was to admit a further 20,000 in January 1976, the financial crisis of 1975 made it impossible to honour that commitment, and we were forced to cut back the number of admissions once more. For these reasons the probability of any given applicant actually being admitted to the University steadily fell (Table 5) from nearly 2 in 3 to less than 1 in 3.

TABLE 5   Probability of gaining a place for courses beginning in January

	1971	1972	1973	1974	1975	1976
Applications	42,992	35,182	32,046	35,011	52,537	52,916
Admissions (Places available)	25,000	20,500	17,000	15,000	20,000	17,000
Probability %	58	58	53	43	38	32

One result of the reduced likelihood of gaining entry to the University was that an increasing number of rejected applicants reapplied for entry a year later. Rejected applicants are sent copies of the new Prospectus and Application form for the following year as soon as they are available; furthermore, their letters of reapplication are antedated by 28 days. They can therefore be very early in the queue for the following year if they so wish. A considerable number of people took advantage of this opportunity and so had to wait only one year for entry to the University.

I am now fairly certain that unless there is a dramatic national recession, the demand for the University will be sustained. We are not dealing with a rapidly emptying pool of potential applicants, for the modal age of applicants has tended to fall over the years, thus directly contradicting the idea that the pool is a fixed one – if that were so, the modal age of applicants would steadily increase.

Various other trends have become obvious over the six years of applications so far. The first of these is the steady increase in the proportion of women amongst the applicants. One of the early fears was that the University would appeal primarily to middle-aged middle class housewives. This was not borne out in practice, for in 1970 the proportion of women amongst the applicants was as low as 25%. This proportion has however increased over the six years to nearly 42% in 1975.

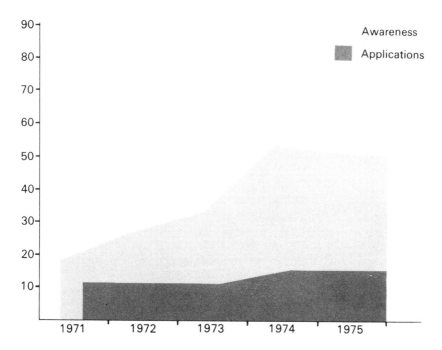

FIGURE 7 Awareness of the Open University and applications, socio-economic groups C$_2$, D and E

The second trend is the steady increase (Figure 7) in the proportion of applicants coming from occupations that could be categorised as working class. This is a slow increase but the fact that it has been a continuous one is of great interest to us. We hope that these people will come forward in increasing numbers as the institution becomes more widely known and as its reputation becomes established. Whether such an increase will be accompanied by a decrease in the success rate of the students in the University as a whole remains to be seen.

A third trend is the decline in the number of applicants who wish to study two courses concurrently. This has quite serious repercussions. The most obvious is that the average student will inevitably take longer to progress through the full number of credits needed to acquire a degree. Thus the total student population for a given rate of admissions per annum is larger than had originally been anticipated. Since the University is financed for a fixed total number of students this has further aggravated the reduction in the number that can be admitted each year. A second effect of this change in pattern is that the number of students subsequently progressing to the second and third level courses is reduced. Clearly if all students were taking two courses concurrently the course populations would be twice as high as if all students were only taking one course. When one considers the spread of students over a large number of more advanced courses this trend means that the less popular courses may attract too few students to justify their cost.

The whole basis of the admissions system has been called into question on a number of occasions within the University. The original 'first come, first served' scheme has been maintained from the beginning. Some members of the Senate believe however that a fairer system could be based entirely on a ballot. This would eliminate the advantage that accrues to those who read the sort of newspapers which give more extensive coverage to the University, and who therefore know about it early enough to be sure of getting their applications in at the head of the queue. Really disadvantaged members of the community may make up their minds more slowly, either because they are slower to become aware of the existence of the opportunity or because they are beset by doubts and delay their application in order to try to resolve them. A ballot would undoubtedly obviate such problems.

There are other members of the Senate who believe that the social purpose of the University can only be served if a very high priority indeed is given to those who come from the most disadvantaged classes of the community. While we eschewed this argument with some relief in 1970, we are now probably strong enough to be able to contemplate such a move. The problem is that one cannot admit more people from one particular occupational category than there are applicants in that category. In 1970 we had a quota for the categories in question that led to the admission of almost all the applicants within them. Only some 10% of applications came from occupations designated as working class. We admitted 25,000 students out of 42,000 applicants. Even if all working class applicants had been admitted they would make up only about 17% of the student population (4,200 out of 25,000). The situation in 1975 is that some 15% of all our applications now come from those in the working class. On the other hand we will admit only 17,000 students from a total of 53,000 applications. Consequently if we were now to accept all applicants from working class occupations they could represent more than 45% of the admissions (8,000 of 17,000). The problem is that amongst the middle class occupational categories also we can find many adults who were in fact deprived of any chance of higher education when they left school. In order to favour one group of occupations one would have to penalise others. It seems to most of us therefore that it is fairer to keep any bias small and to await increased numbers of applications from the working class rather than to set up a barrier against other occupational categories.

Another factor complicating the admission pattern is that for some people education becomes addictive, so that quite a number of students in the Open University do not want to give up studying once they have obtained their degree. The Senate agreed in 1969 (although I personally opposed the decision) that students should be allowed to take a maximum of 10 credits in the University and to count the best 8 results from them in computing the class of their honours degree. This means that students can gain 8 credits and qualify for an honours degree; but they may, if they choose, stay on for a further 2 years to increase their number of credits by 2 and give themselves a chance of improving the class of their degree. This might be a reasonable procedure if there were no limitations on entry to the University, but because of the fixed total number of students in the institution, every student who stays on beyond the 8 credit mark is keeping out one new student who might otherwise have been admitted. It is my hope that the Senate will in the near future reverse this decision and make it impossible for such people to stay on, unless they choose to become 'associate students', paying fees adequate to cover the whole cost of the course. They could then stay on as students without taking up places within the total number subsidised by the government.

It has always been a principle that a student, once admitted to the University, remains a student and has priority over all new applicants for as many years as he or she cares to go on being registered. This is a further complicating factor since some of our students want to have a year in which they do not take any course, possibly to have a baby or to change their job. This means that it is very late in the year before we can be fully aware how many actual ongoing students there will be, and of the number of spaces that are consequently available for new students.

The problem of ongoing registrations is indeed one of the trickiest we have to face. Students are asked in May each year to indicate for which courses they intend to register in the following year, and from these returns we have to make estimates of the ongoing populations of students in each foundation course in the following year, so that we can fix quotas for the admission of new students to these courses. This is especially important in science and technology where the quota is necessarily more restrictive, because each student in the course must be supplied with a Home Experiment Kit and our stock of these is limited. We cannot know for sure whether our estimates are right until the examination results are known in December, since unsuccessful students may opt to repeat their course, but with several years' experience to guide us we can now make fairly accurate estimates.

In part the complexity of the system stems from our large size but it is also the outcome of the fact that all our students are scattered. There is accordingly no way of settling the problems of each individual student by meeting him face to face during the first few days of term, as is the practice in other universities. Our computer-based programmes are vital to our existence, indeed without them we could not operate the admissions system at all. Their existence does not however make for flexibility, but for increased rigidity. It is almost impossible to make changes in the computer programme at a late stage; changes must be very carefully worked out in advance or the whole network of the complex system is put in jeopardy. This is a never-ending source of irritation to both academics and administrators, for it means that, for purely operational reasons, it is often impossible to do what is best for the greatest number of students at the right time. Since there is no feasible alternative, it is nevertheless a cross we have to bear.

10

CREDIT EXEMPTIONS

One of the first letters I received in the Autumn of 1969, just after my appointment as Vice-Chancellor had been announced, came from a man who argued very strongly for a system of credit exemptions. His case was a remarkable one. He had left school without any certificates at all. By the time he wrote his letter he was in his middle forties and had a string of diplomas and certificates of all sorts, each of which he had gained separately and from scratch, because no-one had given him any credit for one when he started another. He put to me the suggestion that he had already successfully completed enough study at the higher education level to warrant the Open University granting him a degree, without his taking any more courses at all.

Although it is true that a number of the claims he made went beyond what was reasonable, his basic thesis was tenable. There is, in this country, no system for cross-accreditation; there is no way in which individuals who have obtained credits towards part of a qualification in one institution can claim that credit, as of right, in another institution. When advanced standing is granted to an applicant to a university, in respect of studies carried out elsewhere, it is granted as a privilege, never as a right. Furthermore, it is a jealously guarded privilege awarded only when the case made is very strong. For studies carried out in institutions other than universities it is granted so rarely as to be almost unknown.

In the United Kingdom, and especially in England, where coherent degree structures are not broken up into modules, so that few intermedicate levels of achievement are recognised, it is correspondingly difficult to award credit in respect of studies carried out elsewhere. A credit system of the kind that I have already described is almost a pre-requisite for transfer of credit. Yet there are a large number of other factors that militate against it even where a credit system is operated.

This can be seen in those British universities which do have a credit system, like the medical schools and some of the Scottish universities. Although the credit system by its existence should make for relatively easy transfer of credit, the amount of such transfer is strictly limited. Thus in medical schools a student can usually transfer credit for a second MB, (the preliminary studies in normal biology) from one university to another, but seldom, if ever, can he transfer credit for any studies in clinical medicine. There is no good reason why this should be so. Similarly, in the United States, where a credit system is uniformly in operation, the transfer of credit is much less easy than one might expect. In discussing this problem with Charles Hitch, then President of the University of California, I discovered, to my surprise, that in his multi-campus university there was actually no automatic right of transferring credit obtained on one campus to another campus, even for a student who wished to follow the same degree course. Thus we have to look further than just the absence of a credit system to account for the reluctance to award credit transfer. One clear reason in the United States is to be found in the widely divergent standards adopted by different universities and colleges. It is reasonable to expect the faculty at Harvard University to be reluctant to award credit in their courses to a student who has passed similar courses in a second or third-rate institution elsewhere in the United States. This argument, however, cannot be applied with any force in Britain, where the standard of performance in any one institution is controlled by external examiners so that there is no comparable divergence of overall standards. The basic reluctance stems, I suspect, from nothing more than false academic pride. Why, say the academics of one institution, should we give our degree away to someone who has done the bulk of his study in other institutions? We must keep our degree for the students who went through our system. Others might argue that the degree that they are awarding bears the stamp of their choice of subject material which, in their view, is the best education to offer to the student. This can be countered, of course, by the sort of argument that I have already mentioned, that adult students know best what they want in study and that the choice should be left to them, rather than imposed by a faculty. Nevertheless, the belief that teacher knows best is widespread and I suspect lies at the root of much of the reluctance to admit a system of credit transfer.

A stronger argument rests on the contention that, especially in sequential programmes of study like mathematics and the sciences, the courses of later years assume knowledge gained in the earlier years of study at the same university; students who have studied earlier courses with a different syllabus in another university would thus be at a disadvantage if they transferred. While this is undoubtedly true it can be argued that, provided the applicant for transfer of credit knows about the disadvantage there is no valid reason to deny him the transfer. It is his own fault if he fails to fill in the gaps in his knowledge and to cope with the later courses.

In the Open University we chose to operate a credit system for reasons quite unconnected with the problems of credit transfer, but we were also determined to act as a catalyst for credit transfer in Britain. While the Open University was still proving itself, it was manifestly hopeless to expect to do this by securing agreements with individual institutions for the mutual recognition of credit. Initially, we would have to act unilaterally in awarding credit to our students. We would have to accept that students wishing to move from the Open University to another institution would for some time be unable to obtain recognition for the credits they had already obtained. We would be able to smooth the path of those adults who were joining us from elsewhere, although we could not do so for those who wished to move from us to other institutions. We therefore set up in 1969 a committee to make recommendations to the Senate about credit transfer, or as it was afterwards called, credit exemption. Once again this question seemed to me to be so important that I myself acted as Chairman of the committee throughout its first two years of operation.

It was clear that we should plan to cope with two different kinds of credit transfer. The first would operate where a student who wished to join the Open University had already achieved, in some other institution, a credit in a course which was nearly identical to the one that he would otherwise have to take in the Open University. At that time we knew that our foundation courses had no counterparts elsewhere – the nearest approach to our kind of course was the Foundation year at Keele University – but apart from that single example, other universities did not have courses of this type at all. Thus it seemed unlikely that many applicants to the Open University could have obtained credit in courses equivalent to our foundation courses, but this might not apply to our more advanced courses, some of which would be single disciplinary courses of a type comparable to those offered in other institutions. For courses of this kind we felt the need for a system of direct transfer and we decided to call it Specific Credit Exemption. In other words, if a student had already successfully completed a course in third-level Mathematics in another university, we would give him a specific credit exemption from our corresponding course in third-level Mathematics.

Next, we had to cope with the very many adult students, like my correspondent of 1969, who had qualifications that could properly be regarded as higher educational qualifications, but which did not conform to the pattern of courses that we would have on offer in the Open University. We decided to recommend the award of General Credit Exemptions, not tied to particular Open University courses, which would simply reduce the total number of credits that the student would require for his degree. We knew that amongst the first applicants there would be a high proportion of certificated teachers who did not have degrees. It was urgent to decide precisely how to treat such entrants. They had spent two and sometimes three years of study in a teacher-training college leading to a certificate qualifying them to teach. How much extra work and extra credit would they need in order to convert that certificate into a degree of the Open University? The answer to that question must be such as could be applied not just to the school teacher but also to many more categories of entrants. We must not give special privileges to school teachers and deny them to other qualified entrants.

Our examination of the particular problem of the school teacher did throw a good deal of light on the problem. There already existed a recognised route in other institutions for a certificated teacher to proceed to the degree of Bachelor of Education. This was a limited route in the sense that a school teacher who obtained his certificate in a college that fell within the Area Training Organisation of a particular university could proceed to a BEd only in that university; he could not proceed in any other university by a system of transferred credit. The time required to proceed from a certificate to a degree was usually two years, but in a few instances universities had made arrangements for the conversion to be completed by one year of further study. Other universities allowed certificated teachers to obtain an Honours BEd degree in a period of two years of further study. These were the limits within which we had to try to arrive at a fair and equitable arrangement of awarding credits in the Open University to certificated teachers.

We decided that each applicant to the Open University having recognised qualifications in the higher educational range would be granted one General Credit Exemption for each completed year of successful study in a recognised institution of higher education. This meant that a certificated teacher who had spent three years of study in a teacher training college, acquiring his certificate, would be granted three General Credit Exemptions in the Open University. He would then require only three more credits to complete a pass degree and five more credits to obtain an Honours degree. He would therefore fall midway within the range of provision of other universities; it would normally take a minimum of one year of full-time study to complete a pass degree and two years to complete an Honours degree. Since our students would all be part-time they would require a minimum of two years of study to complete a pass degree and three years to complete an Honours degree.

At the same time we felt that it was necessary to insist that students who obtained the maximum exemption of three credits should be constrained to follow recommended programmes of study; they would not have a totally free choice of the courses they could take.

This arrangement for General Credit Exemptions also applied to students who came to the Open University having already obtained a degree from another university, and who wished to study for a second first degree in a different area of study. This provision of a second chance, an opportunity to change direction in mid-stream, was felt to be of importance for adult students. The system of General Credit Exemptions could, moreover, be applied to all other forms of certification at the higher education level and it seemed to be a reasonable compromise between doing very little and doing too much in the way of making it easy for people to obtain degrees. The critical feature was that, to get a General Credit Exemption, the study for one year at the higher education level had to have been completed successfully and certified by the institution concerned. The decision as to what constituted a higher education level was one that could not be taken in advance, and that would have to be considered in respect of each application that came in for General Credit Exemption. This was the system that we followed until 1975.

We knew that we were embarking on a very complicated administrative problem in making an offer of General Credit Exemptions on this basis and in 1969 we were not ready to cope with the many claims that might be expected to come in from applicants. We therefore decided that we could not award credit exemptions to them; we would have to restrict the awards to registered students. This gave us an additional year to work out our procedures. The delay also meant however that applicants to the University could not know in advance precisely what credit exemptions would be awarded to them and this was clearly a disadvantage; they had difficulty in determining what their choice of course programme should be. We simplified the matter by deciding that, however many credit exemptions were awarded to a particular student, he would still be required to obtain a credit in at least one foundation course. This was held to be vitally important, since, for example, many certificated teachers might have obtained their certificate many years previously. We felt that our multi-disciplinary, multi-media courses were essential in giving such people a knowledge of recent developments in the subjects concerned. We could, therefore, advise all intending applicants that they could safely embark on the study of one foundation course, knowing that whatever credit exemptions they were subsequently awarded, that course would still be a requirement for the award of an Open University degree.

Of the 25,000 students admitted and registered for 1971, 13,000 applied for credit exemption. We had anticipated that this might be so, and in order to cover the administrative costs of scrutinizing the host of qualifications upon which such applications were based, we imposed a fee for the award of exemptions. The fees thus collected covered the cost of the Credit Exemptions Office, which then embarked on the massive task of classifying all the qualifications which were advanced as evidence of study at the higher education level. This was an invidious process which might cause offence to all sorts of organisations which issued certificates and diplomas, but it was one which we could not avoid. In making these decisions we made use of the expertise that was available amongst our own staff, but we frequently took outside advice as to whether we should recognise a particular qualification or not. Naturally, after the first five years the number of new qualifications that has to be scrutinized each year gets smaller and the system becomes easier to operate.

One of the major difficulties in awarding General Credit Exemptions is that no account is taken of the possibility that students may choose courses in the Open University that significantly overlap the courses that they have previously studied. This is not usually serious but it has been a source of increasing worry in respect of teacher-training certificates, because many teacher-training colleges throughout Britain have by now adopted courses of the Open University as the basis for their own syllabuses. Accordingly, students from these colleges who want to convert their certificates to a degree by entering the Open University may now be studying again courses which are precisely the same as those which have gained them credit exemptions. We have been having discussions as to how best to deal with this problem, which now requires urgent action.

The next problem that arose in relation to credit transfer came as a result of the Conservative White Paper containing a ten year plan for education in Britain[19]. One of the most interesting suggestions made in this document was for the initiation of a Diploma in Higher Education, which would be a final qualification of pre-degree standard representing the successful completion of two years study towards an Honours degree, which in

England usually takes three years. This idea found little favour amongst the universities in Britain, but a number of polytechnics and colleges felt that it was an important innovation that would provide a higher education for many people who might perhaps not wish to proceed as far as a degree, or who were not of a sufficiently high intellectual calibre successfully to complete a full honours degree programme. A Working Party of which I was Chairman was set up to examine the implications of the Diploma in Higher Education, and to prepare guidelines for its award. One main difficulty was that, once again, England was the odd man out in respect of honours degrees. In countries where an honours degree takes four years and a pass degree three, the clear need was for a diploma that would recognise two years of completed work at the higher education level. Yet the Paper prepared by Mrs. Thatcher's department made it clear that the Diploma in Higher Education should be the equivalent of two-thirds of an honours degree programme in the English system. In respect of honours degrees in Scotland and in the Open University, this was very close indeed to the amount of work needed to gain a pass degree. The difference between a pass degree and a Diploma in Higher Education was so small as to make the introduction of the latter a work of supererogation. For example, in the Open University, six credits were needed for a pass degree, eight for an honours degree. For the Diploma in Higher Education, interpreted in the way laid down in the White Paper, a student would require five and one third credits (two thirds of 8). What we really needed was a diploma that recognised the achievement of four credits. My attempts to get the working group to change the terms of the White Paper in this direction were, however, totally abortive.

The implications of all this for the Open University were difficult to foresee. The first question was whether or not we should offer a Diploma in Higher Education. The Senate decided that it would be unnecessary for us to do this since we did have a pass degree that was equivalent to six credits. We decided that, in the meanwhile, we would make no attempt to offer a diploma at a level lower than our pass degree, but we left the way open to do so later. Some of our staff questioned the need for a diploma at all since, in fact, we issue students with certificates of credit for each course that they successfully complete. Thus a student who holds four credits from the Open University already has a qualification which may, in time, come to be just as meaningful for future employers as any diploma given a special name to cover four credits. This is a very big question, and raises the issue as to whether degrees themselves are a necessary feature of higher education once a credit system is used fully. A final certificate that lists all the credits that a student has obtained is just as effective a way of recognising achievement as the award of a degree. Our problem was that we had no choice but to award degrees as long as all other universities did so, for employers and the world in general would not recognise the credit certificate alone.

The other problem that faced us as a result of the publication of the guidelines for the Diploma in Higher Education was that we might in the future have to undertake the topping up of Diplomas of Higher Education into degrees. As people holding the diploma emerged, so, after experience, they might have a legitimate desire to proceed as part-time students to convert the diploma to a degree. It would be wholly inadequate to award only two General Credit Exemptions to holders of the diploma; this would represent an unfair refusal to recognise the achievement of gaining the diploma, which would be two-thirds of an honours degree and equal therefore to at least five of our credits. It was open to us to apply our system of Specific Credit Exemptions. On the other hand there was no guarantee that the sort of course that would be offered by other institutions as part of the syllabus for a Diploma in Higher Education would match the sorts of courses that we in the Open University could offer. By this time, too, we had had to change our notions about our advanced courses. We had already had to modify our original aim of offering specialised honours degrees; thus our courses at third and fourth level would be less likely to match those offered in other institutions. How then were we to proceed?

These developments paralleled our progress in achieving academic recognition in the educational world in general. As a result, other institutions, universities and polytechnics had begun to approach us about the possibility of allowing credit transfer to those students who wished to move from one institution to the other. Such discussions were bipartite between two independent institutions. They were not conducted at a national level.

Clearly, if credit transfer between two universities is to work successfully, it must be on a wholly different basis from the system of General Credit Exemptions that we were accustomed to using. We were now dealing with students who had obtained credit in specific courses in universities and who had done so at the rate of two or even three a year. To offer only one General Credit Exemption for each year of successful study was thus inappropriate. This was indeed a parallel problem to that posed by the introduction of the Diploma in Higher Education.

We considered first a proposed agreement with the University of Lancaster. It was interesting to discover that this university was being approached each year by about thirty students who had obtained credits in the Open University and who wished to move from a part-time into a full-time study programme. We have no evidence as to whether this is a peculiarity of Lancaster University or whether it is common to all universities. If the latter, then the number of our students who might want to return to full-time study in other universities could well be as high as 1,000 or 1,500 per annum. This may be a small proportion of our total of 50,000 students, but it still represents a substantial number of individuals, with a real problem.

The Committee decided that the only way of resolving the difficulty was to assume that one year of full-time study successfully completed in Lancaster University was equal to one third of eight credits in the Open University. On this basis, it would clearly be justifiable to award two full credits in the Open University for each such year of completed study. One could of course argue that the real award should be two and two-thirds credits but, since we did not offer one third of a credit, our only choice was to award either two or two and a half credits. We decided to be less than wholly generous and to limit it to two credits. Thus a student who had completed two full years of study at Lancaster University would have to be awarded four full credit exemptions in the Open University. He could therefore complete a pass degree in the Open University by obtaining only two other new credits by study with us.

This proposal was not wholly acceptable to every member of our academic staff. There was in the Senate a number of people who felt that we were giving away too much and that to award a degree for only two credits-worth of study with the Open University was somehow reducing the special value of that degree, running the risk of bringing us into disrepute. I have never shared this view, which I believe stems from false academic pride. On the other hand, if the institution awarding the first two years of credit is not a university but another type of institution altogether, clearly the academic pride may well not be false and the argument has much more force. In consequence we made it quite clear that this kind of 'credit transfer' (as it came to be called to distinguish it from credit exemption), would be limited to British universities or to institutions awarding CNAA degrees.

At the same time, we obtained similar concessions from Lancaster University in respect of students who wished to transfer from the Open University into full-time study there. Clearly, Lancaster had much greater difficulty than we did in defining the precise credit transfer that would be allowed, since it, like other English universities, operates a much more constrained system of course choice. Thus the programme leading to each particular degree is defined and the choices available to students are limited to a much greater extent than is true for students entering the Open University. We had to recognise that a student who wished to enter Lancaster to read a degree in Science might well not have the right sort of credits to fit him for the Lancaster programme when he had had a completely free choice of courses at the Open University. Thus the award of advanced standing to an Open University student entering Lancaster University would depend on the pattern as well as on the total number of credits he held. Nevertheless, this was a major breakthrough and represented the first case of a bi-lateral agreement between two universities over the award of credit transfer. It is our hope that such arrangements can be multiplied in the future and that in this way our original intent of being a catalyst to the growth of credit transfer in Britain will come to be realised.

Courses of the Open University have been adopted by institutions in other countries. In the United States in particular, some twenty colleges or universities have begun to offer Open University courses, lock, stock and barrel, to external students. I discuss this development in more detail in Chapter 20. The University of Maryland is by far the furthest advanced in this respect. In 1975 they offered no fewer than sixteen Open University courses to students in their external degree programme. Already by June

1975 they had produced their first graduate to have obtained a degree almost wholly by the study of Open University courses. This is a degree of the University of Maryland and it is it, not the Open University, which examines the students and awards credits, although the course materials are identical. Thus a new problem of credit transfer has arisen. What happens to a student who is domiciled in Britain and registers for a degree with the Open University, who obtains a number of credits by examination in our system and who then goes to the United States and wishes to complete his degree by registering with the University of Maryland? Similarly, what happens to a student who, as an external student of the University of Maryland obtains credits in Open University courses, examined and awarded by Maryland, and who then moves to Britain and wishes to complete his degree by registering as a student of the Open University? We have here a perfect example of specific credit exemption; the courses followed have been identical in scope and content. The only problem that remains to be solved is to agree between the two institutions that the standard demanded in the examination for the award of a credit has been the same in both institutions. This is currently being examined in respect of transfers between the University of Maryland and the Open University, but the problems may well grow in size as the use of Open University courses by other institutions throughout the world becomes more widespread.

11

THE INHUMANITY OF THE COMPUTER

It was clear from the outset that it would be utterly impracticable to handle our student records manually, and our first major decision was not only to computerise all records from the start, but also to eschew the temptation of trying to organise any reserve systems that could be operated manually in the event of a computer failure. We thus put all our eggs in one basket – the computer installation.

I passed the responsibility for the development of the installation over to the University Secretary, Mr Christodoulou. In 1969 he spent a lot of time taking advice about the sort of installation that we would require and how best to write the necessary programmes to enable the University to become operative in 1971. The computer was installed at Milton Keynes in January 1971. We could not move any faster because the buildings necessary to house it had not been started until July 1970, and could not be finished in less than 6 months. Nevertheless our first computerised system, for handling all applications for admission, had to start in January 1970. This awkward hiatus was filled by borrowing time on a neighbouring computer at the Cranfield Institute of Technology, which lies only some six miles from the Open University and which operated a computer installation compatible with the one which we chose.

Our computer was not purchased but rented and, by adding new storage capacity and other facilities each year, we were able to use it satisfactorily until 1975. By this time it had become clear that we needed an increase in the size and flexibility of the installation to handle effectively the number of students that were now in the system. After a great deal of discussion, we decided to change from an ICL to a UNIVAC machine. This decision, which involved choosing an American computer instead of a British one, was not easy and we made it only after the most careful consideration, not only by our own Computer Advisory Committee but also with the assistance of external assessors. The changeover from the one installation to the other was a desperately difficult task and involved translating over one thousand individual computer programmes into the rather different language necessary for the new machine. As a result we were able, during 1975, to make few improvements or additions to our suite of programmes, as the available time of systems analysts and programmers over and above that needed to subserve the essential ongoing functions was spent in transferring the existing systems to the new machine. We hope, however, that from 1976 onwards we will be able to modify our programmes where necessary and to add many new facilities to our present range. The new machine offers the potential for much greater flexibility and will allow us to obtain access to selected data with much greater speed.

In 1970 it was necessary to enter into the computer a record of every applicant for entry into the University. I fought hard to keep the entry as simple as possible, incorporating only the minimum necessary amount of information about each applicant. We intended that the information already stored about an applicant would become the basic computer record for him once he was admitted as a student, thus saving considerably on the time of the operating staff. Yet the computer entry was so greatly simplified that we had to make arrangements for storing the further information that was available on the application forms themselves. How were we to do this? There were strong reasons for maintaining detailed student records in the regions where the part-time staff who would come into contact with the student were located but, for the purposes of statistical research and analysis, a central records office was also vital.

We decided that the central records should all be carried on microfilm. Thus each application form, when received at the centre was microfilmed at the same time as the key data were transferred to the computer record. The original application forms were then sent to the appropriate regional office. Regional office records are still handled manually but we are planning to install computer terminals which will give them access to the central computer records.

At the centre, however, the file for each student is maintained only in microfilm form. The file is updated by adding a microfilm copy of all correspondence between the student and the University, and the result is that we can store the records for over a quarter of a million applicants and nearly 100,000 students in one filing cabinet in the Central Registry of the University.

The advantages gained are greater than merely saving on storage space, for the student records are not available to anyone who does not have access to a microfilm reader, and there is no risk of losing a student file because it has been taken, for instance, to another office, for no other office has microfilm readers. This enables the confidentiality of individual student records to be maintained very easily. As a large national institution we were extremely concerned about the confidentiality of our records, especially the names and addresses of all our students. Such a list would be a highly marketable commodity in the commercial world and we were determined that under no circumstances should students' names and addresses be provided to anyone outside the University. The decisions to microfilm all correspondence has been a major factor in enabling us to stick to this principle.

A further point which concerned us was the accessibility of the computer records of each student. Although we hold in the computer only the data absolutely vital to control the progress of students through the University, there is nevertheless a considerable volume of such data, and we were worried about the future legal situation regarding the maintenance of such computer records. There was great anxiety in the country at that time about the potential misuse of computerised records. In order to counter the legitimate fears that students might have, we agreed that any student could have a print-out of his own record, as it was held in the computer, on request. We charge a small fee for this but are prepared to provide such a print-out at any time except during the month of November, when the computer is very heavily engaged in the determination of final grades and the award of credit. It was axiomatic that such a print-out would be available to the student but not to anyone else, except authorised staff of the University. This system, combining free access to and confidentiality of records has worked very well in practice. The one major difficulty is that, operating under these rigid principles, we have been unable to provide the names and addresses of students to our own Students' Association. This undoubtedly has added to the difficulties that our scattered students have in making contact with others who live in the same locality. Nevertheless, we feel that this is a price we must pay in order to maintain the principle of confidentiality in undiluted form.

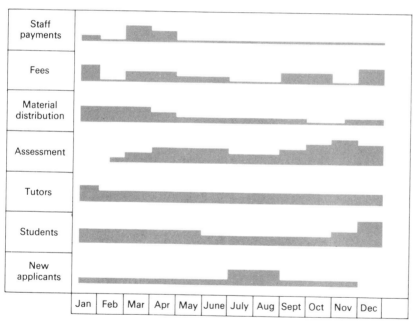

Note   Activities unrelated to student records, such as accounting, marketing, library etc. are not included in the graph.

FIGURE 8   Main activities of the computer

Figure 8 summarises the main activities of the computer in respect of student records throughout the year. When an applicant is accepted, has paid the registration fee and becomes a registered student of the University, the computer records the courses for which he is accepted, and the tutors allocated to work with him in marking his written assignments in those courses. Throughout the year the file is regularly updated with the grades obtained by the student in the two forms of continuous assessment (the CMA and the TMA) and letters informing the student of his grades to date are automatically despatched. At the same time, by our system of monitoring tutors' performance, the student's record will be flagged should his assignments have been marked by a tutor whose marking habits are aberrant – either too stringent, too lenient or too fluctuant.

The computer record also includes an account of payments, by the student, of both fees and deposits for Home Experiment Kits. The computer is programmed to print out at predetermined dates formal letters to the student notifying him that his fee instalment is due, reminding him that it is overdue, and excluding him from the University should he fail to pay his fees. The computer will also, at this stage, remove his name from the printed address list for distribution of course materials. There are many reasons why individual students may fall into arrears in their payment of fees and deposits due to the University. In many cases these reasons are discussed with a part-time tutor or counsellor who can often provide advice and help in solving any difficulties. Yet there is no way of telling the computer to write a sympathetic and understanding letter. In this sense it must always be impersonal and as a result the University will often appear to the student to be equally impersonal and inhumane. The best we can do is to operate two systems concurrently, using the personal contacts between students and part-time staff to counteract the impersonal formality of the communication between students and the computer.

These problems are greatly aggravated when mistakes are made. One classic example occurred in 1971 when a magnetic tape recording the payment of fees by 610 students was damaged in transit. The procedures for checking that the tape was undamaged were not properly followed and as a result the computer file failed to record these fee payments. Because of other delays at that time a decision had been taken to omit any reminder letters about overdue fees; consequently the unfortunate students received printed letters from the computer excluding them from the University for non-payment of fees. The mistake was quickly recognised as soon as the first of these students complained, letters of apology were despatched and students were re-instated. Nevertheless the incident attracted a good deal of sarcastic comment in the press and, although most of our students were very understanding and forgiving, some few were very upset. One letter of complaint remarked 'Not even the Gas Board cuts off supplies without first giving a final reminder!' Fortunately errors of this kind have been few and far between and, as time has gone on, we have tightened up our procedures to avoid the compounding by the machine of the results of human errors.

When the initial computer programmes for maintaining student records were prepared in 1970 there seemed to be plenty of time to prepare one for the award of degrees, since we did not expect to have any graduates before

1973. Unfortunately the growing demands on the data processing staff have over the years, prevented us from completing this particular computer programme. Consequently we have had to handle the award of degrees manually. This has been a Herculean task and has meant long delays between the computerised award of credits and the confirmation of the award of degree. It is manifestly impracticable to continue in this way and we hope to complete this new complex computer programme very soon. We have managed to operate the manual system so far only because the number of honours degrees so far awarded has been very small, but it is fast rising. Clearly no committee can physically scrutinize the detailed results for more than 500 individual students in determining the class of honours to be awarded to each.

During the period when Examination Boards are meeting, in November and December, there are likely to be frequent changes made in the records of students who have sat the examinations. Thus, an Examinations Board may decide that one of the papers that were set was much more difficult than another and as a result may decide to increase the grades awarded. This will require that all the records for the students who sat that examination are adjusted. Similarly they may decide that particular tutors, already flagged in the student records, should have their grades for continuous assessment adjusted upwards or downwards and this also necessitates changes in individual student records. Finally, the decision about how the conflation process is to proceed is one that will vary from examination to examination. This situation provides a further reason why, during the period of flux when a student's record may be changed almost daily, we do not provide print-outs for individual students. It is only after the whole process is over and the decisions about cut-off points of various kinds have been made that the student's record is again in a final form which may be made available to him on request.

The 'turn-round' period between the end of one academic year and the beginning of the next would be busy enough for the computer staff even if the programmes for the award of credits and degrees were the only ones in question. The period (November-January) overlaps the Christmas and New Year holidays, but the computer must work continuously in three eight-hour shifts per day throughout. The reason for this hectic activity is that it is only after the awards of credit have been decided that we can proceed to allocate students to courses and tutors for the following year. The students have made a provisional choice of courses for the next year as early as May and this information is stored in the computer record. In essence, it is only after ongoing students have been awarded credits (or not awarded them) that they can be allocated on a final basis. Secondly, it is only when new entrants have been allocated finally to specific courses that we can know for certain about the allocation of ongoing students to the same courses. The computer must also observe other constraints. For instance, we do not permit a student to register for a second level course if he has not obtained a credit in at least one foundation course. Similarly, he may not register for a third level course until he has obtained credit in at least one second level course. Finally, once the second year allocations to courses have been made, the computer has to match tutors to the students.

Every year we wonder whether we can conceivably complete all the computer work in this relatively short 'turn-round' time. By February the record in the computer for an individual student has started off once again on a new cycle, as he begins his second year courses, and this process will be repeated each year that he stays in the system, until he comes up as a potential graduate. The ultimate stage will be if he completes the maximum permitted number of ten credits. We have not yet reached this point with any student and I am not quite sure what the computer will do at that moment: whether it will print a letter saying 'You may no longer register in the University, You will have to go elsewhere' remains to be seen.

When this complex system of interlocking programmes is described as a single entity it is easy to see why we may appear to be inflexible in handling the problems of individual students. There is simply no time available during the period of maximum pressure to change computer programmes or to search through the computer files to find out individual aberrant entries.

As a result, we have to handle on a manual basis a fairly large number of appeals against decisions taken by our system. We try to deal with them as sympathetically as possible, and certainly a great deal of staff time is spent in trying to sort out the various problems. We find, as a rule, that it is not the computer which has made a mistake, but the student who has misinterpreted the result. However, the computer is an inhuman taskmaster and, if a student does misinterpret the result, it is well worth our while spending a little time straightening out his problem, and writing to him in a more humane fashion than is possible with standard letters printed and despatched on the instructions of a machine.

12

STUDENTS AND THEIR PROBLEMS

I meet fewer students than does almost any other member of my staff, though I do not seek either isolation or insulation. When I worked in Edinburgh I was involved in student activities to an extent quite unusual among Scottish professors, and I enjoyed it. The Open University has, however, made such demands upon my time that there has been virtually none left to spend in an exploration of the grass-roots. I am sure that this has been a positive disadvantage and that I would have done my job that much better if I had been in more intimate contact with our students. Now that the University is a going concern, I hope to be able to rectify this. I am about to become chairman of a course team for a very short course, and this will help to give me some of the insight that, so far, had been denied me. The fact remains, however, that when I try to write about our students, I can do so only at secondhand.

That they have a tough time is indisputable. Ours is the most difficult way of getting a degree yet invented by the wit of man. Our average student has a job and a family that demand attention. We bombard him with written material both academic and administrative. We try to run an open system and make great efforts to ensure that he is kept fully informed, but this often means that he gets so much detailed information that keeping up with it is a task in itself, so that I sometimes wonder if we are not (with the best of intentions) doing more harm than good.

Our student must plan his whole life round his course. He must try not to miss the broadcasts, and they may therefore determine his social activities on at least two days a week. He must submit his assignments on time, which means that he must regularly devote an adequate amount of time to reading and preparing for them: even holidays or family or business crises must not be allowed to upset that regularity. He may feel it necessary to attend his local study centre for tutorials as frequently as once a week, and that may involve him in a complicated, lengthy and costly journey. He must organise his summer holiday so as not to clash with the summer school that he must attend. All this organisation and planning is in itself a considerable demand on his time, his ingenuity, his tact, his patience. We should never forget that the full-time student does not have any such problem; his life is organised for him.

All this can be bearable if things go smoothly. When they do not, his difficulties can soon seem well-nigh insuperable. His job may call for a change in working hours, for an extended period away from home, and all his careful plans must then be recast. The university may make a mistake and leave his name off the list for the despatch of course materials; he then has to chase around to see whether his counsellor, his tutor, his regional office or the central correspondence services department can straighten out the muddle. Putting such a mistake right on the computer is often difficult if the source of the error is unknown; has his name been missed because he has been registered for the wrong course, or is it because of an error in the recorded fee payments? If the primary cause of the error is not corrected, inserting his name will not help because the computer programme will simply remove his name over again. When a mistake occurs the poor student may thus suffer from it for quite a long time, and this can have devastating effects on his work.

If things are often difficult for the student, they are no easier for his family, for their social life is also disrupted and they have no compensating personal satisfaction. They must make considerable sacrifices to support him, over several years. Their loyalty can be put to severe strain.

On the other hand the success of some individuals in overcoming difficulties that at first sight seem insuperable is quite astounding, and can make the sort of problems that I have been describing seem insignificant. One lady has already graduated; she is married and has eleven children, two of whom were born while she was a student. A deep-sea fisherman who spent his days trawling off the coast of Iceland obtained his degree in minimum time although he had left school at 15 with no qualifications whatsoever. He told us that the book he used most frequently was a dictionary because he did not know the meaning of many of the words used in the teaching materials. We receive assignments posted in such faraway places as Singapore from airline pilots or stewardesses who are studying; and we heard an amusing account from the captain of a nuclear submarine of the problems he encountered in carrying out his home experiments while at sea.

It is a never-failing source of amazement to me how pervasive the university now is. Hardly ever do I attend a social occasion, anywhere in the world, without meeting either a student or the relative of a student. This has been true in British embassies in a number of countries, at parties in medical circles to which I accompany my wife, and even on the occasion when I had the honour of lunching with the Queen. Other members of staff have met students while camping in the South of France and on visits to Ethiopia.

When I have managed, very briefly, to attend summer schools I have been, like my colleagues, immensely impressed by the enthusiasm and determination of the students; by the extraordinary mélange of people of all ages and from all walks of life sharing in the same experience; and by the sense of emancipation that so many seemed to have gained from the opportunity to study.

Perhaps, however, the most rewarding experience is to shake hands with the long line of new graduates at each of our graduation ceremonies and to see the faces of those who have been through the mill and come out successfully at the other end. The sense of accomplishment shines through the diffidence and shyness, and I realise that they share with me the feeling that it has all been well worth while.

We soon realised that we had a real chance to do something for some special groups of students, special in the sense that the Open University was virtually the only route, and certainly by far the most practicable one, through which they could obtain a higher education. The categories to which I refer are the severely disabled, long-term prisoners, members of HM Services overseas and their dependents, and merchant seamen. For each of these categories we considered that we had a special responsibility which, in various ways, we have tried to shoulder.

Our first move was to try to make the admission of students in special categories as easy as possible. We therefore exempted them from our regular admissions system based, as it is, on the 'first come first served' principle. We arranged that anyone who, after suitable investigation, was confirmed as belonging to one of these categories, should be offered 'guaranteed admission'. This was often a necessary preliminary to the conclusion of satisfactory arrangements with the authorities concerned. Sometimes it was associated, as in the cases of prisoners and service personnel, with financial arrangements which covered all the direct student costs so that the admissions could be regarded as supernumerary to the total number of students agreed with the Department of Education and Science, whose costs were met by our government grant-in-aid. In such cases the guaranteed admissions policy did not in any sense penalise the general run of applicants for whom the number of vacancies remained unchanged.

Our efforts to cope with disabled students began in 1970. Amongst our first applicants we recognised 25 disabled and offered them guaranteed admission. Each case was examined carefully, for there were some very grave disabilities and, at that early stage, we could usually offer no special facilities and were reluctant to admit those whose studies would consequently be seriously impeded.

We really became aware of the extent of the problem for the first time during the summer schools of 1971. Here a great variety of individual handicaps presented themselves to the summer school staff. It became increasingly apparent that many students, far from declaring any disability, sought to conceal it, believing no doubt that they would be at a disadvantage in competition with the able-bodied. We were dealing with a much larger number of disabled students than our records indicated. All sorts of *ad hoc* arrangements were made by staff to assist these unfortunates, but over the years we have increasingly tried to persuade people to disclose any disability so that we can tell them about all the devices and equipment available to help them. Nevertheless we still come across many who soldier on in ignorance of the existence of such aids.

In 1971 we estimated that at least 50 severely disabled students were admitted through the normal system in addition to the 25 who were offered guaranteed admissions. In 1972 we offered guaranteed admission to 190 applicants. Of these 65 fell within special schemes for the blind, the deaf and for spastics and 81 had other disabilities. The range of such disabilities was extremely wide; virtually all serious disabilities were represented, the most common being severe arthritis and multiple sclerosis. The criterion for guaranteeing admission was primarily whether or not, in view of his disability, an applicant could be expected to attend a full-time institution of higher education. The remaining 44 guarantees of admission went to able-bodied applicants whose personal circumstances amounted to disability in that they were caring for aged or disabled relatives or were unsupported parents. By 1975 the number of disabled students for whom the university was supplying special services had risen to well over 1200. It is interesting to note that in a survey carried out by the National Innovation Centre in 1973, only 554 disabled students were identified in all the institutions of full-time higher education in Britain. Thus the Open University is supplying the needs of more disabled students than all the other universities and polytechnics put together.

This is not done without cost. We estimate that, in very rough terms, each disabled student costs as much as two able-bodied students in terms of actual expenditure. This calculation takes no account of the extra overheads in terms of additional time spent by staff, administrators and academics alike in solving the multifarious problems that arise, and in maintaining special records of these categories of students. Indeed we take our responsibility for these students very seriously and our commitment to them was embodied in a public statement issued by the Council in April 1975 in the following terms:

In the light of (a) the University's experience of the particular value of its courses to disabled people and (b) the recommendations and advice given by the Senate and other bodies, the Council confirms that the University will continue:

(i) to accept its responsibility under Section 3 of the University Charter to meet the educational needs of its disabled students;

(ii) to give special consideration in its admissions policy to disabled students;

(iii) to offer continuing information and advice for full and part-time staff on means of providing for any special needs of disabled students;

(iv) to take all possible practicable steps to enable full participation by disabled students in all aspects of University life;

(v) to treat disabled students as equal members of the University for whatever programme of study they may be registered and to make special provisions only to enable participation (so far as is practicable) on equal terms with all other students;

(vi) to be concerned with the occupational prospects of disabled students and graduates of the University and with the vocational opportunities for disabled people generally;

(vii) to promote and maintain contacts with other institutions concerned with the education of disabled students, both in Britain and in other countries;

(viii) to seek adequate financial support for this area of its work, from central and local government services and other appropriate sources.

Our present arrangement is that any applicant with a disability is invited to state this on the application form. Such applicants are interviewed individually and may be recommended for guaranteed admission. In the regions senior counsellors give special oversight to disabled students, wherever possible helping them to attend study centres. Alternatively counselling or tuition sessions may be held in the student's home, or by linking him by telephone to a seminar.

On a more formal level we have set up a Liaison Committee for the Disabled with representatives from many of the voluntary agencies, and an internal Co-ordinating Committee for Disabled Students. We have also appointed a supernumerary Senior Counsellor who has the special task of co-ordinating all our activities for the support of disabled students. In all these endeavours we have been strongly supported by Mr Alfred Morris, Minister for the Disabled, and by the many voluntary agencies in the country. Each summer school campus is surveyed in advance and students receive information on its suitability or otherwise for particular disabilities. Every student who needs one has a matched personal helper, either a friend or a student volunteer who attends the school with him; and campuses have every kind of aid to enable the student to enjoy as nearly as possible the summer school experience of his colleagues. The Students' Association has played an important role in improving the opportunities for disabled students by providing student helpers, administering 'pairing' systems and organising special educational tours abroad for the disabled.

The development plan for special categories of disabled students will require a greater degree of central and regional co-ordination, and so we have recommended that a development team be formed within the central Regional Tutorial Services. This should be firmly linked to the central areas of student administration and integrated with the support structure in the regions, for we should never forget that these students must be dealt with on an individual basis. The assessment and supervision of the educational needs of applicants and registered students in any of the special schemes is a task for specialists, hence the need for provision of specialist support both in the regions and centrally. Although the precise pattern of counselling support may vary between regions, reflecting differences in local resources, there is a vital need to provide skilled staff and allow time for detailed assessment and continuing oversight.

In 1971 our only special project was for blind students. The Royal National Institute for the Blind and the Student Tape Library were able to give special assistance to those who were taking the foundation course in the humanities. This took the form of tape recordings and braille texts of the course units, assignments and some of the set books. The University arranged for special facilities to be available as required for the summer schools and the final examinations. 17 blind students registered provisionally for the course and all but one went on to final registration. 12 of those who completed their first course in 1971 continued study in 1972, and 16 more blind students were admitted in 1971 for courses in 1972. The Student Tape Library in 1972 offered taped units and braille texts for the social sciences foundation course as well as for that in the humanities. Some students, however, registered for the second level courses, for which neither the University nor the Student Tape Library could offer special help, apart from the facilities at summer schools and for examinations. These include permitting tape recorders for dictation of answers and the allowance of extra time during the examinations. By 1974 the number of courses available on tape and in braille had increased to 11, and the set books for a further 15 courses were also available. The number of blind or partially sighted students was 57.

The Students' Association now administers a scheme whereby a visually handicapped student is 'paired' to a sighted student who is willing to read the course material onto tape for him. This is a particularly useful development since the number of courses for which tapes and braille texts are available is limited.

The project for the blind in 1971 served as a pilot for a similar project for the deaf, starting with those applying for admission in January 1972. For them, scripts of broadcasts are needed, and they also suffer distinct disadvantages in study centres and at summer school, frequently through language defects as well as in ways more obvious to the outsider. Because of the need to give special assistance to them, the project in the first year was limited to the London and Manchester areas. 10 students were admitted in London and 4 in Manchester; in both regions the use of special study centres was arranged. Because of difficulties in transcribing scripts, only the social sciences foundation course was available. Both parts of the project included a 'preliminary course', conducted by the appropriate staff tutor and aimed at familiarising the students with aspects of Open University study before the course began in earnest. These preliminary courses, held in the late autumn of 1971, were highly successful. As with all our projects for disabled students help was given beyond all our expectations by those involved in making the project work.

By 1974 we were catering for 74 deaf students in all of the 13 regions. The Royal Society for the Deaf has provided a full-time liaison officer to work with us in devising suitable equipment to assist in this special project. Some of our summer schools are provided with special visual display units and in some the lecturer can use a microphone linked to special earpieces for the partially deaf.

Statistics about the performance of disabled students are very hard to extract. In the first place the degree of disablement varies enormously and disablement is frequently concealed or its severity minimised. Furthermore, conditions may change with time. For all these reasons the baseline figure for the population of disabled students is frequently changing. The data for our special projects for the blind and the deaf are, perhaps, the most reliable. In 1971, of our 16 finally-registered blind students, one gained distinction, 10 gained credit and 5 failed. By 1974, of 57 blind students, 8 gained distinction and 39 obtained credit, giving a success rate of 82%, at least as good a record as that of able-bodied students.

The comparable results in 1974 amongst the 74 deaf students was 10 distinctions and 59 credits, yielding an overall success rate of no less than 93%.

All in all it seems that disablement is no barrier to successful study in the Open University. Indeed it may well provide an additional motivation which produces an even higher success rate than that achieved by the able-bodied. It is, above all, very touching to meet such students and to discover just how strong is the sense of emancipation that studying with the Open University has induced in them; and just how important the institution has become to them.

In 1970 the Home Office offered to make available, in two prisons, facilities for inmates to take Open University courses. Both were men's prisons and, on security grounds, courses were excluded which involved the use of Home Experiment Kits. The Home Office paid each student's fees, and provided the necessary equipment in terms of set books, projectors, tape cassettes and films. The prisons' tutor organisers were appointed counsellors. The prisons' vetting of applications is designed to discover whether the applicants' motivations are genuine and well-directed and whether security considerations allow them to study, but selection remains a University responsibility. In all, 22 prisoners were admitted for study in 1971, of whom 16 were in Wakefield and 6 in Albany prison.

The experiment of 1971 was extended to other prisons in subsequent years and by 1975 110 prisoners in 11 establishments were registered as Open University students. Prisoners tend to have a relatively high rate of withdrawal from courses before the examinations. In 1974 22% of those registered withdrew and the overall pass rate was 45%. Nevertheless, for those who actually sat the examinations, the results are reasonably good. Over the first four years, 140 prisoners sat for 173 Open University examinations and achieved 131 passes, 12 merits and 11 distinctions, a pass rate of 89%. In 1974 Wakefield prison produced the first Open University prisoner graduate. This experience suggests that within the prison population there are people with the capacity for serious academic study and that it is right to make reasonable provision for them in education programmes.

After discussions with regional directors and the governors concerned, it has been decided in principle that Open University facilities will be extended over the next few years to 18 more prisons. The pace will depend on the availability of funds and the agreement in each case of the Open University.

Whenever Open University facilities have been introduced into a prison for the first time, a memorandum has been circulated by the Home Office describing the detailed action to be taken and the conditions to be observed. It includes the following points:

a) Each Open University prison will continue to recruit its own Open University students from its own population. Transfer, exclusively on educational grounds, from a prison which is not designated for Open University to one which is, cannot be permitted in the existing state of pressure on cell accommodation in closed establishments. This matter, however will be reviewed annually.

b) Only one subject, at foundation course level, may be studied by each Open University prisoner in the first year of the scheme at an Open University prison. This is to keep administration and arrangements for study as simple as possible at the start. In the second year and subsequently, and provided resources are available, the governor, after consultation with the Education Officer and Open University authorities may allow each prisoner who feels able to do so to study 2 subjects simultaneously.

c) For security reasons, the range of subjects which prisoners may study will continue to be limited.

Open University study is regarded as a leisure time activity. For the most part, prisoners study outside working hours, in the evenings, and over the weekends. Prisoners do not, however, have the same opportunities to relax for study as people in the community, or the same ease of access to a wide range of library facilities and academic contacts. Consequently, they may be released from their normal employment to study in the education centre during working hours without loss of earnings. This arrangement has been in operation since Open University facilities were first introduced into prisons in 1971, and it has been decided that this release may amount to 10 working hours a week.

There seems little doubt that, for this small group of students, the Open University is providing an opportunity of retraining that may prove of inestimable value in reclaiming them as active and useful citizens on their release.

In 1971 there were 89 students who, although based outside the United Kingdom, were registered for courses in 1972 by special arrangement with the Ministry of Defence. All were servicemen or 'UK based civilians' (mostly teachers and technicians) and their dependents, stationed in Cyprus. The Ministry supplied books, equipment and tapes and made special arrangements for tutorial reinforcement in lieu of summer schools. Tutorial and counselling services at two study centres were the responsibility of a team of servicemen working, through a senior counsellor in Cyprus, to the Regional Director of the West Midlands region. There were limitations on the number of courses available through this project, and in the first year only the foundation courses in arts, mathematics and social sciences could be offered. Later the foundation course in technology was added.

The experience gained in Cyprus in 1972 led to the institution in 1973 of a similar scheme for servicemen and their dependents in Germany. Here three study centres dealt with 191 students in 1973 and the scheme has subsequently continued with comparable numbers (see Table 6). The scheme is administered by the West Midlands Regional Office which has handed over its responsibility for students in Cyprus to the Yorkshire Office. Again, the courses offered through the scheme are the foundation courses in arts, social sciences, mathematics and technology. Students gaining credit at foundation level and wishing to proceed to higher courses are 'on their own' and cannot be dealt with through the scheme.

The special problems involved and the solutions found have been admirably reviewed by Wing Commander J. Stockton in a paper to our Advisory Committee on Services Education. The emergency in Cyprus disrupted many students' studies because of curfew, evacuation at short notice and intense overcrowding at the sovereign bases. It is remarkable how many students survived and gained credit.

The results obtained over the four years for both Cyprus and Germany are given in Table 6.

TABLE 6

Germany

		Total	Withdrawn	Fail	Resit	Pass
1973	No	191	50	24	n.d.	117
	%	100	26.1	12.6	—	61.3
1974	No	187	57	18	0	112
	%	100	30.5	9.6	0	59.9
1975	No	183	56	19	6	102
	%	100	30.6	10.4	3	55.7

Cyprus

		Total	Withdrawn	Fail	Resit	Pass
1972	No	83	25	5	n.d.	53
	%	100	30.1	6.0	—	63.9
1973	No	150	54	8	n.d.	88
	%	100	36	5.3	—	58.7
1974	No	156	26	28	2	100
	%	100	16.7	17.9	1.3	64.1
1975	No	140	33	6	1	22

Note: Figures for 1975 do not include students who returned to, and completed their courses in the United Kingdom.

Of all our special schemes the most disappointing has been that involving merchant seamen. The scheme was established in 1972, following discussion with representatives of the Seafarers' Education Service, the College of the Sea and other seamen's unions and associations. The first students commenced their studies in 1973.

The features of the scheme include guaranteed entry for applicants and a forwarding office in London for those who cannot make their own postal arrangements. Allocation of tutors and counsellors is made in the normal way but seamen are free to visit the study centre nearest their port of call when in the United Kingdom. Special arrangements are made for examinations to be taken on board ship.

Postal delays are obviously a great problem for this group of students and perhaps our system of despatch is not flexible enough to cope with their occupation. We are still investigating methods of overcoming these problems. What can be done about the low number enrolling each year is another question; perhaps more publicity or information needs to be supplied to seamen, to encourage them to register. Certainly we would be loth to discontinue the scheme as we recognise that for some seamen this is their only chance for higher education, as other educational bodies seem neither concerned nor apt for their particular needs.

In none of these special categories is the number of students very large. Yet the special arrangements required to deal with them are complex and time-consuming and each scheme tends to be expensive. We are prepared, as indeed are the organisations concerned with each project and without whose help we could not operate, to put extra resources into the schemes because of the very special needs of these minorities and because we provide literally their only opportunity for higher education.

13

RESULTS AFTER FIVE YEARS

No account of the students of the Open University would be complete without a description of their performance in this wholly new kind of educational system. The results of the first year or two aroused a great euphoria in us all, for they were very much better than most of us had dared to hope. Yet native caution made me reluctant to extrapolate and to generalise from these early results since there was always a chance, possibly even a likelihood, that the first intakes of students would not be wholly typical. Now that we have completed five years of teaching I am more prepared to analyse the data and to come to tentative conclusions. In each of my Annual Reports I have published statistical data about the students of the Open University and their performance. In 1975 we published the first of an ongoing series of annual digests of statistical information about our students.[20] There is, indeed, a mass of such information. I have tried to select from it data that reflect the progress that we have made and the trends that seem to me to signpost our pathways for the future.

This chapter deals with student performance on a statistical basis and there are those who will find such analysis heavy going. Nevertheless, the figures yield some fascinating information, and there is no other way of effectively presenting it.

Table 7 gives a summary of all applications and admissions over the six year period from 1971 to 1976 inclusive.

From column B of the Table it will be seen that we have now received no fewer than a quarter of a million completed application forms from adults. This is a spuriously large figure because of the fact that a sizeable proportion of the students who fail to get a place in any one year re-apply for the following year, and we do not keep accurate data of the numbers of such re-applications. It is, however, likely that some 200,000 separate individuals have applied for entry.

As I pointed out in Chapter 9, the application rate in the first year, that is from those who wished to start in 1971, was probably unduly high because of the novelty of the institution and its consequent attraction to people who found that, in the event, what was offered was not at all what they had expected. The numbers fell subsequently for two years, began to rise again for 1974 and jumped very significantly for 1975 and 1976. Again, as I have stated, it seems likely that this increase followed the emergence of graduates and the consequent encouragement given to those who saw that other people could succeed in this highly novel institution.

In column C figures are given for those applications which remained in

TABLE 7 Applications and admissions

| Year | No. of applicants | No. of processed applicants | % Withdrawn | Provisionally registered | No. of Admissions | | |
					% of processed applicants	Finally registered	% of provisionally registered
1971	42,992	40,817	5.1	24,220	59.3	19,581	80.8
1972	35,182	34,222	2.7	20,501	59.9	15,716	76.7
1973	32,046	30,414	5.1	16,895	55.5	12,680	75.1
1974	35,011	33,220	5.1	14,976	45.1	11,336	75.7
1975	52,537	49,550	5.7	19,823	40.0	14,830	74.8
1976	52,916	50,340	4.9	16,271	—	—	—
Totals after (5) years	197,768	188,223	4.8	96,414	51.2	74,143	76.9
Totals after (6) years	250,684	238,563	4.8	112,686	—	—	—
A	B	C	D	E	F	G	H

force at the end of the application period and were consequently processed to arrive at the list of those to be admitted. Column D shows that the loss of applicants between the time applications were submitted and the time that the total number of applications was processed has remained constant at an average of about 4.8%. It represents all those who, for one reason or another, like moving jobs or leaving the country, had to withdraw their applications before the final processing took place.

Column E gives the numbers of individuals who were accepted as 'provisionally registered' students in each of the six years from 1971 to 1976, the total number of such students being over 100,000. The number of acceptances in any one year was determined by the amount of government grant available to us and by the number of ongoing students (see Chapter 9). The result of the interplay between the number of applicants and the number who could be admitted to the University is indicated in column F, which shows the percentage of applicants actually admitted in each individual year. The overall figure for the five years is just over 50% so that each applicant had a one in two chance of being admitted to the University; but this chance has declined progressively with time and by 1976 there was less than one chance in three of an applicant being admitted. Thus, although the University is clearly serving a deeply-felt need on the part of a very large number of applicants in the country, it is only partially meeting that need and there is no doubt that, given enough financial support, we could satisfy it very much more fully than we do at present. It is this sort of argument that has led me in the past to say that we were more a 'Half Open University' than an Open University.

Students are required to pay the balance of the tuition fee in April; the number who so pay and are consequently 'finally registered' is given in column G. When this figure is expressed as a percentage of those who were 'provisionally registered' we get the figure in column H; it is a remarkably consistent figure ranging from 74.8% to 80.8% with an average of 76.9%. Thus, over the five years of our existence we have quite steadily lost almost one in every four students who provisionally registered with the University in January. This is a phenomenon which is common to all distance-teaching institutions and we determined that we would regard only finally registered students as having really entered the University in the proper sense of the term.

In 1970 my colleagues and I had no means of estimating what the actual numbers in each of the cells of Table 7 would turn out to be. How far did our guesses agree with the reality? We did not even consider the possibility that applicants would actually withdraw before the selection procedure began; but we did guess that the number of provisionally registered students who would drop out of the system, by opting not to pay the tuition fees after three months, would be about 20%. We were therefore gratified when, in 1971, the first figure turned out to be very close to this – namely 19.2%. Further experience showed, however, that the 1971 figure was aberrant and that the real result is closer to 25%. But it is the consistency of the finding that is so striking; the fact that, year after year, almost the same

TABLE 8

Year	No. of new finally registered students	No. of ongoing students	Total no. of finally registered students	Ongoing students as % of total students of previous year (less graduates)	No. of credits awarded [*]	Credits/ student [*]	No. of degrees	No. of graduates leaving the university
1971	19,581	—	19,581	—	16,346	0.83	—	—
1972	15,716	16,186	31,902	83	27,072	0.85	902	540
1973	12,680	25,744	38,424	82	32,354	0.84	3,641	2,365
1974	11,336	31,300	42,636	86	34,130	0.80	5,188	3,930
1975	14,830	34,528	49,358	89	37,207	0.75	5,421	4,654
Total	74,143				147,109		15,152	11,489
A	B	C	D	E	F	G	H	K

[*] These are full credit equivalent numbers, as distinct from course credit numbers.

† Column E is derived by expressing the total in Column C as a percentage of the total in Column D for the previous year, after adjusting the latter by deducting the number of graduates who have left the university.

proportion of people fall into this category. One might have expected that, as intending students came to have a better knowledge of just what was involved in studying in the Open University, fewer would have made the attempt and failed to stick with it. But this does not appear to have been the case. I am now certain that it was a good idea to allow this period of provisional registration and to refrain from encouraging people to stay on at that particular point. It means that the cost to the University is very much less than it would have been had all the provisionally registered students remained in the system until the end of the year. We save in all sorts of ways, the most obvious of which is that course materials are not despatched to any except finally registered students after the end of April. It also means that the cost to these 'drop-out' students is minimised, for they never become liable for the full tuition fee.

The consistency of these results has, however, another important implication, namely that we are now in a position to make reasonably accurate forecasts before the year starts. In other words, if we know that our government grant is adequate to support another 15,000 new students, we can with confidence admit 20,000 provisionally registered students in the secure knowledge that 5,000 of them will not finally register in the following April. This is of vital importance from the planning point of view and enables us to accept as many applicants as we possibly can without running into the danger of over-stepping our budget. The total number of finally registered students who started in the Open University up to and including the beginning of 1975 was 74,143.

Table 8 gives data about the progress of the finally registered students admitted in the five years from 1971 to 1975.

Column B gives the intake of new finally registered students in each of the years concerned, and Column C the total number of students who were already in the system, having been admitted in previous years, and who registered for new courses in the year under consideration. Column D gives the total number of finally registered students in the University in each year and represents the sum of the figures in Columns B and C respectively. Thus the figures in Column D illustrate the real growth in the size of the University in respect of undergraduate student numbers over the first five years of its operation. By the beginning of 1975, out of 74,143 students who had been finally registered over the period, 49,358 were still students. To the latter figure must be added the number of those who had already graduated and left the University, in order to arrive at an estimate of the success rate of the finally registered students, and this is a very difficult calculation. About 40% of graduates continue as students for one year presumably to top up pass degrees to honour degrees, and of these possibly half stay on for a further year and a quarter for a third year. Thus it would not be correct simply to add the grand total of 15,152 graduates (total of Column H), for many would be double-counted, having already been included as 'ongoing students'; and a more accurate figure, calculated on the basis of the evaluation given above, would be that 11,489 of our graduates had by 1975 actually left the university (total of Column K). Adding this number of 'successes' to the 49,358 students still in the system we get 60,847 successful students out of 74,143 who finally registered, an overall success rate of 82%. Another way of looking at this question is to examine the proportion of finally registered students in any one year who continue into the following year. These figures are given in column E of Table 8. They clearly show an upward trend: whereas only 83% of the students of 1971 continued as registered students in 1972, 89% of the students of 1974 continued into 1975.

Both sets of calculations are, of course, extremely crude and are statistical averages that hide a multitude of reasons why individual students adopt a particular pattern of behaviour. On the one hand, some students do not take any further courses because they have no particular wish to proceed further along the road towards a degree. Others fail to register for courses in a subsequent year because the pressure of their ordinary occupations becomes heavier and precludes their registering for new courses for a period of one or more years; they may still return to the fold after a gap. In 1976 some 2,500 students who had taken no courses in 1975 did exercise this option to register again. On the other hand, the figures of ongoing students do not always represent success, for they include those who have failed their examinations and are repeating the course in order to try and obtain credit in the following year. Furthermore, the nearer a student gets to graduation, and the longer he has been in the system, the less likely is he to drop out, and this is no doubt one reason why the proportion of ongoing students in 1975 is higher than it was in 1972. Indeed the proportion of new students who continue into a second year has not increased but has remained constant at 83%.

Column F of Table 8 gives the total number of credits, in terms of full credit equivalents, obtained by all students in each successive year. Two students, each achieving success in a half-credit course, will appear as one full credit equivalent. In column G the average number of full credit equivalents obtained per student per year is given and is fairly constant at about 0.8. Since the average number of full-credit courses attempted by a student runs at 1.1 the figure provides yet another estimate of the success rate at something like 75%. This figure defines success in terms of obtaining credit and the corollary that failure to obtain a credit implies drop-out is not tenable.

It also follows that if students obtain, on average, 0.8 credits per year, and if all students were eventually to graduate, the average time to graduation would be about 7.4 years, provided that no students had credit exemption. On the other hand, the average number of credit exemptions obtained by a student is 1.2 so that the average time to graduation should be just about six years. The underlying assumptions are, however, untenable. Not all students will proceed to a degree, and furthermore it is probable that those who do not will be predominantly those who take a smaller number of credits in each succeeding year. Thus one cannot press this argument very far.

The number of degrees actually awarded is shown in column H but it is still too soon to come to any conclusion about the rate at which any one cohort of students will actually obtain their degrees (see Table 14). Perhaps the most interesting feature of Table 8 is the relatively constant figure of credits obtained (column G). There is no falling off in the rate of acquisition of credit calculated on this statistical basis until 1975. In the early years, students were, however, more ambitious; they attempted very much more than they now do. They would register for two full credit courses and many would fail to achieve success in both; indeed we suspect that many failed to achieve success in either simply because they attempted both. Over the years their ambition has become less, and more are opting for only one full credit course per annum. I do not know whether the lower success rate in 1975 is aberrant or the beginning of a new trend.

In Table 9 I give the examination results for the same five years of students in some detail.

Column B gives once again the total number of finally registered students in the University; but in column C there appears a new figure which lists the number of student courses that are being attempted in each year. This figure is not in terms of full credit equivalents (FCE's) but represents the total number of courses, whether they be full credits or half credits, attempted by the number of students in column B. In column D the number of courses per student is given for each year and it will be seen that, apart from 1971 when no half credit courses were on offer, it is very constant at about 1.5 courses per student. This figure reflects the fact that about half the students are taking one full credit course while the other half are taking two half credit courses. It is important because it is the operative one for those who are concerned with the operational problems of the University, since for every two additional students that are registered in the University, there is an extra student in each of three different courses. This affects the burden that falls upon the operational units in the University, eg correspondence despatch and examinations.

The total number of students sitting individual examinations is given in column E. Once again, these do not represent individual students because many are sitting more than one examination. In column F the total number of candidates for examinations is given as a proportion of the total number of students registered for all courses. It will be seen that this proportion also is a remarkably constant one ranging from 76 to 79%. Thus, in each year, some 20% of the students registered for courses fail to sit for the examination in that course. No doubt some people do not register for the examination because they feel themselves to be ill-prepared. Nevertheless, there are many more who are taking the course because of an intrinsic interest in the subject, whose performance throughout the year in the written assignments has been uniformly satisfactory, but who do not wish to take the examination for the primary reason that they have no particular interest in acquiring credit. They have no intention of acquiring a degree, so that a piece of paper giving them credit is not an important factor in their lives.

Some of these students, too, do not register for summer schools and there is a remarkable resemblance in the overall statistical figures for the

TABLE 9

Year	No. of students	No. of student-courses (FCE or ½ FCE)	No. of courses/ student	No sitting Exams	Candidates as % of student-courses	Credits (FCE or ½ FCE) gained	Credits per student	Credits per student course	Credits per candidate
1971	19,581	22,327	1.14	17,666	79.1	16,346	0.83	0.73	0.93
1972	31,902	46,956	1.47	36,125	76.9	33,399	1.05	0.71	0.92
1973	38,424	57,798	1.50	45,410	78.6	42,382	1.10	0.73	0.93
1974	42,636	66,432	1.56	51,537	77.6	48,137	1.13	0.72	0.93
1975	49,358	71,512	1.45	54,346	76.0	50,088	1.01	0.70	0.92
A	B	C	D	E	F	G	H	K	L

proportion attending summer schools and for that sitting examinations. There is no direct evidence available to us as to whether the same group of students opts out of both the summer schools and the examinations; but the pass rates in the examinations and the figures for the award of credit both suggest strongly that this is so. In the early years, this particular group of students presented us with major problems; they came to be known as 'sleeping students', and they caused us to overbook accommodation for summer schools (with a consequent financial penalty) and for examinations. We had assumed that anyone taking the course as a serious student would take an active part in all the components of the course. Of late, we have realised that this is not a valid assumption; but the consistency of the proportion of 'sleeping students' has enabled us to adjust all our expenditures on the basis of this expected constant proportion.

Column G of Table 9 gives the total number of credits obtained in examinations, irrespective of whether these credits are in full credit equivalent courses or in half credit courses, and Column H gives the average number of such credits per student. It is clear that on average, apart from 1971, each fully-registered student in the University passes rather more than one individual examination each year. On the other hand in Column K it is equally clear that, if one calculates the number of credits obtained per student course, the average figure lies between 0.7 and 0.73. (The figure in Column K would reach unity only if every student registered for every course succeeded in the examination at the end of that course.) The last column in the Table, Column L, shows the number of credits obtained by each candidate for the examination. Here again, there is a quite remarkable consistency throughout the years. The pass rate in examinations, averaged over all the different courses on offer in that particular year, comes out at a remarkably constant 93%. I would hasten to add that this is not a pre-determined figure, for we do not in any sense start off with an assumption that only seven per cent of all candidates will fail the examination; this would be a disastrous mistake in respect of maintaining standards. Indeed, the pass rates in individual examinations in individual courses vary very widely, from the poor results obtained in certain mathematics examinations to the very high pass rates obtained in certain examinations in the liberal arts. It is however, a striking testimony to the fact that when one is dealing with an extremely large sample of candidates, the overall pass rates are likely to show a remarkable consistency.

In Chapter 9 I mentioned that the differences between the pass rates of students seemed to depend upon their previous educational experience. In Table 10 I compare the pass rates in foundation courses of all students who, on entry, held less than two A-levels, the usually accepted minimum standard for university entrance, with those who already held two A-levels or more. The former are designated as 'unqualified' and the latter as 'qualified'.

In 1971 there was relatively little difference in the level of performance of the qualified as opposed to the unqualified group in the foundation

TABLE 10   Pass rates for foundation course students

	New students	All students		Continuing students	New students
	1971	1972	1973	1974	1974
Humanities					
unqualified	81.7	73.8	75.7	70.0	77.0
qualified	86.8	84.3	85.0	85.0	89.0
Social Sciences					
unqualified	73.5	66.9	69.0	68.9	72.7
qualified	81.8	78.3	83.8	83.6	87.6
Mathematics					
unqualified	41.7	38.7	44.0	36.0	47.6
qualified	65.5	64.8	70.8	70.3	79.5
Science					
unqualified	61.7	58.5	56.8	62.2	68.5
qualified	76.4	76.0	77.5	80.2	85.0
Technology					
unqualified	—	61.7	65.0	65.5	63.3
qualified	—	76.4	78.3	75.6	81.0

courses in humanities and social sciences. The possession of A-levels or their equivalent had little effect on the success of students in these Open University courses. This did not seem particularly surprising. The modal age of students entering the Open University was about 27. The experience of life gained in the ten years between leaving school and reaching the age of 27 is nearly always related in some way to the sort of studies that comprise the humanities and the social sciences. Basic literacy and an awareness of social problems is common to almost all adults in this country. They do not, therefore, start serious academic studies at the age of 27 wholly unprepared, even if they possess no paper qualifications.

The same argument does not hold true for those who begin studies in science or mathematics. In these cases life experience only rarely includes acquaintance with scientific or mathematical principles. It was therefore not surprising to discover that amongst the students beginning studies in science and mathematics, the unqualified group of entrants had a significantly lower success rate than the qualified group. Indeed the figures might be worse than they are if it were not for the fact that a proportion of the unqualified entrants to these foundation courses are drawn from occupations such as that of laboratory technician; from those who have spent their working lives in a scientific ambience and are therefore not as wholly unprepared as their paper qualifications would indicate.

Looking at the results for 1972, 1973 and 1974 however, it is clear that the 'discrimination factor' or the difference in performance between the qualified and the unqualified groups is increasing. The data of Table 10 are taken from the results of all students studying foundation courses: thus for 1972, 1973 and 1974 they include students studying their second foundation course and others who are repeating a course, having failed first time round. For 1974 I have therefore given the figures for students studying their first foundation course, for a more exact comparison with the 1971 record. It is clear that the unqualified entrant has less chance of passing any course than his qualified colleague, and that there was a trend, especially marked in 1972 and 1973, for this discrimination to increase, but that it now appears to have settled down at a reasonably constant level.

In Arts the difference in pass rates between the two groups has increased from 5% to 11% and has settled at about that level. For Social Sciences the difference of 8% in 1971 increased to 12% and has settled at about 14%. In Science the difference started at 15% and settled at around 18%; here it is worth noting that the highest discrimination occurred in 1972 and 1973 and may be due to the difficulty in filling the quotas for entry to the Faculty in those years (see Chapter 9). For Technology the unqualified group has always performed well and the difference in pass rates has been less marked. The most worrying course has been Mathematics. Here the unqualified group perform badly having on average only a 40% chance of passing compared to 70% for the qualified group. This is a matter of concern to us all.

One can speculate as to the reason for these trends. Perhaps the unqualified students in 1971 were 'special', being more highly motivated than in subsequent years, so that this gave them an edge over the unqualified students in later years; there is certainly no evidence that they were better qualified.

When the total number of new applicants was relatively low, as for 1972 and 1973, we sometimes had difficulty in filling the quotas for entry to the science, mathematics and technology courses. Consequently there was a much larger percentage of students on these courses who were studying the course of their second or third choice and one might expect them to perform less well. Similarly some students are 'playing the system'. It is well known that there is a one or two year waiting list for entry to the social science and humanities foundation courses; however all students are required to study two foundation courses and so some opt to do an unpopular course first, in order to gain more rapid entry. Once registered the student may, in the next year, do the foundation course of his choice.

These are hypotheses to explain the fact that the unqualified student appears to be doing less well in 1974 than in 1971, both in relative and absolute terms. Research into this is continuing and one of the more reassuring aspects is that at second and higher levels discrimination appears to diminish and almost disappear, partly due to the fact that having completed a course a formerly 'unqualified' student is more nearly on a par with his 'qualified' counterpart. As with many other areas of our institutional research more data are needed in order to try to eliminate some of the variables.

187

The data in Table 10 pinpoint the difficult problem which faces us over the admission of unqualified entrants to our foundation courses in mathematics. The same problem also arises in science but to a considerably smaller extent; nevertheless what I am about to say of mathematics applies to science also and even marginally to the other faculties.

Both the Advisory Committee and the Planning Committee had, in endorsing a policy of open entry without qualifications, recognised that many such entrants would be inadequately prepared for study at university level. Despite this we made every effort in preparing our foundation courses to make them as accessible as possible to unqualified entrants; to students attempting the foundation course in mathematics, we offered refresher booklets to help them reach the level of knowledge and understanding that we must necessarily assume on entry. Consequently, although we have been fortified by how well unqualified entrants have succeeded in some other foundation courses we have been distressed by our failure to make it possible for them to succeed to the same extent in mathematics. Nevertheless it would be wrong to presume that we were surprised.

We anticipated the problem as early as 1969, and realised that we would probably face a real academic dilemma. One can, of course, argue that adults should be free to try their hand, even if they frequently fail, but that hardly gets the University academics out of their difficulty. It is very depressing to go on offering a course knowing that a great many of your students are not going to succeed; and moreover that the failure is going to be much more frequent amongst those very deprived adults whom one is especially trying to help. We have not yet succeeded in solving this dilemma.

There were clearly strong reasons why entrants to mathematics who are unqualified should be offered preparatory courses which would be easier for them to comprehend and would lead them gradually to the levels that we assumed at the start of our foundation course. It would be relatively simple for us to do this. On the other hand, if we did so, we would be offering a course that would by definition not be of university standard. In 1971 it was inconceivable that we should embark on such a venture. Now that we have shown that we can write and produce courses of high quality at full university level there is no longer the same argument against our doing so.

We endeavoured to persuade other institutions to offer preparatory courses. The first was offered in 1970, the year before we began teaching, by the National Extension College in collaboration with the BBC – the so-called 'Gateway' Course in Mathematics called 'Square Two'. Other courses with similar aims have been mounted by a large variety of institutions of further education, but much more is needed. We need a carefully constructed preparatory course that leads directly into our own foundation course, that is designed primarily for those who have not got any mathematical experience and that is within the capacity of those adults who have not studied mathematics since they left school and had very low achievement levels even when they were at school. Mathematics presents conceptual difficulty to a large number of people. Yet it is often so badly taught that the conceptual difficulty, though real, is magnified out of all proportion by the method of presentation. The great shortage of qualified teachers in mathematics in the schools has compounded the difficulty. One of my sons had no fewer than seven mathematics masters in one year at his school; none of them was skilled, they were all doing the job because there was no one else to fit into the gap at the time. Students are asked to tackle problems without understanding why, without seeing at all what is the underlying purpose of the technique that they are learning. This is quite unnecessary. Mathematics can be made extremely interesting by good presentation. The Open University can make use of skills which are not commonly found among teachers of mathematics to achieve this in its materials. We therefore have a real responsibility to try to raise the general standard of mathematics teaching on a much wider basis than we manage to at present.

Yet we hesitated for a very long time before attempting a preparatory course. The reason was simple. If we were to offer one, we would find it hard to avoid giving preference in admission to students who had taken it. Their chances of progressing satisfactorily would be much higher than those of unqualified entrants who had not taken or had not passed preparatory courses. Thus we would inevitably erode the principle of open entry. The arguments for and against are not yet over. At the moment we are working on our own preparatory materials which are to be made available to applicants for the foundation course in mathematics; but they will only be provided to applicants who have already been accepted as students, so that no question of preferential selection can arise.

It may well be that the ultimate answer, not only in mathematics but for all those who are ill-prepared for the Open University, will lie in the creation of an Open School or Open College which will offer courses only at pre-university level. The qualifications of such an institution need not then be a requirement for the Open University any more than are A-levels. Yet they would be an indication to the prospective student that he or she was ready and able to embark on a higher programme, through the distance-teaching method. A very strong case could be made out for having started such an Open School before ever there was an Open University, but the idea was not politically viable at the time. It would have filled an even bigger social need, and that need is still clamant.

At this point it is perhaps worth summarising what would be likely to happen to a group of 10 applicants who wished to begin study at the Open University. Only five would be admitted provisionally because of the shortage of money. By April, four would have paid the tuition fees and become finally registered students. At the end of the year three would have obtained credit in the course for which they were registered, and would stay in the system for a further year as fully registered students. If the figures for the cohort of 1971 can be used as the basis for such a calculation, then, after six years of study, two would graduate.

TABLE 11   Courses available

| Year | No. of students | No. of courses | | | Full credit equivalent | Full credit equivalent courses at levels | | | | Average No. of students per | |
		Full credit	Half credit	Total		Founda-tion	2	3	4	Total no. of courses	Full credit equivalent
1971	19.581	4	–	4	4	4	–	–	–	4,895	4,895
1972	31.902	9	14	23	16	5	11	–	–	1,387	1,994
1973	38.424	14	24	38	26	5	17	4	–	1,011	1,478
1974	42.636	17	41	58	$37\frac{1}{2}$	5	$23\frac{1}{2}$	8	1	735	1,137
1975	49.358	18	50	68	43	5	26	11	1	726	1,148
1976		24	64	88	56	5	29	20	2		
A	B	C	D	E	F	G	H	K	L	M	N

One can therefore say that of all those adults who have the ambition to join the Open University, only about one in five, on the current record, will succeed in realising his ambition by obtaining a degree at the end of a period of study. Most of the others are denied the opportunity because the university is short of funds. The rest fail to graduate for a variety of reasons. There are those who are the real drop-outs: some have bitten off more than they can chew and cannot find the drive and energy to proceed with a course as difficult as the one that is being offered, while others find the going too hard and beyond their intellectual capacity. Others are by no means drop-outs. They may have a more limited ambition simply to study for the sake of study, or to obtain credits in one or two courses rather than proceeding the whole way to a degree. The fact is that we have no valid criteria for measuring 'success' or 'failure'. That 50% or more of our finally registered students will eventually graduate is, of course, a real indication of a minimum of achievement, but it greatly underestimates the overall success rate in terms of the extent to which our students have satisfied their own ambitions.

Table 11 provides data on the rate of development of new courses offered by the University to its undergraduate students.
    Column B gives the total number of students registered in the University in each year. The next four columns give the number of courses on offer: full-credit courses, half-credit courses, total number of courses, and full credit equivalents. In each year after the foundation course year of 1971, the number of full credit equivalents added to the spectrum has been 12, 10, $11\frac{1}{2}$, $5\frac{1}{2}$ and 13 respectively. The last two figures clearly deserve comment. In the two years since 1974 $18\frac{1}{2}$ full credit equivalents will have been added. This represents a change in our overall planning whereby a longer time is allowed for the preparation of most courses than was true in the early days, when we were in a rush to provide students with an adequate spectrum of choice. Thus many courses were begun in 1976 which will have taken three years in preparation rather than two.
    Overall, therefore, the rate of production by the staff of the Open University of courses has been just over ten full credits per year, since 1972. The rate is steadily declining, the real figures, allowing for the change in the length of the planning period, being 12, 10, $11\frac{1}{2}$, $9\frac{1}{2}$ and 9. This decline is not surprising. It reflects the fact that the larger the total number of courses on offer becomes, the greater is the proportion of the time and energy of the staff concerned that has to be devoted to maintaining and re-making existing courses rather than creating new ones. This is why one can approach a steady state only in an exponential fashion.
    On the other hand it is clear from the figures in columns D and E, that there has been a very rapid growth of choice for students in terms of individual half-credits. This has been the best available way, with a very limited capacity of course production, for us to offer a bigger choice of courses to students quickly.
    In columns G to L of Table 11, I describe the courses in terms of the

TABLE 12 Miscellaneous data on scale of operations

Year	No. of student courses	Millions of packages mailed		Total mailings per student-course †	No. of assignments			No. sitting exams	Exam papers			Exam Centres	
		Bulk	Others		CMAs	TMAs	Total/ student-course		No.	No. of students per paper	No.	No. of students per centre	No. of students per paper per centre
1971	22.327	*	*	*	*	*	*	17.666	8	2,208	139	127	16
1972	46.956	2.28	0.75	64.5	258.087	243.552	10.7	36.125	34	1062.5	147	246	7
1973	57.798	2.6	1.0	62.3	226.293	265.415	8.5	45.410	52	873	138	329	6
1974	66.432	2.85	1.1	59.5	248.200	297.270	8.5	51.337	78	658	129	398	5
1975	71.512	3.4	1.3	65.7	279.500	323.500	8.5	54.346	92	591	137	397	4
A	B	C	D	E	F	G	H	K	L	M	N	P	Q

† This figure is increased by the mailings addressed to part-time tutors and counsellors (about 10% of total)

* No records maintained

level at which each is offered. By 1972, all five foundation courses were available to students. Similarly, the rate of production of new second level courses was very fast in 1972 and 1973, and has got slower in the last two years. The production of courses at third level began very slowly (the first being offered in 1973) but is now rapidly increasing. We have so far made only a handful of courses at level four. This in itself reflects the fact that most of our students obtain their degrees without ever advancing to fourth level, and many without even advancing to third level. The provision of honours degrees has been much slower and more difficult than we anticipated and indeed we have altered our aims and objectives in this respect. Nevertheless it can be expected that in the years following 1976, the proportion of courses prepared at the more advanced levels will increase. All the figures given in columns G to L are in terms of full credit equivalents.

The figures in columns M and N give the average number of students, firstly per course, and secondly, per full credit equivalent course. The figures for 1971 are naturally high, because all students in that year were in one or other of the only four courses available at that time. The figures of students per course have steadily fallen but are levelling off in the last couple of years at about 700. The students per full credit equivalent course have also fallen, but rather more slowly. I shall return to these figures when I discuss the question of University finance in Chapter 16. What is apparent already is that our decision to offer half-credit courses, by increasing the *total* number of courses on offer, has meant that a decreasing number of students can be registered for any one course, so that some of the economy of scale implicit in the Open University's learning system is lost.

Table 12 summarises in three areas, namely the despatch of written materials to students, the handling of assignments, and the organisation of examinations, what the increasing scale of operation of the Open University has meant in terms of complexity.

Here again in column B I give the total number of student courses in each of the years under consideration. In columns C and D, I give in millions, and it is a rough figure, the number of mailings from the correspondence despatch department of the University in each year. Column E, which gives the total number of mailings per student per annum, shows, yet again, a remarkable consistency. Even if we allow a ten per cent average for the mailings to part time staff, there is one mailing to each student roughly every week of the academic year. It is small wonder that the steady increase in postal charges has imposed an enormously heavy burden on the University's finances as the years have gone on.

In columns F, G and H, I give data for the numbers of computer-marked and tutor-marked assignments that have been handled each year by the University: all the figures are of the order of a quarter of a million and upwards. As is evident, there is again a remarkable consistency in the total number of assignments undertaken by each individual student on a course. The figure of 8.5 represents a mean between those studying full

TABLE 13 Summer schools

Year	No. of student/wks attendance	No. of centres	Average no. of students per centre	No. of weeks of summer school	Average no. of students/ week	No. of lines	No. of line/weeks	Average no. of students/ line	Average no. of students/ line/week
1971	17.933	8	2.241	53	338	4	94	4.483	191
1972	24.146	10	2.415	75	321	12	165	2.012	146
1973	25.683	12	2.140	88	291	20	214	1.284	120
1974	26.518	13	2.040	80	331	24	195	1.105	136
1975	30.136	14	2.153	86	350	26	233	1.159	129
A	B	C	D	E	F	G	H	K	L

credit equivalent courses and those studying half-credit courses; and the average is probably six in respect of a half-credit and twelve in respect of a full credit course.

Finally, in columns K to P, I give data about our examinations system. Column K gives the total number of students sitting individual papers, and column L the total number of examination papers that are set and marked in each year. In column M, I therefore give the average number of students who are sitting each particular paper that is set. It is quite clear that this number is steadily falling. Each examination requires a separate examination board; and each paper requires a set of different questions. Consequently the labour involved for each examination is very considerable and the organizational complexity of the timetabling of examinations becomes steadily greater.

The number of examination centres that are operated each year is given in column N and the total number of students on average using each centre is given in column P. When one gets down to the actual number of students sitting one particular paper at any one particular centre, one arrives in the final column of the Table at very small numbers of students indeed.

Table 13 gives data about the summer schools that have been held in each year and the students attending them.

The table illustrates the gradual growth in the total number of student/weeks for which we have to cater. The increase is slower than that for the numbers of students themselves because many of the advanced courses in the liberal arts do not demand attendance at summer school. Thus the number of universities acting as hosts (column C) and the total number of weeks of summer school (column E) have also risen gradually to keep the number of students per centre per week fairly constant at about 325 (column F).

The striking feature of the summer schools is, however, the rapid increase in the number of 'lines' (column G). These lines are each a separate academic programme requiring separate staffing, equipment and preparation. It is the number of lines rather than the number of students that determines the difficulty and complexity of organising the summer school programme, so that the exercise becomes more demanding year by year. The increase in the number of lines is faster than the increase in student numbers so that the number of students per line has fallen dramatically (column K).

In Table 14(a) I have attempted to illustrate the rate at which finally registered students in the Open University have achieved degrees. The figures are given for each cohort of students. Thus all those who started study in 1971 are Cohort A and their progress is analysed separately to show the numbers graduating in each year. After 5 years 43.3% of all Cohort A students have graduated. In Table 14(b) I have expressed the number of graduates as percentages of the number of students in the cohort. It is already clear that Cohort A is an unusual one in that the

TABLE 14a Graduations by cohort of students

Student cohort	Year of starting	Number of finally registered students in cohort	Number of graduates in				Total graduates by 1975	
			1972	1973	1974	1975	No.	As % of finally registered students in cohort
A	1971	19,581	902	3,326	2,644	1,614	8,486	43.3
B	1972	15,716	—	315	2,293	1,740	4,348	27.7
C	1973	12,680	—	—	251	1,851	2,102	16.6
D	1974	11,336	—	—	—	216	216	19.1
Totals			902	3,641	5,180	5,421	15,152	
A	B	C	D	E	F	G	H	K

TABLE 14b Percentage graduations by cohort of students

Student cohort	% of students in cohort who have graduated after			
	2 years	3 years	4 years	5 years
A	4.6	21.6	35.1	43.3
B	2.0	16.6	27.7	
C	2.0	16.6		
D	2.0			

proportion graduating is invariably higher than that for subsequent years; and this may represent the extra high motivation of our first students as well as the extra high proportion of them who were awarded credit exemptions. So far the progress of Cohorts B, C and D looks fairly constant but it is still too early to be sure of this.

It is obviously much too early to give final figures for the number in each cohort who will finally graduate. Even the student cohort A, that is, those students who began study in our first year of operation in 1971, have been studying only for a total period of five years. As will have been apparent from the data given in Table 8 one cannot expect those students who began in 1971 without any credit exemption and who have progressed at a slow rate of credit accumulation per annum (the average being only 0.8 credits per annum, and the lowest rate being considerably below that) to obtain their degrees in a period of less than seven years. In consequence, one must expect graduates from this cohort to appear in all years up to 1979, and indeed probably in very small numbers for several years after that.

It is interesting to note that, by 1975, we had produced more than 15,000 graduates in all. Clearly our alumni will soon make up a considerable force in the community.

Table 15 simply lists in column B the number of graduates in each year since 1973, and in column C the number of those who attended graduation ceremonies at which they were introduced to the Chancellor or to myself.

TABLE 15   Graduation ceremonies

Year of ceremony	No. of graduates of previous year	No. attending ceremonies	% attending	No. of ceremonies	Aver. No./ ceremony
1973	902	601	66.6	1	601
1974	3,641	2,130*	61.3	5	426
1975	5,180	3,238	60.6	9	360
A	B	C	D	E	F

* 167 students in Northern Ireland were unable to attend a ceremony in 1974 since the Belfast ceremony was cancelled owing to the state of emergency that existed. Those students were offered the chance of attending in 1975. Consequently in calculating the percentage attendance these 167 have been assumed to be present in 1974 and not in 1975.

The proportion of those who choose to attend is very consistent, and is high (over 60%) for a voluntary ceremony, for the degrees are actually conferred by post. Students of the Open University are thus just as anxious as any others to mark the end of a long period of blood, toil, sweat and tears by a ceremony, however mediaeval, that suitably marks the occasion.

197

The number of ceremonies has steadily increased, from one in 1973 to nine in 1975, and it looks as if we shall have to hold no fewer than twelve in 1976 in order to cope both with the numbers, and with the fact that our students find it difficult to travel long distances. Our intention is to try to hold ceremonies on a regional basis so as to minimise the trouble caused to the students and to their families and friends. Column F gives the average number of graduates who attend each ceremony. This has naturally fallen as the number of ceremonies has increased.

All in all, the record of the first five years of operation of the University shows a very considerable level of achievement. The success of our students reflects primarily their own quality and dedication; it is only marginally a reflection of the efforts of the staff of the University. The latter have nevertheless shown a dedication to this new task beyond what anyone had a right to expect of them. I hope that in future we can maintain this level of performance and indeed improve upon it, as we become more and more familiar with some of the constant parameters to which this chapter has drawn attention. We should then be able to plan more effectively in order to provide the best possible service to the maximum number of students. But this will not happen of itself. It will require imagination and drive to combat some of the new problems that will arise as we approach a steady state, and to find a new challenge to replace the initial one of achieving what was widely regarded as impossible. There is no room at all for complacency.

4

THE
ADMINISTRATIVE
PLAN

14

THE CHARTER

Most of those who, in the years before 1967, advocated an 'Open University' or a 'University of the Air', envisaged an institution which would work in co-operation with existing Universities; some indeed suggested that the external degree of London University should be awarded to successful students. Mr Wilson, in his early speeches, talked of a consortium of universities getting together to organise the University of the Air. It was only when Jennie Lee appeared on the scene that the first mention was made of an independent university awarding its own degrees; yet, even after this date, there was still a body of opinion that held that a structure which tied the Open University into the existing system would be preferable. Thus, when the report of the Advisory Committee was sent by Mr Crosland, then the Secretary of State for Education and Science, to the Cabinet on 30 September 1966, the proposal that he put forward read as follows:

> I should set up a Planning Committee, composed almost entirely of University Vice-Chancellors, heads of university institutions and other university staff, and ask it (a) to work out a plan for the establishment of the University as a separate institution, to be created by Royal Charter and grant-aided by the Department of Education and Science; (b) at the same time to consider whether these facilities could be provided under the aegis of an existing university or group of universities.

This proposal would therefore have left the Planning Committee free either to follow the line suggested by Jennie Lee and produce a Charter for an independent institution, or to adopt the alternative strategy of coupling the University with existing institutions. When, however, the decision was finally taken, in the autumn of 1967, to create the Planning Committee, the terms of reference given to the Committee were quite specific. They were:

> To work out a comprehensive plan for an 'Open University' as outlined in the White Paper of February, 1966, *A University of the Air* and to prepare a draft Charter and statutes.

Thus the pattern adopted by the Advisory Committee and printed in the White Paper had become the definitive plan, and it was no longer open to the Planning Committee to consider any alternative to an independent University offering its own degrees.

At the first meeting of the Planning Committee, in October 1967, John Scupham, in a paper submitted to the Committee, recommended that a separate working group should be set up on the constitution and organization of the Open University, with specific reference to its Charter and statutes. This suggestion was accepted. The terms of reference of the working party were:

1 To consider and report on the possible constitutional and administrative structure of the Open University; on its relationship with other universities; and on the machinery of government that would be necessary to secure a proper control of finance and administration of the curriculum and of academic standards.

2 To prepare for the Planning Committee (after its adoption of a provisional plan of action) a preliminary outline of the working organization required to implement its decisions.

3 To recommend to the Planning Committee what officers must first be appointed, and whether on a full-time or part-time seconded basis.

It is clear from these accepted terms of reference that the Planning Committee had not, at its first meeting, come to any clear decisions about the nature of the administrative organization of the institution it was going to create. The terms of reference were sufficiently wide to allow the working party a great deal of latitude in drafting a proposed Charter and statutes. Despite this fact, however, at the very first meeting of the working party itself, there was submitted to it the Charter of the University of Warwick as an example of how another new university had tackled the problem. The University of Warwick was a typical university of the conventional type, and its Charter took the form common to the universities that had been created in previous decades. The working party used it as a model and throughout the months that followed, amended it successively to try to cover the special conditions that were anticipated in the Open University. There is little doubt that this course of action in itself was a constraint on the members of the working party, since a study of the papers submitted to the working party shows that no real attempt was made to draft a Charter of an entirely novel kind designed to suit the new institution.

There were, no doubt, two very good reasons for following this course of action. The first was that to use a model of this sort undoubtedly saved a great deal of time. The second was that in the minds of the Planning Committee, there was a much better chance of gaining the agreement of the Privy Council to the Draft Charter if it did not depart too radically from the pattern of the Charters awarded to other new universities over the previous decade. On the other hand, it seems to me, with the benefit of hindsight, that the use of the model did inhibit the Planning Committee from a more radical approach to the drafting of an entirely new Charter for a new, innovative institution. However, members of the Planning Committee were concerned to achieve a deliberate compromise by having a traditional type of Charter for an institution that was otherwise innovative.

Thus, it was accepted at the outset that the government structure of the Open University should be of the traditional kind, with a Council as the main fiscal and financial controlling body of the University, and a Senate as the supreme academic authority. This bipartite control is the standard British pattern and has significant advantages. The pattern evolved at a time when the academic control of the standards to be set, the regulations for the award of degrees, the choice of courses to be offered, and the promotion of research and scholarship, were all decisions that could be taken without significantly affecting the total expenditure of an institution. Furthermore it evolved because the origins of most of the English universities lay in the community within which they were founded. Consequently the community demanded a strong voice in the management of the institution, leaving the academic control largely to the staff.[21]

Over the last thirty years, the picture has changed out of all recognition. It is increasingly apparent that academic decisions have enormous effects on cost and that, in consequence, the Council of the University, as the final financial authority, must play a role in determining academic policy. This has led, in all British universities, to tensions being built up between the Council and the Senate. Members of the Senate tend to regard the Council as arrogating to itself purely academic decisions that should, according to the Charter, fall within the province of the Senate. Members of the Council, on the other hand, tend to think of the Senate as taking decisions for academic purposes that are irresponsible when considered in relation to the financial position of the University. Such tensions are seldom creative and are often destructive of the harmonious working relationship that the bipartite structure is intended to serve. The situation is further complicated by the fact that in most cases the Council is a relatively small body on which members of the academic staff are in a minority and the lay membership, as defined in the Charter, in the majority. A small group of this kind is a relatively efficient way of handling the financial and legal business of the institution. On the other hand, the Senate is usually a fairly large body and is composed wholly of members of the University's employed staff. While it is a useful forum for discussion of overall university academic policies, it is often a relatively inefficient means of taking quick decisions, and this can further aggravate the tension between the Senate and the Council. The reasons for the bipartite structure are, of course, plain. The Senate, although it is very properly the repository of control of academic standards for the institution cannot, composed as it is wholly of employees of the institution, be made accountable for the expenditure of public funds. The Council, with its majority of lay members, is so accountable.

The existence in most British universities of this structure means that the Charter and Statutes must provide for a whole system of checks and balances between the two governing bodies, so that each can subserve its legitimate duties and discharge its proper responsibilities. Whether these balances are adequate or not, they inevitably make for a slow and ponderous mechanism of decision-making. Indeed, no self-respecting commercial organization could possibly live with the cumbersome structure that is imposed upon all our universities. As the size of individual universities has increased over the years, both in this country and abroad, and as the total expenditure for which any one university is responsible has increased out of all proportion to what it was thirty or forty years ago, so the disadvantages of the bipartite structure have become increasingly apparent. Indeed, in one or two instances in the Commonwealth an attempt has been made quite consciously to depart from it and to arrive at a single governing body.

The most notable example of this is the University of Toronto which, following an Act passed in 1971, created for itself in 1972 a new government structure with a single governing body. In the University of Toronto the single governing body consists essentially of four groups of members representing four different 'constituencies'. The first consists of lay members representing the general public. The second is a group of members of the academic staff of the University representing the employees. The third is a group of students representing, as it were, the clientele. The fourth group consists of alumni, of graduates who in a sense bridge all three of the other groups, but who are probably regarded primarily as members of the general public sector. The theory is presumably that the more outrageous demands of any one group will be resisted by the others and the balance thereby maintained. One might expect a priori that accountability for the expenditure of public funds would be adequately safeguarded by the lay members, the alumni and the students; and that the maintenance of academic quality would be adequately safeguarded by the academic staff, the alumni and the lay members. The University of Toronto provides a fascinating test case for the practice of a unicameral government. In a recent letter to me the President of the University of Toronto, Dr John Evans, described the situation as follows:

> The new system of governance at the University of Toronto is successful in several ways. First, it abolishes what has been referred to as the 'double innocence' of a Senate dealing with academic matters but without financial accountability, and a Board dealing with only financial matters without academic understanding. Secondly, it speeds the deliberation of policy issues and ensures that the viewpoint of faculty, student, lay and alumni members of the Governing Council are considered simultaneously rather than sequentially. There has been a broadening of the understanding, and increased tolerance in attitudes on the part of the various constituencies are the result of this exposure.
>
> The principal disadvantage has been the dilution of the role of faculty members in the governance of the University, and specifically in relation to academic matters. This is a function of the relatively small proportion of total membership of the Governing Council made up of faculty members (under 25%). With the abolition of the Senate which was dominated by faculty members, there is a feeling

that the vital academic policies of the University have been given over to others!

Universities in general do not have a hierarchical structure of government. They are essentially cellular in nature, each cell representing one academic discipline or department. The control of the teaching programmes within that discipline is normally vested in the head of the Department, the Professor and his staff. Indeed for the regular kind of academic course offered in a university which is discipline-based, it is difficult to see how any other structure could work. It is not possible for any academics other than philosophers, for instance, to determine the precise nature and content of a course in pure philosophy. Thus, the overriding responsibility of the Senate is exercised to a very large extent by delegation, by trusting the head of the department concerned to maintain the overall policies of the Senate. The Dean of a faculty is normally elected by his colleagues, is *primus inter pares,* and has no authority over his professorial colleagues in respect of their teaching. The powers of the Vice-Chancellor are similarly constrained.

On the academic side, the Open University made a significant break from this normal system. Responsibility for individual teaching programmes is vested not in departments or disciplines but in course teams, which are set up for the purpose. Nevertheless, the course teams are, for their lifetime, just as much cellular components of an overall structure as are departments in other universities. On the other hand, the academic structure of the Open University is a much smaller part of the total University than it is in all other universities. The operational sections of the University, its regional structure and its relatively complex administration, are hierarchical rather than cellular in nature. To operate a hierarchical structure where responsibility must be taken by the individual manager within a system with two separate governing bodies is a very difficult task. It is all very well to have a lengthy and cumbersome system for taking decisions about the creation of courses and their accreditation. It is a wholly different thing to have to work through it when one is dealing with most of the day to day problems of course production and course transmission. In consequence, the bicameral governmental structure of the Open University, which parallels that of other universities, is even more open to challenge than it is in other institutions.

Nevertheless, in 1968, before anyone had a real idea of what the detailed operational structure of the University would involve, this question did not seem to be a pressing one. It was never raised or debated at either the Working Party on Constitution and Organisation or at the Planning Committee itself. When Christodoulou and I joined the Planning Committee after we were appointed in the summer of 1968 we, too, did not question the appropriateness of a bicameral governmental structure. Attention therefore focused on the detailed structure of the Council and the Senate, rather than on whether both bodies should or should not exist.

Three possible structures for the Council were considered. The first envisaged a large, representative group whose members would be nominated by many national bodies and interests. It was felt, however, that it would become very large indeed, rather like the Court of many other universities, and that under no circumstances could it function as an executive body. It would require some sort of executive committee to act for it. It was also doubted whether a nominated body such as this would be able to achieve the cohesion necessary to establish an unusual pioneering enterprise. Nominated members might have undue regard for the interests of the bodies they represented rather than for those of the new institution itself. The second possibility was that of an extremely small group numbering some fifteen in all, but this was held to be too restrictive, especially since it would mean that the Senate could elect only about three members and that only two or three members could be co-opted to bring into the Council particular expertise that it needed and might otherwise lack. Consequently, the third possibility was the one that received most support, namely that of a Council of thirty to forty members, which would still be small enough to act as an efficient executive committee, but would at the same time allow for a slightly larger representation of the necessary interests.

The biggest disadvantage of the solution adopted was that it would inevitably attract criticism from those interests which were excluded from the membership. On the other hand, it could be used to ensure a reasonable balance of external and internal interests, and a continuity of responsible external nominations to preserve the general character of the University. It could also allow for a significant proportion of co-opted members – for the selection of external people of distinction in appropriate fields. The final constitution of the Council as determined in the Charter is as follows:

MEMBERSHIP OF THE COUNCIL

Ex Officio   8   The Chancellor
The Pro-Chancellor (Chairman ex officio)
The Treasurer
The Vice-Chancellor
Three Pro-Vice-Chancellors
The Chairman of the Academic Advisory Committee (while that Committee exists)

External   13   Four members appointed by the Lord President of the Privy Council
Three members appointed by the Committee of Vice-Chancellors and Principals of the Universities of the United Kingdom
Three members representative of Local Education Authorities appointed by the associations of Local Education Authorities and Education Committees

		and the Inner London Education Authority, acting in consultation
		One member representative of education authorities in Scotland, appointed by the Association of County Councils in Scotland, and the Scottish Counties and Cities Association, acting in consultation
		One member appointed by the Royal Society
		One member appointed by the BBC
Academic	8	Six members of the Senate appointed by the Senate including at least two of non-professorial grade
		Two members of the part-time staff appointed by the General Assembly
Students	2	Two students appointed by the General Assembly
Co-opted	8	Eight (maximum) co-opted members not being members of the academic staff or salaried officers of the University or students
	39	

Since 4 of the 8 ex officio appointments and all 8 co-opted members may be regarded as 'external', there are 25 external members of the Council and 14 internal members, so that about two thirds of the members are external and one third internal.

By comparison, the Governing Council of the University of Toronto, which combines the functions of both our Council and our Senate, has 50 members of whom one half are external and one half internal. In Table 16 I give the various categories of membership, as a proportion of the total membership, both for that body and for our own Council.

It is interesting to note, from the last three columns of the Table, that if we were to add to our Council five members of the staff and six students it would very closely match the composition of the Governing Council in Toronto. I do not at all imply that we should immediately rush in and amend our Charter in precisely this way. My intention in making this comparison in some detail is only to indicate that one Commonwealth university is operating successfully with a unicameral government structure and that its governing body is not dissimilar (save in respect of staff and student representation) to our own existing Council. It seems to me that we should be watching the Toronto experiment very closely to see whether, at any time, our own Charter should be amended to provide for a unicameral system of government.

This conclusion is greatly reinforced when one examines the limitations of our Senate. When the Working Party of the Planning Committee was designing the bicameral structure embodied in the Charter, the constitution of the Senate presented a series of very strange problems.

TABLE 16

	Toronto	%	OU		Adjusted OU		
	No.	%	No.	%	Adjustments	New total	%
Ex officio – internal	3	6	4	10		4	8
Staff	14	28	8	21	+5	13	26
Students	8	16	2	5	+6	8	16
Total Internal	25	50	14	36		25	50
Ex officio – external	1	2	4	10		4	8
Government	16	32	4	10		4	8
Other external	8	16	17	44		17	34
Total external	25	50	25	64		25	50
Total	50	100	39	100	+11	50	100

As the supreme academic body, it was necessary, of course, that it include senior full-time academic staff; but it was also considered that it should have a significant proportion of the teaching and tutorial staff of the University in order to be responsive to the needs of the University and its students. A number of members of the Working Party and of the Planning Committee were however concerned about the probability that the Senate might be too large adequately to fulfil its duties, and Lord Ashby made the suggestion that the Charter should define an executive committee of the Senate. This suggestion was not followed, primarily because it was considered that such an executive could be created by the Senate without specific mention in the Charter.

The majority of the members of the Planning Committee considered, at that time, that the total full-time academic staff of the university would be relatively small and that most of the academic staff would be drawn from the members of other universities on short-term secondment. They concluded, therefore, that all full-time members of the academic staff should be members of the Senate. It was felt adequate, as a safeguard against the Senate ever becoming too large, to include in the Charter a provision whereby the Senate could reduce its membership by its own volition to a proportion of the total full-time academic staff.

There was no clear definition of what precisely the term 'academic staff' would include. Obviously the full-time academics working on course construction would fall within this category, but many members of the Working Party and the Planning Committee emphasised that other tasks, especially those concerned with educational technology and with the organization of the correspondence and tutorial teaching, would be undertaken by people who would have just as important a role in the academic organization of the University as would the regular academics in the traditional disciplines. They felt very strongly that the Senate should be constituted so as to specifically include these other categories of staff.

In the event, however, the final draft of the Charter allowed for their membership of the Senate by permitting the Senate to add up to one-fifth of its total membership by co-option. There were thus two ways in which members of staff other than regular full-time academics could be made members of the Senate, first by defining the term 'academic staff' in such a way as to include such people, or, second, by co-opting them.

The Charter, as drafted, left this critical question for decision by the University, since no-one could at that time envisage what the ultimate shape of the University would turn out to be; but, perhaps unwisely, it left the decision effectively in the hands of the Senate itself.

In my opinion, these provisions of the Charter have turned out to be inadequate; although it is only fair to say that this is not a view held by some of my academic colleagues. At the present time the total number of full-time members of the academic staff, as now defined by the Senate, is about 500, so that when the powers of co-option are used, the total size of the Senate is just under 600 people. Such a body can act effectively in only one capacity, namely as a legislature. In a university setting legislation is normally kept to a minimum; it is difficult to frame regulations, other than very formal ones, to control most academic activities. Thus a university Senate only rarely functions as a legislative assembly such as Parliament. Its members are too concerned about the formulation and implementation of policy to be willing to leave such matters to the 'administration', especially since, unlike Parliament, they cannot get rid of the government of the day.

On the other hand a body of 600 members must necessarily be an inefficient agency for the formulation of policy, and can do so only by ratification of prepared papers; and is even more inappropriate to deal with the decisions about implementation of policy which make up the bulk of university business.

Nevertheless the Senate has power to deal with all academic matters: and indeed the Charter does not specifically give it the authority to delegate any of that power. Consequently, for academics who are naturally interested in all aspects of academic policy and sit as of right under the Charter as members of Senate, there is little incentive to vote themselves out of office by invoking the clause in the Charter that permits the Senate to cut down its own size.

I would not at all charge the Senate with having been an irresponsible body – quite the opposite, in fact. It is, however, an extremely cumbersome organisation which, by virtue of its size, can meet only very infrequently, at the moment four times a year, and at a very heavy cost. Six or seven hundred copies of all documents have to be duplicated and distributed by post all over the country. The average attendance, runs at about 30%, or some 200 of the 600 members; and their time plus travel and subsistence costs is expensive. The cycle of business takes at least three months and must take six months if Senate is to have more than one opportunity to debate a matter of principle. It is virtually impossible to take urgent decisions quickly. Furthermore, in the absence of an effective executive, far too much trival business comes before the Senate thus further wasting scarce resources. We have long been aware of the difficulties facing us and I will discuss some of the attempts made within the provisions of the Charter to cope with the problem, in the next chapter. The real point at issue is whether any such attempts can be effective; or whether amendment of the Charter itself will prove necessary.

A third statutory body considered by those drafting the Charter was the General Assembly of all staff and students. This title was chosen in preference to an 'academic assembly' for the same reason that I have discussed already – namely, to give all types of staff and not just the academic staff, a sense of participation in the new institution. It was recognised that the General Assembly would be a very large body and that it should have no executive authority, but should offer an opportunity at the grass-roots for any member of the staff or any student of the University to raise issues of principle. It was thought that the General Assembly might meet on a representational basis once a year at the centre, and once a year in regional sub-groups. When I joined the debates of the Planning Committee, I was appalled at the prospect of trying to organize a General Assembly along these lines. I proposed an alternative structure whereby there would be an assembly in each of the regions and these regional assemblies would themselves elect their representatives to serve on a General Assembly. The General Assembly would then in turn elect representatives of the part-time tutorial staff and of the students to serve on the Council of the University. It seemed to me at that time that the prospect of holding regional assemblies once a year was slightly better than that of holding a General Assembly which students and staff scattered all over the United Kingdom would be required to attend. I turned out to be quite wrong, for the size of any particular regional assembly was, from the outset, so large that it was impracticable to convene actual meetings. We got round this difficulty in the Charter by carrying out the electoral role (the only statutory one) of regional assemblies by post. To provide an opportunity to all staff and students to contribute their ideas and thoughts to the institution, we have devised a system of consultative committees. These are based in the first instance on study centres. Indeed, as it has turned out, the study centre does provide the real grass-roots opportunity. We were not, at the time the Charter was drafted, able to see this with clarity and it would probably have been best had the whole of the participation demanded by the structure of the University been set up on this basis. Here again the Charter is inappropriate for the institution as it has developed and a further modification to take account of this would probably be wise.

The Working Party on the Constitution and Organisation of the Open University and the Planning Committee itself spent a great deal of time and effort on a large number of other clauses in the Charter, trying to amend the model used, namely the charter of the University of Warwick, to make it suit the needs of the Open University. Most of these changes were in fact desirable and successful in practice. If I have seemed throughout most of what I have said about the Charter to be overly critical of the Planning Committee's efforts, it is not to be taken as implying that there was neglect of a very important task. It is merely a reflection of the fact that they were up against enormous difficulties in trying to write a constitution for an institution which did not exist, for which there was no precedent and in a situation where no member of the Planning Committee was able clearly to foresee what the shape of the new institution would be.

A number of comments about the Charter were received from the Privy Council and from other national bodies, such as the National Union of Students, making various suggestions about student representation on the Council and the Senate of the University. After much discussion, two student members were added to the Council. The Privy Council and the Secretary of State had already given an assurance to the National Union of Students that student membership of the Council – and indeed of the Senate – would be written into the Charters of all new universities. We did not in fact incorporate student membership of the Senate into the Charter, but left it open through the clause that allowed for co-option. Students were added to the Senate in 1975 by this mechanism.

After the Planning Committee had considered all the comments received and had made the resulting amendments, the draft Charter was submitted to the Privy Council. It was awarded on 30th May 1969 and was formally presented on 23rd June at the ceremony which I have previously described.

15

GOVERNMENT STRUCTURE

The Charter lays down the statutory bases of the government structure of the University; but the detailed infrastructure that is required both to support the statutory bodies and to implement their policies and decisions is not prescribed in the Charter and has emerged, developed and changed over the years. I would like to be able to claim that my early colleagues and I first devised a master plan and that all the decisions about our emerging government structure were taken so as to fit in with it; but I fear that reality was very different. We did start with one aim, that of remaining relatively committee-free so that decisions could be taken by individuals along well-defined lines of executive responsibility. I fear that we missed our target altogether in the sense that we now seem to suffer from a plethora of committees. What were the reasons why a group of well-meaning – and relatively experienced – people should fail so badly? I think that there were five: the bicameral structure imposed by the Charter, the co-existence of cellular and hierarchical systems, the growing impetus, nationally and internationally, towards participative democracy within organisations, the enormously fast development and growth of the new university, and the interdependence of the various divisions of the University imposed by its very nature. We found it essential to satisfy the demands of the first three; the fourth allowed us no time to think out ways of reconciling those demands in a single coherent plan, and the fifth introduced special obstacles to the solution of all of them.

The major problem of the management of a large complex organisation lies in separating the two major elements, namely the formulation of policy and its executive implementation. This has been recognised by numerous writers on the subject dealing with various kinds of organisations. It also lies at the heart of the difficulties of university government. The formulation of policy is, by popular consent, a matter that should involve the maximum of participative democracy. The implementation of policy cannot efficiently be carried out by the same process. Yet, if implementation is to be left to 'the administrators' there must be trust in them and accountability on their part. Neither of these criteria commonly hold in a university. Administrative officers are in many cases, from the Vice-Chancellor and the Secretary downwards, appointed rather than elected and cannot readily be dismissed if they fail to implement agreed policies. Academics, jealous of their rights as the supreme academic authority, tend to want to retain control of the implementation as well as of the formulation of policy (and the borderline is difficult to draw) and to be hesitant about delegating decision-making about implementation, save in routine and trivial matters, to administrators over whom they feel they have no control. The situation is, of course, aggravated by the fact that the employing authority, the Council, is not the same as the academic authority, the Senate. Thus our original idea of giving decision-making powers to individuals as executives or administrators was frustrated.

What has emerged is an extremely complex system. It surprises me that it works as well as it does, and it is very difficult indeed to describe. I can perhaps best explain it by analysing it in four separate ways, each of which has its own internal coherence, but which, when taken together, appear utterly inchoate. It is as if each of four separate structures were to have been drawn upon transparencies: when one looks at the four transparencies overlaid there does not seem to be any clear structure at all. What then is the role of the Vice-Chancellor in all this, and what is the nature of each of the four separate structures?

Article 8 of the Charter lays down that 'There shall be a Vice-Chancellor of the University who shall be the chief academic and administrative officer of the University . . .'. Later, in Statute 5 iv, it states, 'The Vice-Chancellor shall have a general responsibility to the Council and the Senate for maintaining and promoting the efficiency and good order of the University'. There is, therefore, no room for doubt that the Vice-Chancellor is charged with total responsibility for the running of the University. On looking for the source of the Vice-Chancellor's power to act in this way and to carry this responsibility one finds no clear description in the Charter. In the statutes the powers of the Council and of the Senate are spelled out in great detail, but those of the Vice-Chancellor are restricted to certain powers over students. He may refuse to enrol any person as a student of the University, he may suspend any person from any course and he may exclude a person from any part of the University or premises used by it; but even this authority is circumscribed for he must report any such action to the Senate at its next meeting. Thus, in statutory terms a Vice-Chancellor is in a position opposite to that of the harlot, and holds responsibility without power.

Thus the Vice-Chancellor can wield enormous influence but he does not possess statutory power; he wields influence only with the consent of those over whom he exerts it. He gains that consent to a greater or lesser extent because of such nebulous factors as his reputation as an academic and as a man, his charisma and leadership, and as a result of the reactions that he provokes amongst all his colleagues over the years that he spends in office. His influence could therefore gradually wither and die, be blown away in the turmoil of a storm or even be uprooted by those seeking to do so.

The Vice-Chancellor sits as an ex officio member of the Council and also as ex officio Chairman of the Senate. He is the prime link between the two governing bodies of the institution, but in the one case he must speak with the voice of the whole Senate, and in the other he can speak only as one of the 39 members of the Council. It is therefore normal to be in the position where, wearing one hat, one is committed and vocal in support of a course of action which, wearing another hat, one is committed to deny. I suppose

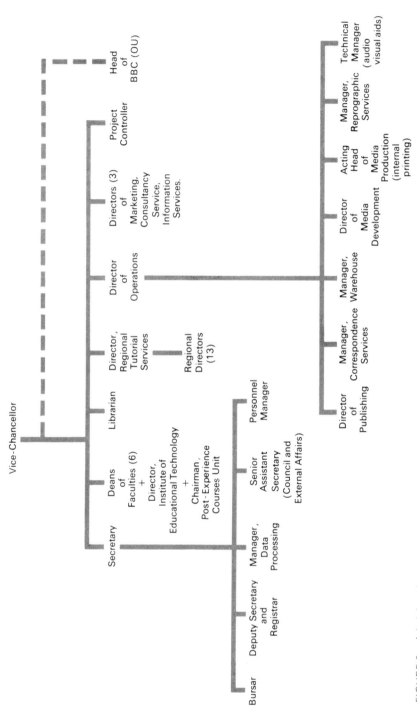

FIGURE 9   Administrative responsibility

it is because this is such a normal state of affairs that one learns to live with it; and the institution seems to survive the dichotomy. The Vice-Chancellor is continually forced by circumstances to take decisions without waiting for the whole of the university machine to operate. In his book *The Open University from Within*[16], John Ferguson quotes me as saying '(My) concept of democracy is to give everyone a full opportunity of expressing (his) views, after which (I) can make up my mind.'

Taken out of context this sounds an arrogant and dictatorial attitude, but in the context of the Vice-Chancellor's job as I have described it, it will be seen to be very far from that. In fact, one could not survive in the delicate position of Vice-Chancellor of the Open University unless one did one's best at all times, having listened to the opinions of one's colleagues, to take decisions which they could be expected to support. Sometimes it takes much longer to educate the University community to the point where they are prepared to support a proposition than the time that is available in which to take a decision to go ahead with it. Thus, if a Vice-Chancellor is doing his job properly, he must take decisions without going through the full democratic process; but they should always be those decisions, which given adequate time, would have been taken by the majority in a democratic vote. It is not, of course, easy to operate in this way and, lacking statutory power, a Vice-Chancellor must not make many mistakes or he will rapidly lose the trust and credibility upon which he relies.

The first of the four separate governmental structures is that of administrative responsibility. As chief administrative officer of the University, the Vice-Chancellor has a very large number of people responsible to him for the execution of policies laid down by the two governing bodies. The University for its government structure has laid down certain major objectives one of which is, 'to establish and maintain clear lines of executive responsibility in order that officials of the University may operate within a properly defined framework and action can be taken quickly and effectively'. This is our unexceptionable aim; the problem is to make it work in practice. I have sketched out in Figure 9 the chain of administrative responsibility as it exists at present. It will be seen that far too many people (17 in all) report directly to the Vice-Chancellor; most management theories would insist that no one man should have more than about six to eight staff directly responsible to him.

The position is further complicated by the fact that, of these 17 people, nine are appointed to their posts by the Council and hold clear-cut positions in an administrative hierarchy, whereas eight (the six Deans, the Director of the Institute of Educational Technology and the Chairman of the Post-experience Courses Unit) are (or ultimately will be) elected by their academic colleagues, the nominations being ratified by the Council. The latter group thus have a dual function, for they are not only administrative officers of the University, they are also the *main* spokesmen of their constituents representing their special interests.

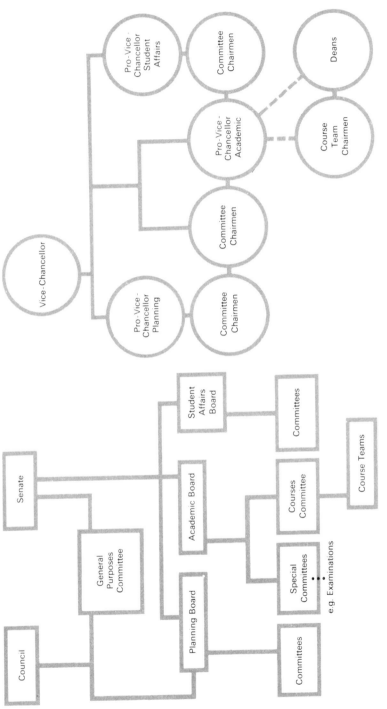

FIGURE 10   Functional areas

Another objective of the government structure of the University is, 'to ensure effective decision taking by allowing problems and issues to be seen in relation to each other at every stage and thus to minimize duplication'. We determined, and it was an arbitrary decision, to organise policy formulation within clearly defined functional boundaries. Thus, the work of the Senate is organised in relation to such functions as student affairs, teaching policy and planning policy; and it is these functional areas which I have delegated to the three Pro-Vice-Chancellors. The overall current structure for these functions in the University is shown in Figure 10. The figure is in two parts. On the left I give the committee structure subserving the various functions; and on the right the chairmen, who often exercise executive authority on behalf of their committees.

In the exercise of this authority a further problem may arise, for there will often be an office of the administration charged with the duty of implementing the policy decisions of the Committee and the administrative officer in charge may well come into conflict with the Chairman of the Committee. In theory I suppose that the Committee itself should formulate the policy, the Chairman should act for the Committee in interpreting it and the administrative officer should implement it, but in practice the distinctions between formulation, interpretation and implementation are usually blurred. It is goodwill and understanding that ensure that, in most cases, the system works.

Deans may thus deal directly with all three Pro-Vice-Chancellors on various matters that affect their faculties, but they remain responsible for the overall running and efficiency of the faculty only to the Vice-Chancellor and have the right of direct access to him. This is a vital factor, giving them a critical influence upon the institution.

A third objective of the government structure of the University is, 'To allow participation by members of the University in its decision-taking processes to the maximum degree commensurate with its efficient operation'. As worded, this objective is little more than a pious hope, for the current number of 'members of the University', which covers academic staff, part-time tutorial staff, all registered students and all graduates, totals well over 70,000 people. How best do we get maximum participation in the formulation of policy and simultaneously keep implementation of policy in the hands of the absolute minimum of executive managers? Large groups of participants find it hard to influence decision taking, small groups are by definition unrepresentative, and there is no way out of this dilemma. But there does exist within the University yet a third structure which reflects the aim of achieving participative democracy (see Figure 11). I have drawn the figure to indicate the two ways in which democratic principles are built into the structure of the University. The first represents the influence that individuals can exert on the employing authority as members of a staff association or union; each group of staff and students is thereby provided with access to the Council as employer (see the upper half of the diagram). I am primarily concerned, however, with how democratic principles can in-

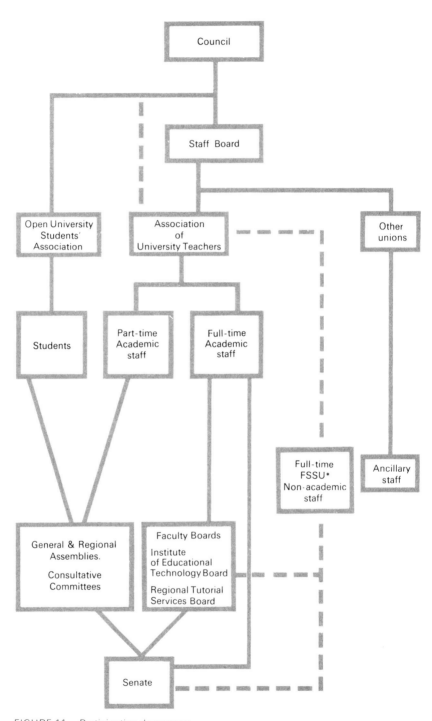

FIGURE 11   Participative democracy
* Federated Superannuation Scheme for Universities

fluence the academic policies of the University and the mechanisms for this are illustrated in the lower half of Figure 11.

Each student and each member of the part-time staff can exert an influence on the policy-making of the University through membership of a consultative committee or of a regional assembly, and can play a part in electing representatives to the General Assembly, the Central Consultative Committee and, since 1975, to the Senate. The full-time academic staff have a dual role – they have, as it were, a double vote – for they are members either of a Faculty Board or of the IET or RTS Boards and can, through the Boards, put proposals of any kind to the relevant functional units of the University. In addition they are all members, as of right, of the Senate itself. It may be that they are in a position to influence policy at too many points within the system. Indeed the sea-lawyers amongst the academic staff can play this complex system most effectively and can sometimes seriously hamper the flow of business. It is only the non-academic staff who have no definitive voice in the formulation of policy, other than that afforded them by co-option as members of Senate or by appointment to Boards and Committees.

The final objective of our government structure is 'To establish and maintain efficient methods of communication before, during and after the decision-taking processes'. We do, of course, disseminate information throughout the University through newspapers, circulars and committee papers. More significantly an informal network of liaison committees and working groups has grown up to ensure that those who are responsible for taking decisions and for implementing policy are kept informed as far as possible about what is happening not only inside the University but also in the outside world. I have tried to sketch this fourth 'government structure' in Figure 12. The 'team' consists of the Vice-Chancellor, the three Pro-Vice-Chancellors, the Secretary and the Registrar. It meets every other week, keeps no minutes and has no formal agenda. Its primary purpose is to ensure that the right hand knows what the left is doing. The 'big team' consists of the same group plus all Deans and Directors and the Bursar. It serves precisely the same function for the larger number of people. Some members of the 'team' each have a number of subsidiary groups that meet to discuss particular problem areas. In addition I hold a series of informal meetings with the Regional Directors who otherwise feel very isolated from what is going on at the centre. Finally I have a standing committee, called the Academic Collaboration Committee, which meets to consider proposed new developments which would necessitate the University working in association with outside organisations.

This structure enables the Vice-Chancellor to take soundings before coming to the decisions which he himself is responsible for making. It also enables the Vice-Chancellor and the administration to channel new matters into the cycle of business of the University at the appropriate place and time. Such an informal sounding-board is essential in enabling the

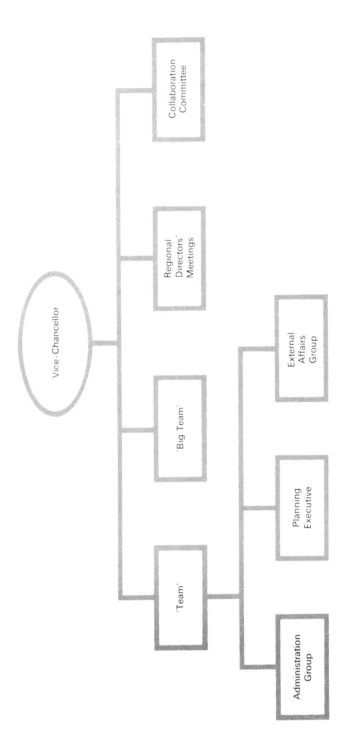

FIGURE 12 Informal liaison

Vice-Chancellor to do the almost impossible job that is required of him under the Charter.

Analysis of our governmental structure reveals three facts which, I believe, lie at the heart of complex systems. The first is that no single tidy chart can ever illustrate the complexity of the real situation, because the various objectives of the institution impose different infrastructures; consequently the system must inevitably exist in a perpetual state of conflict. When this conflict can be controlled in such a way as to induce a creative tension the system will work; the problem facing those charged with imposing the control is to ensure, somehow, that the conflict does not become destructive. The borderline is subtly drawn and keeping the institution on the right side of it is a constant strain.

The second fact is that, however hard one may try to modify the infrastructure – and we have had, in our short life, two major reviews of government structure, each of which was thorough and conducted with a remarkable insight into the nature of the problems – one can never eliminate the sources of conflict. I tend to the view that it is probably a mistake to try. All that can be done is to improve the function of one or more of the concomitant infrastructures. In this respect our two reviews have each been partly successful and this is reflected in the relatively sensible and coherent nature of each of the four infrastructures that I have analysed (Figures 9–12). Further improvements can, I think, be achieved only by amendment of our existing Charter, but even this could never totally remove the sources of conflict. Indeed the experience of the University of Toronto since the fundamental change in its constitution tends to bear this out.

The third fact to emerge from the analysis is that, in any large organisation, which is essentially a complex system, the problems of differentiating between what is policy formulation and what is policy implementation will prove impossible to solve. Consequently delegation of the latter from committees to individuals, which is essential to efficiency, will always be difficult in practice and can be achieved only piecemeal by patient persuasion, and never at a stroke by edict. It is achieved in most instances as a result of 'case-law' by which one example, having been debated at length, may serve as a precedent for individual action in later similar cases. On other occasions it is achieved by the acceptance of 'guidelines' within which individuals can then take decisions.

In short, while I believe that we could still improve very considerably on our present structure, especially by amendment of the Charter, I also believe that the apparent incoherence of our overall system does not reflect a state of chaos; rather it represents a calculated attempt to achieve objectives which individually demand conflicting solutions. In 1969 none of these complex structures had evolved, and we set off along an unknown path with no clear idea of the ultimate size and complexity of the University. To begin with we worked very informally, with the goal of keeping everything informal and of avoiding the fate that had befallen most of us in other universities, that of becoming committee-ridden. I was very anxious that we should have the minimum number of standing committees and that we should operate through project working groups which would be formed to tackle a given problem and then be dissolved. All the other decision making would be done by individuals charged with responsibility for one or other function of the University.

In 1969 it all worked very well; there were only a handful of staff and everyone could meet in the office in Belgrave Square and debate the problems of the week. Everyone who was working there knew all there was to know. We all met for coffee every day. Almost every policy paper was written by me or by one of my close colleagues and there was certainly no piece of paper with which any one of us was unfamiliar. We started monthly meetings of the embryo Senate attended by twelve to twenty members; since both the Planning Committee and, later, the Council of the University met every month, there was a great deal of interplay and there was no difficulty in communication. In those days decisions were taken very fast indeed, in a matter of days; they had to be, and I have no reason to believe that they were less efficient because they were made speedily. To-day they take a very long time indeed and I suspect they are still subject to the same sort of mistakes. We seemed to have found answers to the problems of organisation and management. It is no wonder that nowadays we look back with nostalgia to those halcyon days! As we grew larger and more complex the atmosphere of a 'family business' began quickly to disappear.

The number of full-time staff increased to 116 over the months into 1970 and the size of the Senate to 150. It became necessary to have a smaller executive group, for rapid decisions were still vitally necessary. As early as July 1969 I had begun to hold 'informal meetings of the Vice-Chancellor with Directors of Studies'. These meetings took place weekly and we kept minutes of the matters that were discussed. The proceedings were formalised later in 1969, when the Council and Senate agreed to set up a committee called the Vice-Chancellor's Committee. Its terms of reference were, 'to co-ordinate the short-term planning activities of project working groups and to deal with day-to-day operational problems'. The Committee consisted of the six Deans of the faculties, the three Directors of other units, and two members elected by the Senate to act as 'watch-dogs' and to make sure that this new Committee did not act as a sort of caucus arrogating to itself the powers of the Senate. This was the first sign of the tension, common to all universities, between the academic staff and the administration. The Committee met weekly and held its eighty-seventh and final meeting in June 1971. During that period the Senate and Council met monthly, but the number of day-to-day problems arising in the rapidly developing University that could not wait for the statutory meetings of the governing bodies was unending, and the Vice-Chancellor's Committee acted as the clearing house for them.

The advantage of the system was that it enabled decisions to be taken quickly and business to be processed at the sort of rate necessary if the University was going to work at all. Its big disadvantage was that its existence was widely known and it became the repository of many decisions that should have been taken elsewhere. This enabled individuals and project working groups to pass the buck and have decisions made for them. It was the beginning of the breakdown of what I had hoped to have, namely a University that was not committee-ridden and that relied on individual managers making decisions and taking personal responsibility for them.

Meanwhile, however, there had been other rumblings about the nature of our government structure, which took two main forms. The first arose from the great difficulty of defining what was meant in the Open University context by the term 'full-time academic staff'. The need for such a definition was increased by the difficulties that had begun to arise over the division between those who worked at the centre of the University at Milton Keynes, and those who worked at the periphery, in the various regions. Concurrently the increasing size of the Senate as the governing body had begun to cause concern; how was such a large size to be made compatible with efficient executive action?

In a conventional university there is seldom much difficulty in knowing who is a member of the academic staff and who is not. The teaching staff, those who are in contact with the students as part of the teaching programme, are obviously academic staff. Administrators, technicians, clerical staff are just as clearly non-academic. Problems arise over individuals like the Librarian, who is usually made a member of the Senate, and with research personnel who, although they are nearly always regarded as academic staff, are frequently denied membership of the Senate. This denial is usually based solely on the fact that such staff have no direct concern with the teaching programmes of the University.

Our problem was very different. We had introduced, because we had no choice but to do so, new categories of staff not known in the other universities. These categories embrace the whole of the staff of the Institute of Educational Technology, the entire full-time regional staff, and all the groups, such as graphic artists and editors, who were subsequently collected together in the Operations Division. The Planning Committee had clearly intended that all such staff should be regarded as the equals of the traditional academic staff in the operation of the Open University, and this case was indeed argued vocally by many members of these new and important categories of staff. On the other hand traditionalism was beginning to reassert itself amongst those members of the central academic staff of the more conventional kind. As courses began to be constructed there arose a feeling that it was the people who created them who ought to have the deciding voice in academic matters; and that the extension of the term 'academic staff' to cover all these other categories of people would be to down-grade the status of that term, despite the fact that our method of teaching depended ultimately on both groups. This argument, which has gone on ever since at varying levels of intensity, is nearly always complicated by extraneous factors. Academic staff have terms and conditions of service which provide for study leave, and there is no doubt that this privilege is coveted by other categories of staff; furthermore the Charter provides automatic membership of the Senate for every member of the 'academic staff' so that, if the definition of academic staff were to be widened to include any other category, that category itself would become eligible for automatic membership of the Senate. Thus those who wished to promote a participative democratic form of academic management could do so by widening the definition of the term 'academic staff'.

We tried various ways of circumventing these difficulties, the principal one being to adopt the device of saying that such-and-such an individual was 'deemed to be a member of the academic staff for the purposes of membership of the Senate'. This avoided the necessity of converting his contract and terms and conditions of service to those which pertained to the academic staff.

By April 1971 the Senate accepted the following definition of academic staff: 'Those who, in their role and function, primarily determine the educational and intellectual nature and quality of the University's learning system (of which research activities are an integral part) through devoting a significant proportion of their working time to these matters'. As a definition it left a great deal to be desired; it depended upon a series of value judgments as to the interpretation of 'primarily', 'educational quality' and so on. Indeed, I imagine that it would be difficult to prove that any group of staff in the University was not covered by the definition. For example, those who cook the food in the Refectory may very well 'primarily determine the educational quality' of what is produced in the afternoon and they certainly devote 'a significant portion of their working time' to such matters.

The acceptance of this definition was, however, a critical step in the future of the Senate. It meant that all the full-time educational staff in the Regions became eligible for membership, and this implied an increase in size of the Senate from 150 to well over 300. Furthermore, as the number of staff in the University continued to increase the size of the Senate would grow steadily over the next few years, to reach nearly 600.

There were, at that time, three views on the question. Some people felt that to let the Senate get bigger would be advantageous in that it would be self-defeating; it would become obvious that it had lost any remnant of efficiency and that alteration was essential. Others felt, however, that dilution of the traditional dominance of the Senate by full-time (central) academic staff, would be to alter its nature in such a fundamental way as to change the whole future pattern of University government. There was, however, a third view which held that participative democracy was the most important single factor in the operation of the whole institution and, therefore, that the bigger the Senate the better; this view gained some support from the fact that, within the new and insecure environment of an experimental institution, there was a need to foster a sense of 'belonging'. We have debated these issues on two occasions in the Senate without reaching any consensus about how to proceed, and the whole question is still *sub judice*.

By 1971 it was clear that a new mechanism was needed to carry on day-to-day business and to replace the Vice-Chancellor's Committee, particularly as the frequency of Senate meetings was in future to be quarterly rather than monthly. We therefore replaced the Vice-Chancellor's Committee with a smaller executive, the General Purposes Committee; it would have much less business to do, as the infrastructure of the new Senate was considerably revised to enable sub-groups to deal with business in a satisfactory way. Five boards of the Senate were established covering academic policy, research, tutorial services, staff and student affairs and operations. Most of the standing committees of the University reported to one or other of the boards. It was hoped that the boards would themselves take ongoing decisions on behalf of the Senate and that the General Purposes Committee would only be called in when there was a dispute over an issue that involved more than one of the boards.

The Chairmen of all the boards were members of the General Purposes Committee, which was to become a new, small and efficient group for the solving of urgent problems and for giving advice to the Vice-Chancellor and the administration on matters that arose *de novo* from outside the University. The General Purposes Committee was composed of the three Pro-Vice-Chancellors and the heads of major divisions of the University; to keep it small it was necessary to drop from membership the Deans of the faculties, who had been members of the Vice-Chancellor's Committee from the beginning. This was a necessary step but it was a serious loss to me and, I believe, to the Deans; the contact that I was able to maintain with the affairs of each faculty became very much more tenuous and this had an inevitable effect on the nature of the University. It was aggravated by the fact that I was ill for three months at the beginning of 1971, and that I did not, on my return to work, collect into my own hands quite the number of threads that I had held previously.

It was from this period, as a result of my absence, of the appointment of the first Pro-Vice-Chancellors and of the establishment of the five boards of the Senate, that the University changed from a very tightly controlled and centrally organised institution, to a much more diffuse one with a much wider spread of authority and a consequent lack of tightness of policy control. Looking back, even had the concatenation of circumstances not arisen as it did, it is very doubtful whether a tight central control could have been maintained as the University grew to an unforeseen size and complexity. It was inevitable that the complex organism should develop all sorts of wills of its own, in the nooks and crannies of its administration and operations; and that these wills would not always reflect a central policy determined by a governing body or a chief executive.

Clearly, we have not yet developed a government structure that is wholly satisfactory. I began by admitting that we had no master plan and that we took decisions on an *ad hoc* basis to satisfy needs as they arose. We lived by a process of emergency decision-making. Looking back over the years I do not think that there was any real alternative. We had no clear vision of how development would occur; and, even had we possessed such insight, we had no time to think about its implications. What has emerged appears messier than it really is and we can improve upon it. Even amendment of the Charter would not, in itself, guarantee improvement, but it may be that any significant advance can be achieved only through and after such amendment.

16

FINANCE

Much of the doubt in government circles about the wisdom of starting a 'University of the Air', stemmed from concern in the Treasury about its cost. Its new name, 'The Open University' was seen as implying an open-ended commitment; how was expenditure to be constrained if entry was to be unrestricted and available to unqualified people? Miss Lee's contention, argued repeatedly until February 8th 1966, that a fourth television channel would be a *sine qua non* of the foundation of the new institution, provoked further financial worries because of the very high capital cost that would be involved in setting up the new channel. The first real estimate of the cost of an institution that relied only on broadcasting time available on existing channels was made by Lord Goodman; his estimate of running costs of about three and a half million pounds per annum must have appeared modest, and was probably viewed at the Treasury with suspicion (not altogether unfounded!). He himself now agrees that it was a gross un-derestimate; nevertheless it was an intelligent guess made at a time when there was no factual information on which to make calculations.

The report of the Planning Committee, when dealing with finance, stuck very closely to the figures that could be estimated with some accuracy, namely those that were concerned with the overheads of the University, the costs of maintaining the central establishment to create the courses and of paying the BBC for their production and transmission costs. It was made clear that it had not been possible to calculate the direct student costs. Now it so happened that the figure that the Planning Committee arrived at for the overhead expenditure was very much the same as that which had been forecast by Lord Goodman, namely, something between three and a half and four million pounds per annum. Since no figure was quoted for direct student costs, the press, in reviewing the report of the Planning Committee, latched on to the figure given for the overhead costs and did not qualify it; in other words it appeared in the press as if it would be the total annual cost of the University. This was perhaps a fortunate accident. Clearly, if we were to start with 25,000 students, there would be in addition to the inevi-table overheads a substantial cost involved in teaching each one of them. The trouble was that we did not know what the figure would turn out to be. For every ten pounds that we spent on each student, we would add another quarter of a million pounds to the total cost of the University; and the ex-penditure per student could not be less than fifty pounds and might be much more. Had this been known at the time, the reception of the Report of the Planning Committee would almost certainly have been even less favourable than it turned out to be.

There was so much about the University that was unique or at least very markedly different from the methods of teaching and the conditions pertaining in other universities, that the Planning Committee had resolved (and in this they were wholly supported by the government departments concerned) not to try accurately to forecast the scale and estimate the costs of every one of the new activities. Thus the estimated expenditure was given only in respect of main items of income and expenditure and was not broken down in any significant way. The inability to make accurate forecasts because of these novel characteristics was the primary cause of the decision, taken by the Planning Committee with the full support of Jennie Lee, that it would receive its grant directly from the Department of Education and Science during its initial years of development, and that it should not fall within the ambit of the University Grants Committee. This decision attracted a great deal of publicity, much of it adverse. There is a lot of misunderstanding about the nature and function of the UGC, even within the academic world itself. It is a part-time committee with a full-time chairman, which has the task of advising the DES about the size of the grants to be made to individual universities. It has no significant budget of its own; it advises the Department about the partitioning of one particular line of the Department's budget, a line that covers the expenditure of all British universities.

Over the years, the UGC has accumulated a wealth of experience and knowledge about the ways in which universities spend money in order to achieve teaching programmes in different departments and different faculties. It has in consequence, a number of norms by which to judge the cost and performance of each university and from which to devise mechanisms to decide how much each of them should receive from the overall grant for the universities in the DES's budget. It was perfectly plain that there was no such set of norms to guide the UGC in advising the DES about the size of the grant for the Open University. There was no other university, for instance, that would spend a very large fraction of its total grant in a direct payment to the BBC, and there was no other kind of institution with which such figures could be compared. Similarly, there was no university that would rely for most of its direct teaching on part-time staff and not on full-time staff; thus the staff/student ratio norms in the different faculties of conventional universities could not be applied to the Open University. There was thus very little advice that the UGC could give to the DES which would help the Department to determine how much grant to make available to the Open University. It seemed sensible, therefore, to keep the new institution as a wholly separate line in the Department's budget and to leave it outside the ambit of the UGC, until time and experience had led to the evolution of norms peculiar and pertinent to the Open University.

The force of these cogent arguments was not widely appreciated. Consequently the decision to leave the Open University outside the UGC ambit was viewed by the academic world as a means of protecting the new institution, of giving it favoured treatment and of preventing academic influence from other universities from playing any significant part in determining its nature.

On the other hand, some of us felt that the decision left the Open University in an extremely exposed position in the sense that if there were a change of government or a change of heart on the part of government, it would be very much easier to withdraw grants from the Open University if it were financed by a separate line of the DES budget; we would lack the potential protection afforded by having a buffer, in the form of the UGC, between us and the government of the day.

Within about a year, ministers at the DES were faced with the consequences. They were themselves acting as judges of the proposed expenditure of the Open University and they could not, in defending such expenditure in Parliament, use the existence of an independent advisory group such as the UGC to support their decisions. At that time, approaches were made to the Council of the University asking whether we would prefer, in the long run, to come under the UGC, or to have an independent visiting committee which would stand in the place of the UGC. After long debate, the University responded by rejecting the idea of a visiting committee in favour of being placed under the UGC, once the necessary norms had been determined; and that remains the position to date.

The decision to keep the University separate from the UGC did, however, raise fundamental questions about how direct funding from the DES could be arranged without any erosion of the autonomy associated with the university status granted by Royal Charter. From the outset the DES acknowledged that Government support would be provided as a 'Grant in Aid', under conditions strictly comparable in all main respects with those obtaining traditionally, through the UGC, in British universities. This meant that the University's own governing bodies would be fully responsible for managing the University's financial affairs under professional audit. They would naturally have to work within their total income, including the total block grant allocated by the DES, together with fee income and any income obtained from other sources. The decisions they took about spending that income would be subject only to scrutiny by the Comptroller and Auditor General and Parliament, through its appropriate Committee, on the same terms and conditions as pertain for other universities. It was also taken as axiomatic that, wherever the UGC had established norms, as for example in the levels of academic salary or in the rules governing capital grants for university buildings, the Open University would operate in accordance with them, unless there were some overriding reason that made them inapplicable. This has remained true throughout the entire period of existence of the Open University.

During the latter part of 1968, and the first months of 1969, in a series of discussions between the DES, the Open University Planning Committee and the Treasury, the decision to provide 'Grant in Aid' directly from the DES was confirmed, and thereafter a mutually acceptable set of financial arrangements was drawn up. In one respect, the funding of the institution did differ significantly from the method of funding the other universities by the UGC; and it did so with the agreement of all three parties. It seemed then that, with the rapid development from an outline plan to an institution with many thousands of students, it would be wise to base the planning cycle on a triennium, rather than on the quinquennium normally adopted for the other United Kingdom universities. At that time, such was the lack of advance knowledge of the pattern of our expenditure that we suggested that we should operate on a 'rolling triennium', so that, after each year, the remaining two years together with the next following year should be re-planned as a new triennium. This suggestion, however, was not accepted and has never been put into operation.

We have now lived through the whole of the first triennium and are currently in the final year of the second triennium. It is not however possible to judge the efficiency of the triennial arrangement, because throughout the whole six years of the two triennia, we have been living in a period of unprecedented inflation which has made budgeting extremely difficult. There has therefore been argument each year, between ourselves (and indeed all institutions in receipt of government funds) and the Departments concerned, about how much supplementary support is needed to cover inflationary rises in expenditure beyond the control of the institutions; and the net result of this is that instead of working to a triennial, or quinquennial grant, one is effectively in the position of working to an annual budget.

Furthermore, as we had anticipated, a whole series of unforeseen developments arose over the critical foundation years of the first triennium. Each development which involved new expenditure had to be justified step by step with officials of the DES. In the second triennium unforeseen developments were naturally much less common; but an additional complication arose from the large increase in the number of applicants. We had then to justify an adjustment upwards of the target number of students to enable us to admit more students than had been budgeted for when the second triennial settlement was arrived at. I have tried to indicate (Table 17) the amounts of money agreed at the time of the triennial settlements and to relate these to the real value of money (taking account of inflation) and to the actual grants paid.

The Table shows in line 7 that, in all three years of the first triennium, the actual grant paid, even after adjustment for inflation in the year concerned, was considerably greater than the agreed triennial settlement. For 1971 the grant paid was 9% higher than the original settlement and for 1972/3 the percentage increased to over 13%. These adjustments for inflation were agreed, furthermore, by a Conservative government which had been out of sympathy with the idea of the Open University when it was begun, and they are an indication of just how sympathetic and understanding the ministers and the officials were, both at the DES and the Treasury, over the problems that the new institution was facing.

When one remembers that it was not until the end of 1973 that there was any significant number of graduates from the new university, it is all the more remarkable that two successive and opposed governments should

TABLE 17　Triennial settlements and the effects of inflation

	69/70	71	72	73	74	75	76
		£m	£m	£m	£m	£m	£m
1 Triennial settlement		5.49	6.86	7.87	10.6	11.2	11.8
2 Triennial settlement (adjusted Oct 1970)		5.46	6.50	7.30			
3 Actual grant paid	3.19	6.01	7.90	10.01	12.65	16.26	21.9
4 Tress-Brown inflation index (%)		8.4%	10.3%	9.3%	21.1%	25.0%	
		£m	£m	£m	£m	£m	£m
5 Actual grant adjusted to 1971 prices*		6.01	7.24	8.23	9.43	9.48	9.57
6 Settlement adjusted to 1971 prices		5.49	6.36	7.27	8.71	9.20	9.70
7 Grant as % of settlement (all at constant 1971 prices)		109%	114%	113%	108%	103%	99%
					£m	£m	£m
8 Actual grant (second triennium) adjusted to 1974 prices					12.65	12.73	12.84

* These figures are calculated by applying a correction to the grant for one year based on the Tress-Brown index *for the previous year.* Actual supplementation was calculated by different methods in various years but this correction gives the nearest approximation to constant prices.

support an experimental institution so well and enable it to get off to such a good start. Thus, up to the end of 1971, before any student had gained any credit even in one course, there had been a total recurrent expenditure by the government on the Open University of £9.2 million and a total capital expenditure of £3.5 million, so that some £12.7 million had been spent as an article of faith that the new institution would be a success. It is the history of this gigantic gamble that excites the admiration of the governments of many of the other countries which have been interested in this kind of educational venture; none has, until very recently, been prepared to invest to this extent in a comparable institution. The fact that the British government, with a tradition of extreme conservatism in its educational policies, should have been the one to embark on such a venture is all the more remarkable.

When one looks at Table 17 in respect of the second triennium, it can be seen that there was a big increase in the actual grant paid for 1975. This increase was a result of the agreed increase in the intake of new students in that year, due to the very large increase in the number of applications.

The quinquennial system used by the UGC is an extremely useful one for universities. It enables them to know, five or six years in advance, how much additional money they can expect to have for new developments, and is a period long enough to plan such developments sufficiently carefully. It also enables building programmes to be planned so as to take account of new developments and provide the necessary space for their housing. In recent years, however, the system has been working less and less well. Governments have been progressively more dilatory in settling the total university bid for money for the next quinquennium. This was perhaps inevitable, because over the period in question, the total amounts being spent by universities were increasing by leaps and bounds: the total University Grants Committee expenditure in 1950 was only £15 million, but by 1970, this figure had increased to £230 million. The net result of these delays, however, has been that universities have not known the quinquennial settlement until a date too late to enable them to make significant changes in academic planning for the first year of the new quinquennium. Indeed, in latter years, the habit grew whereby the first year of the quinquennium was settled separately from the later years, so that effectively the period became a quadrennium, with an annual settlement every fifth year. Furthermore, the quinquennial system depends on an agreement between the universities and government that, in the final year of the quinquennium, no new developments are introduced which would themselves demand additional funding in the following quinquennium, so that the final year of each quinquennium has become a period of consolidation. This effectively means that only in three years out of five can universities introduce new developments. For the Open University, working on a fixed triennium, the position could well be even worse in the sense that only in one year of the triennium could new developments be effectively introduced, and since the rate of building is now so slow, it would be impossible to plan capital expenditure to fit in with new developments over such a relatively short timescale.

During the recent period of massive inflation all systems of long-term financial planning have had to be abandoned, and we have all operated virtually on an annually determined budget. But the quinquennial system worked well when the country was in a stable financial situation and when the total government expenditure on universities was a relatively small fraction of the gross national product. There were two conventions that had come to be accepted as rules. The first was that the estimates submitted by the UGC for the following quinquennium would be accepted in full by the government of the day. This convention was first broken in the mid 1960s, when the UGC estimates were cut by the Treasury. This action came as a very rude shock to the university community, who until that point had lived in the happy faith that the convention was sacrosanct; it was therefore a significant turning-point in the confidence of the universities as a whole in the UGC system. The second convention was that once a quinquennial settlement had been agreed it would be honoured by the government of the day. In the recent period of massive inflation the spirit of this convention too has been broken. For, although the quinquennial grants have been paid in full, the real value of the money granted has been greatly reduced, and supplementary grants to counteract inflation have not been large enough to restore the purchasing power of the original settlement. Neither convention had ever been a rule. Since government expenditure is authorised by Parliament annually it had always been open to government (or indeed to Parliament) to refuse to honour in any one year amounts that had been agreed for that year at an earlier date. Despite the fact that the conventions can no longer be regarded as sacrosanct the quinquennial system is still a better one than any other yet devised and is the envy of most other countries.

Over the last year or two we have quite rapidly been approaching a situation where norms for our expenditures can be established; and many of these have been described in the Report of the Gavin Committee[22] (see Chapter 18). Although these have not yet been fully accepted by government, it is probable that they soon will be. When this happens it seems to me, although many of my colleagues would not agree, that the Open University should be placed within the ambit of the UGC which will then be able to advise government, as an independent assessor, about the level of grant that is appropriate to it. Although our student population is at present a very different one from that served by the other universities, this may well change over the years if the other universities come to accept more students on a part-time basis. In that case it will be all the more necessary that a single advisory body should have an overview of the provision of university-level education in the country as a whole. Nevertheless, this decision is in turn likely to be influenced by what the future may hold for the national provision of continuing education (see Chapter 21).

As Table 17 shows, the Tress-Brown index of inflation in all three years of our first triennium ran at about 10%, whereas, in the second triennium, the rate of inflation in 1974 was 21.1% and in 1975 about 25%. Clearly such rates of inflation are incompatible with the maintenance of services in any institution on a fixed grant. During the first triennium, the conditions that had applied for many years to other universities also applied to us. These were basically that any nationally agreed increase in academic staff salaries was automatically compensated by supplementary grants made to each university. In respect of other inflationary increases, there was no automatic supplementation of this kind, but negotiations between the universities, the UGC and the government led to supplementation to cover agreed increases in costs of particular categories of expenditure. From 1974 the University agreed with the DES that the basis of assessing supplementation should be changed to become the Tress-Brown index. In other words, rather than assess increases in costs for particular budget heads, a common percentage increase, based on the Tress-Brown index, would be applied to all eligible expenditure. So that payment for supplementation would not always be retrospective, the Department agreed that, from 1974, recurrent grant payments should be assessed at mid-year price levels, based on movements in the index during the preceding year (i.e. an attempt would be made to estimate the rate of inflation in advance).

On these general bases, the financing of the University remained reasonably stable throughout the first triennium, despite the annual 10% increase due to inflation. The situation was to change very radically in the second triennium, with the rapid increase in the national rate of inflation. There were two government announcements during 1974 that marked the change. The first concerned the relationship of supplementation to the level of student fees. The University was advised that supplementation from 1975 onwards would relate only to the proportion of expenditure not covered by student fees, the implication being that either the University increased the level of student fees to maintain the real value of its total income or it would have to make cuts in real expenditure. This was likely to be particularly damaging to the Open University since our fees constituted a larger proportion of our total income than did the fees in other universities.

A little later, there was a general government announcement to the effect that universities financed through the UGC would receive no general supplementation for inflation in the financial year 1974–75. The effect of this decision would clearly be to cut the real level of spending of all universities. Were this decision to have been applied to the Open University, it would have had highly discriminatory effects. Supplementation for increases in full-time academic staff salaries was to remain automatic. Such salaries account for more than 50% of the expenditure of other universities but for only about 14% of Open University expenditure. Consequently, if the balance of expenditure were not supplemented we would be hit much harder than the others.

The Council of the University made strong and successful representations to successive governments in the hope that our special problems would be sympathetically considered, and the general ruling was not in the event applied to the Open University. As Table 17 shows, the degree to which our grant was supplemented in 1974 and 1975 effectively offset the effects of inflation.

In Table 18 I give figures for the total grant paid by the government per fully registered student in the University in each of the years of the first two triennia and also figures for that grant adjusted to take account of the rate of inflation over these years. The grant received by the University per fully registered student was just over £300 in 1971. This was an aberrant figure since much expenditure was being incurred in the preparation of courses for second-year students and we had only first-year students in the system. Consequently there was an abrupt fall in 1972 to £248 per student, but since then the grant per student has risen steadily each year, reaching £406 in 1976. It seems probable that this increase was due primarily to inflation. I have therefore calculated the grant per student in each year allowing for inflation at rates determined by the Tress-Brown index so that grants can be expressed in terms of constant purchasing power, and obtained the figures in the last line of Table 18. It is clear that 1971 (the first year of our operation) remains aberrant for the reasons just given. There was an abrupt fall in 1972, when the second intake of students joined the University, and since 1972 the grant per student has remained remarkably constant in real money terms, falling very slowly year by year as the number of students has increased.

TABLE 18   Grant per student and the effect of inflation

	71	72	73	74	75	76
	£m	£m	£m	£m	£m	£m
Actual grant paid	6.01	7.90	10.01	12.65	16.26	21.90
Actual grant adjusted to constant 1971 prices	6.01	7.24	8.23	9.43	9.48	9.57
	000	000	000	000	000	000
No. of student (Finally Registered)	19.6	31.9	38.4	42.6	49.3	53.4
	£	£	£	£	£	£
Actual grant/student	307	248	261	297	327	406
Adjusted grant/student	307	227	214	221	193	179

The grant paid per student is not the full cost of educating each student. It makes no allowance for the contribution paid by the student himself as tuition fees. It does, however, represent the direct cost to the government of each fully registered student. I have already explained why only finally registered students should be regarded as real members of the University community; thus the number of finally registered students should be used as the base-line of the total student population. A larger number of students are actually registered in the University from January to April each year, but they are provisionally registered and pay only a registration fee. This registration fee does not in fact cover the whole cost of a provisionally registered student to the University, although it makes a significant contribution thereto. Thus, by calculating the cost per student in terms only of finally registered students, one gets a slightly inflated figure, because one conceals the additional costs of the provisionally registered students. Nevertheless, it is a fair base from which to calculate costs per student, since such figures must clearly be related to success rates in the University.

Table 19 gives data about the fees paid by students. Tuition fees (line 1) are added to the component of the summer school fees that covers tuition costs (line 3) giving the total income for tuition. (The balance of the summer school fee covers board and lodging charges levied by the host institutions.) When the total income from tuition is divided by the number of finally registered students (line 5) one gets (line 6) the average tuition fee paid by a student. This sum must then be added to the grant paid by government per student (line 7) to arrive at the total cost of educating a student (line 8). The actual cost of educating one undergraduate in the Open University in 1975 was thus £369. Of this total sum, some 11% was obtained from fees paid by the student and 89% from government grant.

TABLE 19   Undergraduate fees 1971–1975

	71	72	73	74	75
	£m	£m	£m	£m	£m
1 UG fee income	0.48	0.77	1.18	1.26	1.41
2 UG summer school fees	0.41	0.74	0.91	1.03	1.29
3 Summer school (tuition) fees*	0.21	0.37	0.46	0.52	0.65
4 Total tuition fees	0.69	1.14	1.64	1.78	2.06
	000	000	000	000	000
5 No. of finally registered (FR) students	19.6	31.9	38.4	42.6	49.3
	£	£	£	£	£
6 Tuition fees/FR student	35	36	43	42	42
7 Grant/FR student	307	248	261	297	327
8 Income/FR student	342	284	304	339	369
9 Tuition fees as % of income	10%	13%	14%	12%	11%

* Calculated as 50% of summer school fees

When one turns to the calculation of how much it costs to produce a graduate in the Open University, one has a very much more difficult task. In the first place, we have not yet reached a steady state in terms of graduate production. It is still too early, as I showed in Chapter 13, to calculate the true number of students who will graduate from any given intake, and it is also too soon to know what will be the average time taken by a student to graduate. Even when we know the average time to graduation we will still have to adjust the figures, because there is virtually no cost to the University for a student who takes a year out in which he does not register for any courses. Indeed the total number of finally registered students for any one year takes no account of additional students who may still be in the system but who have decided, for one reason or another, not to take a course in that particular year.

It is relatively easy to calculate the crude uncorrected cost per graduate simply by dividing the total cost of the University in any one particular year by the number of graduates coming out of the system in that year. Figures of this kind are given in Table 20, and indicate that the adjusted grant per graduate has fallen each year and was running in 1975 at something like £1750, the actual grant per graduate being about £3000 in that year.

TABLE 20   Cost per graduate

	71	72	73	74	75
Actual grant paid	6.01	7.90	10.01	12.65	16.26
Actual grant adjusted to constant 1971 prices	6.01	7.24	8.23	9.43	9.52
No. of graduates	—	903	3641	5188	5421
Grant/graduate	—	8749	2749	2438	2999
Adjusted grant/graduate	—	8018	2260	1818	1756

We realised from the start that the University's recurrent expenditure must be seen as having two basic components, the first representing unavoidable overheads, largely but not wholly independent of student numbers, and the second being a direct student cost component, related to supporting the individual students themselves. Overhead expenditure can be sub-divided into, first expenditure by the University itself on full-time staff, maintenance of plant, buildings and course development and, second, the payments made to the BBC, to meet the costs of production and transmission of the audiovisual components of courses. Direct student costs comprise a wide variety of items, the main ones being the printing, packing and postage of correspondence material, the hiring and equipping of study centres, the provision of libraries of cassetted audiovisual material, the payment of a large number of part-time staff and the administrative costs at the centre and the regions that arise directly from services to students. In the first triennium the accounts published by the University show figures for direct student costs. But these figures unfortunately did not include all expenditure that could properly be attributed to students; there are many more items of expenditure, such as examination costs, that are included in the 'overheads' rather than in the direct student costs. Later analysis (see below) indicates indeed that expenditure that is 'student-related' could be some three times greater than the crude figures in the accounts. Nevertheless in Table 21 I have re-arranged the accounts for the four years from 1971 to 1974 inclusive to show this split of expenditure; all figures being given as expenditure per student. These may be compared with those for income per student given in Table 19. It is apparent that despite the inflationary pressure nearly all the figures are consistent over the years.

This relatively crude analysis was found to be inadequate, as the institution became more complex. For the second triennium, a new system of costing was adopted at the instigation of Professor Ralph Smith, one of the mathematicians in the University who has acted as Pro-Vice-Chancellor for planning purposes for the past five years. He pointed out in an elegant paper (reprinted in the Report of the Gavin Committee[22]) that the University was involved in two sets of variable costs and not in just one. In other words, there was a variable increase in costs as the number of courses offered by the University increased as well as a variable component of costs related

TABLE 21   Comparative cost per undergraduate student 1971–74

	1971	1972	1973	1974
Total no. finally registered students	19,581	31,902	38,424	42,636
Expenditure Head	£	£	£	£
Administration	39	39	39	49
Regional Services	43	42	42	46
Academic Faculties	60	47	49	58
BBC Recurrent	75	54	58	67
	217	182	188	220
Direct student costs	71	57	57	59
	288	239	245	279
Other	44	49	41	40
Total cost per student	332	288	286	319

to the increase in the number of students. His more sophisticated approach led to an approximate identification of three sets of expenditures, first an overhead component, second a course related component and third a student related component. In other words, the equation could be written not as T =A + Bn as we had used in the first triennium, but as

$$T = A + Bn_1 + Cn_2$$

where T =total expenditure, n_1 equals the number of courses on offer and n_2 equals the number of students in the system, and A, B and C are constants. He calculated that, at 1975 prices, for student numbers between 40,000 and 70,000 and for course numbers of 60–100, the values of B and C could be taken as £80,000 and £192 respectively. Thus each extra course that we offer will cost £80,000 per annum; and each extra student will cost £192. The latter figure is thus a reasonably accurate estimate of the marginal cost for one extra student.

In 1974, at the request of the Treasury, the DES set up a joint working party under the chairmanship of Professor Gavin, with representatives from the Department and from the University, to report on the norms that might be used to establish the levels of staffing (mainly academic staffing) in the Open University. Their report was published in 1975[22]. The working party accepted Professor Smith's formal analysis of expenditure and recommended it as a basis for the DES to calculate overall University expenditure and thus to arrive at the level of grant.

However one tries to make a comparison of the cost of educating a student in the Open University with the cost of educating a student in a conventional university, and whatever basis one uses for making those comparisons, one is forced to the conclusion that education through the

Open University is relatively very cheap. The cost per student per annum is very much lower: even if we consider the cost per graduate, which is the comparison least favourable to the Open University (see Table 20), we find that our crude estimate for 1973 of £2749 (which can only be an overestimate) may be compared with a figure for the comparable faculties of other universities of £5250 (UGC figures).

It is also obvious that the Open University, if it had to exist alone, would cost a very great deal more. It is a system complementary to the conventional system of higher education and parasitic on that system. Most of the teaching of the Open University is carried out by the part-time staff (some 6000 of them) most of whom are employed on a full-time basis by other educational institutions. In paying them for their Open University work the University does not have to provide them with the services that have already been provided by their primary employer. Thus for example we have no need to provide them with office space, with superannuation contributions, or with support for their research. We do not supply them with secretarial help. We give them no vacations on a paid basis. We do not provide them with study leave. All this is provided by their primary employing institution. Clearly, if we had to employ our tutorial staff on a full-time basis and meet all these additional expenditures, both capital and recurrent, the whole cost of the Open University system would be very much higher.

In the second place, we do not incur capital costs for our teaching accommodation. We hire the space for our study centres from existing educational establishments and we pay for this a relatively small fee that meets the additional costs falling on the host institution, but makes no real contribution to the capital investment involved in putting up these buildings (which, during the day, serve wholly different purposes). Similarly, for our summer schools, we occupy space in fourteen existing British universities which would otherwise not be fully utilised during the vacations. Thus, we are able to provide these services relatively cheaply.

From a national point of view this makes a great deal of sense, because it increases the utilisation of the capital tied up in the buildings of other institutions and enhances the educational services given by members of the staff of a host of educational establishments all over the country. In this sense, the complementary nature of the two systems is wholly advantageous; but the comparatively low cost of the Open University system is to some extent the result of the method of costing. Nevertheless, even when one has made allowances for the parasitic nature of the Open University, it is still true that our method of education incorporates real economies of scale which make it possible for a large number of people to be offered an opportunity of education at a cost considerably below that which would be incurred by traditional methods.

In 1969 we had to fix the fees that would be charged to our first students in 1971. The pattern adopted in the whole of the higher educational system in Britain was that students were required to pay tuition fees that covered only a small fraction of the total cost of their education, the rest being met by direct government subvention, through the UGC, to the institution itself. In the university system, the actual fees charged had not increased greatly over a period of years, during which the total cost of education had continually risen. In consequence, the fees, expressed as a proportion of the total cost of education, had been declining steadily over that period.

The figure in 1969 for the fee income of other British universities was £17.746 million, representing 7% of total income. We felt that it was proper that the Open University's fees should more than match this figure: and we planned to charge students fees which would yield about 10% of the total cost of their education. We set our fee level rather higher than that which was current in the other British universities, because we were aware that there was pressure from the other universities to increase their fees. The cost to the student worked out, on this basis, at £20 per credit, so that an ordinary degree of six credits would cost £120 and an honours degree £160. To this, of course, would be added the annual costs of attending summer schools, of buying books, and of travel to and from study centres.

When the Conservative government came to power in 1970, one of the pressures that were put upon the University was to increase the tuition charges so as to make the University more nearly self-sustaining and less dependent on government grant. This was resisted very strongly by the University Council on the grounds that to increase tuition charges would be to price the opportunity out of reach of the poorest members of the community who were, many of them, the most deprived educationally. Fortunately, we were able to sustain this argument at the time. As inflation increased in its impact, so the proportion of total expenditure recovered from fees declined and increasing pressure was put on the University by successive governments to increase fee income in order to keep pace with inflation and to maintain the proportion of total expenditure recovered from fees.

The University made one significant increase in fees in 1973, and in doing so attempted to set a new level of fees which would remain unchanged for several years. Consequently, there was an increase in that year in the proportion of expenditure recovered from fees, as shown in Table 19.

In 1975, the government insisted on assuming a sizeable increase in fees and used the 1973 proportion as the baseline for its calculation of the new fee levels that it wished the University to charge. It is of course true that autonomous institutions like the Open University may charge whatever fee they wish, but if the grant is calculated by the government having taken into account a fee income at an assumed level, then, if the University chooses to charge smaller fees, it must adjust its total expenditure to the reduced grant. There is thus a very effective means for the government to insist on an increase in fees.

During 1975 there was therefore a very long, and in some cases bitter campaign, conducted primarily by the students but with our support, designed to persuade the government to drop its demand for the increase in fees. The battle was, however, lost and the charge for each full credit course was increased in 1976 from £25 to £40.

It is true that inflation between 1971 and 1976 more than justified an increase of this magnitude. On the other hand, the ability of the poorer students to meet such charges was still very much in doubt and when coupled with parallel increases in the cost of summer schools, which the University had decided should be self-sustaining, in the cost of books and of travel, the burden falling on the student was very considerably greater than we had anticipated in 1969. In 1971 the minimum cost of obtaining a BA Degree was £200; by 1976 this minimum cost had risen to £327. It must be remembered that this is the absolute minimum cost; for students undertaking several post-foundation courses involving summer schools the total cost can be in the order of £500–£700.

The position is made much worse by the rulings that pertain in respect of grants paid to students through local authorities. The position in Britain is that all full-time students are awarded mandatory grants by their local authority. Thus if a student gains admission to an ordinary university, he is awarded a minimum grant of £50, and this can increase, on a means test of parental income, to a current maximum figure of £810. In addition, all his tuition fees are paid. Thus, although the fees charged to students by other universities were increased in 1976 to about £140, the burden falling on the poorer student has not been increased at all since the total cost of his education is met by the mandatory award of a local authority grant. The same does not apply to the part-time student, where the system of mandatory awards does not operate. Thus the Open University student who is in need may apply to his local authority for a grant, but it is awarded on a discretionary basis. In other words, the local authority may or may not accede to his request. The inflationary pressures in the country have hit local authorities' budgets especially hard, and consequently it is possible that local authorities may become very much less inclined to award discretionary grants. The increased fees of the Open University are thus unlikely to be met to any significant extent by an increase in discretionary grants to the poorer students. The government is very well aware of this fact but it is difficult for it to take any significant action in the matter. There are nearly 2 million part-time students in the country, and it would be difficult to exempt the Open University part-time student from the discretionary system and award him a mandatory grant while refusing it to all other part-time students. We are currently very worried that the welcome trend, whereby more and more of the really deprived working class population in the country have been applying for entry to the Open University, will shortly be reversed by the financial pressure that is being put upon them.

The best we have been able to achieve so far is an increase in the grant to the Open University for the provision of a hardship fund, to enable us to waive or assist with the fees of the students most in need. This will provide some small alleviation of the harsh facts of life but will be extraordinarily difficult to operate in practice, for it means that the University will be put in the position of having to operate its own means test and to decide whether its students merit awards from the hardship fund or not. Thus, in the current financial situation, the particular objective of the Open University of providing educational opportunities to deprived adults is being placed in serious jeopardy by the decision of government. We can only hope that the overall financial situation in the country will stabilise fast enough to remove this threat to the future well-being of the University.

I have been dealing so far with the recurrent expenditure of the University. Its capital expenditure differs very significantly from that in other educational establishments. In Table 22, I show the total capital expenditure of the University over the two triennia, which amounted by the end of 1975 to only £9 million. It covers the costs of buildings erected at the campus at Milton Keynes, general furniture and equipment, the equipment for the BBC studios and for the research laboratories and the library of the University. This is a very small capital expenditure to cover the education of some fifty thousand students a year. In comparison the capital expenditure involved in creating a new conventional British university capable of producing 6000 graduates per annum would be of the order of at least £60 million. In the current financial situation where the cost of money is so high, this capital economy is particularly attractive to government.

TABLE 22   Capital expenditure

| | Up to end of | | | | | |
	1970	1971	1972	1973	1974	1975
	£m	£m	£m	£m	£m	£m
Building works and fees	0.953	0.596	0.560	0.478	0.390	1.843
Furniture and equipment	0.620	0.449	0.208	0.163	0.396	0.323
Library books	0.026	0.004	0.002	0.067	—	—
BBC equipment	0.504	0.348	0.100	0.153	0.652	0.216
Totals	2.103	1.397	0.870	0.861	1.438	2.382
Cumulative totals	2.103	3.500	4.370	5.231	6.669	9.051

The amount made available for capital expenditure is nevertheless smaller than we had hoped, and one of our major problems has been the almost continuous freeze on new university buildings that has been a feature of our first six years of life. We are in consequence very short of space and this is a major factor in holding back the progress of the University and in causing frustration and distress to its full-time staff. Our essential building programme is two or three years behind schedule; I can only hope that happier times lie ahead and that this deficiency will be corrected in the very near future.

5

THE FUTURE

17

RESEARCH AND POSTGRADUATE STUDIES

There was never any doubt in the minds of those concerned with the creation of the Open University that it should be a University not only in name but in fact. The distinctive feature of a university as opposed to other educational institutions is that it engages in research, giving it as much priority as teaching; and that it is funded and staffed at a level sufficient to enable the research function to be satisfactorily pursued. It was made abundantly clear in the Report of the Planning Committee that the Open University, like other universities, should possess this feature; paragraph 48 of the Report reads 'The full-time academic staff will thus be expected to devote a significant fraction of their time and energy to private research so that they can keep pace with the advances in their subjects, and suitable arrangements will be sought to provide them with adequate facilities, both library facilities and, where necessary, laboratory facilities.' This objective was confirmed in more general terms in the Charter of the University as follows,'it is expedient that we should constitute and found a University for the advancement of learning and knowledge by teaching and research . . .' Throughout her long association with the University, Jennie Lee constantly emphasised that it must be nothing less than the equal of all the other universities in the United Kingdom.

This clear intention was a major factor in attracting me to join the University, and I have always acted on the assumption that it was a policy endorsed by the government when they accepted the Report of the Planning Committee. I advertised for academic staff in 1969 in terms similar to the advertisements for all other universities and made it clear to applicants that opportunities for research would be equal to those in other universities. In explaining this I did, however, enter two caveats. The first was that, like all other new universities, we could not expect to be able to provide in the early years of development of the University adequate buildings for the library or for laboratories; and that even if we did have these facilities, the pressure of creating our first undergraduate teaching programmes would leave little time left for research activity during that period. This was understood by all those who joined the University in the first years and accepted as a necessary feature of starting a new and innovatory institution. Nevertheless, it was implicit in that acceptance that the institution intended to support an active research programme just as soon as the facilities were available and the pressure of preparing the initial courses relaxed.

My second caveat was a rather different one. We knew that the total size of the full-time academic staff of the new institution was bound to be very small by comparison with the staff of universities which depended on normal traditional face-to-face teaching methods; our initial concept was of individual disciplines being represented by only about four members of staff. Furthermore, in the larger disciplines like chemistry and biology, the four members of staff would have to cover very widely different areas within the same discipline so that there could be no more than two people with a similar research interest. This implied that, within the Open University, there would be considerable benefits if the subjects of active research were broader and more inter-disciplinary in nature than was the pattern normal in most universities. Thus it would be desirable to mount research programmes in each of which a larger number of members of the academic staff could be involved. This kind of arrangement would make it easier to attract postgraduate students on external research grants to supplement the teams working on each particular problem. I therefore pointed out that the opportunity to carry out research in the individual disciplines might be harder to organise than it was in a conventional university, although there would be no question of frowning upon it; and that inter-disciplinary research teams might be preferable. In practice three such broad areas of research have already emerged, namely the Brain Research Unit, the Energy Research Group and the New Towns Study Unit. These have been amongst the most successful of our research programmes to date.

General discussions with early applicants for full-time academic jobs almost always followed these lines. It is also true to say that a number of members of the Planning Committee who served on the selection panels were seized of the idea that the new innovative teaching methods of the Open University would themselves form a fascinating subject of study. They often suggested to candidates that they probably would, within the context of the Open University, develop an interest in the methodology of teaching in general and in particular in the development of methods of making disciplines more directly understandable by distance teaching systems. Might they not, with the passage of time, become even more interested in this aspect of their work than in their private individual research interests? Such suggestions had a mixed reception at the time they were made. Nevertheless in practice a small but significant number of academic staff have indeed developed real interests of this kind.

I am quite certain that it was precisely because jobs on the academic staff were advertised and discussed in these terms that we were able to attract high quality applicants from other universities in this country and abroad; in turn, it was because we did appoint high quality academics that we were able to prepare and offer to our students courses of such high quality. Had there been any suspicion at the outset that the Open University would be primarily a teaching institution and not be an active research one, we would probably have failed quite miserably. It is arguable that such an institution would have been unworthy of the title 'University'; its current standing and reputation as an institution offering degrees of high quality could not have been achieved quickly if, indeed it could have been achieved at all.

Because of this basic philosophy we have always made every effort to lessen the obstacles which prevented people being really active in research. We decided that there should be postgraduate degrees offered both to internal and external students (see below). The primary purpose of the University was to serve external students at a distance and we deemed it necessary to provide for their needs at postgraduate as well as undergraduate level. Nevertheless we also felt that, to promote active research programmes amongst the staff of the University, it was vitally necessary to have internal postgraduate students of a conventional kind in residence on campus. Opportunities for such students to acquire postgraduate degrees up to and including the Doctorate of Philosophy were needed from the outset.

At that time the official government policy on postgraduate students was that funds to support them within the Universities should be channelled through the Research Councils and not through the University Grants Committee. Grants to maintain the universities were intended to cover the basic facilities that made research possible, but proposed research programmes would be judged by the Research Councils and, if approved, would attract money from them to cover *inter alia* the stipends of postgraduate students and the necessary special equipment and general research expenditure for them. I felt that the Open University must try as quickly as possible to put itself in a similar position so that our staff could attract such grants from the Research Councils. For this reason we included in our early budgets three rather unusual heads of expenditure. First, if any member of the academic staff could arrange to have access to laboratories in any other institution during the years when the University had no research space of its own, we would undertake to pay the rental charges involved in housing him in that host institution. Second, we provided each discipline with one research assistant. The general idea was that the senior member of staff in any discipline had probably been involved before joining the Open University in a particular research programme. Because he would himself be heavily involved in developing the early teaching programmes he could continue to carry out this research only if he had the help of a research assistant who would work under his direct instruction. I hoped that senior members of staff might be able to attract as research assistants the sort of person who had already had some postgraduate experience, but who was not particularly ambitious, and would be happy to continue working under supervision for a number of years. In practice, however, the posts were filled by ambitious and able young graduates who were anxious to complete a research degree and go off to further and more rewarding jobs in the academic world. Third, we decided that it would be justifiable, despite the current government policy, to devote a small fraction of our total grant-in-aid to the creation of research studentships. We felt that initially it might be difficult for our members of staff to attract grants from the Research Councils, and to get them started we should therefore be prepared to support research students from government funds. We were by no means certain that the DES would support this proposal, but it did in fact approve expenditure on these research studentships at the rate of one to each of the academic disciplines in the University. While doing something to help maintain the research activities of our new academic staff these measures were also an earnest of our intent to promote the research activities of the University as soon as circumstances would allow.

At that time I wrote to the Secretaries of all the Research Councils pointing out what we were trying to do and asking for their co-operation. I made it clear that, insofar as it was possible for us to do so, we would be offering that level of general support in the form of ancillary staff, space and equipment which was normal in other universities and that, in consequence, requests for grants would not be inflated by including the costs of services normally provided by a university. Despite the doubts in the academic world about the future of the Open University, and despite the fact that we had almost no facilities on campus, the Research Councils accepted the proposition that I had put to them; and in practice there was at that time no discrimination against our staff on the grounds that the University was unable to provide appropriate back-up services.

Thus in 1969 we did everything we could, as far as was practicable, to create a favourable climate for research. In the years that followed, however, we came up against a number of unforeseen difficulties which have prevented the rapid development of research facilities in the University.

In all new universities the creation of the library presents a major financial problem. The UGC usually recognises this by providing an initial starting grant to enable the new library to stock up with books and back numbers of journals in such a way as to make it possible for literature research to be carried out. The size of the starter grants, and indeed the scale of the recurrent expenditure on libraries, is very largely determined by a method of formula financing, depending on the number of undergraduates, postgraduate students and staff making use of the library. Although the allowances payable in respect of postgraduates and staff are much higher than those payable in respect of individual undergraduates the money provided on behalf of the latter represents a large fraction of the total sum. Our undergraduates, although much more numerous than in a conventional university, were not offered any service at all from our central library since this was regarded as an impossibly difficult logistic task. In consequence we were faced with the need to create a good library for staff without being able to claim funds for the servicing of large numbers of undergraduates. We have thus been unable so far to build up an adequate stock of books and back numbers of journals. The most recent figures indicate that the number of volumes held in the library per member of the academic staff runs at 123 as compared with over 1000 in other universities.

I have considered the possibility of making a public appeal for library funds, but the time has never been propitious. The scepticism with which we were viewed at first made it seem unlikely that we would succeed in any attempt to raise private money; and, more recently, when we have become reputable, the national recession has been a potential brake on fund-raising.

We have tried to mitigate the difficulties by making extensive use of the inter-library loan system that operates in this country. It is not, however, an adequate substitute for a good library that can provide a proper service for people engaged in literary research. Most of our staff in the arts-based faculties have been forced to use other libraries, a factor which puts an additional and time-consuming difficulty in the way of making rapid progress in research projects.

Successive governments over the years of our development have imposed freezes on university building. The basic laboratory building for the faculties of Science and Technology was originally intended to start in 1971 and to be open in 1973. It was actually begun in October 1975, so that we have already lost four years; and furthermore only a part of the building, as it was originally planned, has so far been approved and funded. In 1969 we built a small laboratory block intended only as preparation laboratories where home kits could be developed and experiments to be shown on television could be worked out. This building, which provided only one small room per discipline, has for six years been our only science-technology laboratory on the campus. Despite this disgraceful state of affairs many of our staff have managed to continue their research, which is greatly to their credit. The preparation laboratories have been used to their full capacity for research programmes; a Research Unit was set up in Oxford, in a rented house, to provide for the needs of some of our physicists and technologists; and a number of staff have continued to carry out active research work in space in other universities made available to them by the good offices of their hosts. Nevertheless it has become a matter of increasing frustration and bitterness that the promises, made in good faith by the University to its staff when they were recruited, have not been honoured. This has not been for any lack of endeavour on the part of the University itself; we have simply been unable to persuade successive governments to provide the necessary buildings fast enough.

The delays in the provision of adequate facilities are serious enough for those who were appointed as professors and senior lecturers in the Open University. However, they came to the University with established reputations, and a hiatus in their research output would not put their future employment and prospects at risk. It has been much more serious for the younger people who came with research reputations still to be made. It is a matter of grave concern to me and to the Council of the University that they should continue to remain in this state of limbo and we have continually pressed the government for more research facilities.

A third aggravating factor arose from the success of the first students. In two ways they outstripped our expectations: first in the high proportion who obtained credits, and second in the smaller but still relatively high proportion who attempted more than one course at a time. As a result there was a need to provide more quickly than we had anticipated a selection of more advanced courses, to keep up with the legitimate aspirations of our most successful students. All decisions about the rate of course provision have been and must be made by the Senate, which is formed of the very people whose research has been put at risk; and the members of Senate have, on each occasion that the matter has been debated, voted in favour of continuing a high rate of course production to meet the needs of the students. In so doing they have implicitly denied themselves enough time to carry out their own research work. This is no doubt an extremely altruistic attitude but it is not one that the University can permit indefinitely, because of its effect on the whole research programme of the Open University.

For all these reasons there has been a long delay in setting up an active research programme. This has had an unfortunate side effect in that an increasing number of people all over the country have come to think of the Open University as primarily a teaching institution and not as a research-based one, despite all the protestations that we have made to the contrary. During late 1974 and early 1975 occasions arose when members of staff who applied for research grants were informed that had the proposal come from any other institution it would have been supported, but that it was being rejected because it was not considered that the Open University was a research-based institution. I was horrified to discover that there had been such a serious change in attitude. Urgent action was needed to counteract it and I had no difficulty in persuading the Council to publish the statement which I reproduce here, and which embodies the philosophy of the University in simple and straightforward terms.

The Open University has, over the five and a half years of its life, introduced a wholly new system of distance teaching and has used it with great success for over 60,000 students, of whom nearly 10,000 have already obtained degrees. During this period a total of the equivalent of some 45 full credit courses has been written and produced. Each is an integrated multi-media course and many are interdisciplinary and of innovatory content and design. Each represents some 400 hours of student work; it takes many hours of academic staff time to prepare one hour of student work. As a result, during these years the full-time academic staff of the University, who now number some 300, have given unstintingly of their time and energy to an extent far beyond that which would be expected in the normal course of duty. In doing so, many of them have foregone their full leave entitlements, postponed their entitlements to study leave, and have been able to devote too little time to private study and research.

The academic staff of the Open University were recruited in precisely the same ways as the academic staff of other universities.

They have virtually the same conditions of service as do the academic staff of other universities. The senior staff came with established reputations in their own fields of scholarship and research. From the outset the Open University undertook to supply them, as soon as possible, with facilities for private study and research on a level comparable with that available in any other university; and the Council has never deviated from its intention of honouring that undertaking at the earliest possible date. It is of particular importance to do so in the case of younger staff whose efforts have been so much directed towards course writing at the most crucial time in the establishment of their careers. Active consideration is being given therefore to the encouragement of research; each year rather more of the University's resources are being directed towards its build-up within the limits imposed by the facilities currently available; and the teaching load for members of staff is gradually being adjusted in order to allow them more time for research.

Regrettably, it remains true that the Council's plans to provide adequate research and library facilities for the staff have suffered setbacks from a series of government cuts in capital expenditure on university buildings so that, even now, the faculties of Science and Technology have no permanent buildings and the temporary arrangements that have been made are much less than adequate. But plans are at last at an advanced state and have been approved by the Government, and it is hoped that the first phase of the building will be started early this year. Nevertheless, it will be several years before a reasonably adequate provision is achieved.

It should be emphasised that despite the considerable difficulties encountered, many members of staff have been determined to keep up their research activity. The Open University's Oxford Research Unit and Brain Research Group are outstanding examples of this. In 1974 nearly 100 research publications and books were produced and over eighty visits to international conferences overseas were undertaken, which show that the academic staff have every intention of continuing their research studies.

It should also be noted that the academic staff of the University have, in many instances through their commitment to innovatory new courses, developed new research interests in complex problems involving many disciplines. Cases in point are research groups in energy, in communication theory, and in new town planning. These research groups are themselves investigating problems in areas which, in turn, form the material for the more advanced courses to be offered by the University. This pattern is identical, though in entirely new fields of study, to the pattern upon which honours degree teaching in the classical university disciplines has always been based; namely that the advanced level teaching is sustained in the context of the Open University, for failure to do so will inevitably lead to eventual reduction of standard in the teaching materials.

Because of the very success of the Open University in developing as a new and innovatory teaching institution over a period of years during which research has been inhibited by shortages of both time and facilities, there has grown, in certain quarters, an impression, no doubt for the reasons described above, that that is all that it is; and that it is not, and, indeed, should not be, an institution firmly rooted in the tradition of research and scholarship that is characteristic of other British universities. The Council wishes to make it incontrovertibly clear that this impression is false, that the future of the University as a university depends utterly upon dispelling it, and that, as with every other British university, it is not possible to teach effectively at the Open University without firmly basing the teaching programme on the research and scholarship of the staff. Furthermore staff for the Open University courses could neither be recruited nor retained on any other basis.

It is because of its deep concern for this intimate relationship between teaching and research that the Council has decided to make this statement. The Council is aware that it is quite impossible to provide all the necessary accommodation, equipment and time for research immediately; and that demands for further resources must be tempered to the present economic climate. This statement does not in itself call for immediate further resource. It does call for a reconfirmation by the Government of its commitment, implicit in its acceptance of the Report of the Planning Committee and in the award of the Charter, to the aims of the University, including, as they did, the aim of promoting research. The statement is further intended to induce awareness, within the academic world, that the Council firmly intends to achieve, as soon as possible, all these aims, including the promotion of research; and that it hopes that such awareness will ensure that, in so far as any individual member of staff of the University has access to the facilities necessary for undertaking a particular research project, all grant-giving authorities, including the Research Councils and the research foundations and trusts, will consider applications for the support of that research project on the same basis as they would consider applications emanating from any other university. Only under such circumstances can the morale and enthusiasm of the staff of the Open University be sustained through a difficult and prolonged formative period.

So far the DES has failed to answer the call contained in the last paragraph; and in disussions with the Minister of State, Lord Crowther-Hunt, I became aware that he himself was in doubt about the validity of this case, arguing that it has never been overtly accepted by government. Since, to my knowledge, the philosophy behind it has been tacitly accepted from the beginning and is well documented, these new reservations are distressing and appear to stem largely from the current financial strains. It may be that the Department considers that to admit the Open University to the ranks of research-based institutions would be to weaken their hand in resisting similar pressures from other educational institutions.

The publication and reception of the Report of the Gavin Committee[22] became a crucial factor. The Committee had been set up jointly by the Department and the University with the remit of making recommendations about how the level of academic staffing of the Open University should be determined. The Report, published in 1975, came out unambiguously in favour of staffing the University in such a way as to provide each member of the academic staff with adequate time to devote to private study and research. Acceptance of this Report would make it explicit that the research-based nature of the University was recognised. Expenditure on the academic staff of the Open University is only some 14% total expenditure (as compared with over 50% in other universities) so that the cost of implementing the Gavin Report would be relatively small.

As I write, the prospects for the future are decidedly rosier. A start has been made on the laboratory building for the faculties of Science and Technology; the Gavin Report, which firmly endorses the concept of a research-based university, awaits acceptance by the government; and the Council has publicly recorded its views on research. Thus I have great hopes for the future. These hopes are considerably enhanced by the fact that the staff of the Open University has managed to carry out more research than could have been expected under the circumstances. At the last meeting of the Council at Milton Keynes in September 1975 the research activities of the University were demonstrated and provided an impressive display. We have, on our staff, a number of people who have such determination to continue to produce research papers of quality that they will not allow any difficulties, however great, to stand in their way. Such results augur well for the future.

We had decided that we must mount a programme of postgraduate degrees that would be dual in nature, providing both for conventional internal students and for part-time external students. The internal programme began in 1969 with a handful of students and has grown as fast as our limited accommodation has permitted. By 1972 there were some 50 registered internal postgraduates and by 1975 the total had reached 79.

The Planning Committee had taken the view that the main emphasis of our postgraduate programme should be on the provision of opportunities to study for higher degrees for those who could not satisfy the residential requirements commonly required by other institutions; in other words that we should try to provide a postgraduate service parallel to the undergraduate teaching service we were already undertaking. Schoolteachers, scientists in industrial laboratories, civil servants – there were many graduates who were unable to leave their jobs and go back to full-time residential postgraduate study. Could we arrange a suitable pattern of study for them?

We knew that the Council for National Academic Awards was already offering higher degrees to external students by a carefully monitored system of appointing two supervisors for each student, one local to his place of work, and one from a suitable university or college department. After investigation we felt that we might usefully extend this system, since we could use as 'internal' supervisors our own full-time academic staff – a facility not available to the Council for National Academic Awards. But we were very conscious of the need to keep our regulations closely in step with those of the Council, so that a strict parity of standard could be maintained, and we consulted the Council's officers at all stages in drawing up our own scheme. As a result of these discussions we were able to publish our first Postgraduate Prospectus[23] in July 1972.

While we knew that we could begin with only a relatively small number of students, there was no means of knowing what the demand might be, except that there had been a growing number of applicants to CNAA. We decided therefore to start with about 100 and to let the number grow to some 400 by 1976. Whatever the demand might be there was a strict limit to the extent to which the activities of our academic staff could be dispersed.

We had to ensure that our part-time external students would be able to work at their own speed and subject to the requirements of their jobs. Higher degrees, apart from those based on course work, are normally awarded on the fulfilment of two basic requirements: first a minimum period of study and research under supervision and, second, a minimum standard of achievement judged by the thesis or dissertation finally submitted. We therefore had to devise a means of quantifying the time spent on research and to do this for students scattered all over the country and working in a multitude of different patterns of study. This was a much more difficult task than that of determining the minimum standard of achievement, which we could do by wholly conventional means. The problem was solved by inventing the 'research credit' which can be defined as a period of study and research equivalent to three months of full-time study and research. We require the supervisors of a registered postgraduate student to certify the completion of each such 'research' credit; and insist that such credit is completed within an overall period of one calendar year. In other words the minimum part-time commitment must be 25% of a student's time, but within this restriction he can accumulate research credits in his own time.

One advantage of this system is the extent to which it allows a rationalisation of the fee structure for higher degrees. We decided to charge a supervision fee payable in advance for each period of study for a research credit. In other words the fee for a period of three academic years of study under supervision towards a PhD is split into nine equal instalments. This makes it easier for the student to meet the charges made, and also helps the University in paying supervisors.

Originally it was also intended that we should offer 'course credits' for postgraduate students so that they could supplement their research programme with any necessary formal studies. As yet, however, we have been unable to devote any resources to the creation of special postgraduate courses, nor does it appear likely that we will be able to do so in the near future.

It was decided to offer degrees for one, two and three years of satisfactory work beyond first degree level. Just as we had decided to have only one undergraduate degree, the BA, so we agreed – after much agonising thought – to have only one degree for each of these periods of postgraduate study. Furthermore we were quite sure that, notwithstanding the potential importance of course credits, there was minimum number of research credits that must be gained in order to qualify for these higher degrees. In consequence we devised the scheme shown in Table 23.

TABLE 23   Postgraduate degree structure

| Degree | Required number of credits | |
	Minimum 'research' credits	Minimum 'total' credits
B Phil	0	3
M Phil	3	6
Ph D	6	·9

The first Postgraduate Prospectus attracted some 450 applicants for registration. Of these 60% were from teachers in schools, colleges or universities; 80% were graduates, and the remainder had other qualifications claimed to be equivalent to a degree, which we required as the minimum qualification for acceptance as a postgraduate student.

Table 24 shows the distribution of applicants by major subject area and indicates the overwhelming concentration on the arts side (nearly 80%).

TABLE 24   Distribution of postgraduate applicants by subject area

Subject Area	Applicants %
Arts	28
Education studies	26
Education technology	3
Mathematics	2
Science	8
Social sciences	24
Technology	6
Other	3

In Table 25 I have shown the age distribution of applicants, which is very much what one would expect it to be.

The requests for supervision were so various that it proved impossible to cover all interests from the full-time staff of the University. In the event 80 students were registered in 1972, of whom 45 were supervised by the method originally envisaged, that is by one internal and one external supervisor. The others were supervised by a method more akin to that used by the CNAA, whereby we appointed as internal supervisor a member of staff from another university. The readiness of such staff to help us in this way has been a feature of our programme and we are very grateful to them.

TABLE 25   Age range of postgraduate applicants

Age group	Applicants %
21–29	26
30–39	37
40–49	26
50–59	9
60 and over	2

Over the years the number of external postgraduate students has increased, and reached 209 in 1975. The progress made by these students in acquiring research credits is shown in Table 26. Thus, although the number of students graduating with postgraduate degrees has to date been very small, there is every reason to expect that this situation will soon change, and that the programme will shortly be seen to be an extremely effective one, filling an obvious need.

TABLE 26   Award of research credits

Year of Regist- ration	No. who have acquired research credits										Total no. of students	Total no. of research credits acquired by 1975	Credits/ student
	0	1	2	3	4	5	6	7	8	9			
1972	–	–	11	4	9	2	4	–	2	2	34	138	4.0
1973	–	17	8	10	3	3	3	–	1	–	45	116	2.6
1974	24	12	8	4	3	–	–	–	–	–	51	52	1.0
1975	65	13	3	–	–	–	–	–	–	–	81	19	0.2
Total	89	42	30	18	15	5	7	–	3	2	211	325	—

18

THE STEADY STATE

During 1974 and 1975, we became aware for the first time that we were gradually approaching a situation where the undergraduate programme in the Open University would reach a steady state. We had for such a long time been working on *ad hoc* principles, making guesses about the future, that it came as something of a shock to realise that we were now so well established that we could make forecasts for the future based on relatively firm estimates. This applied to the number of courses, the number of staff, the number of students, the number of graduates and the total cost. It also came as something of a shock to members of the academic staff to realise that the period of innovation was not an unlimited one and that, sooner or later, conditions of work in the Open University would change significantly. I have, in previous chapters, described many of the factors involved in this gradual realisation of and approximation to a steady state, but should like now to summarise what the future undergraduate programme is likely to be.

There is now agreement that the total profile of full credit courses offered in the undergraduate programme will be 87 and I have discussed in detail the reasons why we arrived at this magic number. A total profile of this size has two major implications for the steady state. In the first place each course on offer requires to be maintained; and we have discovered over the years that the maintenance load runs at about 10% of the initiation load, based upon the amount of staff time involved in each case. Thus, when we have a profile of 87 full credit courses on offer, there will be a necessity each year for the same amount of staff time to be devoted to maintaining them as would be required to create, *de novo*, 8.7 full credit courses. The second implication arises from the length of life of an individual course. If each course has to be re-made every five years, then we require one other parameter in order to calculate the load on staff. We have very little experience so far of re-making courses, only one course having been totally re-made, namely the foundation course in social sciences; but we have estimated that on average it will take, in terms of staff time and effort, 50% of that required to create the course *de novo*. Thus, when the total profile of 87 full credit courses is in operation, one fifth of all these courses will have to be re-made every year – the equivalent of creating 8.7 new courses each year. Putting together the load that will fall on the University in providing for both maintenance and re-make at the steady state, we must be in a position to carry out the same amount of work as would be involved in creating about 17 new courses each year. This will be an on-going commitment for all time, if the standard of teaching materials offered by the University is to be maintained. Realisation of this perpetual load, without the stimulus of innovatory creative work, comes as a horrifying prospect to many of the academic staff.

The current rate of course production is running at about 9 new or remade full credit courses per annum, plus the maintenance load on the existing 54 courses, which amounts to the equivalent of another 5.4 courses per annum. It is generally recognised throughout the University that this is too high for current staff numbers to cope with. Thus the total capacity of the University, albeit an over-strained capacity, is about 14 full credit courses per annum. In other words, if there were no change in staffing we could not maintain the steady state.

The Report of the Gavin Committee[22] makes it clear that additional staffing is required in the University if it is to fulfil its obligations in terms both of teaching and of research; and the steady state that we must reach by about 1983 will depend absolutely on acceptance by the government of the recommendations in the Gavin Report. It demands an increase of approximately 15% in the total full-time academic staff of the University. The increase is needed now, not just when we reach the steady state, in order to provide the existing staff with proper opportunities for research. On the other hand, it would be virtually impossible to accomplish an increase of staff of this magnitude overnight, even if the money were available; there is no space at the moment in the buildings available to house them. But the matter is, nevertheless, extremely urgent.

The existing staff have from the outset been entitled as of right to two months of study leave for each year of service in the University, and this study leave can be accumulated up to a total of twelve months. The pressures inherent in providing courses for undergraduate students at the earliest possible time has meant that the majority of staff have deferred taking study leave in order to devote themselves to course production. As a result, the University has built up a large debt of study leave to its staff. Thus a moderate increase in the staffing of the Open University, if it were permitted immediately, would not necessarily cause a severe accommodation problem, since it would permit an increased proportion of the staff to take study leave and the accommodation thus freed would be available for the additional staff. On the other hand, at this time of financial stringency, it seems unlikely that additional funds will be forthcoming to enable this to happen, even if the implications of the Gavin Report are accepted by government in principle. Thus it seems likely that to reach the steady state in terms of staff numbers will be a slow process. Nevertheless, it is vital that the aim is accepted and that we attempt each year to come closer to the achievement of that aim within the limits of available funds.

The high initiation costs involved in making a course make it economically necessary that, on average, a substantial number of students register for that course in each year. We have never accepted that we should choose courses only on the basis that they attract a large number of students. We have been aware that some courses which will not themselves attract large numbers of students will be necessary to provide coherent study programmes, and will have to be subsidised, as it were, by those courses which attract more than the minimum necessary number of students for cost effectiveness. In other words we must plan on an average number of students per course, rather than insisting that every course should attract a minimum number of students. With a profile of 87 full credit courses it will be necessary that on average, each course should attract about 800 students a year, giving a total number of student courses per year of approximately 70,000, if we are to maintain our cost effectiveness. If each student in the system registers for an average of 1.1 full credit equivalents each year, then 64,000 students will be required in order to produce a total of 70,000 student courses.

How do we envisage the total number of students in the system increasing over the next few years? Mr Prentice, then Secretary of State for Education and Science, agreed in 1974 that for the following two years we should aim at admitting 20,000 students in each year. If this total admissions figure were to be maintained in the steady state, then it would lead eventually to a total number of students in the system of about 60,000 on our current figures. An increase in the admission rate to 25,000 new students per course would similarly yield a total student population of about 75,000. At the moment we are limited by the funds available to a total student population of 50,000; and to reach 75,000 would involve us in considerable additional direct student cost expenditure. Nevertheless, we have to assume that once the current financial stringencies are over this would be a reasonable projection for our future activities. It would certainly not outrun the apparent demand for the University.

Thus, in our long term planning, we envisage an annual admission rate of 25,000 students and a total student population in the University of 75,000; and consequently, a total of student courses of over 80,000, more than enough to sustain the profile of 87 full credit courses that will be on offer at the steady state.

Furthermore, if applications continue at the current rate of some 50,000 a year, then even if the demand is very heavy for some courses and much smaller for others, we will still be able to fill all the course quotas and thereby maintain a balance of students in the more advanced courses in each of the six faculties. These are clearly important factors in providing for national needs, as well as for the self-fulfilment of students who wish to register for these different types of study in the undergraduate programme.

The results of our first five years indicate that the total number of graduates that might be expected each year at the steady state would run at an average of something around 7000 to 8000, that is, about 40% of the finally registered students of each intake. Similarly the total expected accumulation of credits in each year would amount to 75,000. These are both predictions based on reasonably accurate figures.

Our building programmes have been submitted to the Department of

Education and Science, but will call for a further capital investment in the Milton Keynes campus amounting to £21 million over the next eight years, if we are to be in a position adequately to house the total staff. This total capital expenditure on the Open University is still very much less than that which would be involved in providing conventional university space for this number of students. Given adequate capital funding, there is no question but that by 1983 a capital building programme of this magnitude could be completed, and the University enabled to maintain the steady state without accommodation difficulties.

In our ten-year plan for the Open University, we have calculated what the total cost of running the University at this steady state would be. The total annual grant then required, given the Gavin expansion and the necessary expansion in the total number of students, would be £27 million in 1975 values.

For the purposes of comparison with our costs in 1971, I have calculated this figure back to the value of money at that time and it comes out at £16.3 million. It is therefore possible to make projections about the cost per student per annum and the cost per graduate at the steady state. I have tried to summarise the whole position in 1971 money values in Table 27, which shows that our forward projection, on the bases that I have described, will lead to no further increase in such per capita costs.

TABLE 27

		1972	1975	Steady state
No. of students	(thousands)	31.9	49.3	75
Total grant	(£m)	7.09	12.1	16.3
Grant/student	(£)	222	245	217
No. of graduates	(thousands)	0.9	5.5	7.5
Grant/graduate	(£)	7851	2200	2170

One other feature of the University in the steady state, on which we would lay great stress, is the achievement of adequate methods of evaluating our courses. The Planning Committee laid great stress on the need for an innovatory institution, embarking on a highly experimental form of teaching, to build in from the beginning ways of estimating how far it had succeeded in meeting the needs of the students. The main protagonist of this aspect of the new University's activities was Professor Hilde Himmelweit, whose work in this field has long been known and respected. We have tried our best to fulfil these aims and to organise an adequate feedback from the students so that we could gradually improve and refine the whole of our teaching/learning system. The main problem has been to devote enough of our limited funds to the task of analysing and evaluating the programmes we were offering.

Amongst the first appointments to the Open University staff were two research officers. In 1969, their main task was to analyse the performance of students in the 'Gateway' courses that were offered for intending students of the Open University by the National Extension College in co-operation with the BBC. In preparation for 1971, when our first students began work, we assimilated the research officers into the new Institute of Educational Technology; and gradually, inside the Institute, there developed what is known now as The Survey Research Department, headed by Naomi McIntosh, one of the original research officers. The Survey Research Department works very closely with the Registry, to try to determine what precisely is the effect of our teaching programmes on the students. A sample of students studying each course is asked to return weekly questionnaires describing their reactions to the various components of the teaching material. The questions are essentially simple ones, requiring very little time to complete. The students are asked, for instance, how much time they devoted to each particular unit of the course, which parts of the course they found interesting and essential, which parts they found did not matter and could be missed, and whether there are any major comments about particular units that they would like to make. The general idea was to feed back the results of the surveys to the course teams so that they would have some guidance in how to re-plan the teaching materials for the following years.

A mass of material is collected on a continuing basis, and undoubtedly it sometimes is of great value in helping the course teams to decide what to do. For instance, in the first year we were able to isolate a particular unit in the foundation course in science which was taking students an inordinately long time to complete. In the second year of this course, the unit was divided into two, thereby making it a much more reasonable task for the students involved. In terms of the evaluation and amendment of courses it is, however, essentially a blunt instrument which can only be of value in relatively crude ways. On the other hand, it is of absolutely crucial importance for many administrative aspects of the University work. Matters such as the timing of television and radio broadcasts are significantly affected by the sort of information that is collected through the Department on, for example, the availability to students of television sets and recording equipment, and the hours of the day when students are free to watch and listen to programmes. Many papers have been written by members of the Department on the various ongoing projects involving student progress, withdrawal and study patterns; of particular interest is a longitudinal study of the first intake of students, which was funded by the Social Science Research Council.[24]

A larger amount of detailed criticism of the components of individual courses probably reaches course teams via the faculty mechanisms of feedback. These are dependent on the existence of a large cadre of part-time tutors and counsellors, to all of whom students make comments and criticisms about the courses that they are studying. These filter back to the faculties through the staff tutors and senior counsellors working in the regions who are in direct contact, both by telephone and by visiting Walton Hall, with the faculty staff and the course teams.

Although we have evolved a series of formal reporting mechanisms to pick up the particular problems of individual students, these are mainly confined to difficulties of an administrative type and there is no comparable mechanism for the reporting of detailed criticisms of the text and other components of the teaching material. It is much more an informal liaison process whereby the part-time staff and the regional full-time academics are able to influence course teams in re-designing certain parts of the course. This informal feedback often leads also to the urgent and rapid correction of mistakes in the teaching material, or to expansion on points which students have found difficult to comprehend. This is sometimes done by making use of radio broadcasts. Each course team leaves certain of its allocation of radio programmes to be recorded at a later date, so that from time to time it is possible to make radio tapes very quickly so as to give prompt help.

One of the functions of the Institute of Educational Technology is to carry out major programmes of investigation into the evaluation of our teaching methods. Unfortunately such programmes are extremely costly and time-consuming and we have been unable to divert or to attract sufficient funds to cover the full range of studies which would be desirable.

Detailed content analysis of individual teaching units, to discover the most satisfactory methods of approaching the distance learner, is an extraordinarily laborious exercise. It takes a research worker a whole year to do such a content analysis on one unit, which is one week's work for a student; in an institution which is producing some 300 units in any one year, it is much too expensive to use this as a routine method of evaluation and feedback. Nevertheless, attempts have been made to carry out studies to this degree of depth on selected course units.

Another large programme was mounted, with the help of the Ford Foundation, to study the different learning methods of particular groups of students. People vary in the way they respond to teaching material presented by different media; some students learn better by listening than by watching, others by reading than by either listening or watching. The research programme was designed to discover whether students could be divided into sub-groups according to their particular ability or lack of ability in these respects; and whether, as a result, alternative methods of presentation of the same material could be offered to the different sub-groups so as to improve the learning capacity of each. This is an on-going programme and full reports have not yet been published.

Another group within the Institute of Educational Technology has been doing comparable studies of the effectiveness of open-circuit broadcasting as a teaching medium and has already produced some fascinating data.[25]

Both the Consultative Committee structure, by which the University takes account of student opinion, and the Students' Association, which exists to make student views known, have provided valuable additional feedback from students about their courses. This information tends to arrive too late to enable the University materially to change the courses currently on offer, but should be of great value when the re-making of courses becomes a major part of the activity of each faculty. Argument within the student organisations tends to have centred largely on such things as the proportion of face-to-face tutorial help available, and on the precise balance between tutorial and counselling work offered by the University. The student organisations have also been very interested in the methods of assessment and in the precise mechanisms by which credits are awarded to individual students; useful information about the attitudes of students to television and radio broadcasts as integral parts of their teaching programme has also been collected in this way.

We are not at all satisfied that we have solved the major problem of evaluating what we have been doing, and we would very much like to improve and extend such studies. It is sad that, during our most experimental period, when we would have benefited most from feedback of this sort, shortage of resource curtailed our activities so severely. It is vital that during the steady state, when less effort will be devoted to the creation of innovative courses, but when opportunities will continue to exist for modification of courses through detailed evaluation of our programmes, further money both from external and from internal sources should be found to permit an adequate programme of such evaluation.

19

THE UNIVERSITY AND THE BBC

Almost the first firm decisions taken about the new university were those that concerned the role of the BBC. Long before the political decision to create the University was taken, Lord Goodman had obtained the agreement of Sir Hugh Greene, then Director-General of the BBC, to provide the necessary air-time on BBC2 and on radio; and detailed plans and costings for the whole operation had been prepared by the BBC (see Chapter 2).

During the period 1968-71 the University lagged behind the BBC in its preparation for the start of the venture; at the same time both sides were exploring the nature of their educational partnership. At this stage, partly because the BBC was more advanced in its planning and partly because the old name, the University of the Air, had evoked a general expectation that broadcasting would be the major medium of teaching, the University was widely regarded as a creature of the BBC. As a result many of the enquiries, both from within Britain and from abroad, were directed to the BBC and not to the University itself.

The equipping of the existing studios at Alexandra Palace for the sole use of the Open University led to the development there of a separate BBC team, first of television and later of radio production staff now numbering some 400, which gradually became as committed to the partnership as was the University team at Milton Keynes. It fell under the general guidance of the Controller of Educational Broadcasting, first Richmond Postgate and later Don Grattan who had been Postgate's television aide, with Michael Stephens on the radio side. As leader of the team actually working at Alexandra Palace we were fortunate in having first Peter Montagnon, who had been responsible, as one of the joint producers, for Sir Kenneth Clark's enormously successful series *Civilisation,* and later Bob Rowlands, formerly editor of *Panorama.* The contribution of all these men to the development of the Open University was critical. The relationship between them and the senior officers of the University was always a happy one; and together we quickly won first the support and later the enthusiasm of other senior BBC staff who had been doubtful about our future and concerned at our demands for scarce air-time; both Huw Wheldon, formerly Managing Director of BBC TV and David Attenborough, formerly Director of Programmes have told me about their gradual conversion.

It became increasingly clear to all those engaged on the project, and particularly to those near the coal face, that a prodigious amount of teamwork was required if the broadcasts were to be of the highest quality in educational terms. It says much for both parties that the programmes have proved to be as effective and as polished as they are. It has been said to me by BBC colleagues that, in the process of making programmes, some old and revered shibboleths were destroyed. Perhaps the most important one was that academics do not make good broadcasters; I am assured that they do, and on a scale that surprises people used to the yardsticks of general programme making. And, conversely, it is often held that producers and directors are hardly likely to make good academics. Again, I am happy to say that our own experience points rather in the opposite direction. Our BBC colleagues are manifestly concerned with the totality of the enterprise, rather than the narrower confines of the broadcasts themselves.

Concerning the programmes themselves, we have seen a steady, if small, change in the content. In television, progressively greater use has been made of film specially shot on location. This emphasis on observing the world where it exists, of going to people and events rather than bringing them into the studio was to be expected, particularly in the areas of the social sciences and the arts. To meet the needs of the course teams, film crews have been to the Netherlands, Germany, France, Italy, Iceland and North America. Although until 1975 our studio productions were in black and white, we shot as many as possible of these film programmes in colour.

Overall, the consensus of opinion seems to be that we have not seen the emergence of any radically new styles of programme. We tried, as far as possible, to eschew the 'talking face' and to use television only when there was a pedagogic need for a video-signal. The attempt has rather been to consolidate proven techniques and to concentrate on the educational content. I think that this perhaps rather conservative approach was justified. So much of our institution and its methods of operation was new, that it was proper to be wary of innovation for its own sake.

The detailed financial arrangements for the partnership took longer to determine. The University was to pay all the costs incurred by the BBC in making Open University programmes so that no burden would fall upon the revenues obtained from licence fees. This was rightly regarded by both parties as a critical feature of the agreement. It meant that our programmes could be prepared wholly for the student audience. There was no need to make them set out deliberately to appeal to a wider segment of the general public, at any sacrifice of educational objectives, in order to justify the use of licence fee income for their production; a constraint that applied to all other adult educational programmes.

On the other hand the BBC was in total control of the budgets for both production and transmission and the University simply paid the bills. This raised two problems. In controlling its expenditure the University needed to know in advance the size of the BBC bill, which was one of its largest commitments. What happened if BBC expenditure outran the estimate? This was a very difficult question to answer. Stopping production could have only marginal effects since the cost of production was very largely made up of inescapable BBC overheads. Their staff would have to be paid even if the studios were not in operation, so that savings could, even by drastic action, only amount to about 20% of the total bill. The problem has hardly arisen in practice; but the legal wording of the agreement was indeed difficult. The second problem concerned the auditing of the BBC accounts. The University's accounts were subject to the scrutiny of the Controller and Auditor General and the items concerning payments to the BBC were not expected. Yet the BBC's own accounts were not so scrutinised. Questions were thus bound to be asked about the control of this expenditure and satisfactory answers had to be built in. The Agreement was signed on 19 Dec 1971 and lasted originally for 5 years; it was later extended for up to seven years with only minor amendments.

During the early stages of discussion it was agreed that the BBC should renew its lease of Alexandra Palace, in North London, until 1977 to provide a production centre for the University's television programmes, while the radio programmes would be produced in Central London studios. The BBC also decided during this time not to create new production departments for these programmes, but to call on the experience of its existing Further Education Departments in radio and television and to enlarge them appropriately to meet the rising production demands of the University from year to year.

Arrangements were made for the extensive conversion and re-equipment of one television studio at Alexandra Palace, on which work began in 1969. By the beginning of May 1970 the studio and supporting services at Alexandra Palace were available on time and were officially opened. At this point programme production began in earnest, and the studio from which the world's first public television service had been started became the home of this latest advance in educational communication.

It was evident, from the start of 1971, that plans for an alternative site to Alexandra Palace would have to be prepared. A joint working party was set up by the Open University and the BBC to examine this problem. Our first concern was to discover whether there was any prospect of an extension to the lease from the Greater London Council, which owns the building. We were informed – as indeed was the DES which repeated the enquiry – that there was no prospect of a renewal.

All the advice, architectural and technical, that we could muster was unanimous: that we must start planning in 1972 for a new building that was to provide studio services in 1977. We therefore appointed architects and consultants for the new Audio-Visual Production Centre. An early approach was made to the government about the timing of the provision of funds for the new building; but the initial response was a further question about the renewal of the lease of Alexandra Palace and a request to examine the availability of existing studio facilities throughout the country. A very careful survey of all available studios was made by a team of experts but the conclusion reached was that no suitable premises were available, and in the light of this the working party recommended that the new centre be erected on the campus at Milton Keynes. This advice was accepted by the BBC and the Council, and subsequently by the DES. Two further questions were raised by the DES, concerning who should run and operate the building, and the extent to which it might serve wider educational needs than those of the Open University alone. After a prolonged and searching analysis it was agreed that the University should own the building, which would be operated by the BBC primarily for our programme production; but that any spare capacity could be used to provide for the needs of other educational users. On this basis general approval for the project was given by the DES and the detailed work of design began.

The delays that have affected all our building programmes applied also to the new studio centre. In consequence it became impossible for it to be ready by 1977 and we were faced with a possible hiatus in production. The Greater London Council, however, had also been affected by the national financial crisis and the BBC began negotiating for an extension to the lease of Alexandra Palace. By this time, too, we felt that the need to make our programmes in colour had become urgent: although we had previously intended to install colour equipment only in the new studio, we arranged to convert the Alexandra Palace studio to colour in 1975. Thus at the time of writing we are well ahead with the plans for the new Studio Centre at Milton Keynes and we look forward to making a start on the building.

The opening of the new Studio Centre will undoubtedly alter the relationship between the staffs of the BBC and of the University. With such geographical proximity there will be an immense gain in closeness of contact and in the saving of time spent at present commuting in both directions between Alexandra Palace and Milton Keynes. It may well be that progress in educational broadcasting will be greatly accelerated as a result of the move. On the other hand the conditions of service for BBC and University staff differ considerably; and while this does not matter when we operate from separate centres, there may be great problems when we live cheek by jowl as staff doing the same sort of work but having different pay scales and holiday entitlements are bound to start making invidious comparisons. We have had many discussions about these problems and I believe that all of them can, with patience and tact, be overcome.

The initial agreement with the BBC provided the University with 30 hours per week on BBC2 television and 30 hours on Radio 3 or Radio 4. It did not, however, determine the time-bands during which these hours would be provided. Problems arose over this question almost from the outset.

By 1973 the number of courses on offer was such that we were using virtually all the suitable time slots that were available. We broadcast every weekday evening in the band from 5.00 pm until 7.00 pm and we used the valuable band from 7.30 am until 1.30 pm on Saturday and Sunday mornings. Until 1973 we could, within these bands, broadcast all our programmes, each repeated once. Since then, as the number of courses has further increased, this has become less and less feasible and we have been forced to use less suitable slots. Matters can only get worse; and very soon we shall have to face up to the fact that some radical change will be necessary. Either we must obtain an extension of the number of hours available beyond 30 per week, making use of even more unsuitable time-bands, or we will have to abandon the principal of broadcasting each programme twice. The latter decision could be implemented in many ways, of which the most important are, first to select those courses which are repeated or, second, to select some courses which we will offer to students only every second year. So far no firm decisions have been taken but they cannot long be deferred.

The situation has been allowed to remain unresolved largely because of the uncertainty about the whole future of broadcasting. The government has set up a Committee under the chairmanship of Lord Annan to report on this matter and we have made two submissions to it, setting out our proposals and needs for the future. Nevertheless it will be some time before the Committee reports; and even when it has reported it will probably be much longer before its recommendations can be implemented.

One critical question will be the decision that is taken about the allocation of the fourth television channel. Even after it was agreed that we should make a start by using BBC2, Jennie Lee always hoped that, ultimately, the fourth channel would be made available to us. In our submissions to the Annan Committee we have reiterated the need for time on the fourth channel; but we have also argued the case for retaining some broadcasting time on the existing channels to reach, as it were by stealth, that segment of the general public which might ignore a channel devoted primarily to education.

We have no idea whether the fourth channel will be devoted to such a purpose, or whether it will be used for an extension of commercial television, for a growth of 'participative television' or for other minority groups. Even if the claims of education are met, we do not know whether control will be vested in the BBC or in some other authority. We must be prepared for all eventualities. It will inevitably be many years after the decision about the fourth channel is made before it can be made available for use. Thus we will be faced with a period of years during which our broadcasting needs will have to be fitted into existing TV channels.

The position in regard to radio is much the same, although there is some hope that new VHF channels may become available rather sooner; and the competition for radio time is unlikely to be as keen as that for TV time.

We have always assumed that broadcasting is an effective medium of education, and indeed there is ample evidence to support the assumption. Nevertheless, it is a very expensive medium and not unnaturally the Open University staff, struggling with all the problems of distance teaching, have from time to time questioned whether the expenditure, especially on television, brings a commensurate return in educational value. Television accounts for only about 5% of the time taken when studying our courses but for about 20% of our total expenditure. Is it worth it? The question becomes even more pointed when some graduates tell us that they managed to get their degrees without ever watching the television programmes.

I still believe that the answer must be 'yes'. It is not really surprising that some students can manage without it. Some students in conventional universities can manage without ever attending a class; it does not follow that all classes are a waste of time. For most students of the Open University the television broadcasts are interesting, stimulating and an important part of the teaching. On average, at foundation level, over 90% watch each programme[25]. The broadcasts have, as I have mentioned, a function as a 'pacing' mechanism. In science they are vital for demonstrations. They also offer a quality of glamour in an experience that is otherwise fairly drab; and they probably have a subtle effect in fostering a spirit of comradeship amongst distance learners. We cannot afford to do without them. On the other hand it seems not improbable that more advanced courses can be prepared that make minimal demands, or even zero demands, on air-time. This offers a further possibility for overcoming the shortage of broadcasting time in the future.

The need for a continuation of the educational partnership with the BBC has also been questioned. The BBC has provided the broadcasting time, the studio production facilities, expertise, experience and, not least, access to its own archives. Are these still vital to our future? What would be the advantages of 'going it alone'? The problems of obtaining access to broadcasting time might be eliminated after the Annan Report. If they were so eliminated, could we not run the new studios ourselves, recruiting our own producers and studio crews? I think that we could, but that we would be very unwise to try. We could offer little in the way of career prospects to the specialised staff and might therefore attract only the second best. We would not have access to the archives or to the wealth of facilities and expertise available within the vast organisation of the BBC.

We would give all this up for gains that could be only marginal. We could indeed make, more cheaply, programmes of lower technical quality which might still have the same pedagogic value. We could more easily experiment with new ideas for audio-visual teaching materials. The emphasis in both these cases is on freedom to change. The partnership does not deny such freedom; it only makes it more difficult, for both partners must agree. At first sight it would appear that we could more readily control expenditure; but I suspect that our own overheads would be as inflexible as those of the BBC. I am therefore sure that the partnership should continue and that we should modify it only in so far as the recommendations of the Annan Report make it necessary to do so. It has been a successful partnership that has brought credit to both sides, and that is much studied by other countries aiming to start similar educational ventures. There is no reason to doubt that it will continue to be a vital feature of the Open University in the future.

20

COMMERCIAL ACTIVITIES

In 1969 Lord Crowther, the first Chancellor of the Open University, was rash enough to suggest in public that the University, through selling its course materials on a large scale throughout the world, might become the first ever self-supporting university that the world had ever seen. This was undoubtedly an over-sanguine estimate of the potential of the University in commercial markets. Nevertheless, we realised from the very beginning that, through preparing our course materials, we would gradually amass a wealth of material in permanent form, printed and audio-visual, which was of enormous potential value to users all over the world and which could therefore be exploited commercially. On the other hand many of those who joined the staff of the Open University at the beginning were much less interested in the commercial possibilities of the material they were producing than in the altruistic notion that they could benefit people everywhere who had, for one reason or another, been deprived of the opportunity of education. This particular altruistic aim was directed much more strongly towards the Third World than to the developed countries of the Western world. Yet the markets of the Western world were much richer and we would be foolish to ignore the possibility of increasing the income of the Open University, thereby decreasing our dependence on whatever government was in power, by exploiting our materials for sale in this sort of way. It was clear that such commercial enterprise would not mix happily with university enterprise of a conventional kind and that we would be up against difficulties all along the line.

This sort of reasoning led us, from the very beginning, to vest the copyright in all course materials in the University and not in the individual authors. Collaboration between universities and other institutions of higher education had long been bedevilled by copyright problems. Members of the academic staff of a conventional university who write textbooks are, of course, properly entitled to receive royalties from the publishing company which produces their work. This principle had, however, been extended to the reproduced teaching materials that might be used in a particular university. Thus, when a lecture programme was produced by a member of staff in written form for the benefit of his students, it was not possible for the university concerned, his employers, to provide these materials to other universities without paying the individual member of staff a royalty on them. This was an odd situation in view of the fact that he was a full-time employee of that institution and that his main task as an employee was precisely the production of teaching materials of this kind. We could see that if a similar principle were to be adopted in the

Open University, it would make the commercial exploitation of our teaching materials virtually impossible. Consequently, the terms of appointment of all our staff made it perfectly plain that, for all materials produced in the University, as part of the courses themselves, copyright would be vested not in the member of staff or members of staff or course teams involved but in the University itself. On the other hand, we made it equally plain that if a member of staff were to produce written materials which were not part of the course materials, he would hold the copyright in them just as he would in any other institution.

This principle was accepted by all those who joined the academic staff of the Open University and was clearly understood. Nevertheless, it left very difficult grey areas between the course materials produced for students of the University and other materials written by members of staff. Two of these areas are perhaps worth particular mention. The first is the textbook produced by a member of staff which is subsequently adopted as a set text for students of the Open University. Clearly, if the book has been written before the member of staff joined the Open University, the individual's right in the matter is indisputable; but if a member of staff, knowing the future programme of course production, were to write an appropriate textbook for a projected course as a set book, a problem did arise. With sales of the potential size conferred by such an Open University adoption, it is necessary to be absolutely sure that no individual member of staff can persuade or indeed coerce the University into adopting his own text. We therefore arranged that if a course team proposed as a set book a textbook which had been written by a member of our staff, it could only be adopted if the Academic Advisory Committee, as an independent external assessor, were to concur. A second grey area appeared when it became obvious that we would have to include, as set texts in a number of courses, anthologies of original writings to which our students might not have access, since the University could not offer a direct library service to them, and since the public library service could not normally provide such source materials. The preparation of these anthologies was a task that fell upon the course teams concerned, but it was a task additional to that of preparing the course materials themselves. Consequently the University, after much debate, adopted a middle course: it was agreed that those members of staff who undertook the additional task of preparing anthologies should be paid for so doing, but paid an outright sum rather than a royalty on the number of copies sold. As might have been expected, these were not wholly popular decisions in the University, since many members of staff felt that the product of their creative imaginations was being arrogated by the University to itself without proper recognition. On the other hand, it seemed to be wrong for the University to pay its full-time staff out of public funds for undertaking tasks which were precisely those for which they had been appointed in the first place.

It also seemed wrong that because particular courses had a very large popular appeal, resulting in the sale of large numbers of copies of the course materials to the general public, those who wrote such courses should benefit financially, whereas other academics who put the same amount of effort and imagination into the production of courses which did not have the same wide public appeal, would not benefit in this way at all. This dilemma was resolved by deciding that, if the University were to make a significant amount of money from sales of course materials, some part of the profit should be set aside in a General Purposes Fund for the non-monetary benefit of all members of staff equally. This would ensure that the money did not go only to those particular individuals who happened to be working in popular fields. This solution is, however, fraught with difficulty, because the University is supported by a grant-in-aid. This means that the government provides sufficient funds to cover the costs of an approved budgeted programme, these funds being calculated after taking into account all other sources of income, including fee income and sales income. Thus, if we were to make profits from the sales of course materials, our grant-in-aid would be reduced accordingly. This problem has arisen in other universities, usually on a fairly small scale and usually in those cases where they have been involved in engineering consultancy work or other services of that kind. The general pattern has always been that the government has recognised that if it were to take back, by a reduction of the grant-in-aid, all the income achieved by a university in offering such services to the public, it would remove all incentive for the extra work involved in providing them. Consequently, although the grant-in-aid might sometimes be reduced to take account of these other sources of income, it was never reduced by quite as much as the amount of money actually obtained by rendering the services. We felt that we should proceed on the assumption that a similar attitude would be adopted in our case and that, therefore, there was something to be gained by promoting sales of course materials on a wide scale and thereby increasing our gross income and, probably, our net income.

Whether or not this turned out to be the case, we would undoubtedly gain in public regard if we were seen to be capable of raising funds by our own endeavours. This particular conclusion was reinforced in the summer of 1970, when the Conservative government took power; for when the continuation of the grant to the University was agreed it was specifically indicated that we would be expected to increase the proportion of our income obtained from sources other than public funds by all means at our disposal. The original idea underlying this indication was that we should increase the student fees, but we successfully resisted it on the grounds that we would achieve the same end by maximising our income from the sales of materials.

There was one major hindrance to the commercial exploitation of our materials. The academic staff knew that they were writing integrated multi-media courses; the written texts were not designed to be self-sufficient and might have frequent cross-references to the radio and television programmes and to supplementary materials of various kinds. They might be dovetailed with home experiment kits, with the Student Computing Service, with all sorts of other bits and pieces that were provided to the student as part of the overall integrated teaching package. Consequently, many academics were very worried that the University would damage both its own reputation and their reputations as contributors to a course if it were to sell any individual bit of material as a single isolated unit and not the whole course as an entity. Much of our early attention was therefore devoted to ways in which we would market whole courses, rather than to the problem of marketing whatever we could sell, wherever we could sell it, in order to maximise our profit margins. This argument has raged ever since and is still unsettled.

The problem does, however, tend to be much more acute in respect of sales outside Great Britain and there are cogent reasons for this. Everyone realised that, in Britain, sales of whole courses were extremely improbable. The scepticism, to which I have referred on so many occasions, about the future of the University, made it seem unlikely that any other institution would wish to adopt whole courses of the Open University as part of their own teaching programmes. On the other hand much of our teaching material might be used by teachers rather than by students, as guidelines to the planning of their own teaching; and indeed, this has been a clearly visible development from the beginning, especially in Colleges of Education in Britain. If one examines the prospectuses of such colleges one frequently finds courses with the same title, and even the same syllabus as courses of the Open University. This usually means, however, that our course materials are sold only to the teachers; the teaching methods used being tradititional and the much larger number of students not being required to buy our course materials.

It is, of course, flattering to the University that its courses should be used in this way, but it does not significantly increase our income from marketing. It may, however, satisfy the innate altruism of our academic staff that teachers in other institutions should want to use their work. Knowing that such teachers in Britain would be aware of the integrated multi-media nature of the Open University courses, they did not feel any particular pang in allowing our Marketing organisation to sell individual units or parts of units to them. From the very beginning, as far as the United Kingdom is concerned. our course materials have been available in bookshops up and down the country and direct from our Marketing Division as individual items for sale, and we have not tried to persuade institutions to adopt whole integrated courses. The home market has been tackled in fairly conventional ways through marketing representatives making direct contact with the teaching staffs of institutions up and down the country.

The situation overseas was very different. Most members of the University felt that members of the staffs of universities and colleges overseas might not fully appreciate the integrated nature of our courses, and that the purchase and use by them of individual units in their teaching programmes would therefore give a misleading impression of the Open University. Our first thoughts when we created our Marketing Division were therefore that we should attempt to sell overseas either whole courses or, indeed, our whole system. We knew that the biggest potential market for English language educational materials in the world was the USA, where there were some 3000 colleges and universities which were potential users of such pre-packaged courses. We therefore devoted a large amount of time and energy to trying to exploit this potential American market.

It is not easy to persuade any institution in any country in the world to adopt a whole course prepared by the Open University. One is invariably up against academic resistance. No academic likes to think that any group of other academics can produce a better course than he can himself. Also there has been, throughout the period of our existence, a declining educational market; academic staff are as a result fearful of the consequences of adopting pre-packaged courses, since it may run the risk of making them or their colleagues redundant.

In exploring the American situation, we found that the chief administrative officers of many American universities were extremely interested in the prospect of using Open University courses. The attraction for them was that it was much cheaper to buy such pre-packaged material than to recruit more staff. The prospect of increasing the number of students and thereby increasing the fee income, which in the USA is often a very large fraction of the total income, without a comparable and parallel increase in the expenditure on staff, was a very beguiling one. Chief administrative officers of universities are not, however, dictators and they subsequently found that they could not adopt Open University courses in their own institutions without the agreement of their own academic staff; and to persuade the academic staff to go along with this economically attractive proposition turned out to be very difficult. Furthermore, in the USA, there is a strong view that Americans can do anything better than anybody else. Why should they adopt courses prepared in a British institution, rather than rely on what was being done in the USA? This was a very understandable attitude in a country which had been, on the whole, far more innovatory and imaginative about educational experiments and non-traditional methods than we had in Britain. The trouble in the USA had been that, because education is controlled by the individual states rather than the Federal government, no individual state could afford the amount of money necessary to start an institution like the Open University. Although there had been many experiments, there was a paucity of high quality software because the investment necessary to produce it had not been available. Nevertheless, it was widely known that all sorts of new ideas were being tried out, and it came as a rude shock to them that Britain, with its traditionalist attitudes, should be the place where they had borne fruit, owing to the very large government investment in the Open University.

One of the consequences of this rather insular attitude was that most academics who considered using Open University materials felt that, although they might be very suitable and successful for use in the UK, they would require considerable amendment and change in order to suit American students in the American educational scene.

I therefore devoted considerable time and effort to trying to mount an experiment whereby our course material would be used in American institutions by American students, to see whether British-designed materials would actually work in the different ambience. It was quite clear that it would be very difficult to do this using methods of transmission similar to those adopted in the UK. I decided to try to run the experiment on the basis that the courses and the course materials would be transmitted by whatever method was appropriate to the institution concerned in the USA. In this way the experiment would test, not the Open University's transmission system, but only the Open University's course materials.

It was also true that, as would have been the case in the UK, American institutions were very much more willing to experiment with courses prepared by the Open University if they were to be offered to adult students on a part-time basis rather than to whole-time students on campus. This is a further reflection of the fact that most academics are primarily concerned with their own full-time students and are only marginally interested in the teaching programmes offered in external degree programmes.

I found three universities in the USA which were willing to participate in this way in a trial of Open University courses; namely, the University of Maryland, Rutgers University in New Jersey and the University of Houston in Texas. There remained the problem of finding a source of funds which would enable an experiment to be mounted and a report to be written on its result. The Carnegie Foundation was willing to put up the money for such an experiment. They had long been interested in non-traditional methods of higher education in the USA and had produced a whole series of monographs on the future of education. On the other hand, their rules of procedure made it impossible for them to make a grant directly to any organisation which was not based in the USA and I had therefore to find a local sponsor for the trial. The College Entrance Examination Board agreed to apply to the Carnegie Foundation for funds to run the experiment, and to ask the Educational Testing Service in Princeton to undertake the task of analysing the results of the experiment.

The Open University contributed to the cost of the whole exercise by providing the course materials at cost and, in the event, by providing a large amount of informal advice and help to the participating institutions. The experiment was run in 1972, and the results were published in a report by the Educational Testing Service in 1974[26]. It commented favourably on the Open University courses and came to the conclusion that they could be used satisfactorily by American students in American institutions. The report did suggest that they could be improved by amendment to suit the American scene, but this was not regarded as a major difficulty. We were very pleased with the outcome of this experiment and looked forward to the use of materials by other institutions as a likely follow-up. Unfortunately, however, the financial wind in the USA blew very much colder over the following years and the growth of user institutions of whole courses there has been much slower than at one time we had thought likely.

Those institutions in the USA which have adopted whole courses have

275

almost invariably found that they are highly satisfactory and that the students who have studied them have been uniformly pleased and excited and stimulated by the experience. Indeed, when I have met such students, I have usually found them even more enthusiastic than our own students in this country. The University of Maryland, and to a lesser extent the other two initial institutions, have increased the number of students in this experimental programme and the number of Open University courses adopted.

In the summer of 1975, the first student of Maryland University to obtain a degree almost wholly through courses of the Open University, graduated. At the time of writing, there are now nineteen colleges and universities in the United States which have adopted one or more courses of the Open University and are teaching them to external students. In parallel with these developments our Marketing Division arranged to sell our course materials in the USA through an American publishing house, acting as sole agent. The latter was enthusiastic about the prospect of sales, and particularly so in the light of the report from the Educational Testing Service on the experimental use of our courses. Unfortunately, however, the cold financial climate and the consequent lack of funds for educational development has so adversely affected the adoption of Open University courses by institutions in the USA that these sanguine expectations have not been realised.

Our sole agent and indeed the three institutions which took part in the trial, were inundated with requests for further information about the Open University, about the courses, and particularly about the ways in which these courses should be taught; that is, all the back-up services in the form of supplementary material, set books, tutorial systems, examination systems and so on, without which the course materials in themselves could not stand on their own feet. Neither the sole agent nor the user institutions were staffed or equipped to deal with this volume of requests and we therefore felt it necessary to open an office in the USA to act as a source of information to all the user institutions and to persuade other institutions to become users. The office opened in 1974, and has been running for two years at the time of writing. It is almost impossible to assess what influence it has had, but I feel sure that the increase in the number of user institutions which has occurred is at least partially due to its existence; it is unfortunate that the financial climate has been such that its efforts have not been crowned with a greater degree of success. The office serves other aims and objectives to which I shall refer later.

We also hoped to market individual units or parts of units on a much wider scale to the general educational public in the USA. In terms of printed materials this effort has been unsuccessful, for two main reasons. The first is that many of the Open University courses turn out to be too sophisticated for the average college market in the USA. The main interest centres on our foundation courses and on a few of our second level courses. This is perhaps a reflection of the fact that American college work is set, on average, at a level below that of university work in the UK. The second difficulty stems from the fact that our course materials have a very high initiation cost; consequently, the selling price in the USA is higher than normal. To some extent we have tended to price ourselves out of that market. As a result, 90% of our total sales of course books in the USA has been to whole course users.

On the other hand, this barrier does not apply at all to the sales of our audio-visual materials. Here, our sales to whole course users amount to only 30% of overall sales; most of our audio-visual sales in the USA are thus going to other institutions, presumably as back-up material to wholly different courses taught in those institutions. There seems little doubt that the sales of our audio-visual materials in the United States are potentially much greater than the total so far reached. We have great hopes that they can be expanded, especially now that we have been able to colourise our television studios and produce our videotapes and films in colour, for black and white products are increasingly less acceptable in the American market.

This policy in the USA of moving away from the marketing of whole courses to the marketing of individual items and particularly of audio-visual items was reflected in the strategy which we adopted from the outset in other countries. The pattern of marketing in other countries has been for us to select a sole agent in each country or region of the world and to offer to that agent the opportunity to stock whatever materials he chooses from our catalogued lists. We have not in any sense enforced a contract which required the agent to stock whole courses. All our agencies have been reasonably successful, but perhaps the most successful of all has been that in Australia, where the total volume of sales exceeds that in the USA, although the total potential market is very much smaller.

Marketing in countries where the language of teaching is not English presents additional problems. The course materials have to be translated before they can be adequately marketed and, here again, we have put ourselves in the hands of sole agents who are responsible for selecting those materials to be translated. The initial expense of commissioning the translations is a serious factor in limiting the amount of material that the agent can handle, but the sales of materials in translation has continued to rise. It seems quite clear that the potential sales in Spanish, mainly in the South American market, are extremely large by comparison with those in any other language and it is here that we consider our largest potential market for translations to lie.

It has always seemed to me that the problems associated with successful marketing operations demanded a method of decision taking which was so different from the methods normal to universities that we would do well to consider splitting off the marketing activities of the University into a separate limited liability company. Such a company would be wholly owned by the University, but governed by a board of directors and able to take quick decisions based on motives more commercial and less academic than those which governed the normal decision taking methods of the

University. However, when I mooted this idea in 1972, it did not find favour amongst the other Officers of the University and it was decided to continue to operate the Marketing Division as a separate section of the University itself. In 1975, however, our new Treasurer, Sir Henry Benson, came forward with a similar suggestion to the one I had made before and this was accepted by the University in the rather new circumstances that pertained by that time. At the time of writing, we anticipate that a separate marketing company will have been set up during 1976 to which will be passed the responsibility for running an efficient sales service and for increasing our income from this potentially large source.

The following table summarises the income accruing to the University from sales of our course materials, and from royalties on translations, television rights overseas etc., in the years 1971–5.

TABLE 28   Marketing income 1971–5

	1971 £	1972 £	1973 £	1974 £	1975 £
Tapes	3,162	6,734	13,652	29,584	28,637
Books	58,423	143,280	267,791	236,937	253,401
Films	9,229	58,170	96,307	155,537	207,212
Records	—	1,092	1,875	916	3,691
Equipment	13,579	78,325	52,343	24,855	46,393
Royalties	11,645	4,863	18,732	33,115	36,769
Totals	96,038	292,464	450,700	480,944	576,103

From the beginning we were faced with a series of visits from Ministers of Education and other officials of the governments of the many foreign countries which were interested in creating educational systems similar to that provided by the Open University. We were, of course, flattered by this interest and anxious, wherever possible, to give what help and advice we could. This was relatively straightforward when confined to general discussion, but became increasingly burdensome as more detailed enquiries were made and as answers to these enquiries became harder to give. We also came to realise that we had developed over the years a great deal of what the commercial world would refer to as 'knowhow', which enabled us to operate our system successfully and which, in commercial terms, was a highly marketable commodity.

As our overriding priority was still to serve our own students, and as the demands for help of this kind increased, we were faced with the necessity of clamping down on the amount of help and staff time we could give free. The most efficient mechanism for doing this seemed to be to sell the knowhow, rather than give it away. By this means, we hoped to be able to finance supernumerary staff to continue the services to other governments that were being demanded. It was this philosophy that led us to start the Consultancy Service. We had initially thought, especially in the context of the USA, that we could provide such a service commercially to individual institutions but it rapidly became apparent, first, that they expected such services to be provided as a courtesy between comparable institutions, and second, that, even if we insisted on a payment for such advice, few of them would be able to afford the scale of charges that was necessary before we could make ends meet in providing the service. It therefore became increasingly obvious that it was only governments or similarly sized organisations that could possibly afford to employ us as consultants.

The main problem was that we could not provide a Consultancy Service at all unless we already had supernumerary staff in post; and that we could not employ such staff unless we had funds to do so. Such funds must be available for at least a year in advance of undertaking any service, since it would take at least that long to train new members of staff in the operations of the Open University to the point where they would be able to pass on authoritative information to the client. We therefore needed risk capital if we were going to take on such supernumerary staff and be in a position to offer the sort of service we wished. Risk capital could not be supplied from our grant-in-aid, as this was by no means the sort of purpose for which central government funds were being supplied. We accordingly explored the possibility of providing the service in the early stages by making use of members of our ordinary staff who would be interested and willing to act as consultants. We could then hope, with the money paid by our first clients, to employ supernumerary staff, who would not in fact act as consultants, but would spend their time replacing those more experienced staff who acted as consultants in the early contracts. This solution depends entirely on the willingness of the members of the ordinary staff of the University to act in this way.

Our first contract was with the Free University of Iran, which was financed and created by the Iranian Government. We undertook to supply them with help, advice and knowhow, over a period of two years, 1975 and 1976, at a fee of some £140,000. We carefully arranged that half of this fee should be paid in advance so that we could take on some six supernumerary staff, in the hope that we would be able to spare more experienced staff to undertake the consultancy work.

I should emphasize that, although I describe our work with this overseas university as a contract, it is in spirit as well as practice very much more of an educational partnership. Even if there are strong reasons why we must ensure that the university gains rather than loses financially from its consultancy work (which implies a contractual basis for all such arrangements), both our own staff and the staff of our client institution very properly regard themselves as conjoined in an effort to create in partnership the best possible educational system for the circumstances prevailing locally.

It was clear that, to operate a successful service, we must consult the Senate before accepting any contract and have, on our staff, a number of people who were contractually bound to undertake consultancy work – who would fill any gaps that we were unable to fill from amongst our regular academic and professional staff.

Since it is not possible to do this without obtaining risk capital in advance from sources other than the clients themselves, we have been exploring the possibility of obtaining such capital, first, in respect of countries who are in need of educational aid such as Pakistan and, second, in respect of countries like Venezuela, where there is no question of overseas aid and where the new concept of paid educational services has become the operative one.

Overall it seems clear that, as is the case with marketing, we have a very large potential income from clients who would like us to help them in sundry ways to set up new educational ventures suitable to their own internal conditions, their methods of distribution, and their problems in education; and that we could in fact help greatly in such cases if only we were staffed and equipped to do so. This in turn has led to the concept that the Consultancy Service might, like marketing, be made the responsibility of a separate company, and such may well be the long term future for it. However, at the moment we are completely dependent on the goodwill of our own full-time staff and it seems premature to separate this service from the source of the expertise that is required. In many cases, members of our full-time staff will not wish to undertake such additional work unless there is some financial incentive for them to do so, and clearly we must arrive at acceptable methods, both to the University and to the staff concerned, of rewarding them for it. These are problems for the future and I hope that we will find satisfactory solutions to them before too long.

The need for educational reform in the world at large and for educational development in the Third World is so great that the Open University would be guilty of negligence if it did not help in such a worthy and deserving cause. At the same time, we cannot afford altruism; we cannot afford to spend the very limited resources at our command, given for the support of our own internal students in Britain, on providing help which should be paid for either by the country concerned, or by other agencies which are set up to provide overseas aid. The financing of such help involves highly complex negotiations which will require a great deal of patience and perseverance before they can be satisfactorily concluded.

21

CONTINUING EDUCATION

The concept of continuing education is one which has been developed in detail only in the last two decades. It has been variously referred to as 'éducation permanente', 'recurrent education' and 'continuing education'. What is it all about? Why has it suddenly taken hold of the imagination of individuals, and especially of international agencies? I attempted to answer these questions in my Rede Lecture of 1974[27], and am indebted to Cambridge University Press for permission to use part of it in the following account.

The concept of initial education, namely the preparation of the child for adult life, has never, until recently, been seriously challenged as the main method of providing for the needs both of the individual and of society. There have, however, been a number of developments in this century that have made people wonder about its validity ... The sum total of human knowledge in any one field or discipline is now so large that initial education has become longer and longer and now continues until the age of 25–30 or even 35. The Admirable Crichton who, in 1579 at the age of 21, was able to challenge and worst the Faculties both of Paris University and of Genoa University over the whole range of human knowledge and in seven languages, is today admittedly an unreal figure, even if we admit the existence of the prodigy. But is it really acceptable that the most able young people should be unable to contribute to society until they have virtually reached middle age? The rate of acquisition of new knowledge is now so fast – and it is still accelerating – that the idea that a man, during his initial education, can be so fully educated that he can cope successfully with his chosen career throughout his working life is no longer tenable. The rate at which jobs become obsolescent because of new technological developments is now such that an increasing proportion of adults have to change from their chosen careers to new ones. Thus re-education becomes an increasing need. There has been a growing realisation of the fact that selective systems of initial education take no account of the late developer, who may awake to a realisation of the importance of education all too late for the system. In an age where there is an increasing availability of leisure time, the problems of satisfactorily filling the leisure time take on a new importance, and the most satisfying of all leisure activities is, for many intelligent people, the pursuit of knowledge and new interests. A system based almost wholly upon initial education makes little provision for them.

For all these reasons, people all over the world have begun to suggest that we are putting too great an emphasis on initial education and too little emphasis on education provided at various stages throughout life – namely on continuing education; and that, indeed, the ordering and structure of the established patterns of initial education are themselves very inefficient.

May I look, for a moment or two, at this suggestion as it relates to higher education? . . . The suggestion incorporates two separate issues which are all too readily confused. If we say that there is too much emphasis upon initial higher education and too little on continuing higher education we could mean *either* that too many people are getting an initial higher education *or* that everyone should have a shorter initial higher education, *or* we could mean a bit of both.

Those who have argued against the expansion of initial higher education have often based their arguments on the 'more means worse' principle, and have often been motivated by the fear that the expansion would put at risk what Ashby has called 'the thin clear stream of excellence'. To nurture that stream is, I believe, a vital necessity. . . . But there is another necessity, . . . namely to provide everyone with an opportunity to be educated to the limit of his or her capacity. To meet this need there has been a massive expansion of initial higher education. Was this the right solution? Did we choose the right method of meeting the need?

It is at least arguable that we did not; that we would have done better to meet the need by providing a system that combined a different form of initial higher education with continuing higher education; a system that could exist side by side and closely integrated with the existing system of initial higher education.

I believe that Ashby's 'thin clear stream of excellence' refers to a particular kind of excellence which is best described as the excellence of scholarship; and that there are many other kinds of excellence. The characteristics of excellence in scholarship are much more to be found in an attitude of mind, in a particular bent, in an attribute of character than in the ability to pass any kind of examination. Even when, before the expansion of the universities, the number of entrants was small, only a select few turned out to be scholars. Thus we cannot segregate the thin clear stream of excellence in scholarship from the wide and muddy river of ability; one must go on providing opportunities for scholars to emerge – and emerge they will – and then, whatever their age or their background, one must nurture them.

But one must also recognise other kinds of excellence, the kinds that are found amongst those whose attitudes of mind, whose particular bent, whose attributes of character, lead them to want to *do* things rather than to *study* things. Such people want to study only when they find that it is necessary to study in order to be able to do something. But once they begin to study, just a few of them will emerge as scholars; their attitude will have changed. For the great majority, however, study will always be towards a practical end; they will never be scholars; they are not, in either sense, excellent. But their education matters.

I believe that, for the scholars who emerge at school, prolonged initial higher education . . . is ideal. For the rest I believe our current initial education is already too long and is to a large extent counter-productive. Were a shorter period of initial study to be supplemented by a ready access to periods of continuing higher education, this problem could be overcome. But it would require the proviso that, when scholars emerge from this new programme, the door is always open for them to return to those universities catering specifically for scholarship.

Is this all a pipe-dream? With all the talk about continuing education, all the lip service paid to it, why has so little been done about it? There are, again, a number of answers and all of them are powerful reasons for doing nothing. There is an enormous investment in initial education and a very large number of people with vested interests in maintaining and, indeed, expanding the provision thereof.

The inertia in a massive and complex system is very large indeed. There is a very large – and wholly understandable – measure of resistance on the part of educated men and women to the idea that, having struggled hard to acquire their qualifications, they may nevertheless rapidly lose touch with the skills and knowledge that their qualification claims for them. They tend to reject any suggestion that periodic requalification is necessary. The cost of initial education is now so high, and makes such demands upon the national purse, that there is little incentive to add to it the very large cost of establishing continuing education. Indeed it seems to me that most attempts to do so will inevitably be self-defeating; and that the introduction of a programme of continuing education in any sphere of activity will usually demand a concomitant reduction in the length and cost of initial education in that sphere. . . .

[Take, for example, medical education.] The initial education of doctors was always based on the concept that graduation was associated with a licence to practice medicine in any branch of the profession – i.e. that the aim of a medical school was to produce the toti-potential graduate. More and more information was fed into its students and the course of study both became longer and became more closely packed. At the same time each branch of the profession became more and more dependent upon highly specialised knowledge, the amount of which grew at an accelerating rate. Thus the medical graduate has steadily moved from a position of being toti-potential to being properly prepared for nothing in particular.

I do not believe that we can afford to let this state of affairs continue – for it can only get worse. I can see no cure at all unless there is a completely radical change in the pattern. It seems to me that it should be possible to devise a three-year degree course that would produce graduates perfectly capable of taking on limited responsibilities in junior hospital work and in general practice. At the end of such a period of service to the public, rendered at the age of 20–22, the majority of these graduates would have a clearer vision of the branch of medicine which particularly attracted them. To return at this stage to a second period of study which would render them fit to practise in this particular branch – to be trained to practise *only* in this particular branch – would also mean that the courses required could be properly selective in a way that is currently impossible – so that once again the duration and complexity of the educational provision could be reduced. I can thus see the new system producing specialists, fully trained over a more limited range, at a much earlier age than is currently possible. I will be accused of iconoclasm in making such a suggestion. Yet it is my basic contention that the introduction of continuing education in any sphere *must* inevitably be an iconoclastic procedure. . . .

I mentioned as [one] reason for the slow development of continuing education the high cost of initial education. But initial education, on its present scale, makes *other* demands that militate against the development of continuing education. One is the preoccupation of the limited number of qualified teachers with initial education programmes and the consequent shortage of teachers for any programmes of continuing education. Thus, once again, it is difficult to introduce continuing education without a concomitant reduction of provision for initial education.

Then, again, the patterns of employment militate very heavily against continuing education; for they are based on the concept of the toti-potential graduate emerging after a prolonged initial education. To release highly trained and expensive men for long periods of full-time continuing education is a very unattractive prospect for employers – as well as a costly one for the nation.

As I said, all these are very strong reasons for doing nothing; and it is not, therefore, surprising that virtually nothing has been done. Some of the reasons for doing nothing are, as we have seen, subjective and emotional; others are objective and severely practical.

What I think our Open University experience, short as it is, has shown is that we can offer a way of achieving a compromise; a way of trying out a practical system of continuing higher education without a simultaneous and radical change in the pattern of initial higher education.

Thus it is no longer *hopeless* to think of adding a leavening of provision of continuing education to a system primarily dependent upon initial education, if a system like the Open University delivery system is used. For the system of course delivery which we have developed in the Open University makes it possible for one expert teacher to reach a very large number of students. We are not labour-intensive. Nor does our system require any disruption of productive work; our students can remain in full-time employment studying part-time at home. And, finally, on a large scale, we can do the job *relatively* cheaply. Once continuing education is available, the whole question of radical changes in the pattern of initial education can be re-opened. For one has then decided which is the horse and which the cart. Then, and only then, could we approach the ultimate goal: a system of higher education which would provide for the needs of all, the scholar and the practical man, the excellent and the able, the school-leaver and the adult, without the risk that providing for the one will prejudice the best provision for the other.

What then, have we done so far in trying to play this sort of catalytic role? We had almost unlimited authority to undertake such a role in our Charter, which listed amongst the objectives of the University 'to promote the educational well-being of the community generally'. Although our first activities were directed towards the provision of undergraduate courses, we had all intended to move into a wider sphere of activity as early as possible.

The most crying need, first outlined by the Planning Committee, was for a series of post-experience courses intended to serve as refresher, updating or retraining courses for adults. We did not assume that they would all be at postgraduate level; we envisaged that many might be para- or even pre-undergraduate in level but might still offer an important service to society. It was for these reasons that we used the term 'post-experience' courses to cover all such courses. It is not a wholly satisfactory term since, as we deal with mature undergraduates, all our courses can properly be termed post-experience. In certain circles 'post-experience' has been used in a narrow sense to imply very highly vocational courses, so that this again can cause confusion.

The main problem that we faced when we embarked on the preparation of post-experience courses was that they must be self-supporting. The fees must cover all the costs. Furthermore, we had a particular difficulty in that even though the fee involved could, over the life of the course, cover the cost of production, none of it could be collected until the expenditure on production had all been incurred. In consequence we began to develop acute cash flow problems. We spent a lot of time exploring ways in which grants could be obtained to finance the necessary development costs but without very much success. It also became clear that the financial and administrative problems of the whole post-experience course area would require a particularly energetic drive – for the primary loyalty of all the staff concerned was still inevitably to the undergraduate courses. Consequently we set up an administrative unit, under a Director, to try to supply that drive. But this in time gave rise to another problem, for we began to find that problems of demarcation arose between the responsibilities of the academic staff who wrote the courses and those of the Director who was responsible for ensuring that they attracted sufficient students to make them pay. Nevertheless we did succeed in making three or four post-experience courses. Sadly the demand for them was small and did not parallel the demand for the undergraduate programme, and we were at pains to try to discover the reasons. Were they the right kinds of course? Were they priced too high? Was the market for them not researched adequately in advance? Are people not yet ready to admit they need to update their own knowledge? Was the publicity insufficient? We had no real answers to these questions.

We therefore realised that we must re-assess the whole of our policy concerning post-experience courses; including examination of academic control, cash flow, demand and, especially, fee structure. The programme, unlike the undergraduate programme, is not subsidised by government grant. Thus the fees payable by the students are inevitably high even if the numbers taking the course are large. When the numbers are small the economic fee is wholly unacceptable. It follows that we can succeed only if the government agrees to subsidise a continuing education programme, or if employing authorities agree to subsidise individual courses in a continuing education programme which meets the needs of their employees, or if we mount only courses which attract sufficiently large numbers of students and are sufficiently cheap to produce for fees to be kept at an acceptable level.

This reassessment was carried out in 1974. The outcome was two-fold. First we decided to continue our post-experience programme only on a very limited and experimental scale for the next few years; and, second, we decided to set up a Committee to study the whole of the next phase of our activities. By this time the need for courses at pre-university level offered by the distance-teaching method had become very obvious. Furthermore there was an increasing national interest in the whole problem of providing educational programmes for those who had left school at 18, and many of us felt that the Open University could offer significant help in contributing to such programmes. The new Committee, which included members from outside the University, was given the broad remit of advising on what role we might play in the whole field of continuing education. We were fortunate in being able to persuade Sir Peter Venables, who had by this time retired from the Pro-Chancellorship, to become Chairman of the Committee. At the time of writing we await the publication of the Report of the Committee, which will, I hope, draw an imaginative and acceptable blueprint for the next great phase of development of the Open University; and which may have far-reaching effects in determining the ultimate balance in the national provision of initial education on the one hand and continuing education on the other.

EPILOGUE

That, then, is my story. I found that, in telling it, there were many things that I had been anxious to say, and saying them has been a catharsis. The result is inevitably patchy for I have left great gaps when I was either ignorant or not particularly interested. Since it has been a story and not a history I have also failed to include some absolutely critical changes. The most important of these – and it is one that I must now rectify – is that we have lost all our original lay Officers and have had to find new ones.

When Geoffrey Crowther died I felt that one of my main props had gone; but in Lord Gardiner we found a Chancellor who brought wholly new qualities to the task and new honour to the University. Not only does he bring to the top of the pyramid his wisdom and humanity; he is to be found at its very base, as an undergraduate student who has completed and passed two full credit courses, and who knows what it is like to be on the receiving end of our complex system.

When Peter Venables resigned as Pro-Chancellor we lost one of the key characters in my tale; but we found to replace him Sir Frederick Warner, who had sat as a member of Council from its first meeting, had served as its Vice-Chairman and whose appointment then ensured continuity and insight in its Chairman. He has more than adequately filled shoes that many of us thought would fit no-one. To replace Paul Chambers, our first Treasurer, we brought in new blood. We had grown very rapidly and our financial systems, under his guidance, had had the necessary flexibility; but the time had come in a period of consolidation for a new look and we were delighted when Sir Henry Benson agreed to join us, and to bring his wealth of experience as an outstanding member of the accountancy profession to our service.

All these changes have brought a new style with them befitting an established institution. The links with the past are necessarily severed; and the memory of the early struggles fades. This is as it should be, for there are new struggles to be faced, no easier and no less challenging than those that have already been met. There are five that I would pick out.

The first may, in a period of national recession, be a struggle for survival in our present form; if fees continue to rise the opportunity that we offer to the poorer and more educationally deprived section of the community could easily disappear. The second challenge will be to come to terms with the new situation of the 'steady state' in undergraduate course provision, which will call for a readjustment of attitudes and a new pattern of activities for the staff. The third is closely related and vitally important to that new pattern; it is to build the university up to its proper level as a research-based institution. I believe that the chores of the 'steady state' can be willingly accepted only by a staff that achieves fulfilment at least in part from the prosecution of research. The fourth challenge will be to achieve a proper balance within the established and ongoing university. I have explained in some detail the way in which we responded by ingenious improvisation to the problems that arose and the lack of time properly to solve them. There is a desperate need to re-organise; in particular I would single out the whole suite of computer-based systems, the regional structure, the staff structure (especially in relation to the imbalance of age – some 80% of our academic and professional staff are between 30 and 45), and the government structure. The last of these problems may well call for amendment of the existing Charter. Finally we will have the biggest challenge of all in determining, on the advice of the Venables Committee, just what role the university should play in the development of a national programme of continuing education. This will be the next great step into the future, the extension of the teaching programme beyond the provision of courses leading to a first degree.

There has been no time to worry; there has not even been time to think. I hope that in the years to come there will be more opportunity for thinking; I cannot yet foresee us having time to worry. The opportunity to take an active part in the early development of the Open University has been the most exciting one currently available in education. We have all been privileged in having it. I have no fear that our successors will face merely a dull routine; they, too, will have a real chance to change the face of education not only in Britain but in the world.

REFERENCES

1 DEPARTMENT OF EDUCATION AND SCIENCE (1973) *Adult Education: a plan for development,* HMSO (Russell Report 1973).

2 PRIME MINISTER'S COMMITTEE ON HIGHER EDUCATION (1963) *Higher Education,* Appendix 1: The demand for places in higher education, Cmnd 2154–1, HMSO (Robbins Report, 1963).

3 MINISTRY OF EDUCATION. CENTRAL ADVISORY COUNCIL FOR EDUCATION (ENGLAND) (1959) *15–18: a Report,* Vol. 1, HMSO (Crowther Report, 1959).

4 BRITISH BROADCASTING CORPORATION (1928) *New Ventures in Broadcasting: a study of adult education,* BBC.

5 BRIGGS, A. (1965) *The Golden Age of Wireless* (Vol. 2 of *The History of Broadcasting in the United Kingdom*), Oxford University Press.

6 WILLIAMS, R. C. G. (1962) in *The Electrical Journal,* 23 Feb 1972; and in a speech at Guildford (1963).

7 YOUNG, M. (1962) 'Is your child in the unlucky generation?', *Where?,* no. 10, Autumn 1962, pp. 3–5.

8 GENERAL POST OFFICE (1962) *Report of the Committee on Broadcasting,* Cmnd 1753, HMSO (Pilkington Report 1962).

9 GENERAL POST OFFICE (1962) *Broadcasting: memorandum on the Report of the Committee on Broadcasting,* Cmnd 1770, HMSO.

10 JACKSON, B. and MARSDEN, D. (1966) *Education and the Working Class,* Penguin (Rev. edn.).

11 STUDY GROUP ON HIGHER EDUCATION (1963) *Report to the Labour Party,* unpublished (Taylor Report).

12 WILSON, H. (1963) Speech to a Labour Party rally, Glasgow, 8 Sept 1963.

13 TUNSTALL, J. (ed.) (1974) *The Open University Opens,* Routledge and Kegan Paul.

14 MINISTRY OF EDUCATION (1966) *A University of the Air,* Cmnd 2922, HMSO.

15 OPEN UNIVERSITY PLANNING COMMITTEE (1969) *The Open University: Report of the Planning Committee to the Secretary of State for Education and Science,* HMSO.

16 FERGUSON, J. (1975) *The Open University from Within,* University of London Press.

17 BATES, A. W. (1975) Submission to the Annan Committee on the Future of Broadcasting.

18 DOUGLAS, J. W. B. *et al.* (1968) *All our future: a longitudinal study of secondary education,* Peter Davies.

19 DEPARTMENT OF EDUCATION AND SCIENCE (1972) *Education: a Framework for Expansion,* HMSO.

20 OPEN UNIVERSITY (1975) *Annual Digest of Statistics,* Open University Press.

21 MOODIE, G. C. and EUSTACE, R. (1974) *Power and Authority in British Universities,* Allen and Unwin.

22 WORKING GROUP ON THE REVIEW OF ACADEMIC STAFF (1975) *Report to the Department of Education and Science and to the Council of the Open University,* unpublished (Gavin Report, 1975).

23 OPEN UNIVERSITY (1972) *Postgraduate Prospectus 1973,* Open University Press.

24 MCINTOSH, N. E., CALDER, J. A. and SWIFT, B. (1976) *A Degree of Difference: a study of the first year's intake of students to the Open University of Great Britain,* Society for Research into Higher Education.

25 BATES, A. W. (1975) 'Student use of Open University broadcasting: a survey of 10,537 students carried out in November 1974', *IET Papers on Broadcasting,* no. 44, Open University Institute of Educational Technology.

26 HARTNETT, R. T. *et al.* (1974) *The British Open University in the United States; adaptation and use at three universities,* Educational Testing Service.

27 PERRY, WALTER (1974) *Higher Education for Adults: where more means better,* Cambridge University Press (The Rede Lecture, 1974).

INDEX

projected numbers of, 259, 260
special categories of, 169–76
see also Applications for Student
Places; General Assembly, Students'
Association
Students and Curriculum Working Group
see Planning Committee
Students' Association, 163, 171, 172,
262–3
Student Tape Library, 171, 172
Study Centres, 76, 106, 110, 112–13,
114–16
Subjects of Courses, 72–73, 190–93
Summer Schools, 76, 117–19, 130, 168,
185, 194–5, 235
Supplementary Materials, 88, 91
Survey Research Department, 143,
144, 261
Swann, Professor Sir Michael, ii, 31
Syllabuses, 86, 100
Systems, Technological, Course in, 73

Taylor, Baron, of Harlow, 8, 10, 11
Technology, Faculty of, 68, 90–91, 251, 253
Television,
see British Broadcasting Corporation;
Channel Four;
Independent Television Authority;
colour, 267
Television Centre,
see Alexandra Palace
Thistlethwaite, Frank, 122
Treasurer, 45, 46, 206
Treasury, 22, 40, 48, 139, 142, 227,
229, 230
Technical Colleges, 3
Technology, Courses in, 73
Technology, Ministry of, 14
'Televarsity', 6
Telewriter, 120
Thatcher, Margaret, 3, 30, 104
Third World, 270, 280
Thwaites, Dr Bryan, 122
TMA,
see Assignments, Tutor-Marked
Toronto, University of, 204–05, 207, 221
Tunstall, Jeremy, 85
Turnstile, Magnus, 19
Tutors, Part-time, 110, 112, 115–16, 127,
128, 261

UCCA,
see University Central Council for
Admissions

UGC,
see University Grants Committee
Union of Soviet Socialist Republics, 7
correspondence teaching in, 6, 8
educational broadcasting in, 8
United States of America:
academic credit system in, 60–61
educational broadcasting in, 6, 7–8
hardware systems in universities of,
119, 120
Open University courses available in,
159–60, 275–6
Open University materials marketed in,
274–7
Units of work, 86, 87
Universities Council for Adult Education
(UCAE), 6, 7, 19
University Central Council for Admissions
(UCCA), 136
University Grants Committee
(UGC), 14, 21, 40, 48, 228–9, 230, 232,
233, 234, 240, 247
University of the Air:
academic scepticism about, 15
ministerial attitudes towards, 15–16
parliamentary questions on, 23–4
press comments on, 18–19, 23
proposals for, 8–9, 10–11, 12, 16, 69–71
name of, changed to Open University, 24
White Paper on, 17–18
Urwick Diebold Ltd, 44

Venables Committee, 286, 288
Venables, Sir Peter, 24, 25, 26, 29, 31, 45,
46, 47, 139, 286, 287
VHF Channels, 268
Vice-Chancellor, ii, 20, 27, 31, 46, 84, 121,
206, 213–15, 216, 219
see also Perry, Sir Walter
Vice-Chancellor's Committee, 222, 225
Vice-Chancellors and Principals of the
Universities of the United Kingdom,
Committee of, 206
Video-Recordings, 104–5
Viewers' and Listeners' Association, 7
Viva voce, 125, 130

Walton Hall, 39, 40, 42
Warner, Sir Frederick, 287
Warwick, University of, 202, 210–11
WEA,
see Workers' Educational Association
Wedgwood Benn, Anthony, 15